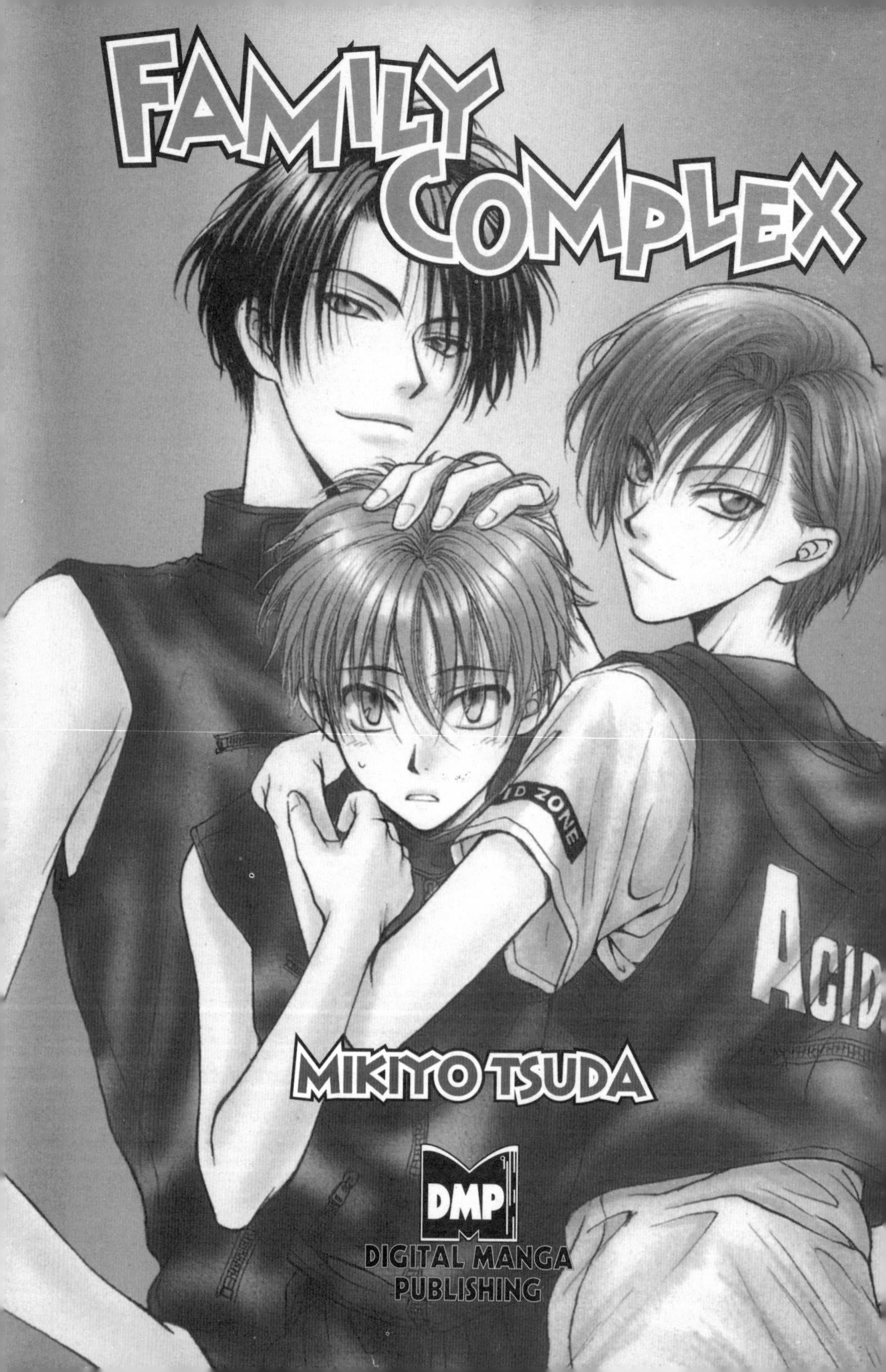
FAMILY COMPLEX
MIKIYO TSUDA
DMP
DIGITAL MANGA PUBLISHING

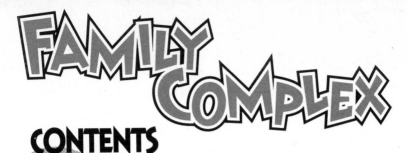

CONTENTS

SECOND SON • AKIRA 003
FIRST SON • HARUMI 035
FIRST DAUGHTER • NATSURU....................................079
SECOND DAUGHTER • FUYUKI....................................115
SAKAMOTO FAMILY • MOM AND DAD......................167
MIDWORD..152
DETACHED RETINA DIARY 153
AFTERWARDS..179
4-PANEL COMIC THEATRE..184
AFTERWORD..188

Translation	Duane Johnson
Lettering	Ed Brisson
Graphic Design	Wendy Lee / Daryl Kuxhouse
Editing	Daryl Kuxhouse
Editor in Chief	Fred Lui
Publisher	Hikaru Sasahara

T 251609

English Edition Published by
DIGITAL MANGA PUBLISHING
A division of DIGITAL MANGA, Inc.
1487 W 178th Street, Suite 300
Gardena, CA 90248

www.dmpbooks.com

First Edition: January 2008
ISBN-10: 1-56970-771-5
ISBN-13: 978-1-56970-771-5

1 3 5 7 9 10 8 6 4 2

Printed in China

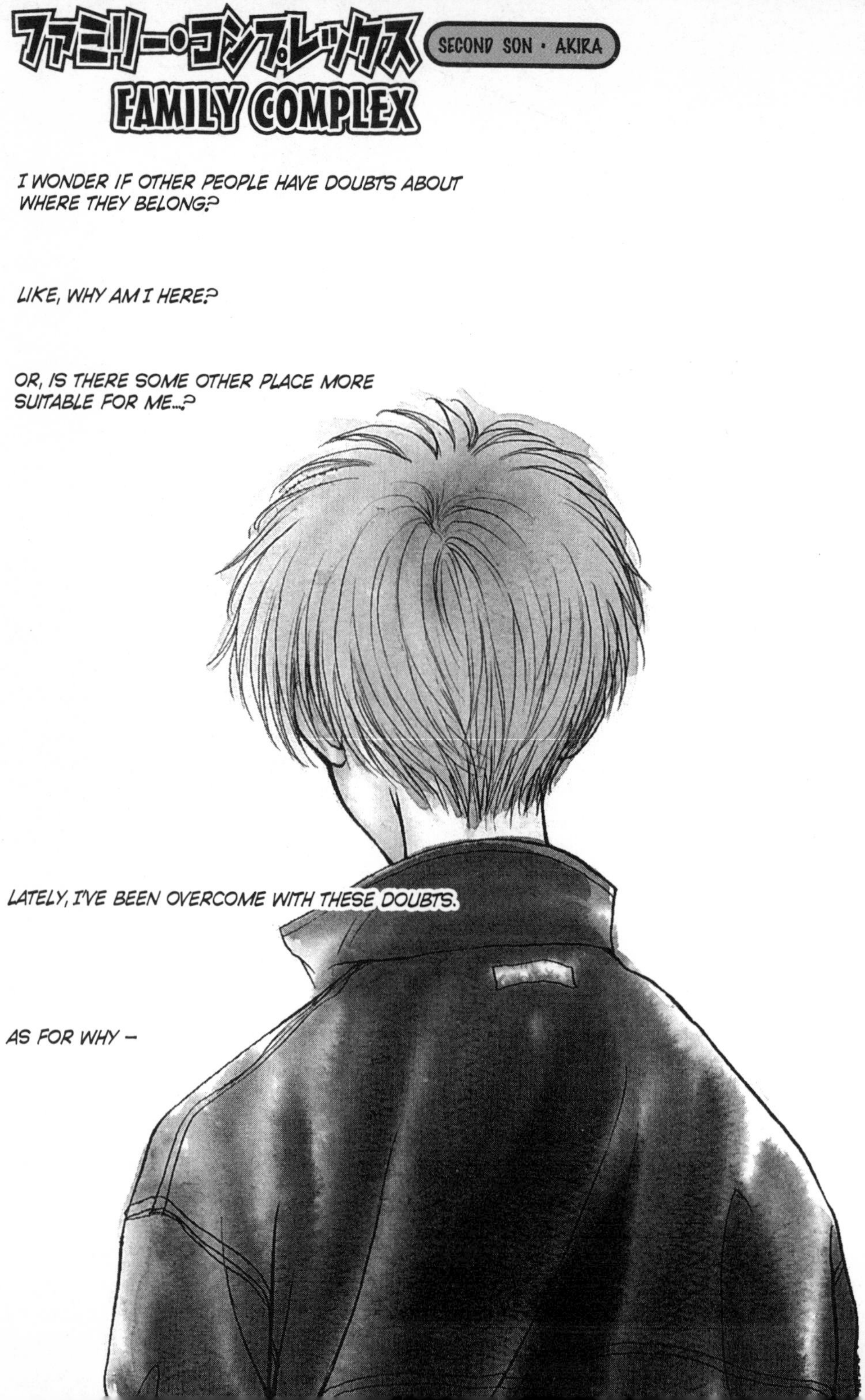
ファミリー・コンプレックス
FAMILY COMPLEX
SECOND SON • AKIRA
I WONDER IF OTHER PEOPLE HAVE DOUBTS ABOUT WHERE THEY BELONG?
LIKE, WHY AM I HERE?
OR, IS THERE SOME OTHER PLACE MORE SUITABLE FOR ME...?
LATELY, I'VE BEEN OVERCOME WITH THESE DOUBTS.
AS FOR WHY –

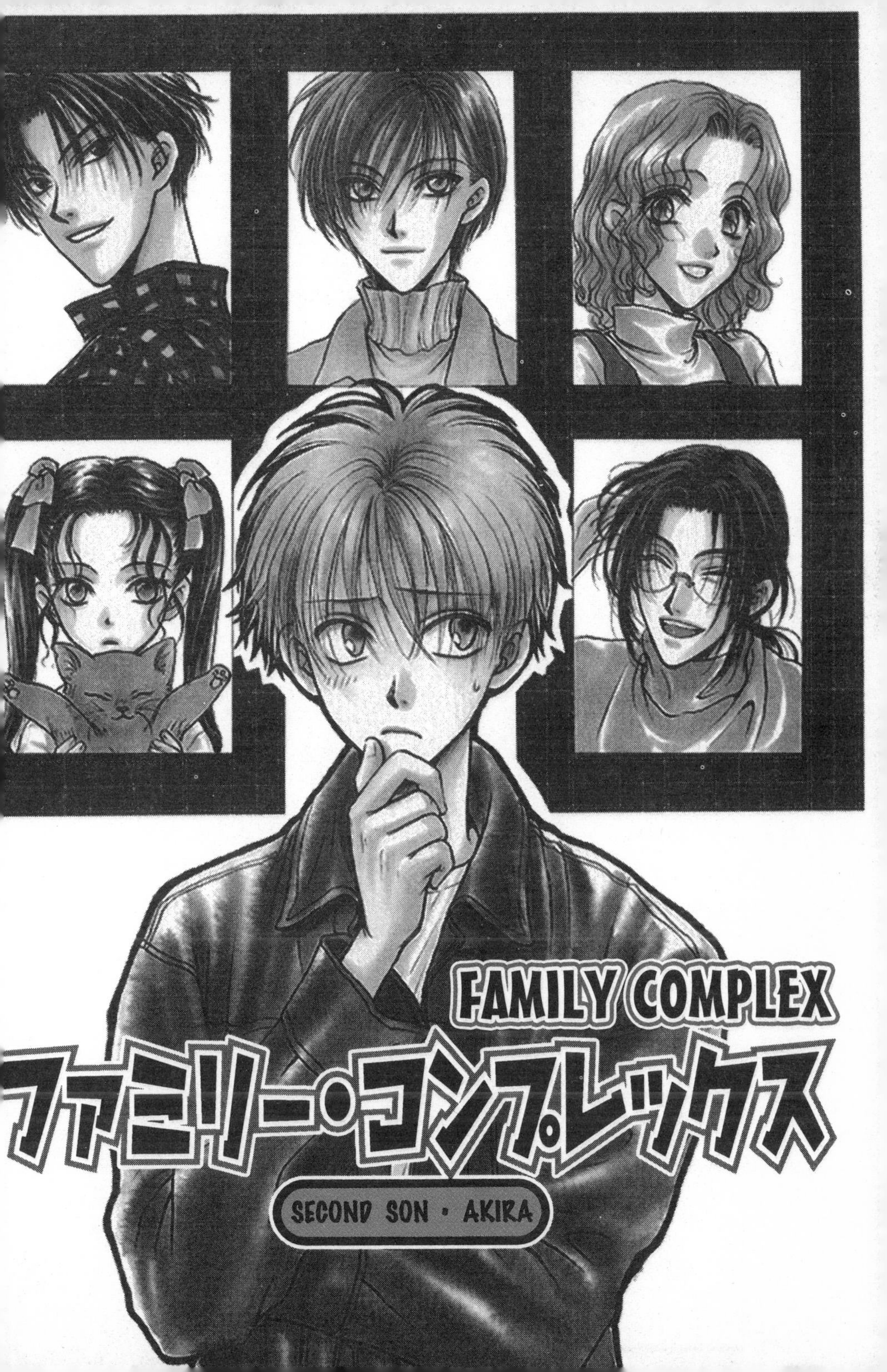

FAMILY COMPLEX
ファミリー・コンプレックス
SECOND SON・AKIRA

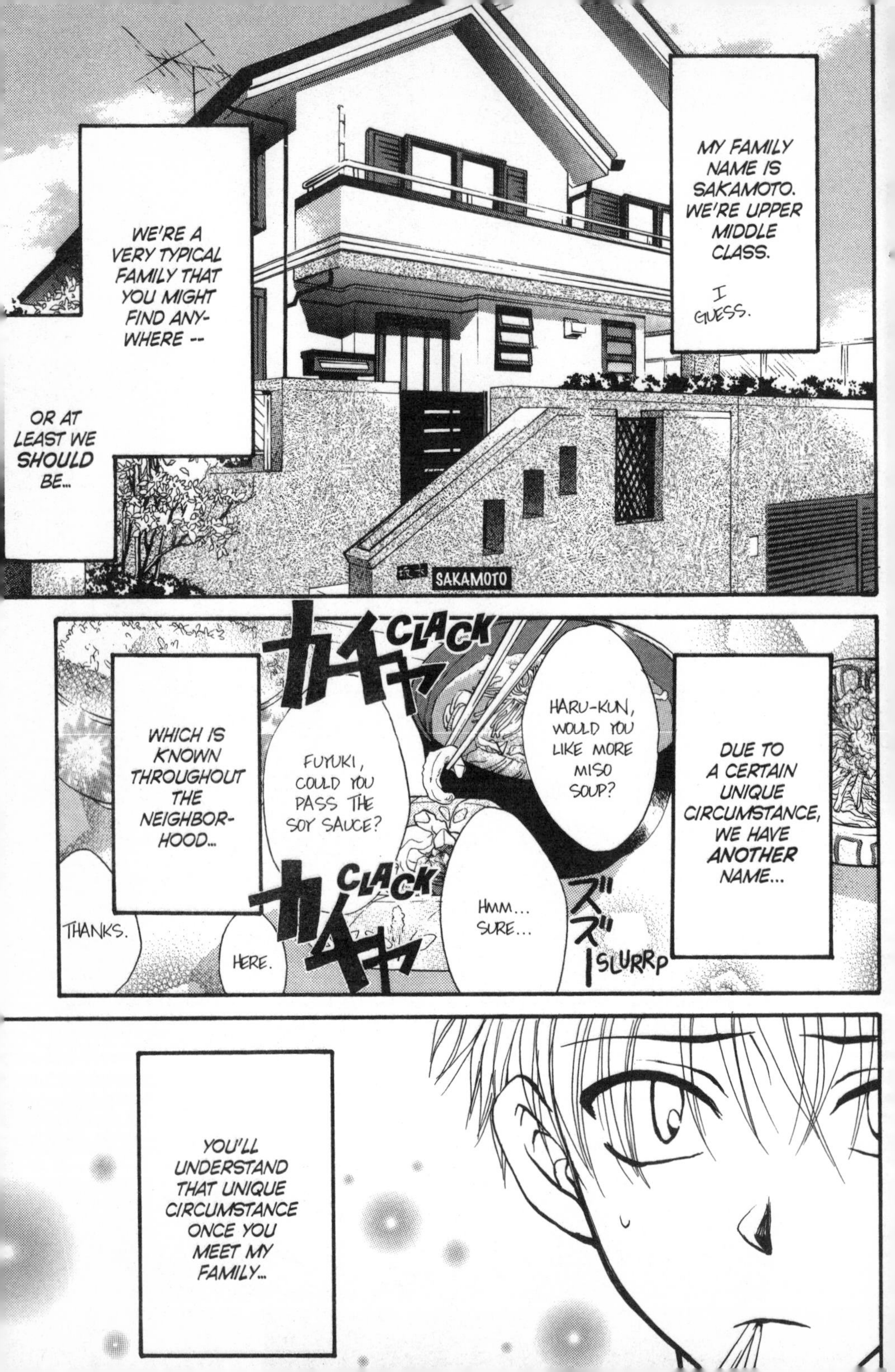
MY FAMILY NAME IS SAKAMOTO. WE'RE UPPER MIDDLE CLASS.
I GUESS.
WE'RE A VERY TYPICAL FAMILY THAT YOU MIGHT FIND ANY-WHERE --
OR AT LEAST WE SHOULD BE...
SAKAMOTO
DUE TO A CERTAIN UNIQUE CIRCUMSTANCE, WE HAVE ANOTHER NAME...
HARU-KUN, WOULD YOU LIKE MORE MISO SOUP?
CLACK
FUYUKI, COULD YOU PASS THE SOY SAUCE?
WHICH IS KNOWN THROUGHOUT THE NEIGHBOR-HOOD...
SLURRP
HMM... SURE...
CLACK
HERE.
THANKS.
YOU'LL UNDERSTAND THAT UNIQUE CIRCUMSTANCE ONCE YOU MEET MY FAMILY...

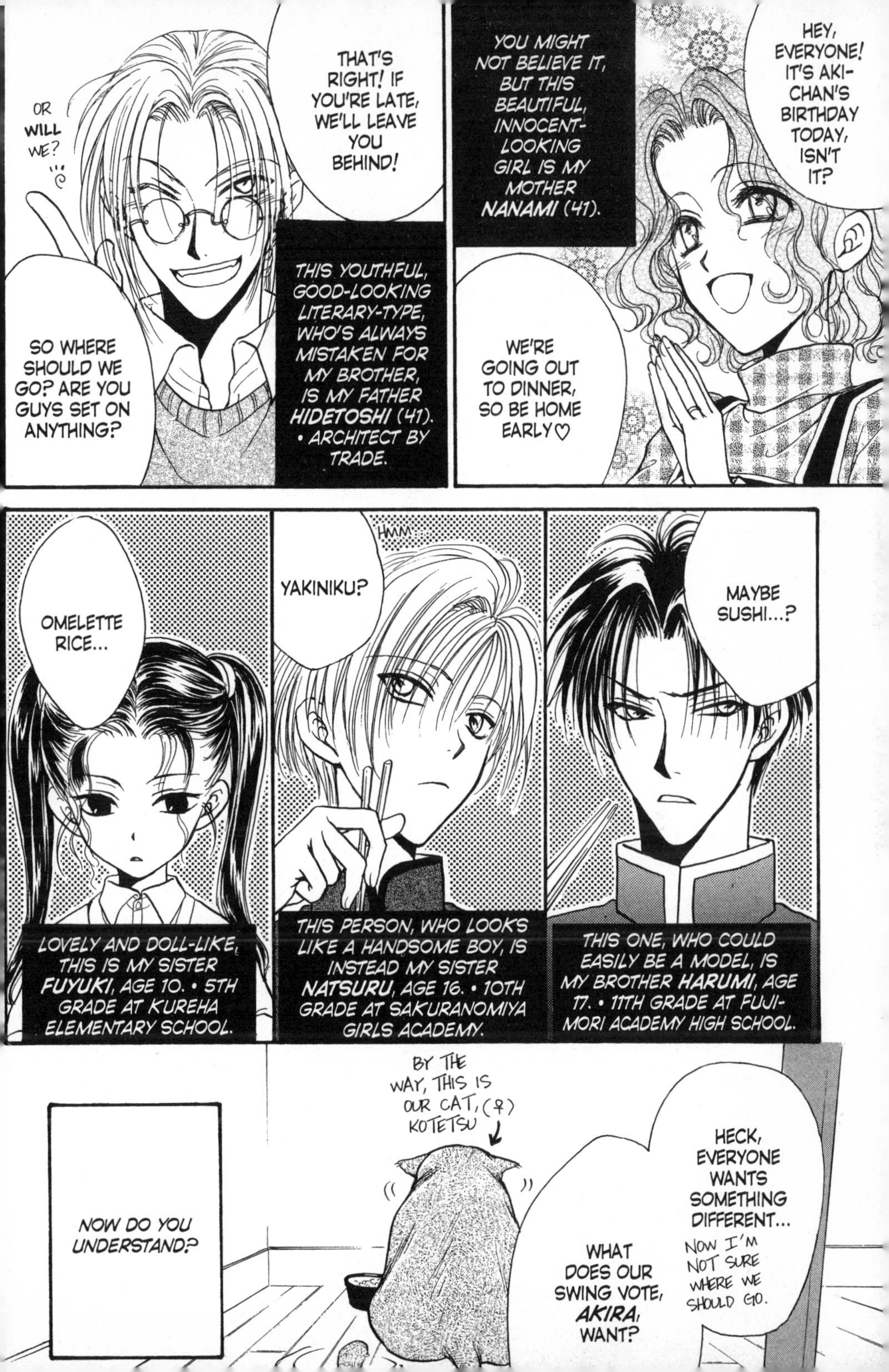
HEY, EVERYONE! IT'S AKI-CHAN'S BIRTHDAY TODAY, ISN'T IT?
YOU MIGHT NOT BELIEVE IT, BUT THIS BEAUTIFUL, INNOCENT-LOOKING GIRL IS MY MOTHER NANAMI (41).
WE'RE GOING OUT TO DINNER, SO BE HOME EARLY♡
THAT'S RIGHT! IF YOU'RE LATE, WE'LL LEAVE YOU BEHIND!
OR WILL WE?
THIS YOUTHFUL, GOOD-LOOKING LITERARY-TYPE, WHO'S ALWAYS MISTAKEN FOR MY BROTHER, IS MY FATHER HIDETOSHI (41). • ARCHITECT BY TRADE.
SO WHERE SHOULD WE GO? ARE YOU GUYS SET ON ANYTHING?
MAYBE SUSHI...?
THIS ONE, WHO COULD EASILY BE A MODEL, IS MY BROTHER HARUMI, AGE 17. • 11TH GRADE AT FUJI-MORI ACADEMY HIGH SCHOOL.
HMM
YAKINIKU?
THIS PERSON, WHO LOOKS LIKE A HANDSOME BOY, IS INSTEAD MY SISTER NATSURU, AGE 16. • 10TH GRADE AT SAKURANOMIYA GIRLS ACADEMY.
OMELETTE RICE...
LOVELY AND DOLL-LIKE, THIS IS MY SISTER FUYUKI, AGE 10. • 5TH GRADE AT KUREHA ELEMENTARY SCHOOL.
BY THE WAY, THIS IS OUR CAT, KOTETSU (♀)
HECK, EVERYONE WANTS SOMETHING DIFFERENT...
NOW I'M NOT SURE WHERE WE SHOULD GO.
WHAT DOES OUR SWING VOTE, AKIRA, WANT?
NOW DO YOU UNDERSTAND?

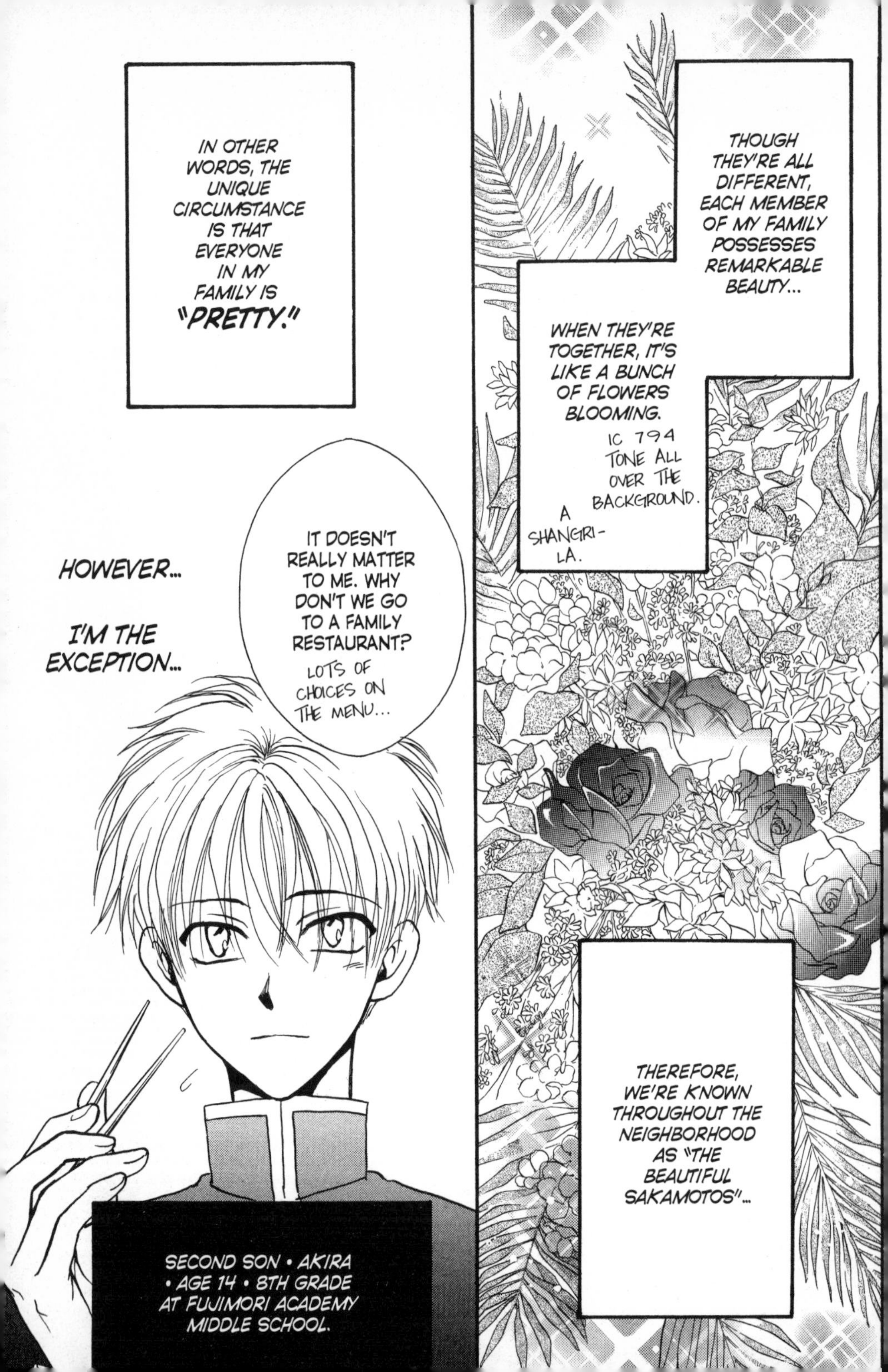
THOUGH THEY'RE ALL DIFFERENT, EACH MEMBER OF MY FAMILY POSSESSES REMARKABLE BEAUTY...
WHEN THEY'RE TOGETHER, IT'S LIKE A BUNCH OF FLOWERS BLOOMING.
IC 794 TONE ALL OVER THE BACKGROUND.
A SHANGRI-LA.
THEREFORE, WE'RE KNOWN THROUGHOUT THE NEIGHBORHOOD AS "THE BEAUTIFUL SAKAMOTOS"...
IN OTHER WORDS, THE UNIQUE CIRCUMSTANCE IS THAT EVERYONE IN MY FAMILY IS "PRETTY."
IT DOESN'T REALLY MATTER TO ME. WHY DON'T WE GO TO A FAMILY RESTAURANT?
LOTS OF CHOICES ON THE MENU...
HOWEVER...
I'M THE EXCEPTION...
SECOND SON • AKIRA • AGE 14 • 8TH GRADE AT FUJIMORI ACADEMY MIDDLE SCHOOL.

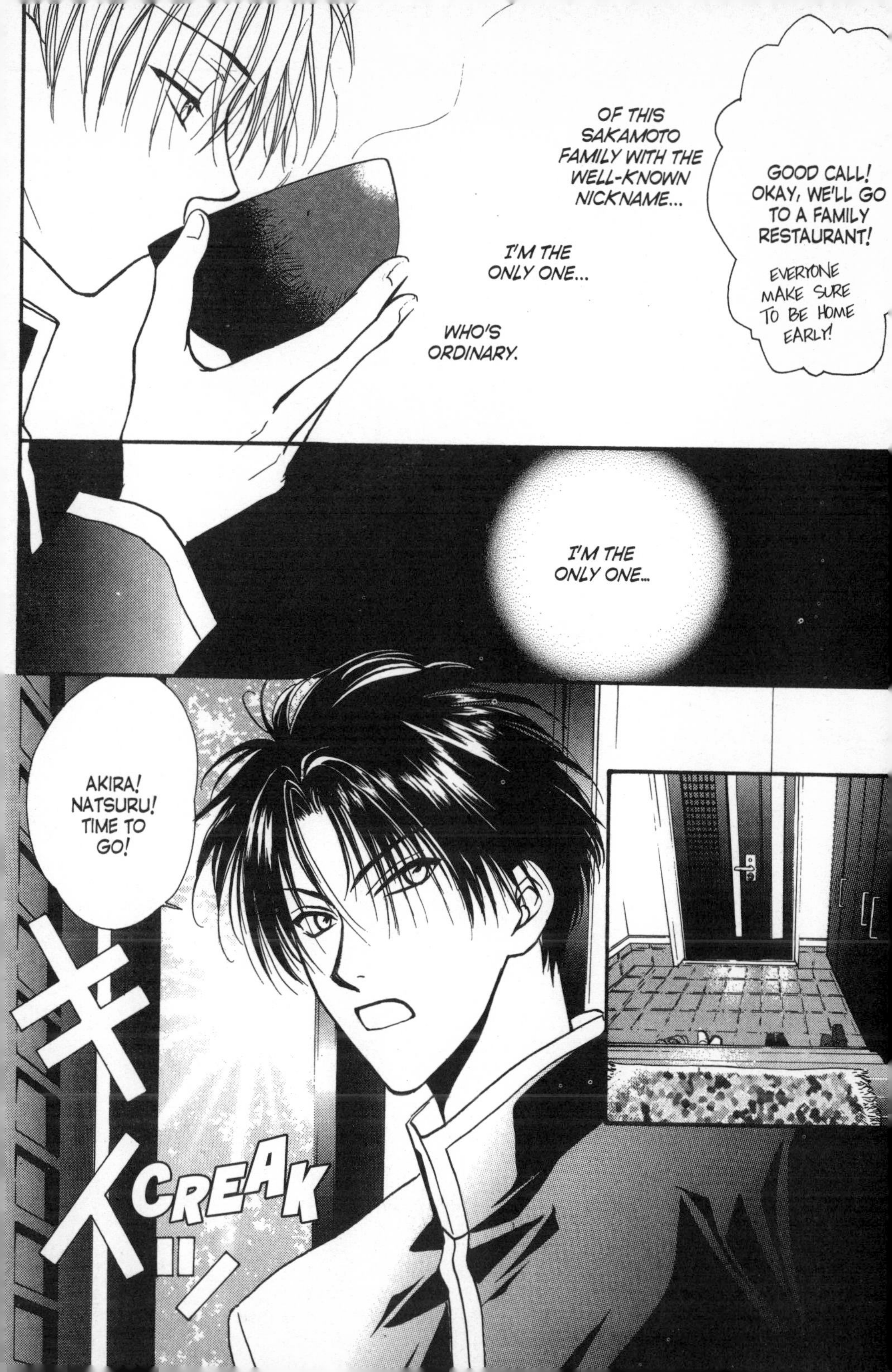
GOOD CALL! OKAY, WE'LL GO TO A FAMILY RESTAURANT!
EVERYONE MAKE SURE TO BE HOME EARLY!
OF THIS SAKAMOTO FAMILY WITH THE WELL-KNOWN NICKNAME...
I'M THE ONLY ONE...
WHO'S ORDINARY.
I'M THE ONLY ONE...
AKIRA! NATSURU! TIME TO GO!
CREAK

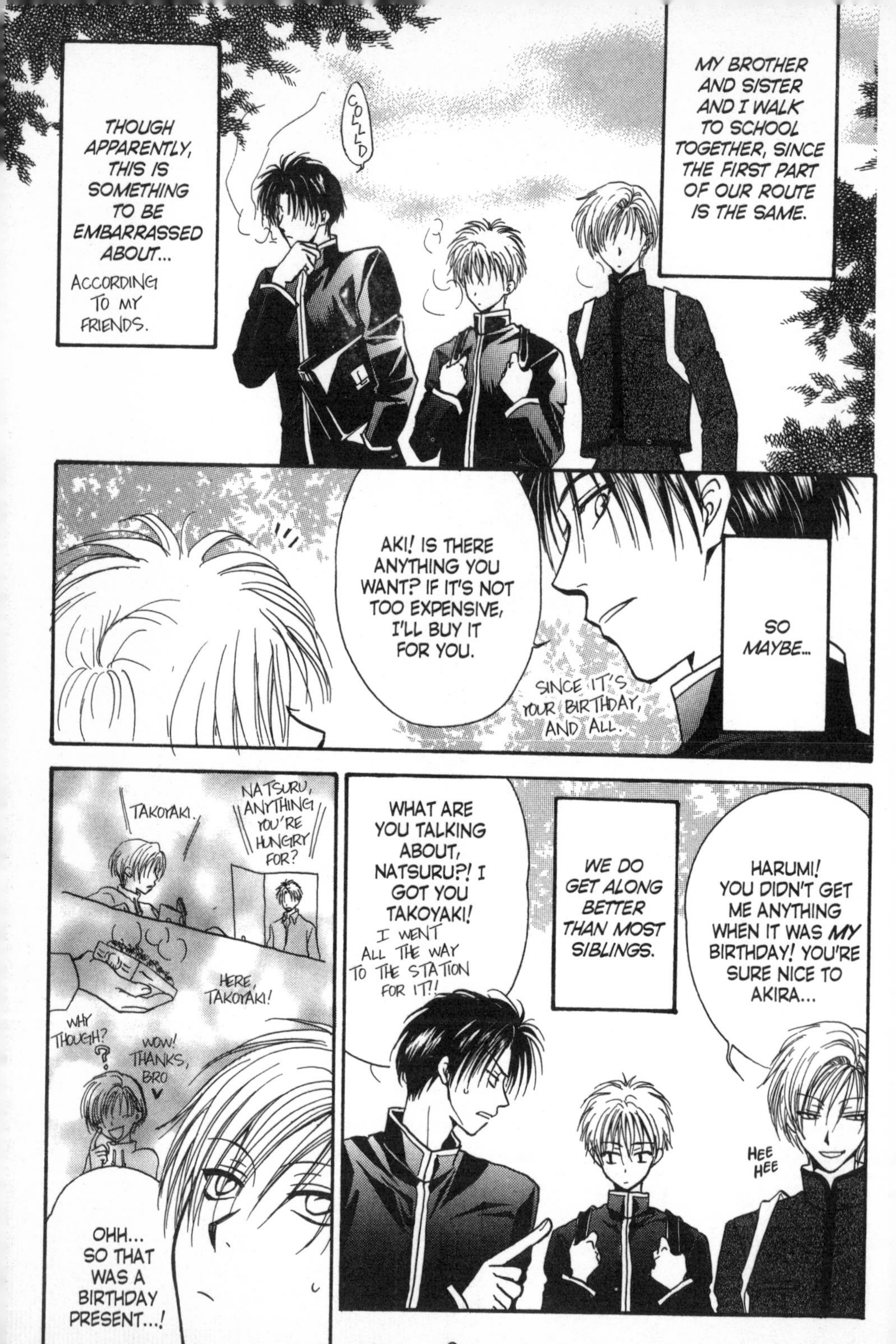
MY BROTHER AND SISTER AND I WALK TO SCHOOL TOGETHER, SINCE THE FIRST PART OF OUR ROUTE IS THE SAME.
COLLLD
THOUGH APPARENTLY, THIS IS SOMETHING TO BE EMBARRASSED ABOUT...
ACCORDING TO MY FRIENDS.
SO MAYBE...
AKI! IS THERE ANYTHING YOU WANT? IF IT'S NOT TOO EXPENSIVE, I'LL BUY IT FOR YOU.
SINCE IT'S YOUR BIRTHDAY, AND ALL.
HARUMI! YOU DIDN'T GET ME ANYTHING WHEN IT WAS *MY* BIRTHDAY! YOU'RE SURE NICE TO AKIRA...
HEE HEE
WE DO GET ALONG BETTER THAN MOST SIBLINGS.
WHAT ARE YOU TALKING ABOUT, NATSURU?! I GOT YOU TAKOYAKI!
I WENT ALL THE WAY TO THE STATION FOR IT!!
NATSURU, ANYTHING YOU'RE HUNGRY FOR?
TAKOYAKI.
HERE, TAKOYAKI!
WOW! THANKS, BRO
WHY THOUGH?
OHH... SO THAT WAS A BIRTHDAY PRESENT...!

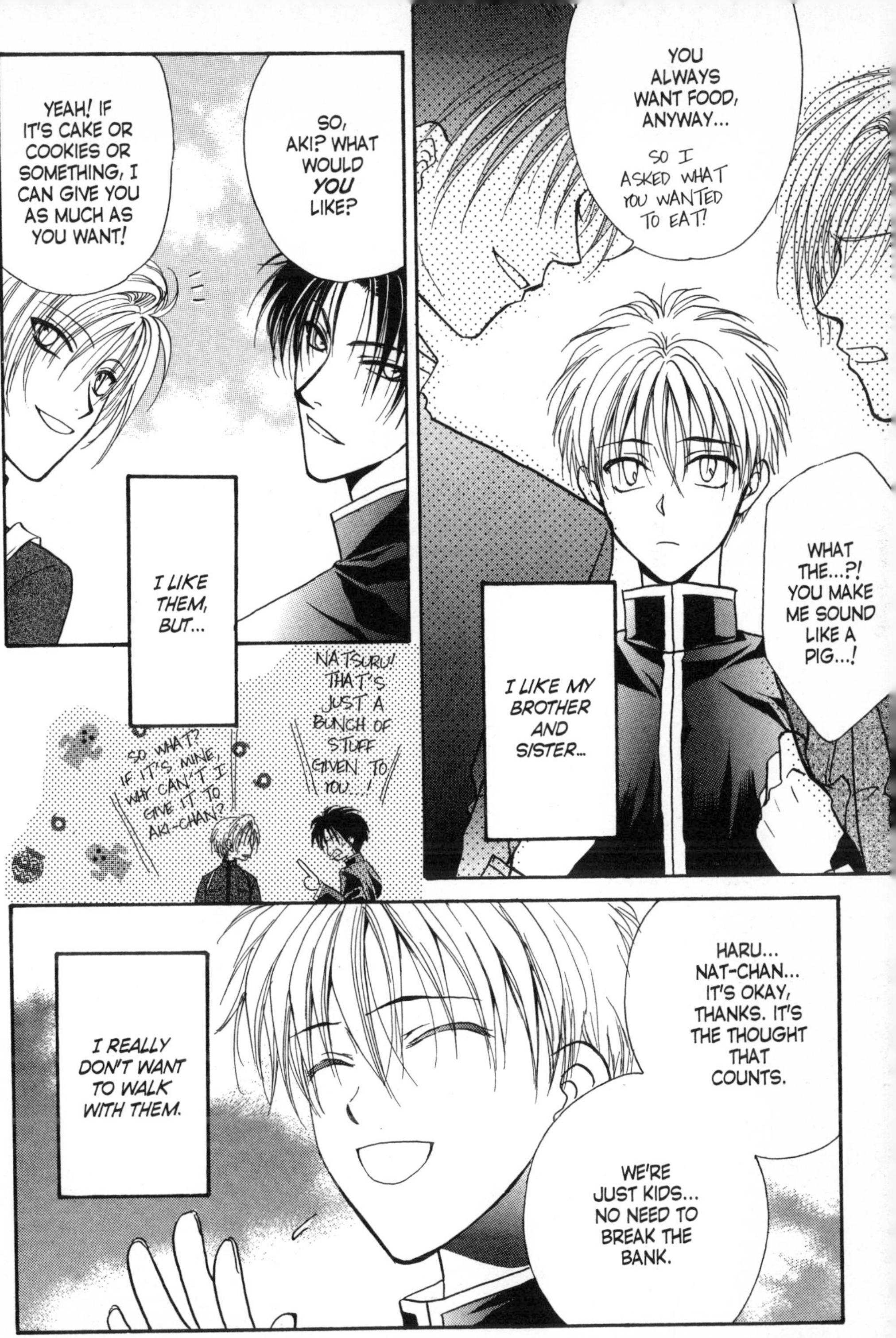
YOU ALWAYS WANT FOOD, ANYWAY...
SO I ASKED WHAT YOU WANTED TO EAT!
WHAT THE...?! YOU MAKE ME SOUND LIKE A PIG...!
I LIKE MY BROTHER AND SISTER...
SO, AKI? WHAT WOULD *YOU* LIKE?
YEAH! IF IT'S CAKE OR COOKIES OR SOMETHING, I CAN GIVE YOU AS MUCH AS YOU WANT!
I LIKE THEM, BUT...
NATSURU! THAT'S JUST A BUNCH OF STUFF GIVEN TO YOU...!
SO WHAT? IF IT'S MINE, WHY CAN'T I GIVE IT TO AKI-CHAN?
HARU... NAT-CHAN... IT'S OKAY, THANKS. IT'S THE THOUGHT THAT COUNTS.
WE'RE JUST KIDS... NO NEED TO BREAK THE BANK.
I REALLY DON'T WANT TO WALK WITH THEM.

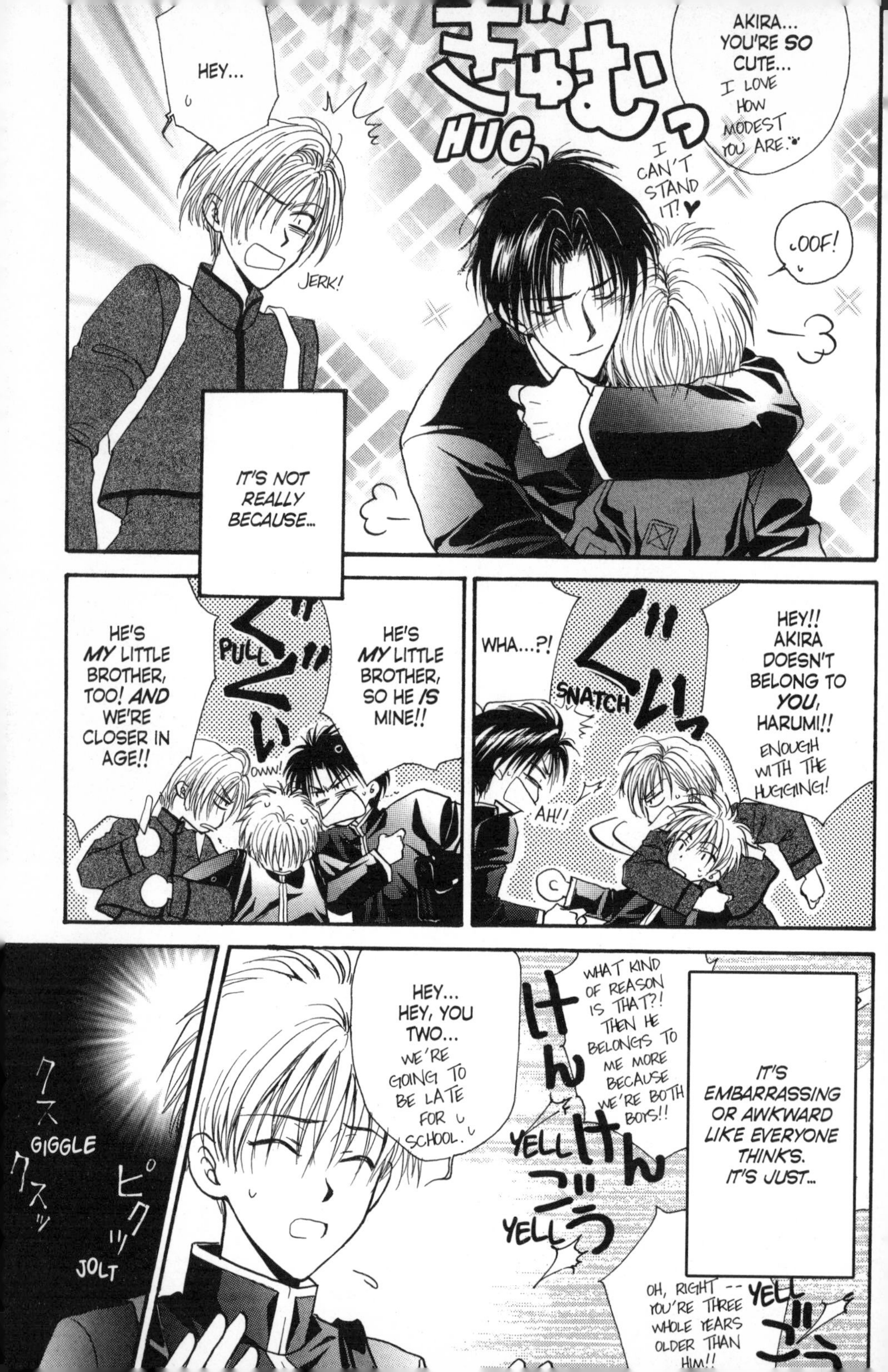
ぎゅむっ
HUG
AKIRA... YOU'RE SO CUTE... I LOVE HOW MODEST YOU ARE.
I CAN'T STAND IT!♥
OOF!
HEY...
JERK!
IT'S NOT REALLY BECAUSE...
HEY!! AKIRA DOESN'T BELONG TO YOU, HARUMI!! ENOUGH WITH THE HUGGING!
ぐいっ
SNATCH
WHA...?!
AH!!
HE'S MY LITTLE BROTHER, SO HE IS MINE!!
ぐぐい
PULL
HE'S MY LITTLE BROTHER, TOO! AND WE'RE CLOSER IN AGE!!
OWW!
IT'S EMBARRASSING OR AWKWARD LIKE EVERYONE THINKS. IT'S JUST...
WHAT KIND OF REASON IS THAT?! THEN HE BELONGS TO ME MORE BECAUSE WE'RE BOTH BOYS!!
けんけんごうごう
YELL
YELL
OH, RIGHT -- YOU'RE THREE WHOLE YEARS OLDER THAN HIM!!
YELL
HEY... HEY, YOU TWO... WE'RE GOING TO BE LATE FOR SCHOOL.
ピクッ
JOLT
クスクスッ
GIGGLE

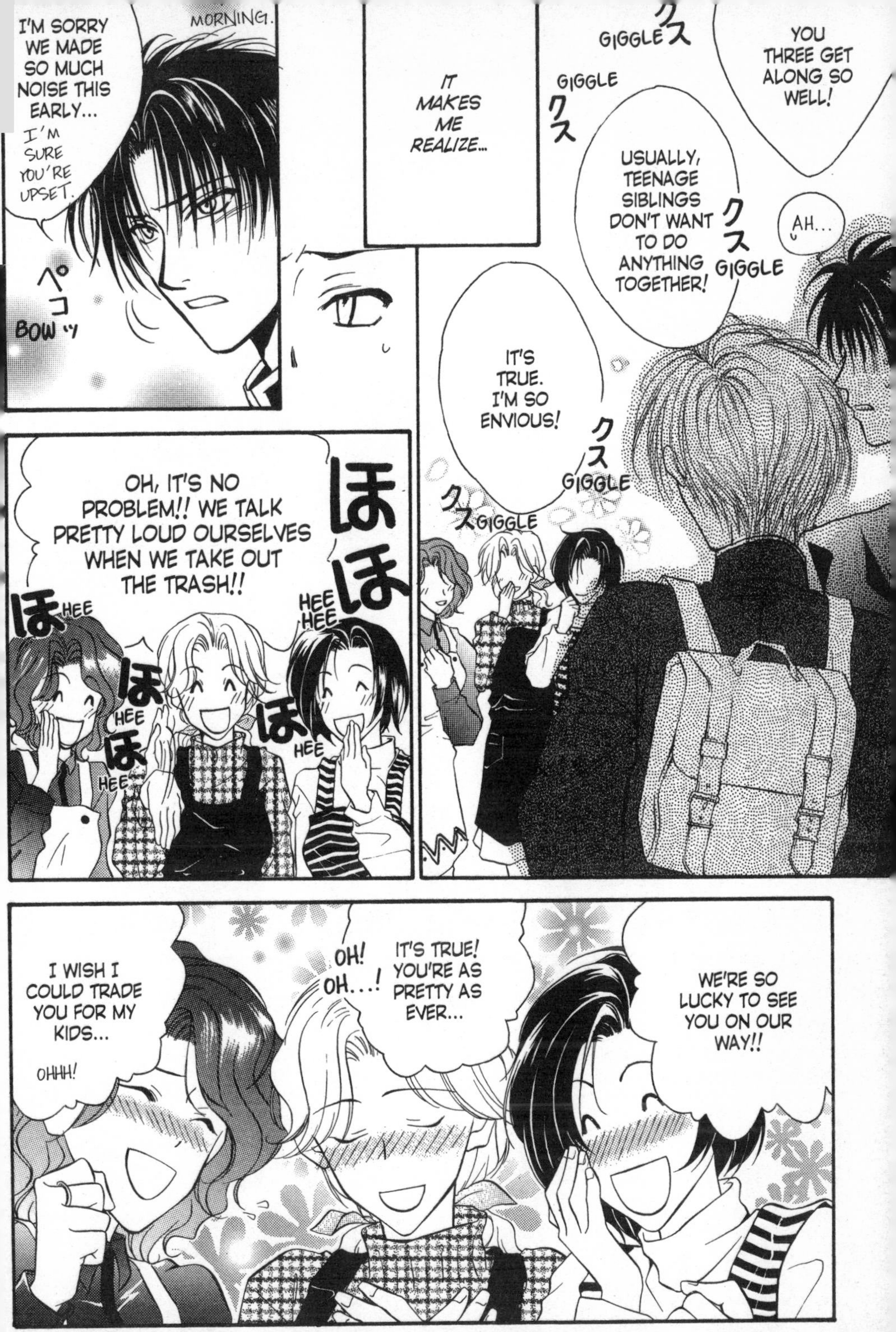
IT MAKES ME REALIZE...
YOU THREE GET ALONG SO WELL!
クス GIGGLE
GIGGLE クス
USUALLY, TEENAGE SIBLINGS DON'T WANT TO DO ANYTHING TOGETHER!
クス GIGGLE
AH...
IT'S TRUE. I'M SO ENVIOUS!
クス GIGGLE
クス GIGGLE
MORNING.
I'M SORRY WE MADE SO MUCH NOISE THIS EARLY...
I'M SURE YOU'RE UPSET.
ペコッ BOW
OH, IT'S NO PROBLEM!! WE TALK PRETTY LOUD OURSELVES WHEN WE TAKE OUT THE TRASH!!
ほほ
HEE HEE
ほ HEE
ほ HEE
ほ HEE
ほ HEE
WE'RE SO LUCKY TO SEE YOU ON OUR WAY!!
IT'S TRUE! YOU'RE AS PRETTY AS EVER...
OH! OH...!
I WISH I COULD TRADE YOU FOR MY KIDS...
OHHH!

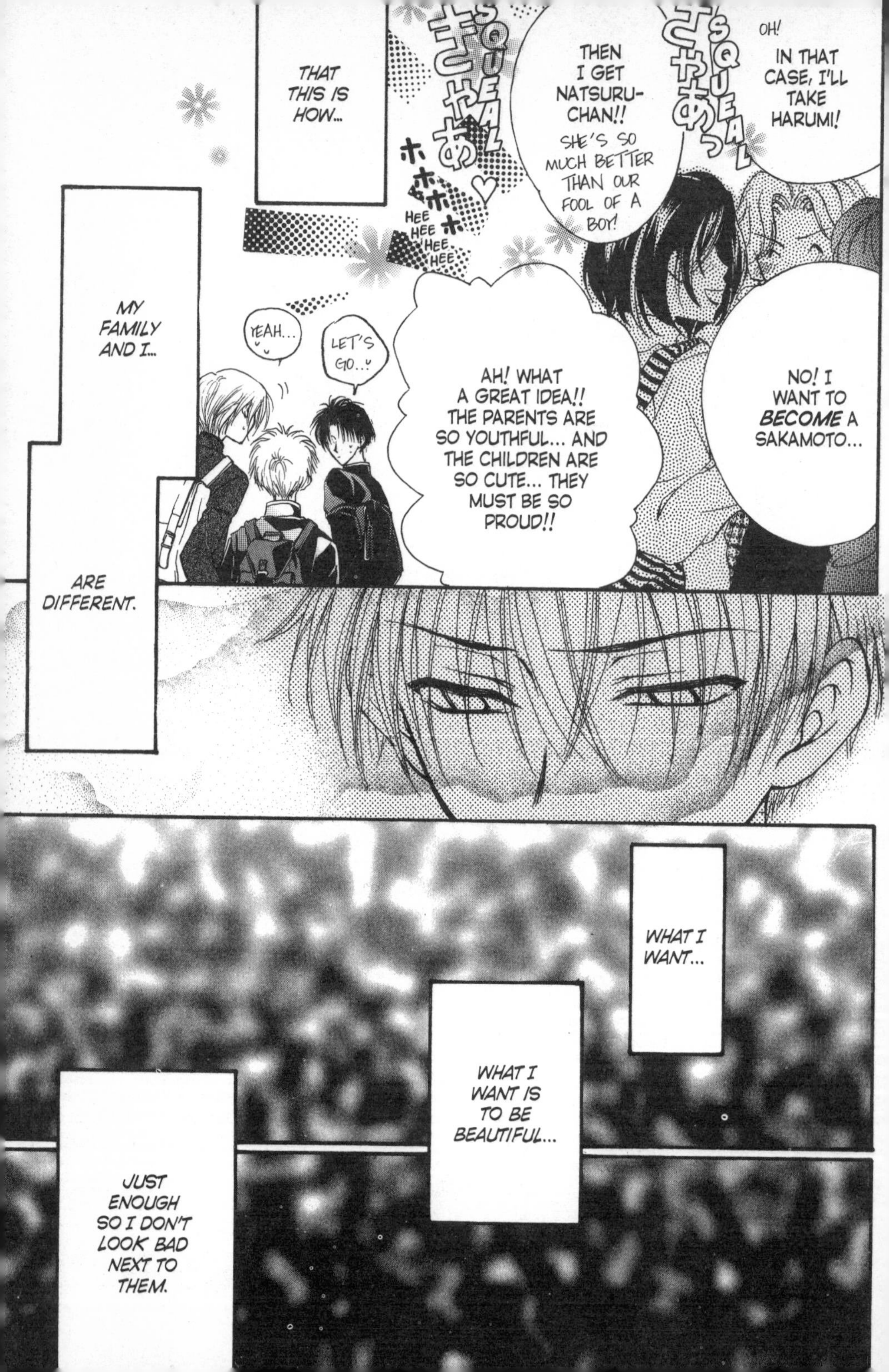

OH!
IN THAT CASE, I'LL TAKE HARUMI!
きゃあっ SQUEAL
THEN I GET NATSURU-CHAN!!
SHE'S SO MUCH BETTER THAN OUR FOOL OF A BOY!
きゃあ SQUEAL
ホホホホ HEE HEE HEE HEE
THAT THIS IS HOW...
NO! I WANT TO BECOME A SAKAMOTO...
AH! WHAT A GREAT IDEA!! THE PARENTS ARE SO YOUTHFUL... AND THE CHILDREN ARE SO CUTE... THEY MUST BE SO PROUD!!
LET'S GO...
YEAH...
MY FAMILY AND I...
ARE DIFFERENT.
WHAT I WANT...
WHAT I WANT IS TO BE BEAUTIFUL...
JUST ENOUGH SO I DON'T LOOK BAD NEXT TO THEM.

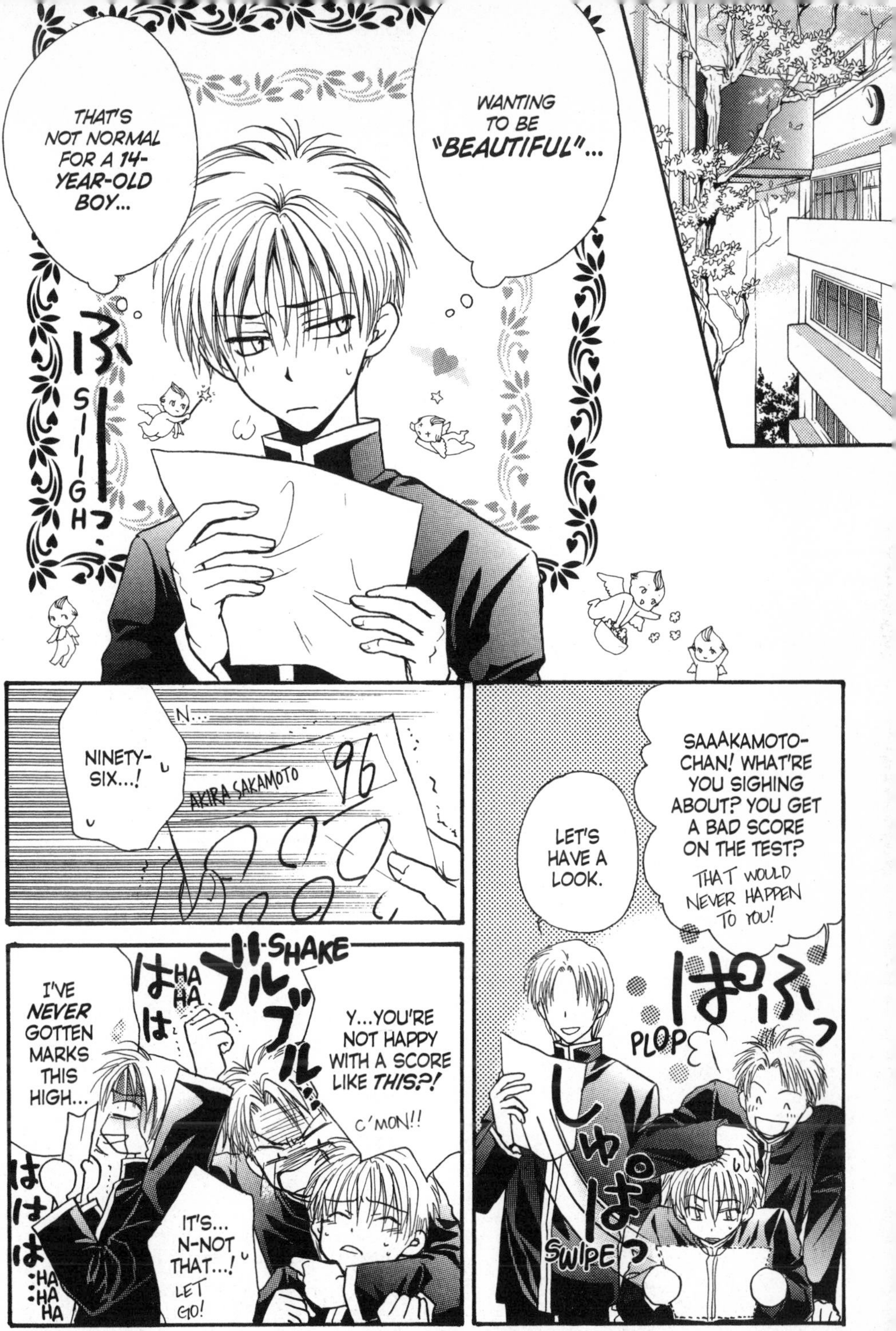
WANTING TO BE "BEAUTIFUL"...
THAT'S NOT NORMAL FOR A 14-YEAR-OLD BOY...
ふーっ
S-I-I-I-G-H
SAAAKAMOTO-CHAN! WHAT'RE YOU SIGHING ABOUT? YOU GET A BAD SCORE ON THE TEST?
THAT WOULD NEVER HAPPEN TO YOU!
LET'S HAVE A LOOK.
ぱふっ
PLOP
しゅぱっ
SWIPE
N...
NINETY-SIX...!
AKIRA SAKAMOTO
96
Y...YOU'RE NOT HAPPY WITH A SCORE LIKE THIS?!
C'MON!!
ブルブル
SHAKE
はは
HA HA
I'VE NEVER GOTTEN MARKS THIS HIGH...
ははは
HA HA HA
IT'S... N-NOT THAT...!
LET GO!

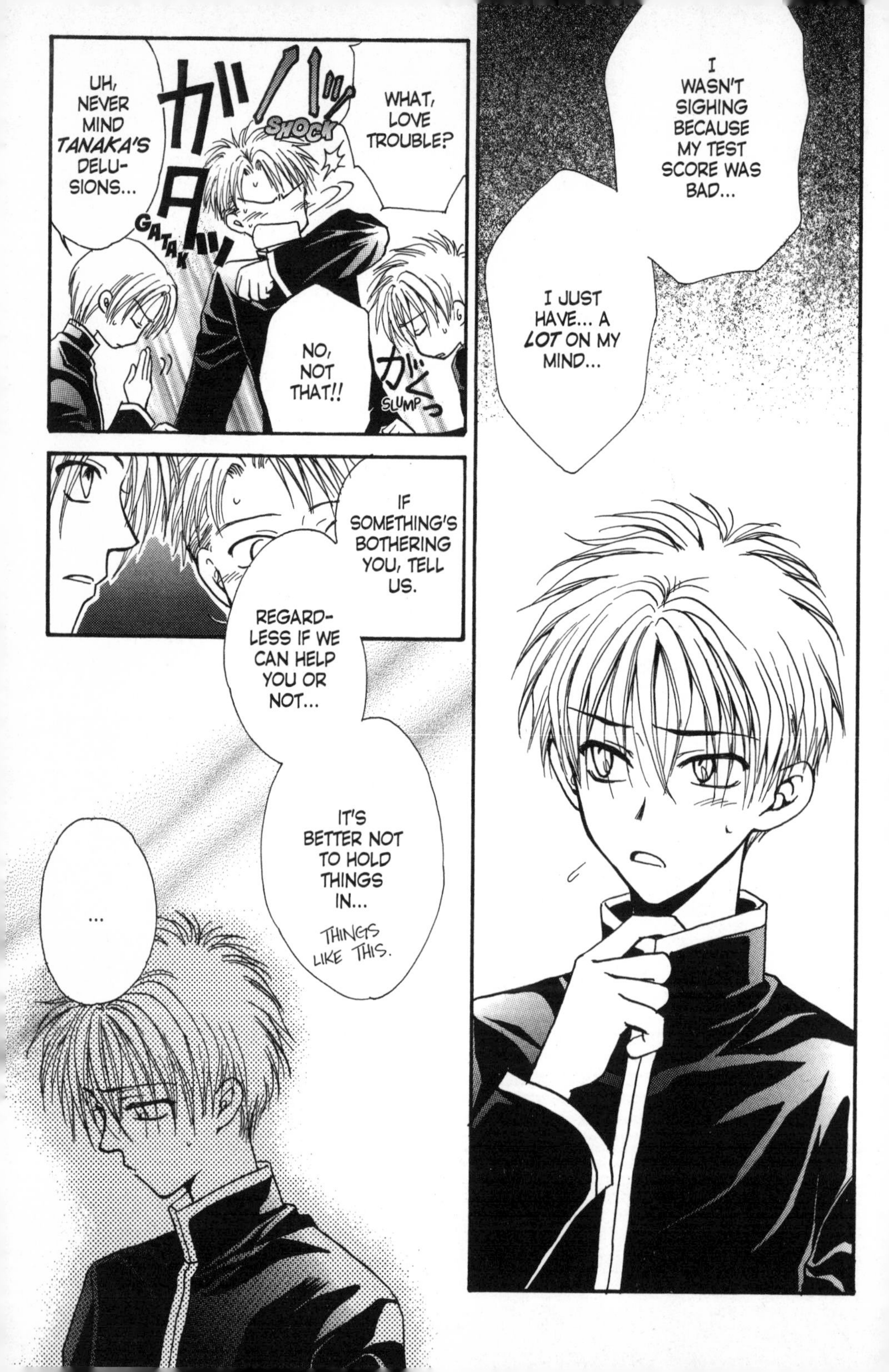
I WASN'T SIGHING BECAUSE MY TEST SCORE WAS BAD...
I JUST HAVE... A *LOT* ON MY MIND...
WHAT, LOVE TROUBLE?
SHOCK
UH, NEVER MIND *TANAKA'S* DELUSIONS...
ガタ
GATAK
NO, NOT THAT!!
がくっ
SLUMP
IF SOMETHING'S BOTHERING YOU, TELL US.
REGARDLESS IF WE CAN HELP YOU OR NOT...
IT'S BETTER NOT TO HOLD THINGS IN...
THINGS LIKE THIS.
...

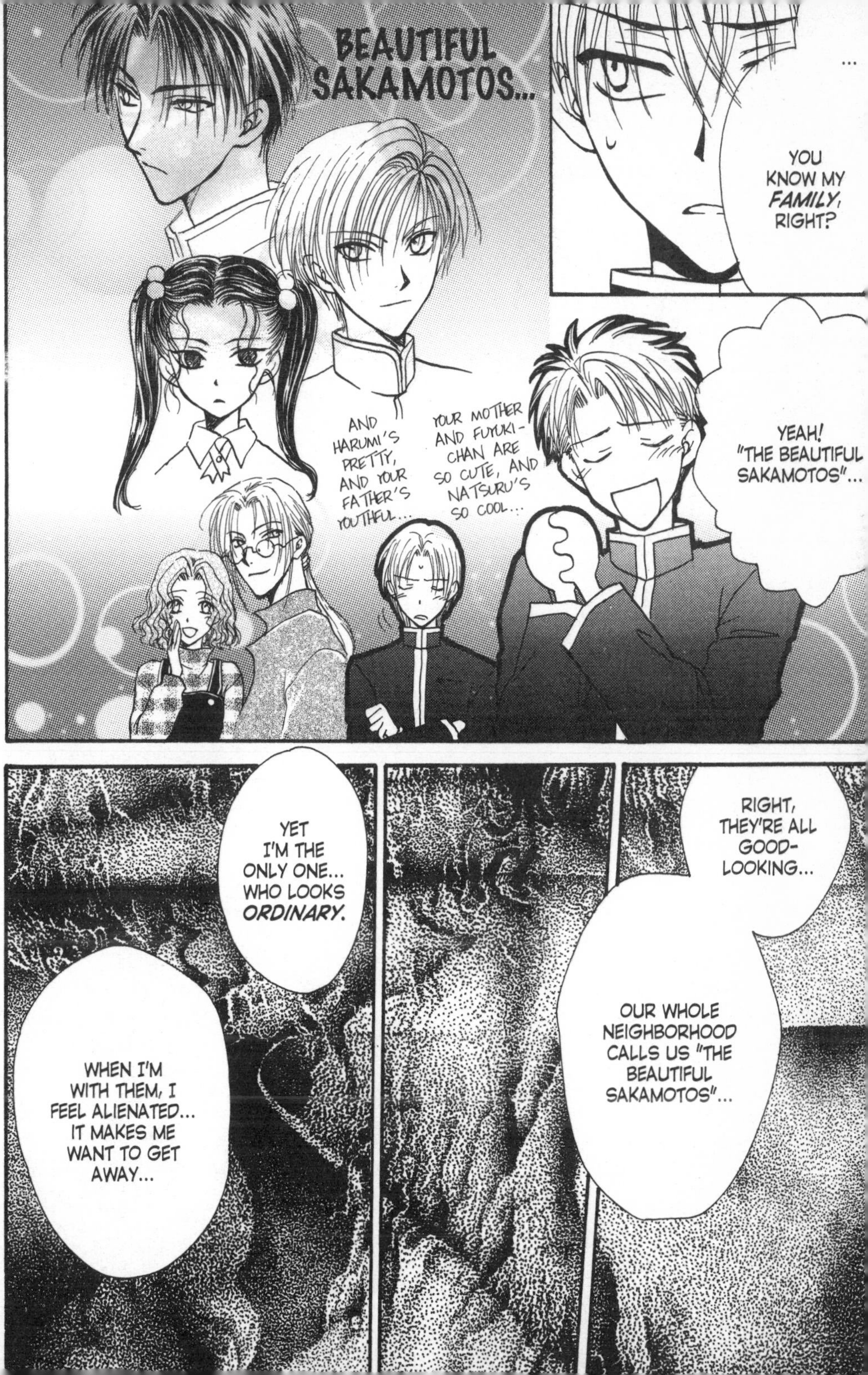
...
YOU KNOW MY *FAMILY*, RIGHT?
YEAH! "THE BEAUTIFUL SAKAMOTOS"...
BEAUTIFUL SAKAMOTOS...
YOUR MOTHER AND FUYUKI-CHAN ARE SO CUTE, AND NATSURU'S SO COOL...
AND HARUMI'S PRETTY, AND YOUR FATHER'S YOUTHFUL...
RIGHT, THEY'RE ALL GOOD-LOOKING...
OUR WHOLE NEIGHBORHOOD CALLS US "THE BEAUTIFUL SAKAMOTOS"...
YET I'M THE ONLY ONE... WHO LOOKS ***ORDINARY.***
WHEN I'M WITH THEM, I FEEL ALIENATED... IT MAKES ME WANT TO GET AWAY...

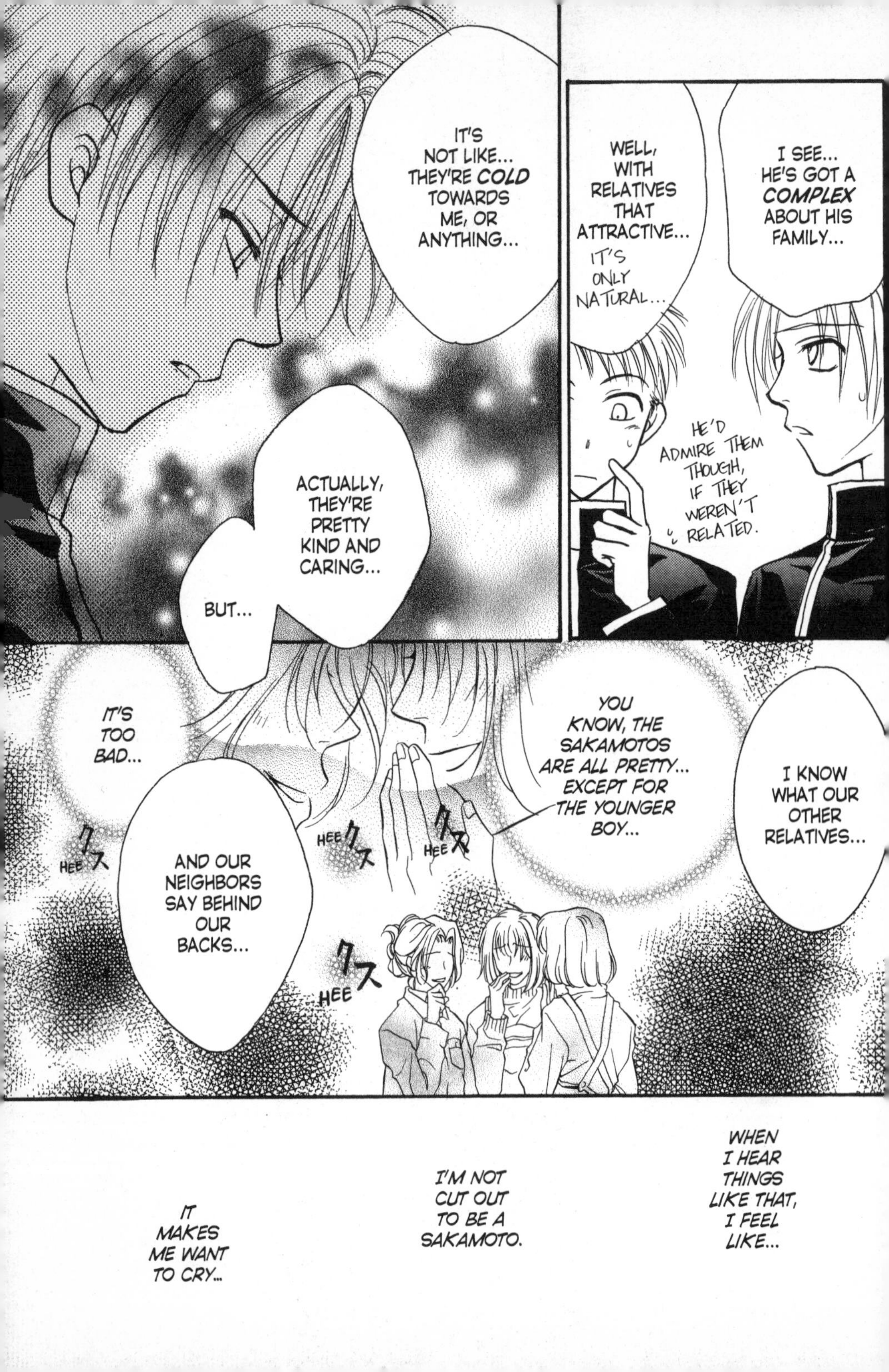
I SEE... HE'S GOT A COMPLEX ABOUT HIS FAMILY...
WELL, WITH RELATIVES THAT ATTRACTIVE... IT'S ONLY NATURAL...
HE'D ADMIRE THEM THOUGH, IF THEY WEREN'T RELATED.
IT'S NOT LIKE... THEY'RE COLD TOWARDS ME, OR ANYTHING...
ACTUALLY, THEY'RE PRETTY KIND AND CARING... BUT...
I KNOW WHAT OUR OTHER RELATIVES...
YOU KNOW, THE SAKAMOTOS ARE ALL PRETTY... EXCEPT FOR THE YOUNGER BOY...
HEE クス
HEE クス
IT'S TOO BAD...
AND OUR NEIGHBORS SAY BEHIND OUR BACKS...
HEE クス
HEE クス
WHEN I HEAR THINGS LIKE THAT, I FEEL LIKE...
I'M NOT CUT OUT TO BE A SAKAMOTO.
IT MAKES ME WANT TO CRY...

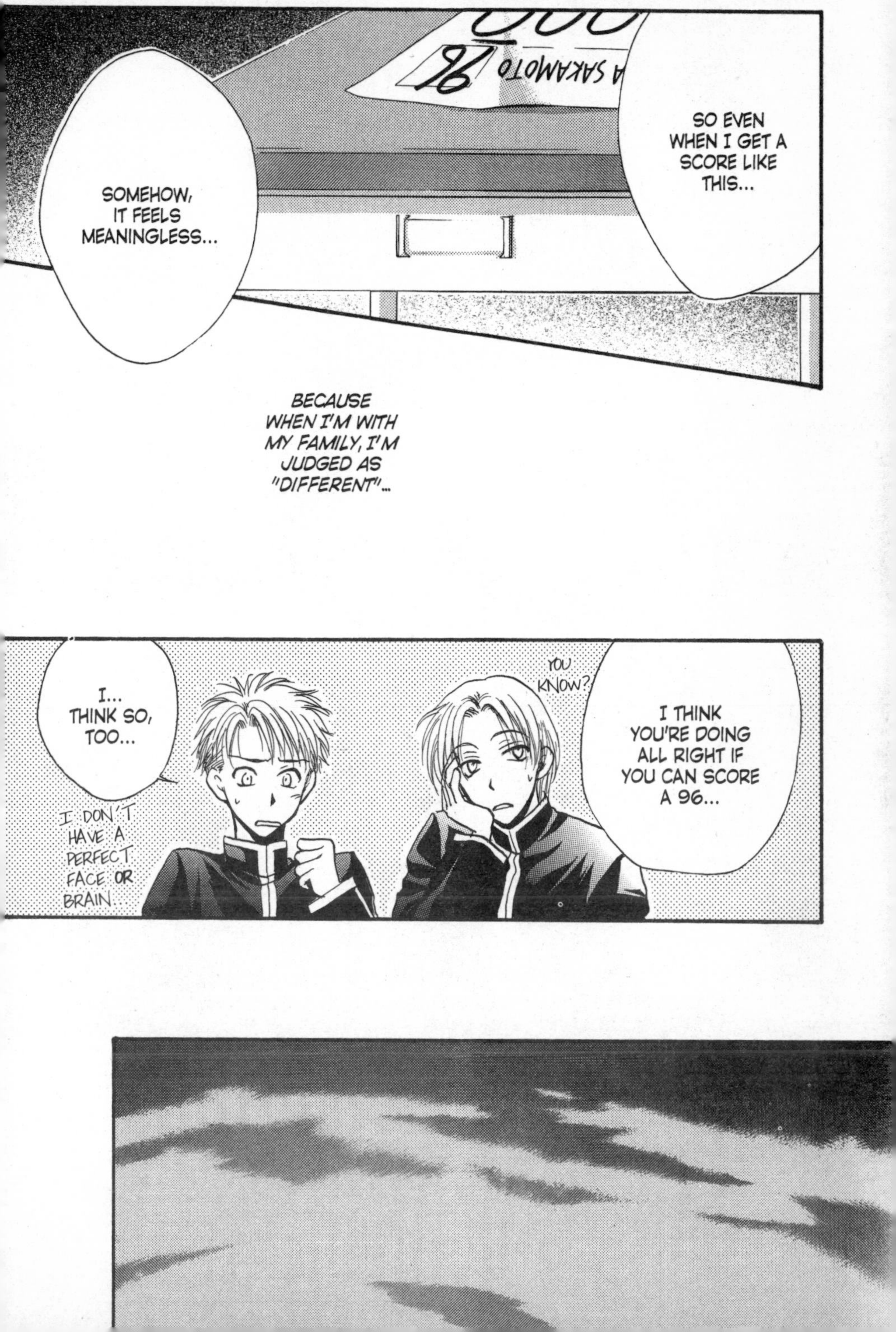
SO EVEN WHEN I GET A SCORE LIKE THIS...
SOMEHOW, IT FEELS MEANINGLESS...
BECAUSE WHEN I'M WITH MY FAMILY, I'M JUDGED AS "DIFFERENT"...
I THINK YOU'RE DOING ALL RIGHT IF YOU CAN SCORE A 96...
YOU KNOW?
I... THINK SO, TOO...
I DON'T HAVE A PERFECT FACE OR BRAIN...

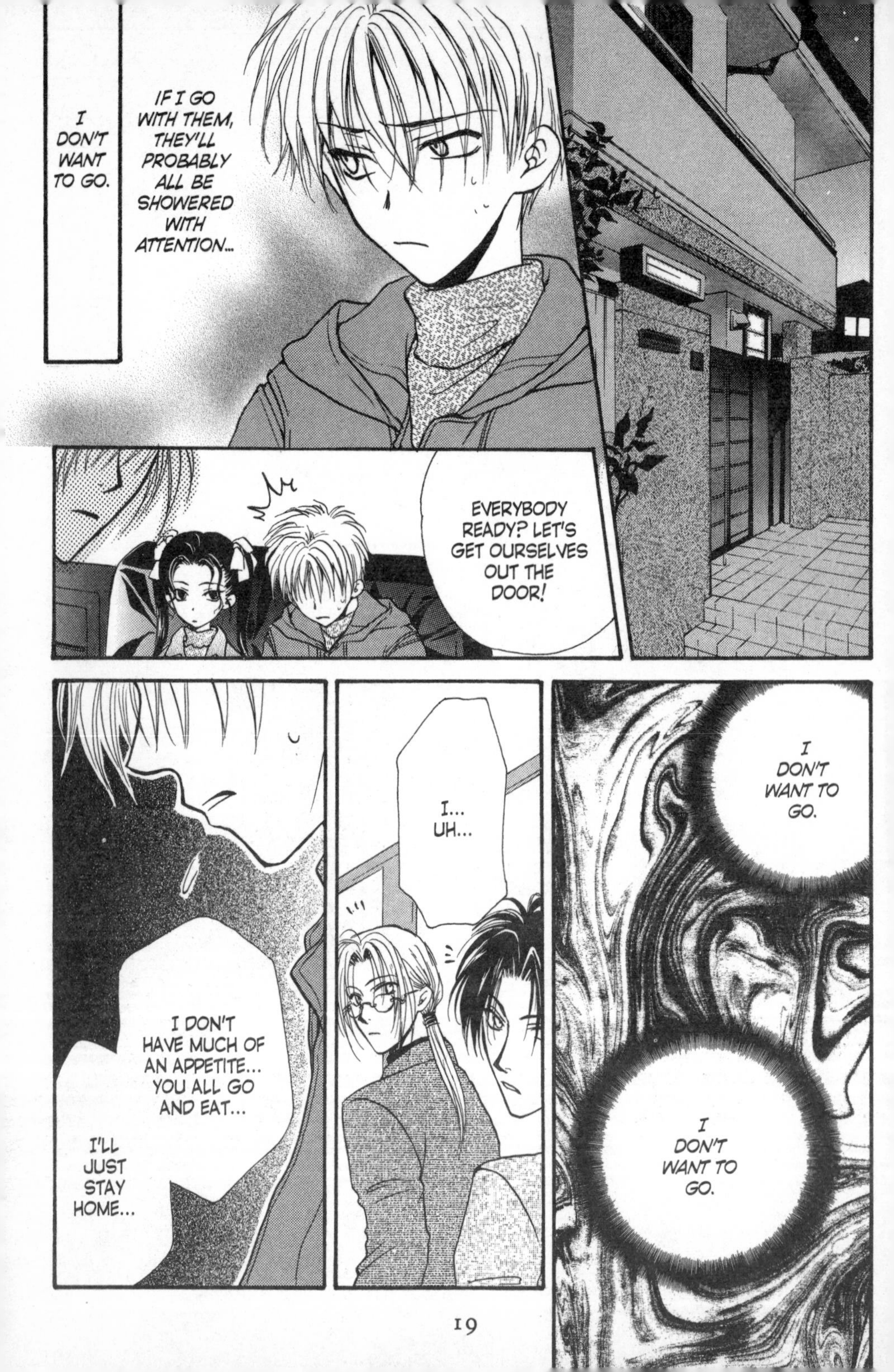
IF I GO WITH THEM, THEY'LL PROBABLY ALL BE SHOWERED WITH ATTENTION...
I DON'T WANT TO GO.
EVERYBODY READY? LET'S GET OURSELVES OUT THE DOOR!
I DON'T WANT TO GO.
I DON'T WANT TO GO.
I... UH...
I DON'T HAVE MUCH OF AN APPETITE... YOU ALL GO AND EAT...
I'LL JUST STAY HOME...

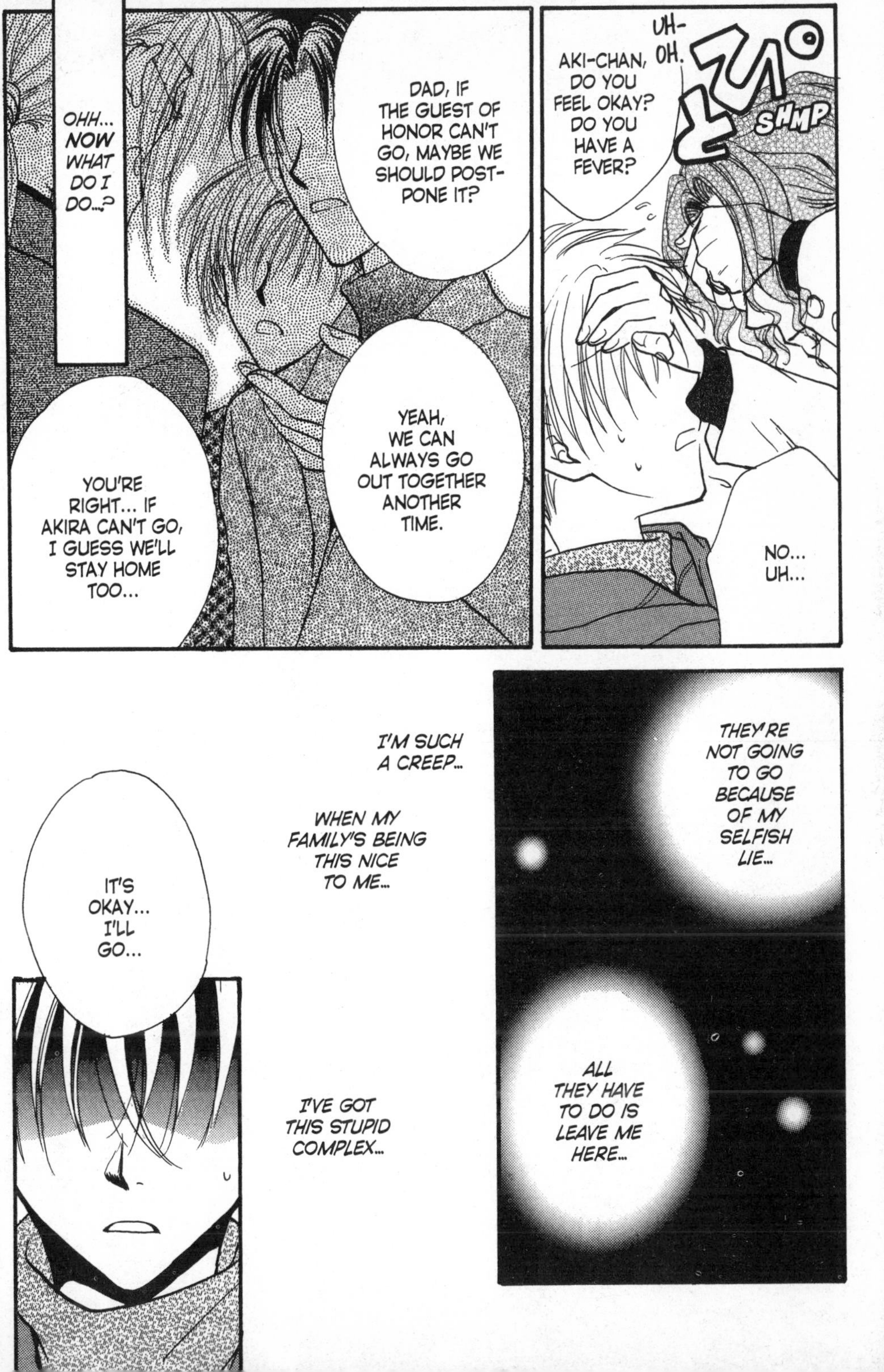
UH-OH.
AKI-CHAN, DO YOU FEEL OKAY? DO YOU HAVE A FEVER?
SHMP
NO... UH...
DAD, IF THE GUEST OF HONOR CAN'T GO, MAYBE WE SHOULD POST-PONE IT?
OHH... NOW WHAT DO I DO...?
YEAH, WE CAN ALWAYS GO OUT TOGETHER ANOTHER TIME.
YOU'RE RIGHT... IF AKIRA CAN'T GO, I GUESS WE'LL STAY HOME TOO...
THEY'RE NOT GOING TO GO BECAUSE OF MY SELFISH LIE...
ALL THEY HAVE TO DO IS LEAVE ME HERE...
I'M SUCH A CREEP...
WHEN MY FAMILY'S BEING THIS NICE TO ME...
I'VE GOT THIS STUPID COMPLEX...
IT'S OKAY... I'LL GO...

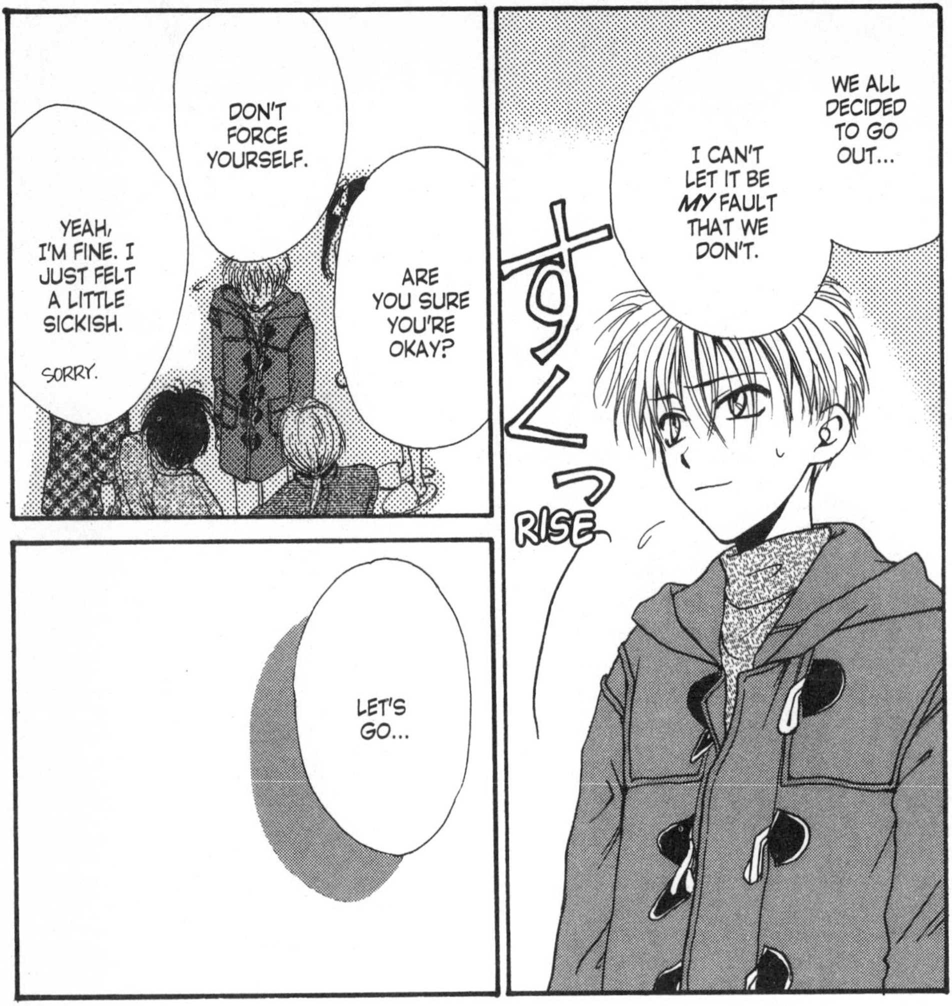
WE ALL DECIDED TO GO OUT...
I CAN'T LET IT BE *MY* FAULT THAT WE DON'T.
すくっ
RISE
ARE YOU SURE YOU'RE OKAY?
DON'T FORCE YOURSELF.
YEAH, I'M FINE. I JUST FELT A LITTLE SICKISH.
SORRY.
LET'S GO...

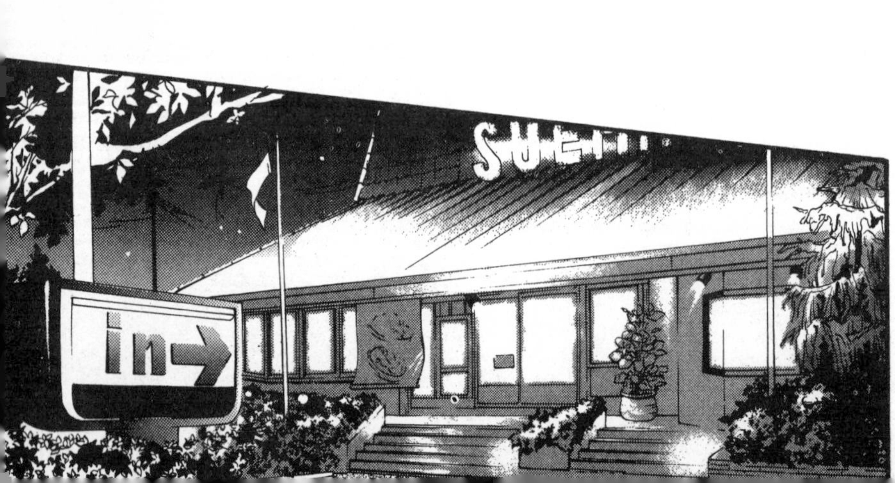
in

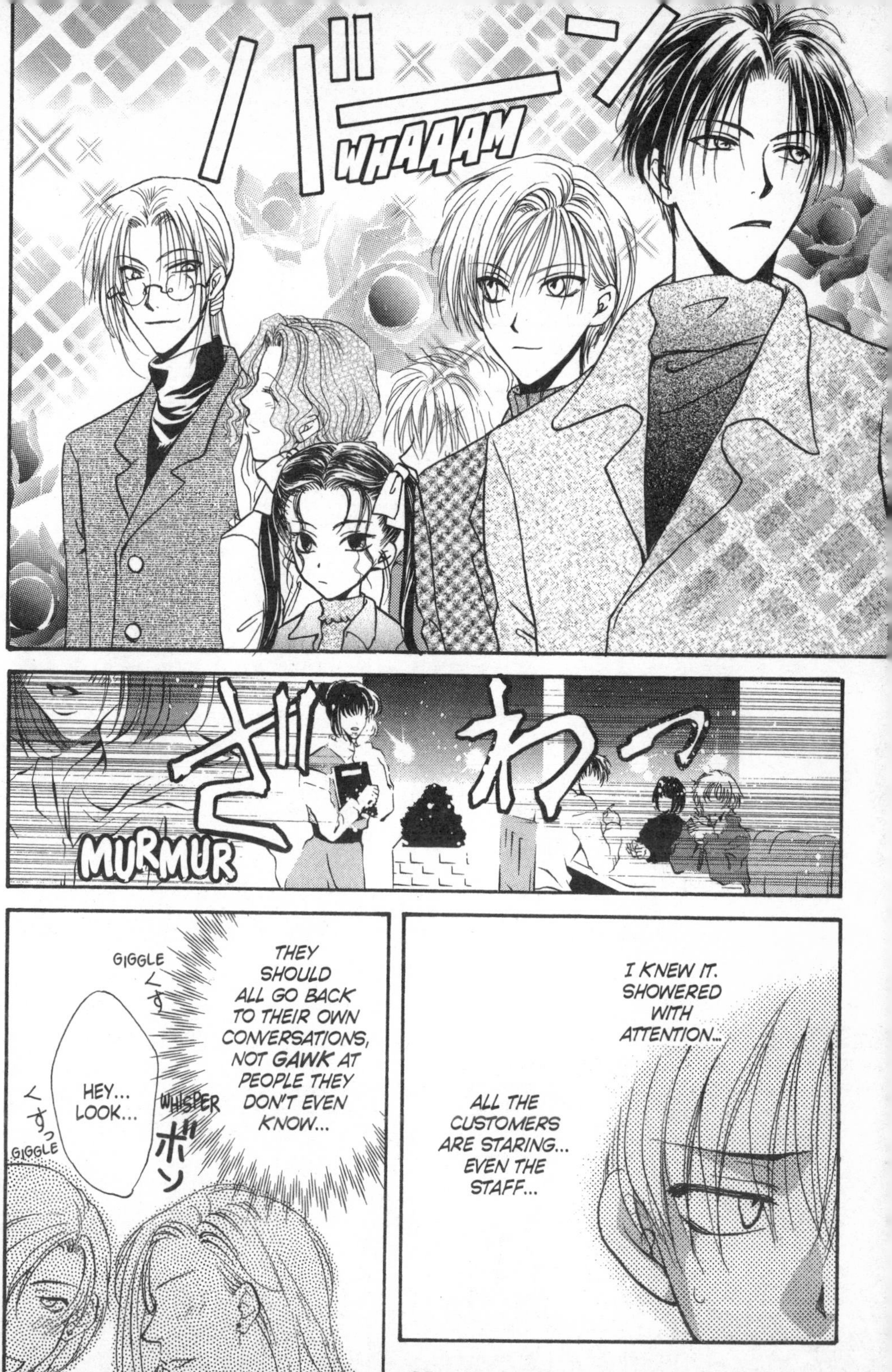

バーン
WHAAAM
ざわっ
MURMUR
I KNEW IT. SHOWERED WITH ATTENTION...
ALL THE CUSTOMERS ARE STARING... EVEN THE STAFF...
THEY SHOULD ALL GO BACK TO THEIR OWN CONVERSATIONS, NOT GAWK AT PEOPLE THEY DON'T EVEN KNOW...
GIGGLE
くす
HEY... LOOK...
WHISPER
ボソ
くすっ
GIGGLE

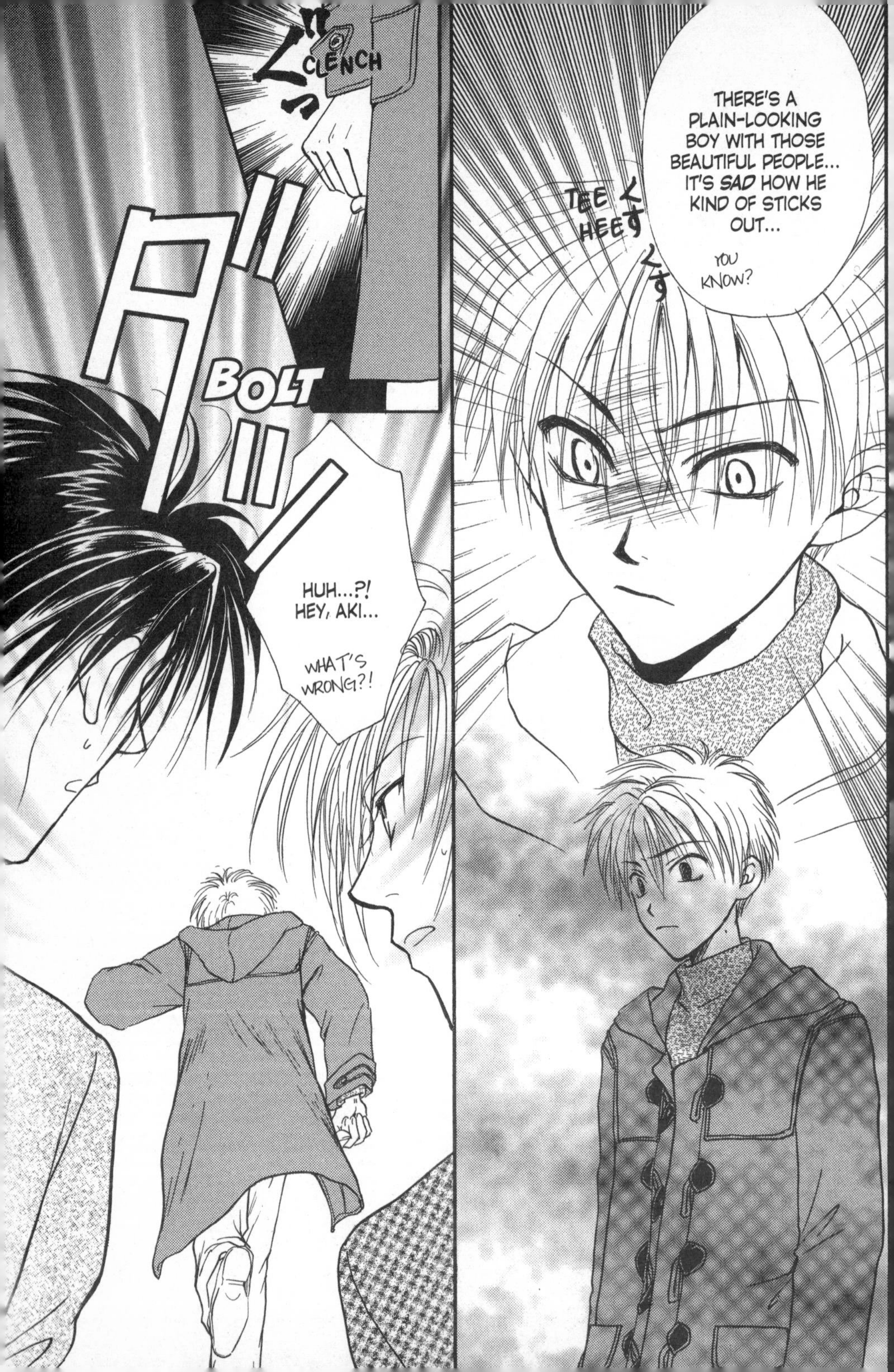
THERE'S A PLAIN-LOOKING BOY WITH THOSE BEAUTIFUL PEOPLE... IT'S SAD HOW HE KIND OF STICKS OUT...
YOU KNOW?
TEE HEE
くすくす
CLENCH
BOLT
HUH...?! HEY, AKI...
WHAT'S WRONG?!

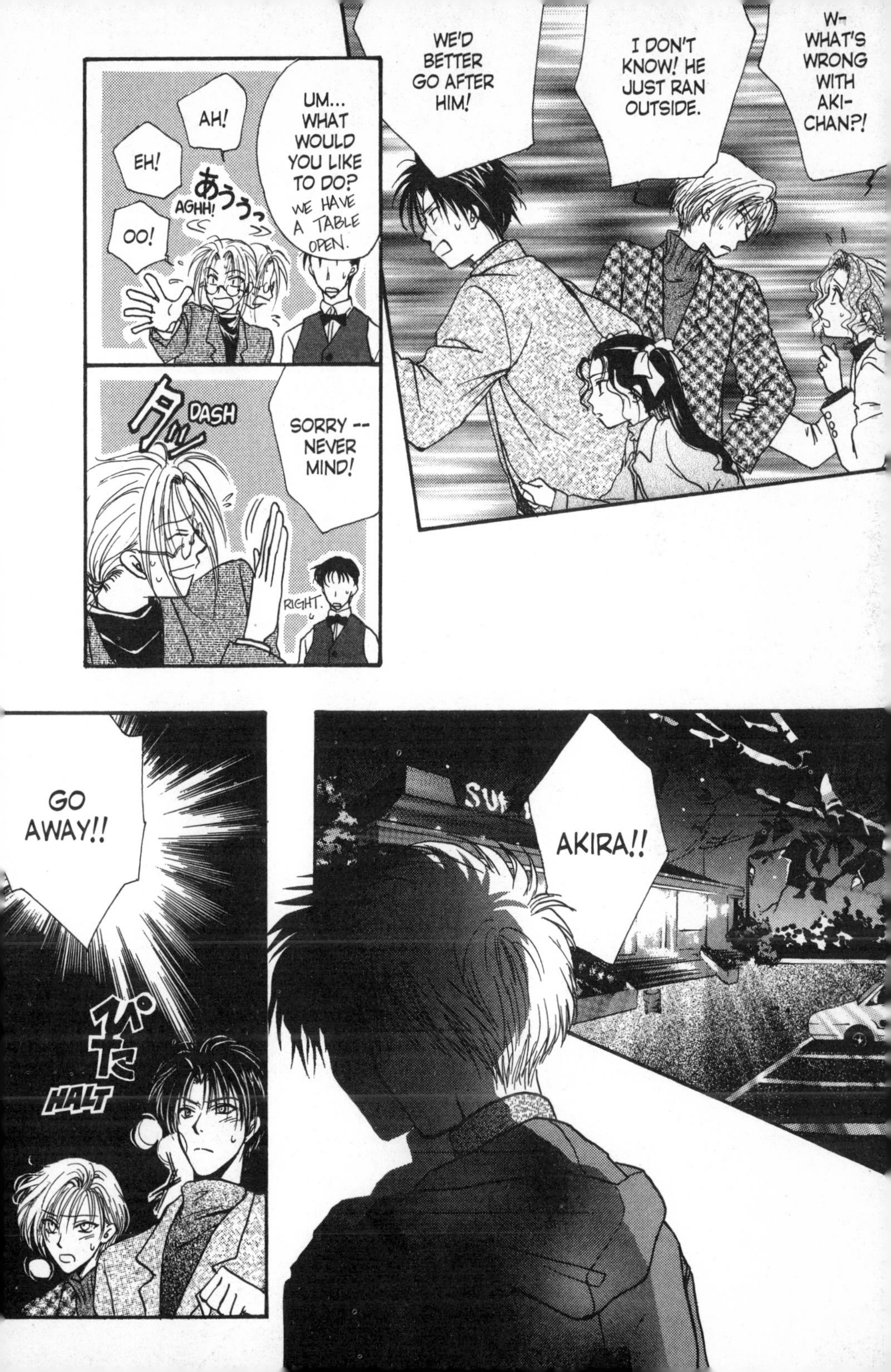
W-WHAT'S WRONG WITH AKI-CHAN?!
I DON'T KNOW! HE JUST RAN OUTSIDE.
WE'D BETTER GO AFTER HIM!
UM... WHAT WOULD YOU LIKE TO DO? WE HAVE A TABLE OPEN.
AH!
EH!
あうぅっ
AGHH!
OO!
SORRY -- NEVER MIND!
タッ
DASH
RIGHT.
AKIRA!!
GO AWAY!!
ぺた
HALT

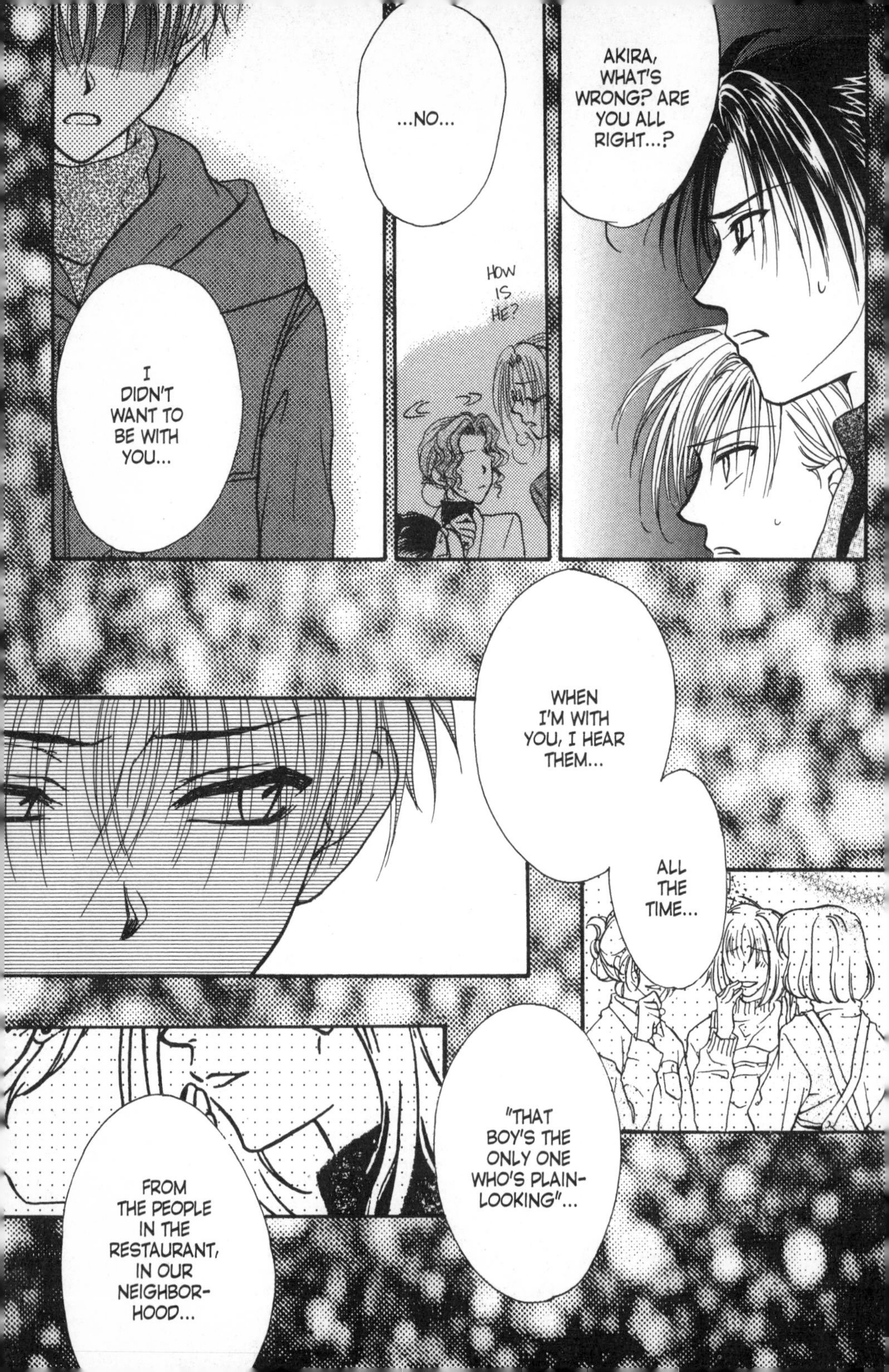
AKIRA, WHAT'S WRONG? ARE YOU ALL RIGHT...?
...NO...
HOW IS HE?
I DIDN'T WANT TO BE WITH YOU...
WHEN I'M WITH YOU, I HEAR THEM...
ALL THE TIME...
"THAT BOY'S THE ONLY ONE WHO'S PLAIN-LOOKING"...
FROM THE PEOPLE IN THE RESTAURANT, IN OUR NEIGHBOR-HOOD...

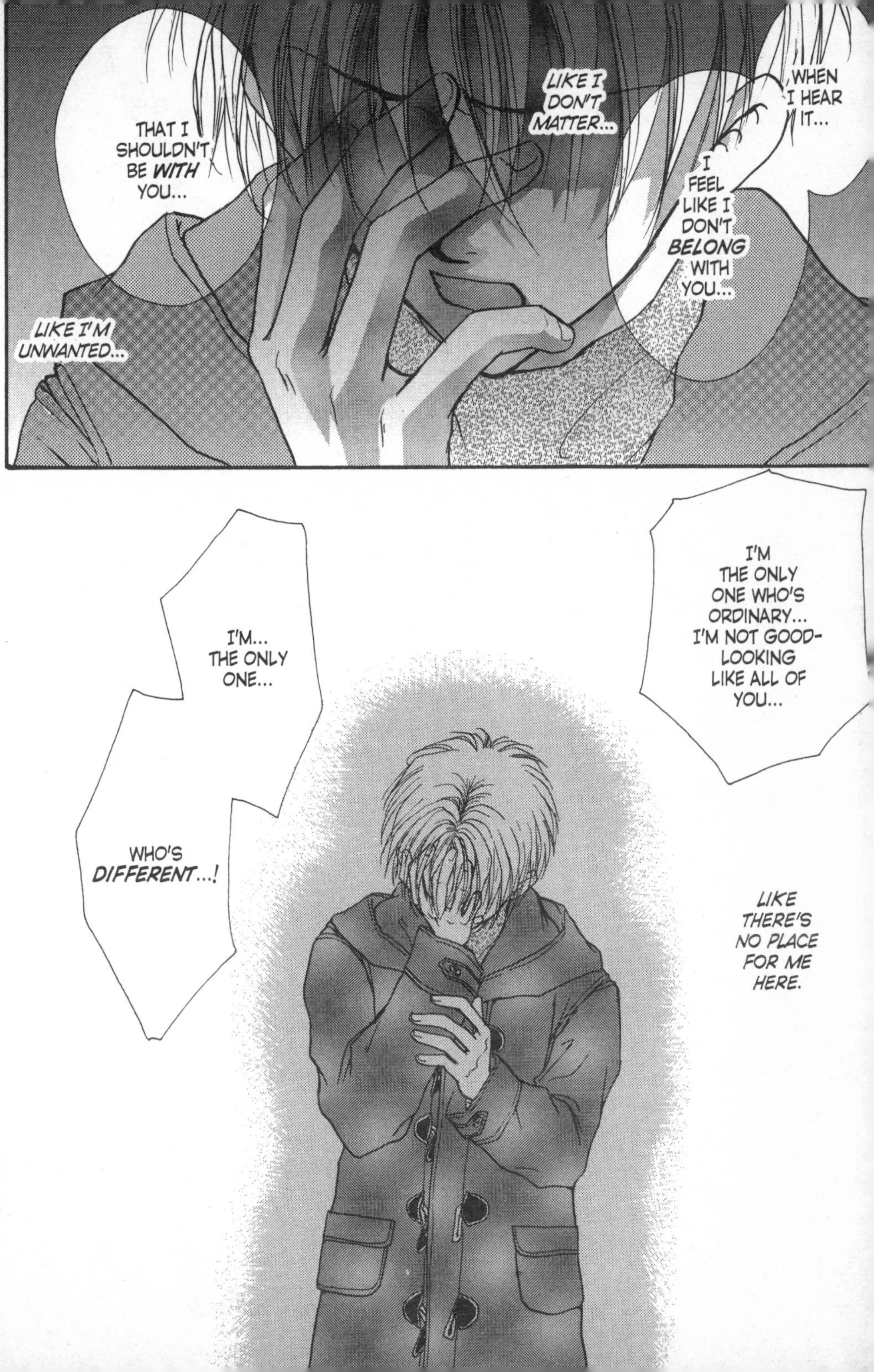
WHEN I HEAR IT...
I FEEL LIKE I DON'T BELONG WITH YOU...
LIKE I DON'T MATTER...
THAT I SHOULDN'T BE WITH YOU...
LIKE I'M UNWANTED...
I'M THE ONLY ONE WHO'S ORDINARY... I'M NOT GOOD-LOOKING LIKE ALL OF YOU...
LIKE THERE'S NO PLACE FOR ME HERE.
I'M... THE ONLY ONE...
WHO'S DIFFERENT...!

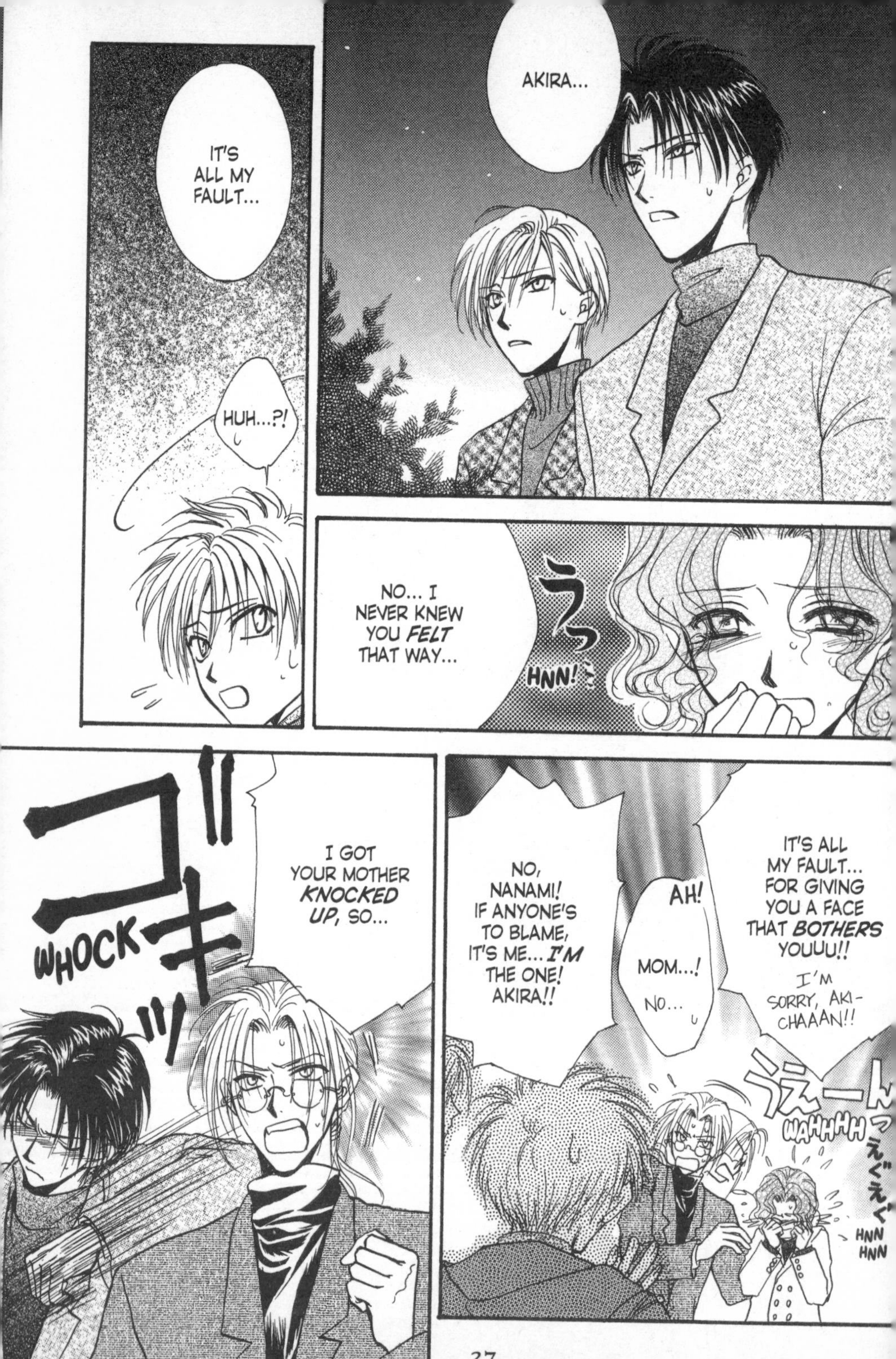
AKIRA...
NO... I NEVER KNEW YOU *FELT* THAT WAY...
う
HNN!
IT'S ALL MY FAULT...
HUH...?!
IT'S ALL MY FAULT... FOR GIVING YOU A FACE THAT *BOTHERS* YOUUU!!
I'M SORRY, AKI-CHAAAN!!
うえーん
WAHHHH
えぐえぐ
HNN HNN
AH!
MOM...!
NO...
NO, NANAMI! IF ANYONE'S TO BLAME, IT'S ME... *I'M* THE ONE! AKIRA!!
I GOT YOUR MOTHER *KNOCKED UP*, SO...
ゴキッ
WHOCK

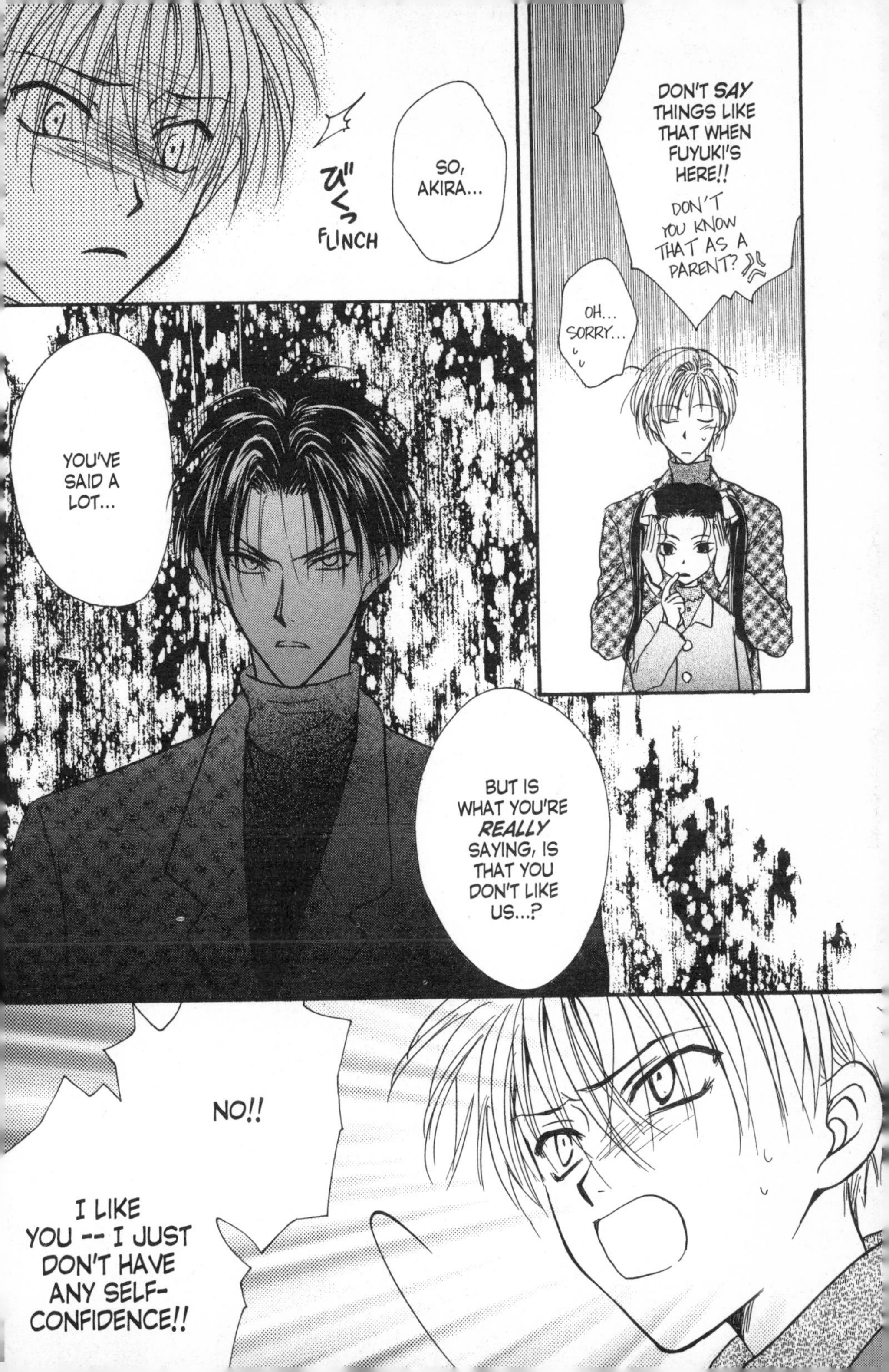
DON'T SAY THINGS LIKE THAT WHEN FUYUKI'S HERE!!
DON'T YOU KNOW THAT AS A PARENT?
OH... SORRY...
びくっ
FLINCH
SO, AKIRA...
YOU'VE SAID A LOT...
BUT IS WHAT YOU'RE REALLY SAYING, IS THAT YOU DON'T LIKE US...?
NO!!
I LIKE YOU -- I JUST DON'T HAVE ANY SELF-CONFIDENCE!!

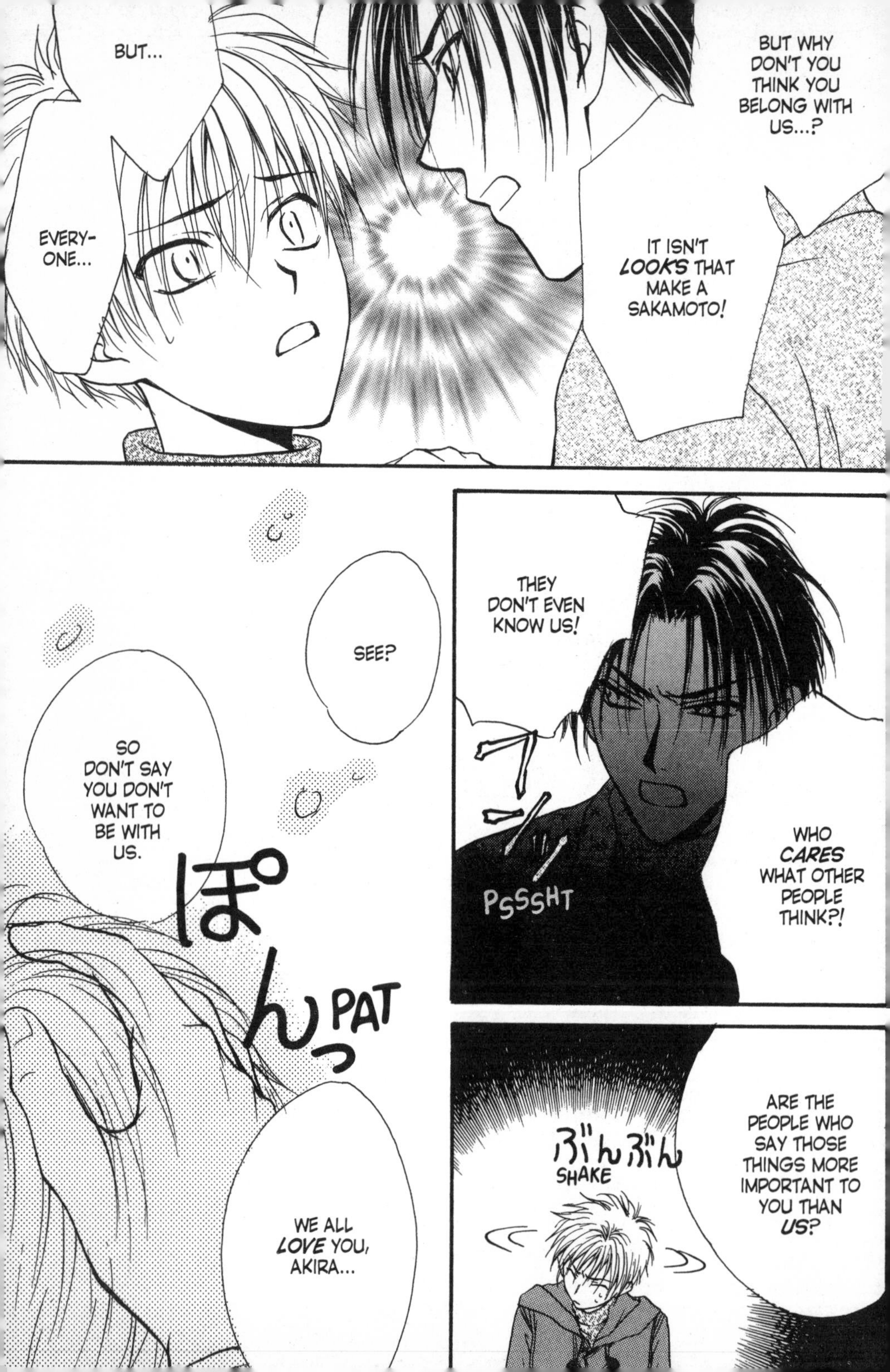

BUT WHY DON'T YOU THINK YOU BELONG WITH US...?
IT ISN'T *LOOKS* THAT MAKE A SAKAMOTO!
BUT...
EVERY-ONE...
THEY DON'T EVEN KNOW US!
PSSSHT
WHO *CARES* WHAT OTHER PEOPLE THINK?!
ARE THE PEOPLE WHO SAY THOSE THINGS MORE IMPORTANT TO YOU THAN *US*?
ぶんぶん
SHAKE
SEE?
SO DON'T SAY YOU DON'T WANT TO BE WITH US.
ぽんっ
PAT
WE ALL *LOVE* YOU, AKIRA...

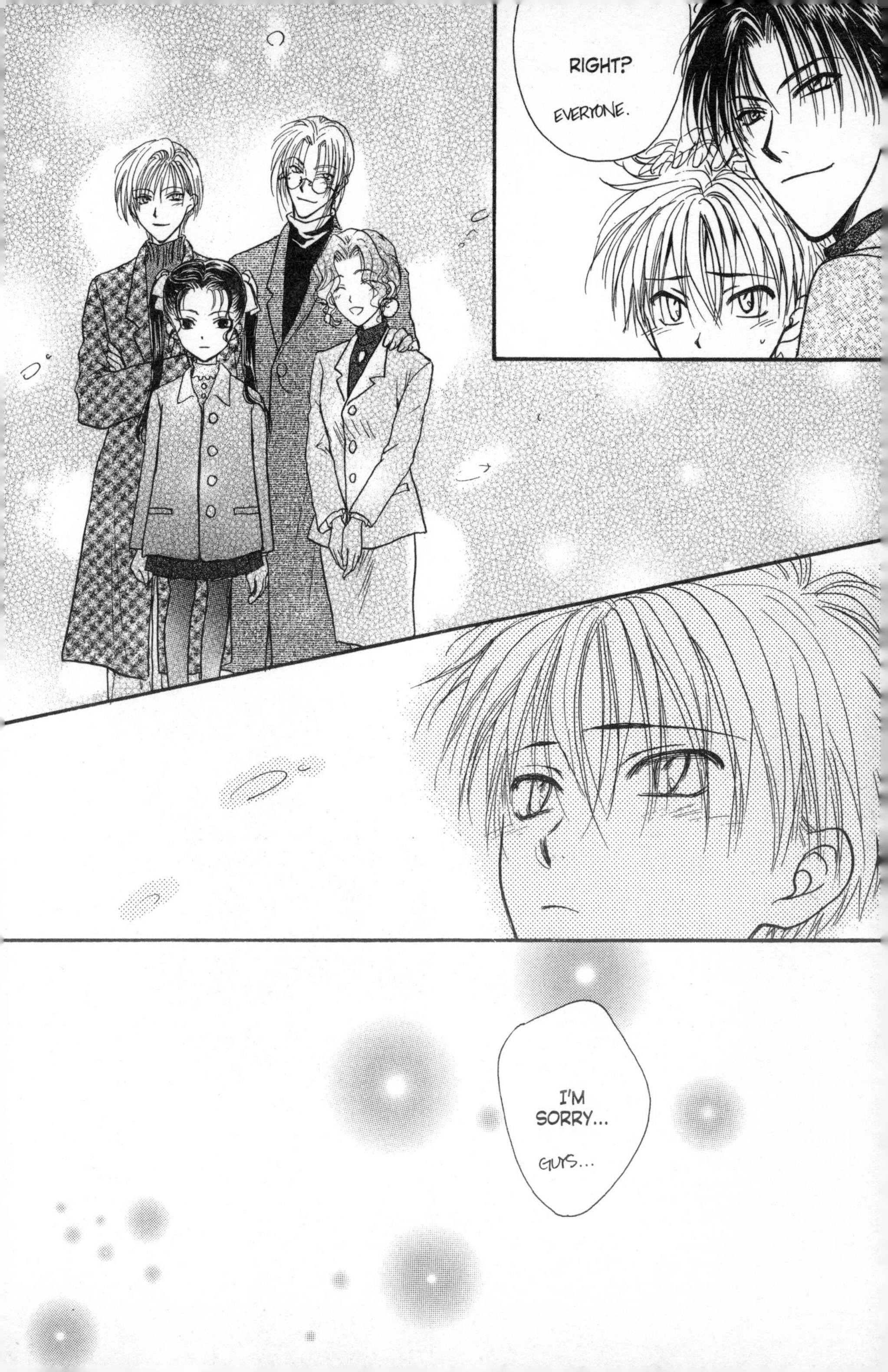
RIGHT? EVERYONE.
I'M SORRY... GUYS...

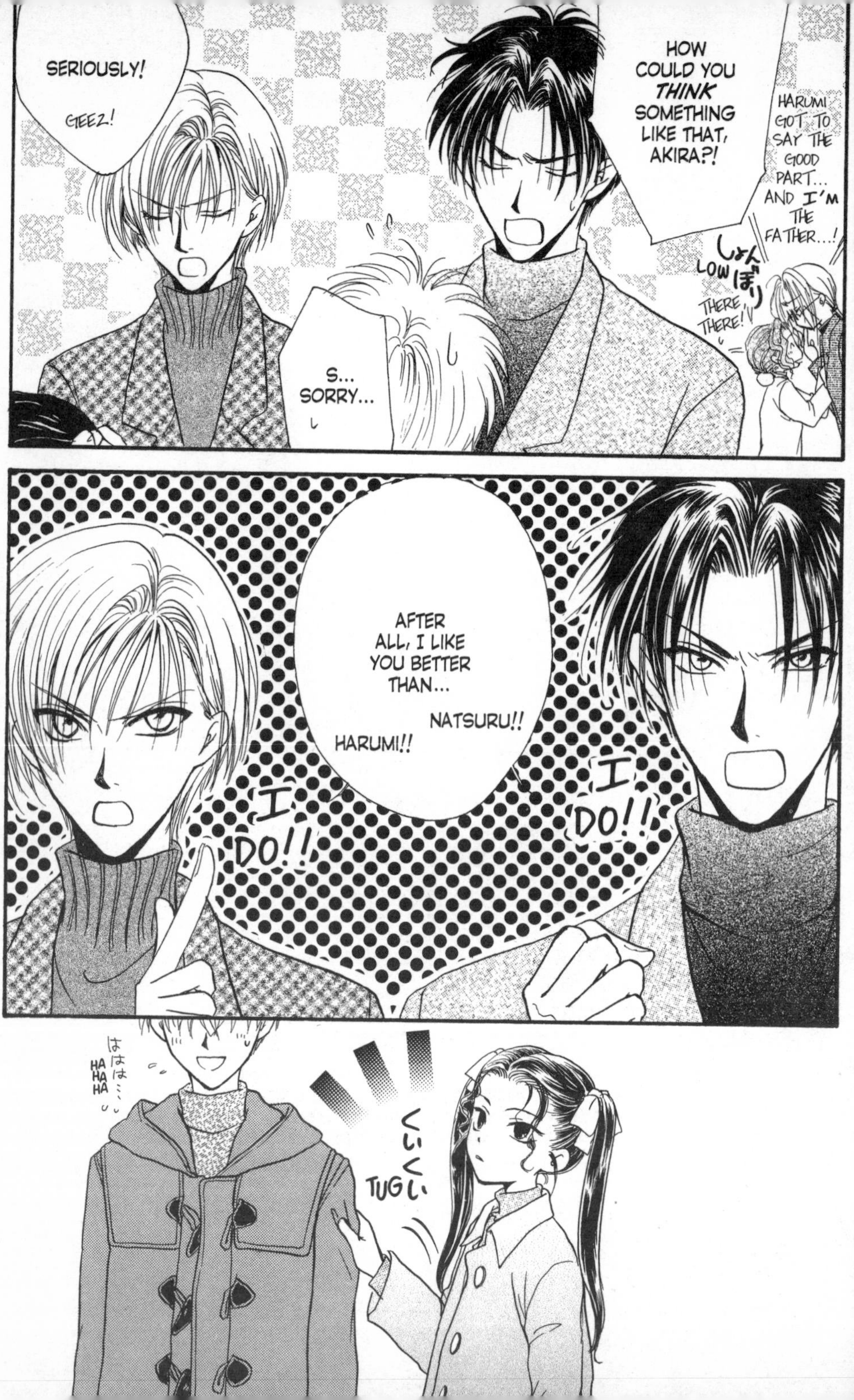
HOW COULD YOU THINK SOMETHING LIKE THAT, AKIRA?!
HARUMI GOT TO SAY THE GOOD PART... AND I'M THE FATHER...!
しょんぼり
LOW
THERE THERE!
SERIOUSLY!
GEEZ!
S... SORRY...
AFTER ALL, I LIKE YOU BETTER THAN...
NATSURU!!
I DO!!
HARUMI!!
I DO!!
くいくい
TUG
ははは
HA HA HA

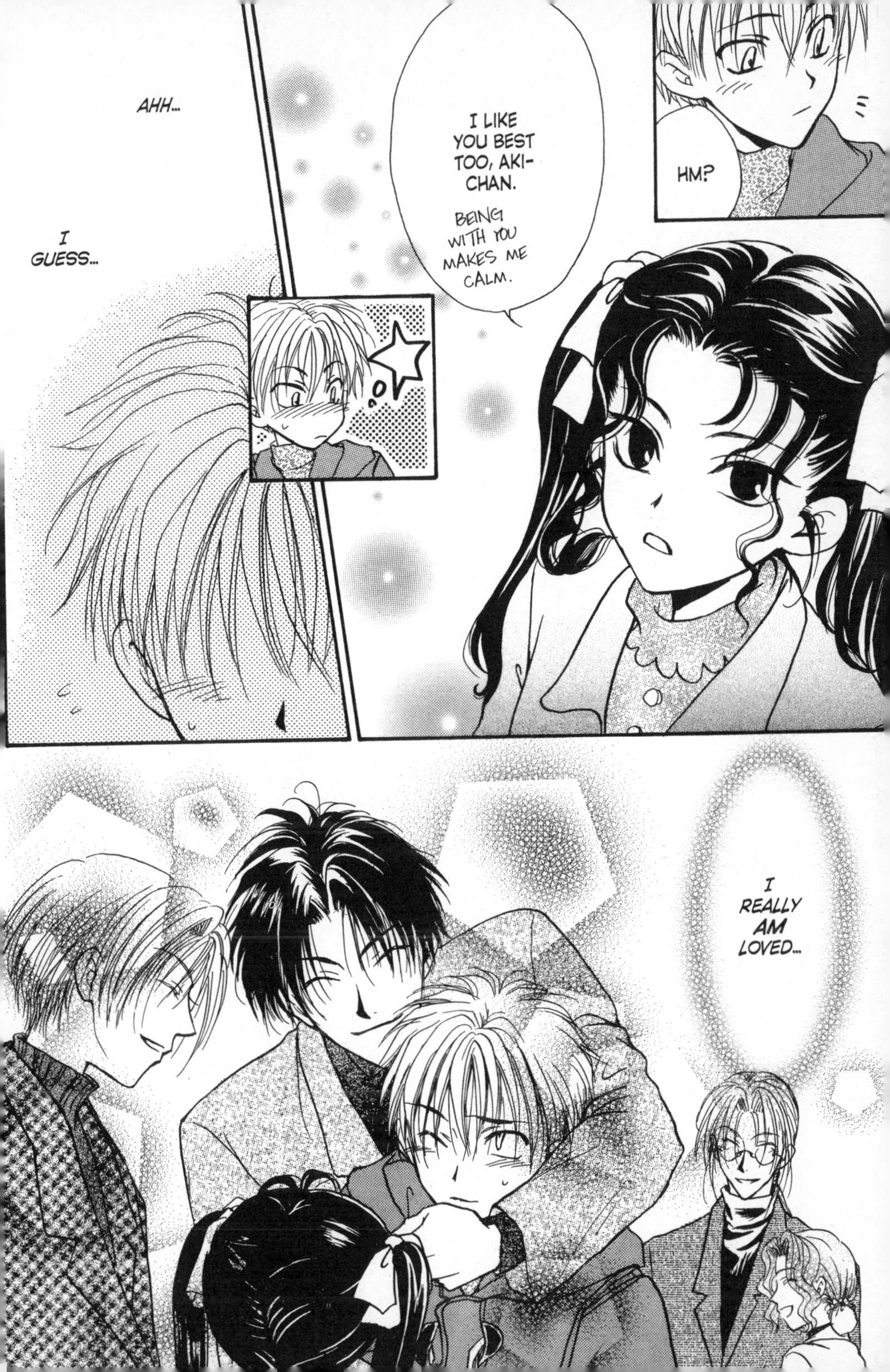
HM?
I LIKE YOU BEST TOO, AKI-CHAN.
BEING WITH YOU MAKES ME CALM.
AHH...
I GUESS...
I REALLY AM LOVED...

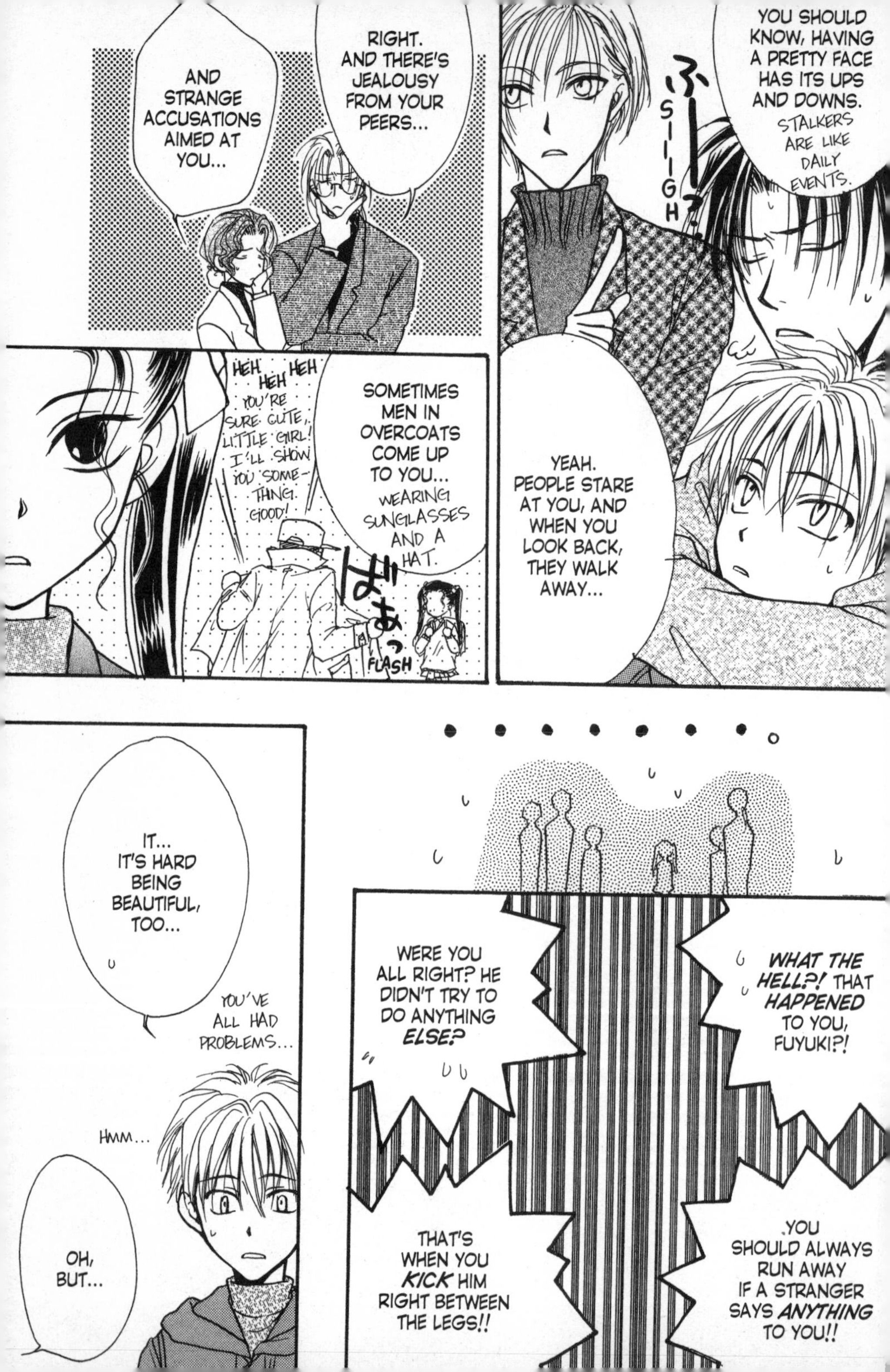
YOU SHOULD KNOW, HAVING A PRETTY FACE HAS ITS UPS AND DOWNS.
STALKERS ARE LIKE DAILY EVENTS.
ふーー
SIIIGH
RIGHT. AND THERE'S JEALOUSY FROM YOUR PEERS...
AND STRANGE ACCUSATIONS AIMED AT YOU...
YEAH. PEOPLE STARE AT YOU, AND WHEN YOU LOOK BACK, THEY WALK AWAY...
SOMETIMES MEN IN OVERCOATS COME UP TO YOU...
WEARING SUNGLASSES AND A HAT.
HEH HEH HEH
YOU'RE SURE CUTE, LITTLE GIRL! I'LL SHOW YOU SOMETHING GOOD!
ばあっ
FLASH
.........。
WHAT THE HELL?! THAT HAPPENED TO YOU, FUYUKI?!
WERE YOU ALL RIGHT? HE DIDN'T TRY TO DO ANYTHING ELSE?
.YOU SHOULD ALWAYS RUN AWAY IF A STRANGER SAYS ANYTHING TO YOU!!
THAT'S WHEN YOU KICK HIM RIGHT BETWEEN THE LEGS!!
IT... IT'S HARD BEING BEAUTIFUL, TOO...
YOU'VE ALL HAD PROBLEMS...
HMM...
OH, BUT...

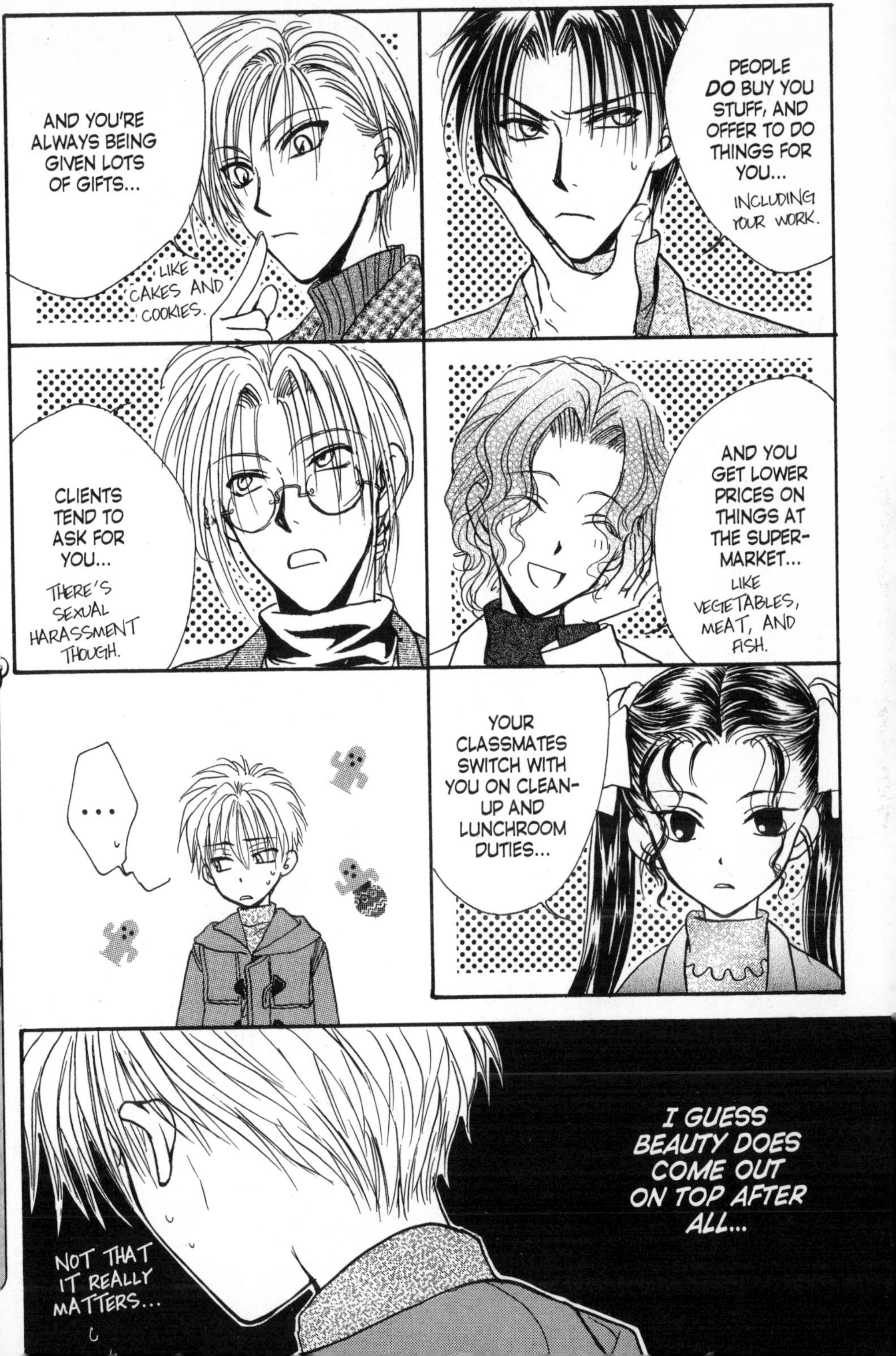
PEOPLE DO BUY YOU STUFF, AND OFFER TO DO THINGS FOR YOU...
INCLUDING YOUR WORK.
AND YOU'RE ALWAYS BEING GIVEN LOTS OF GIFTS...
LIKE CAKES AND COOKIES.
AND YOU GET LOWER PRICES ON THINGS AT THE SUPER-MARKET...
LIKE VEGETABLES, MEAT, AND FISH.
CLIENTS TEND TO ASK FOR YOU...
THERE'S SEXUAL HARASSMENT THOUGH.
YOUR CLASSMATES SWITCH WITH YOU ON CLEAN-UP AND LUNCHROOM DUTIES...
...
I GUESS BEAUTY DOES COME OUT ON TOP AFTER ALL...
NOT THAT IT REALLY MATTERS...

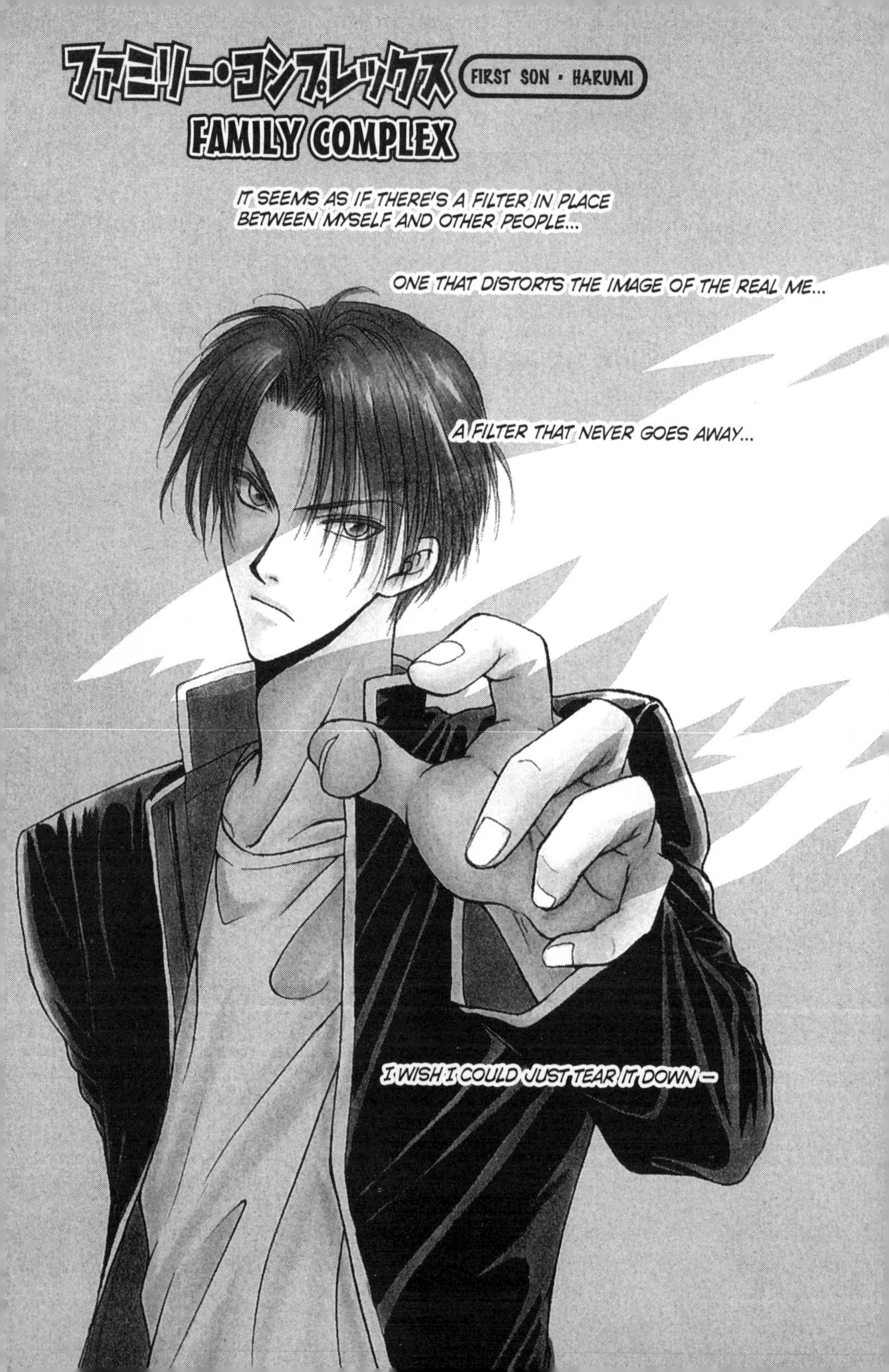
ファミリー・コンプレックス
FIRST SON · HARUMI
FAMILY COMPLEX
IT SEEMS AS IF THERE'S A FILTER IN PLACE BETWEEN MYSELF AND OTHER PEOPLE...
ONE THAT DISTORTS THE IMAGE OF THE REAL ME...
A FILTER THAT NEVER GOES AWAY...
I WISH I COULD JUST TEAR IT DOWN —

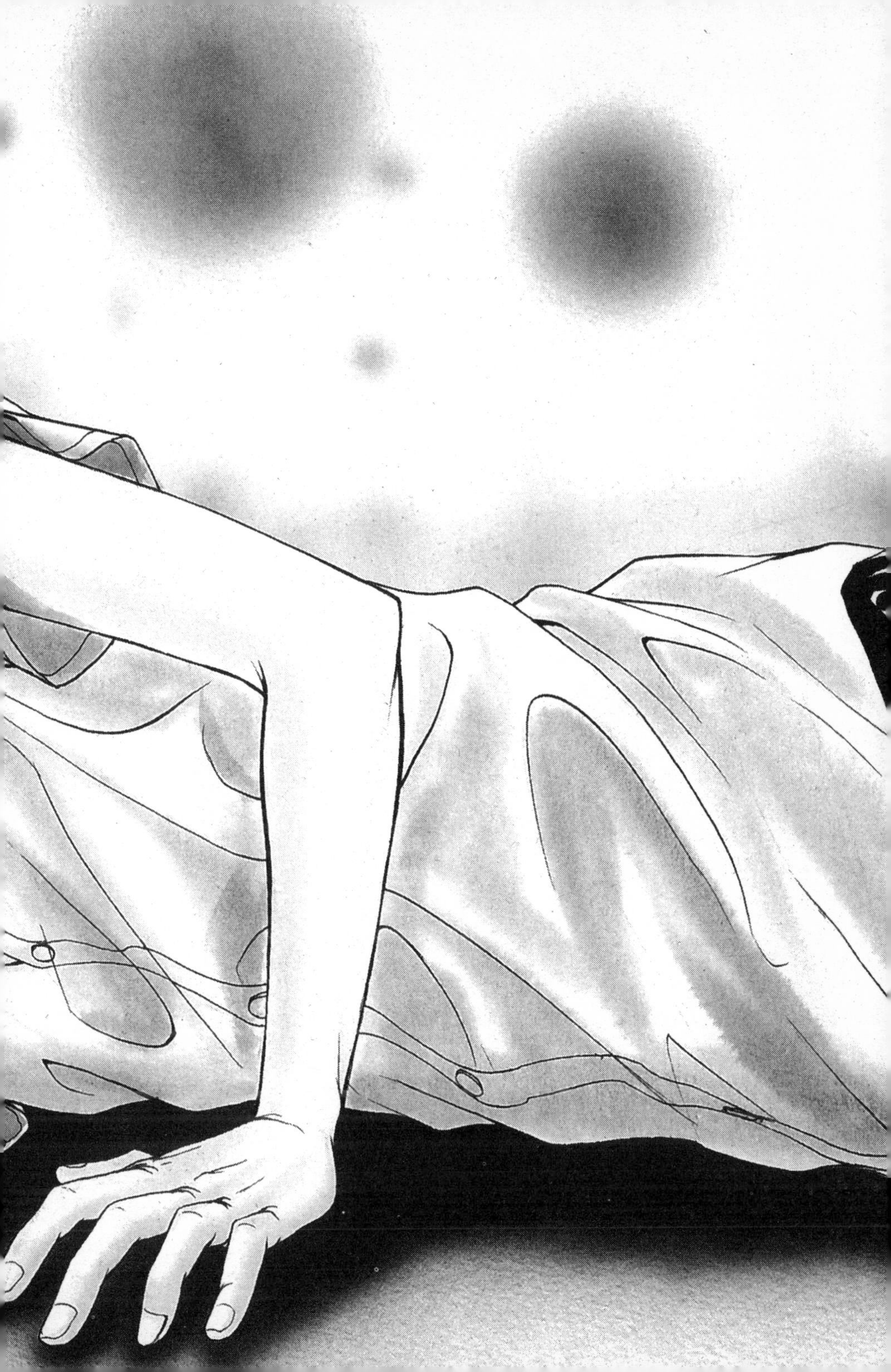

ファミリー・コンプレックス

FIRST SON • HARUMI

FAMILY COMPLEX

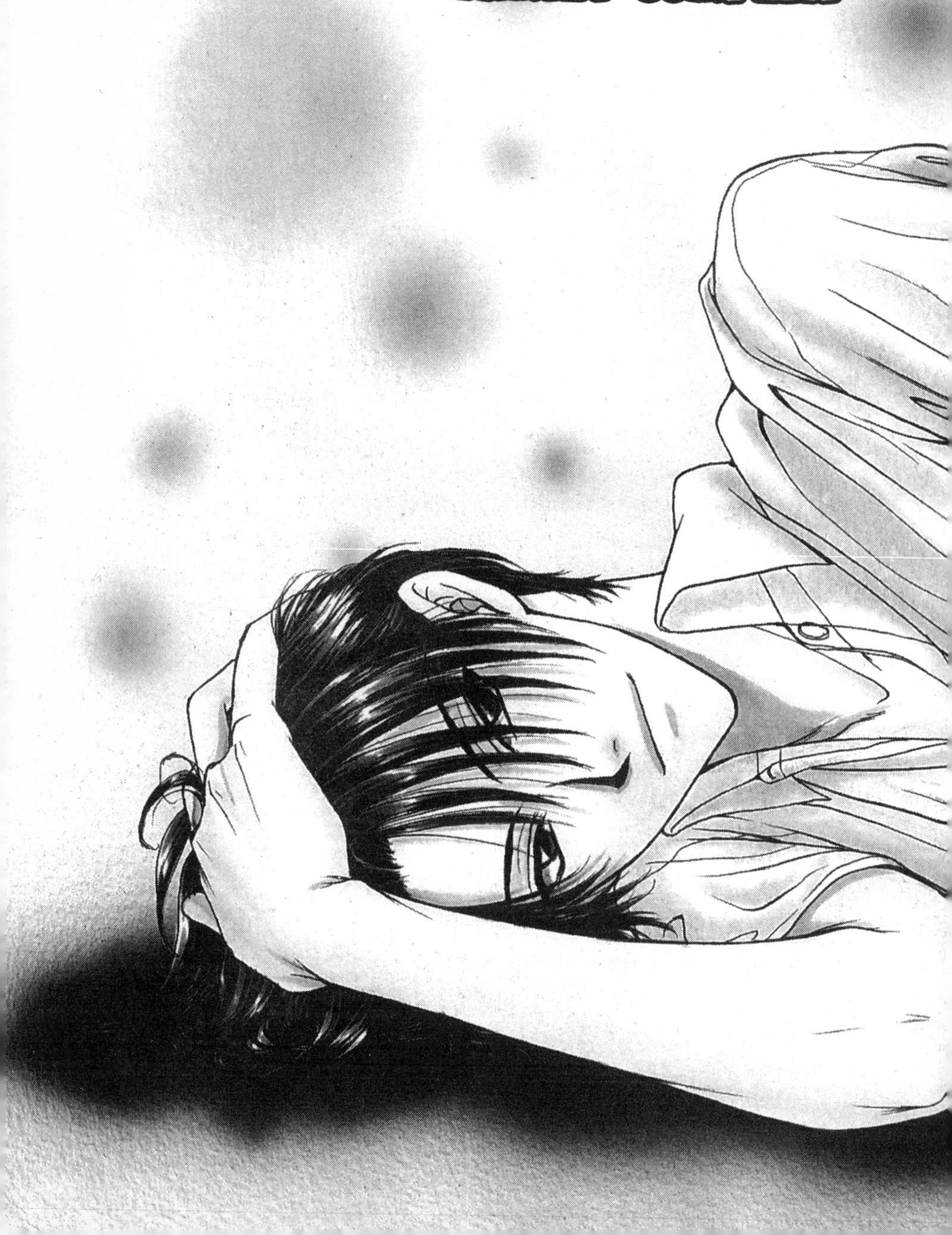

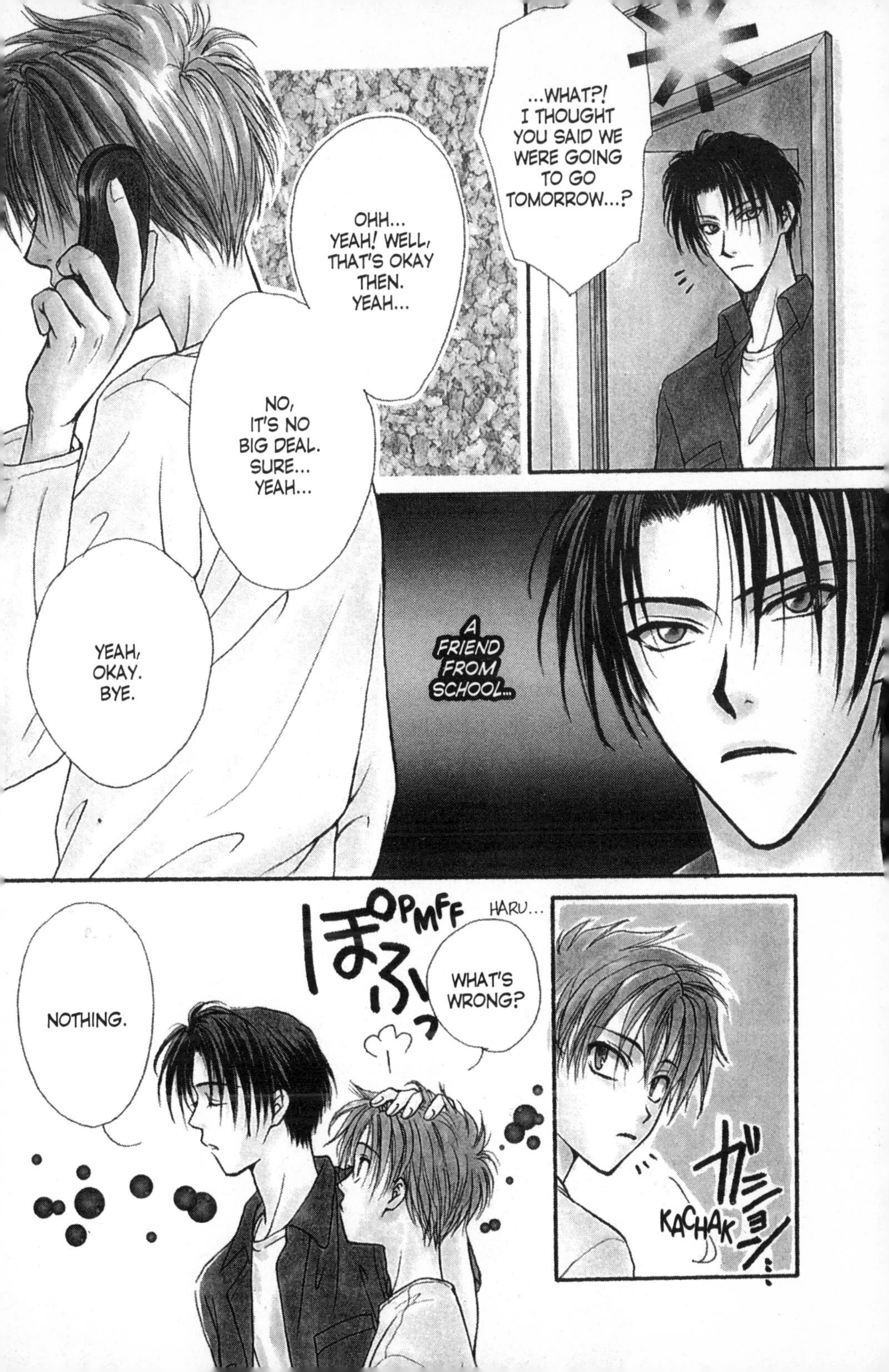
...WHAT?! I THOUGHT YOU SAID WE WERE GOING TO GO TOMORROW...?
A FRIEND FROM SCHOOL...
OHH... YEAH! WELL, THAT'S OKAY THEN. YEAH...
NO, IT'S NO BIG DEAL. SURE... YEAH...
YEAH, OKAY. BYE.
ガションッ
KACHAK
HARU...
WHAT'S WRONG?
ぽふっ
PMFF
NOTHING.

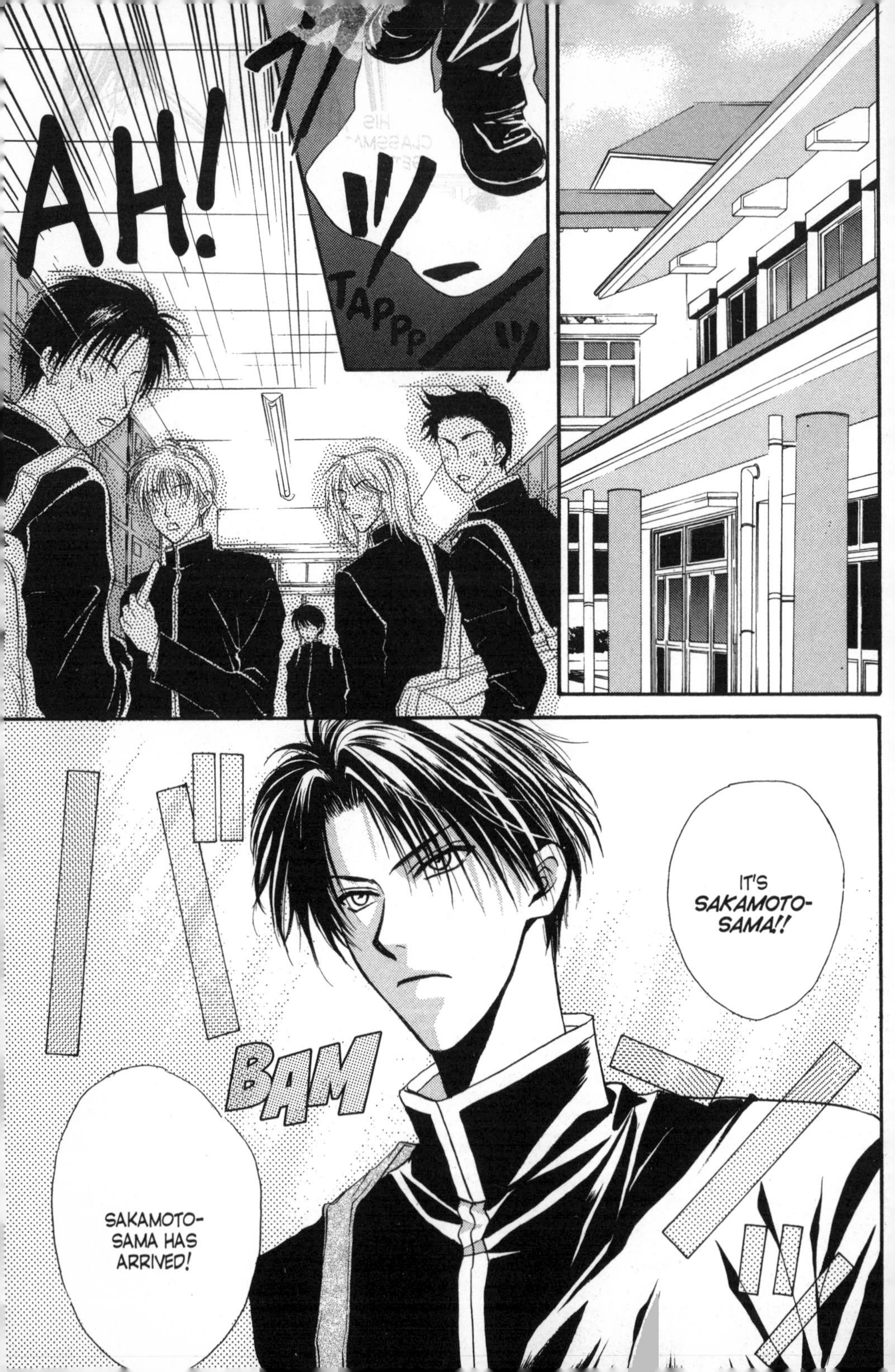
AH!
TAPPP
IT'S SAKAMOTO-SAMA!!
BAM
SAKAMOTO-SAMA HAS ARRIVED!

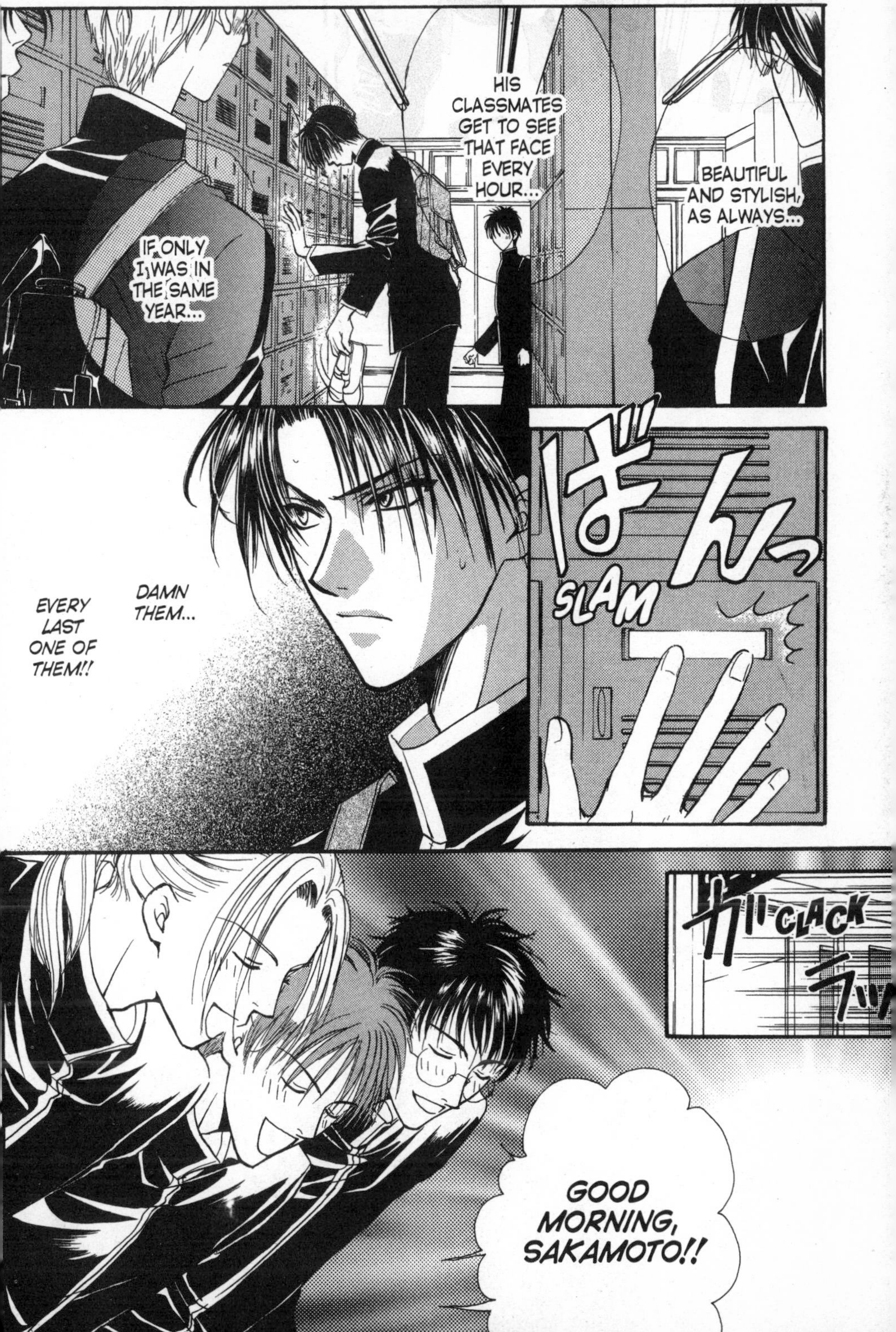
BEAUTIFUL AND STYLISH, AS ALWAYS...
HIS CLASSMATES GET TO SEE THAT FACE EVERY HOUR...
IF ONLY I WAS IN THE SAME YEAR...
ばんっ
SLAM
DAMN THEM...
EVERY LAST ONE OF THEM!!
カラッ
CLACK
GOOD MORNING, SAKAMOTO!!

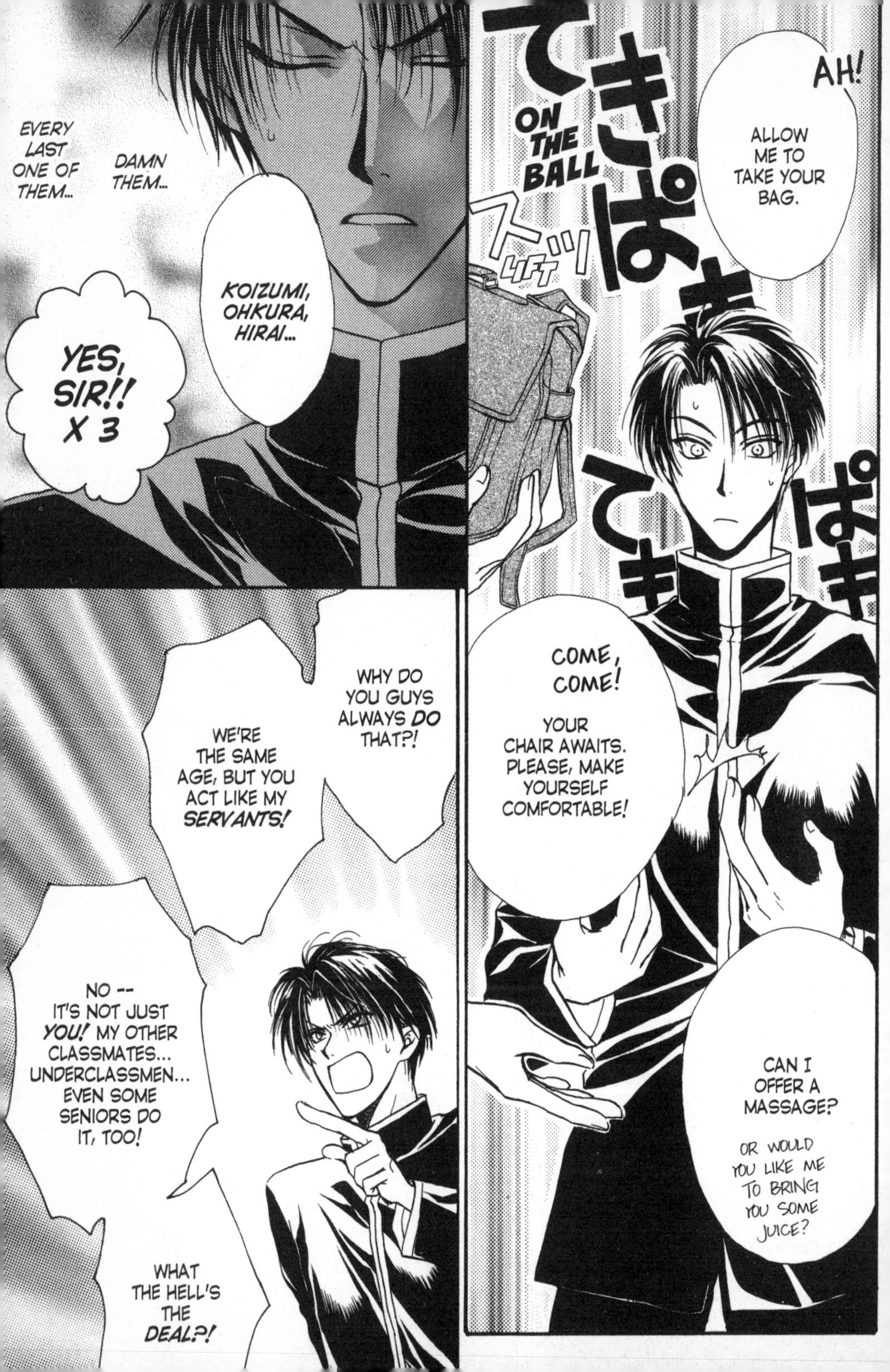

AH!
ALLOW ME TO TAKE YOUR BAG.
てきぱき
ON THE BALL
LIFT
てきぱき
COME, COME!
YOUR CHAIR AWAITS. PLEASE, MAKE YOURSELF COMFORTABLE!
CAN I OFFER A MASSAGE?
OR WOULD YOU LIKE ME TO BRING YOU SOME JUICE?
KOIZUMI, OHKURA, HIRAI...
YES, SIR!! X 3
DAMN THEM...
EVERY LAST ONE OF THEM...
WHY DO YOU GUYS ALWAYS DO THAT?!
WE'RE THE SAME AGE, BUT YOU ACT LIKE MY SERVANTS!
NO -- IT'S NOT JUST YOU! MY OTHER CLASSMATES... UNDERCLASSMEN... EVEN SOME SENIORS DO IT, TOO!
WHAT THE HELL'S THE DEAL?!

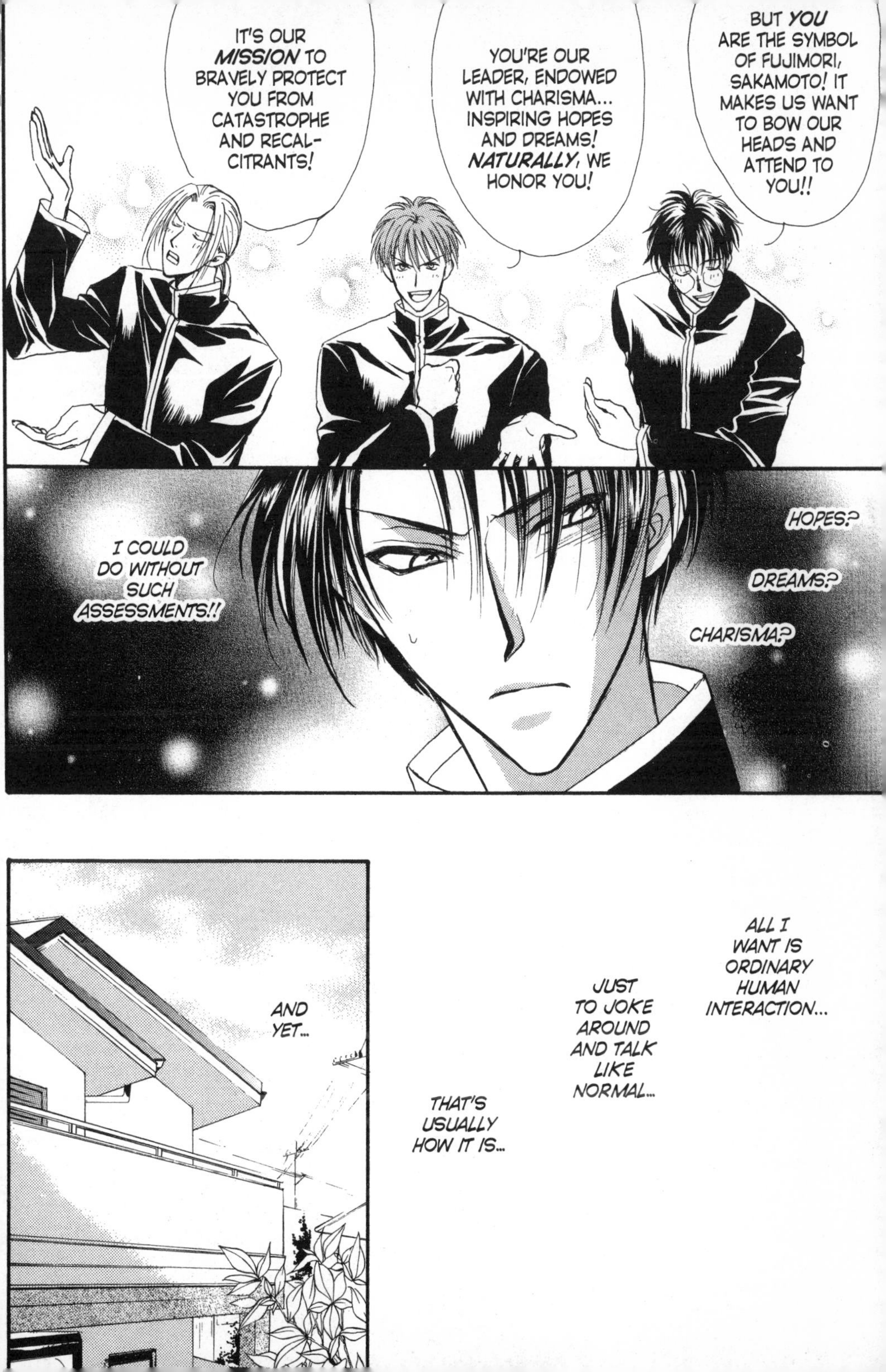

BUT YOU ARE THE SYMBOL OF FUJIMORI, SAKAMOTO! IT MAKES US WANT TO BOW OUR HEADS AND ATTEND TO YOU!!
YOU'RE OUR LEADER, ENDOWED WITH CHARISMA... INSPIRING HOPES AND DREAMS! NATURALLY, WE HONOR YOU!
IT'S OUR MISSION TO BRAVELY PROTECT YOU FROM CATASTROPHE AND RECAL-CITRANTS!
HOPES?
DREAMS?
CHARISMA?
I COULD DO WITHOUT SUCH ASSESSMENTS!!
ALL I WANT IS ORDINARY HUMAN INTERACTION...
JUST TO JOKE AROUND AND TALK LIKE NORMAL...
THAT'S USUALLY HOW IT IS...
AND YET...

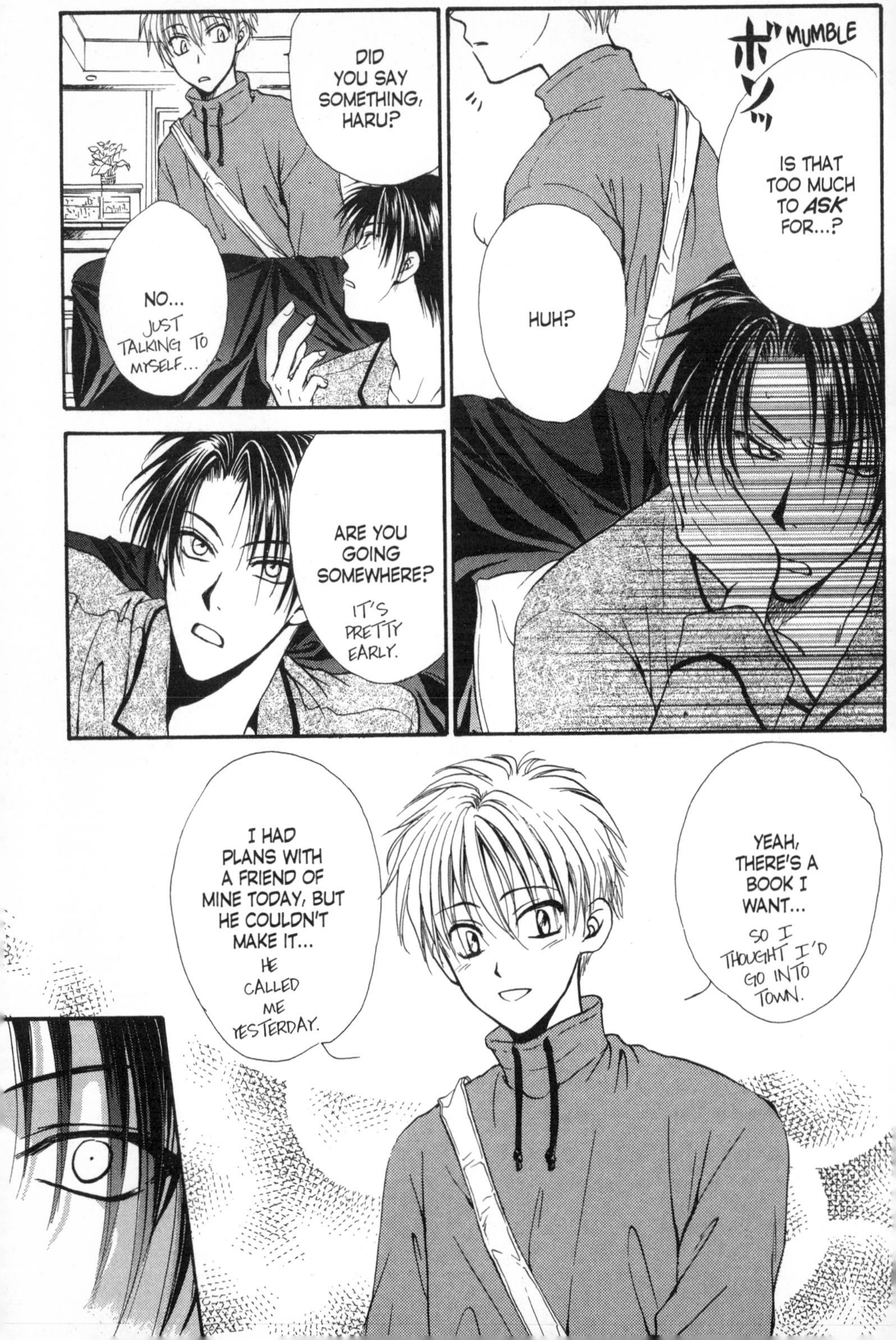
ボソッ MUMBLE
IS THAT TOO MUCH TO *ASK* FOR...?
HUH?
DID YOU SAY SOMETHING, HARU?
NO... JUST TALKING TO MYSELF...
ARE YOU GOING SOMEWHERE? IT'S PRETTY EARLY.
YEAH, THERE'S A BOOK I WANT... SO I THOUGHT I'D GO INTO TOWN.
I HAD PLANS WITH A FRIEND OF MINE TODAY, BUT HE COULDN'T MAKE IT... HE CALLED ME YESTERDAY.

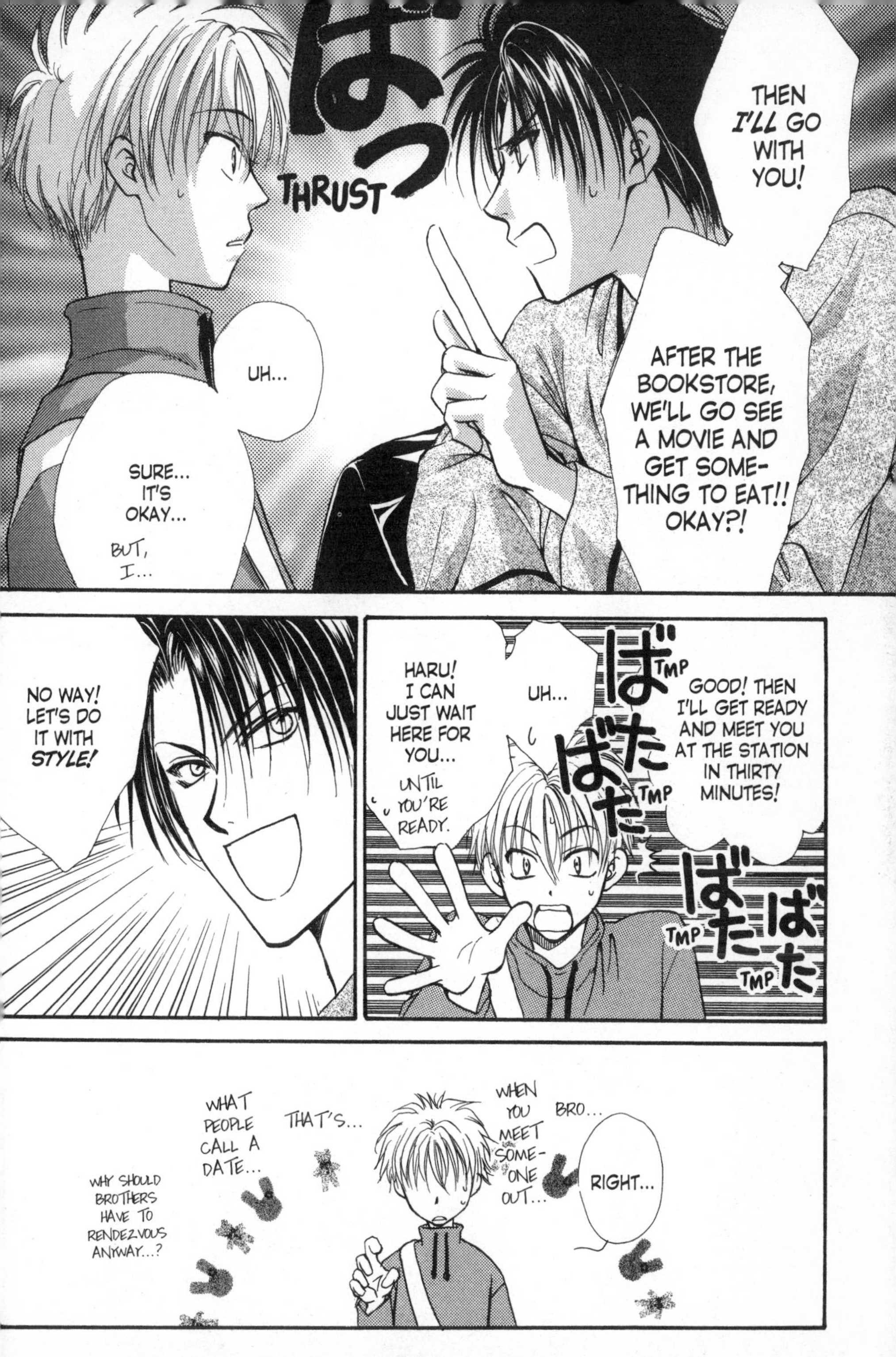

THEN I'LL GO WITH YOU!
ぼっ
THRUST
AFTER THE BOOKSTORE, WE'LL GO SEE A MOVIE AND GET SOME-THING TO EAT!! OKAY?!
UH...
SURE... IT'S OKAY...
BUT, I...
GOOD! THEN I'LL GET READY AND MEET YOU AT THE STATION IN THIRTY MINUTES!
ばたばた
TMP TMP
ばたばた
TMP TMP
UH...
HARU! I CAN JUST WAIT HERE FOR YOU...
UNTIL YOU'RE READY.
NO WAY! LET'S DO IT WITH STYLE!
RIGHT...
BRO...
WHEN YOU MEET SOME-ONE OUT...
THAT'S...
WHAT PEOPLE CALL A DATE...
WHY SHOULD BROTHERS HAVE TO RENDEZVOUS ANYWAY...?

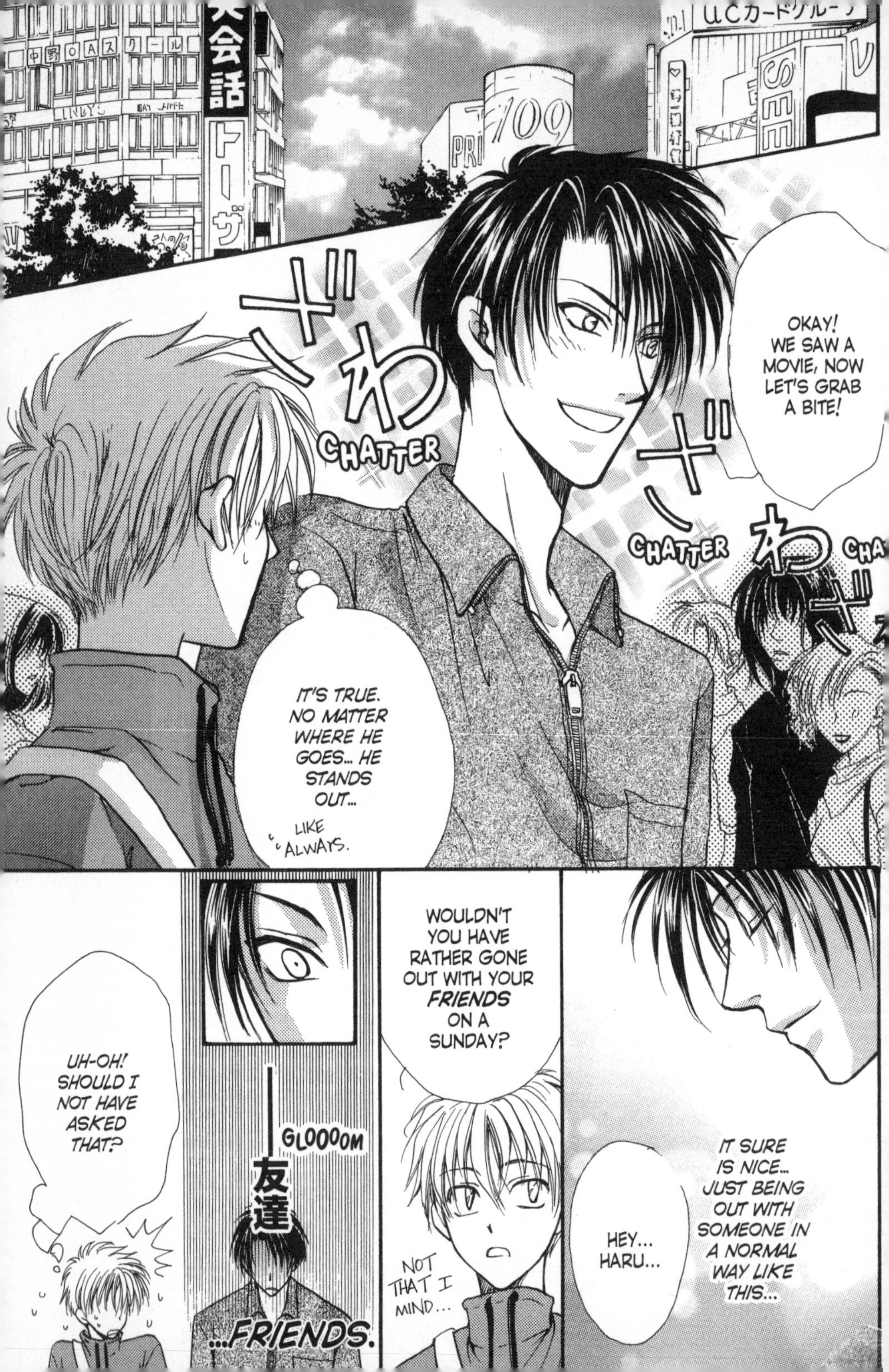

OKAY! WE SAW A MOVIE, NOW LET'S GRAB A BITE!
ざわ
CHATTER
CHA
ざわ
CHATTER
IT'S TRUE. NO MATTER WHERE HE GOES... HE STANDS OUT...
LIKE ALWAYS.
IT SURE IS NICE... JUST BEING OUT WITH SOMEONE IN A NORMAL WAY LIKE THIS...
HEY... HARU...
WOULDN'T YOU HAVE RATHER GONE OUT WITH YOUR FRIENDS ON A SUNDAY?
NOT THAT I MIND...
GLOOOOM
友達
...FRIENDS.
UH-OH! SHOULD I NOT HAVE ASKED THAT?

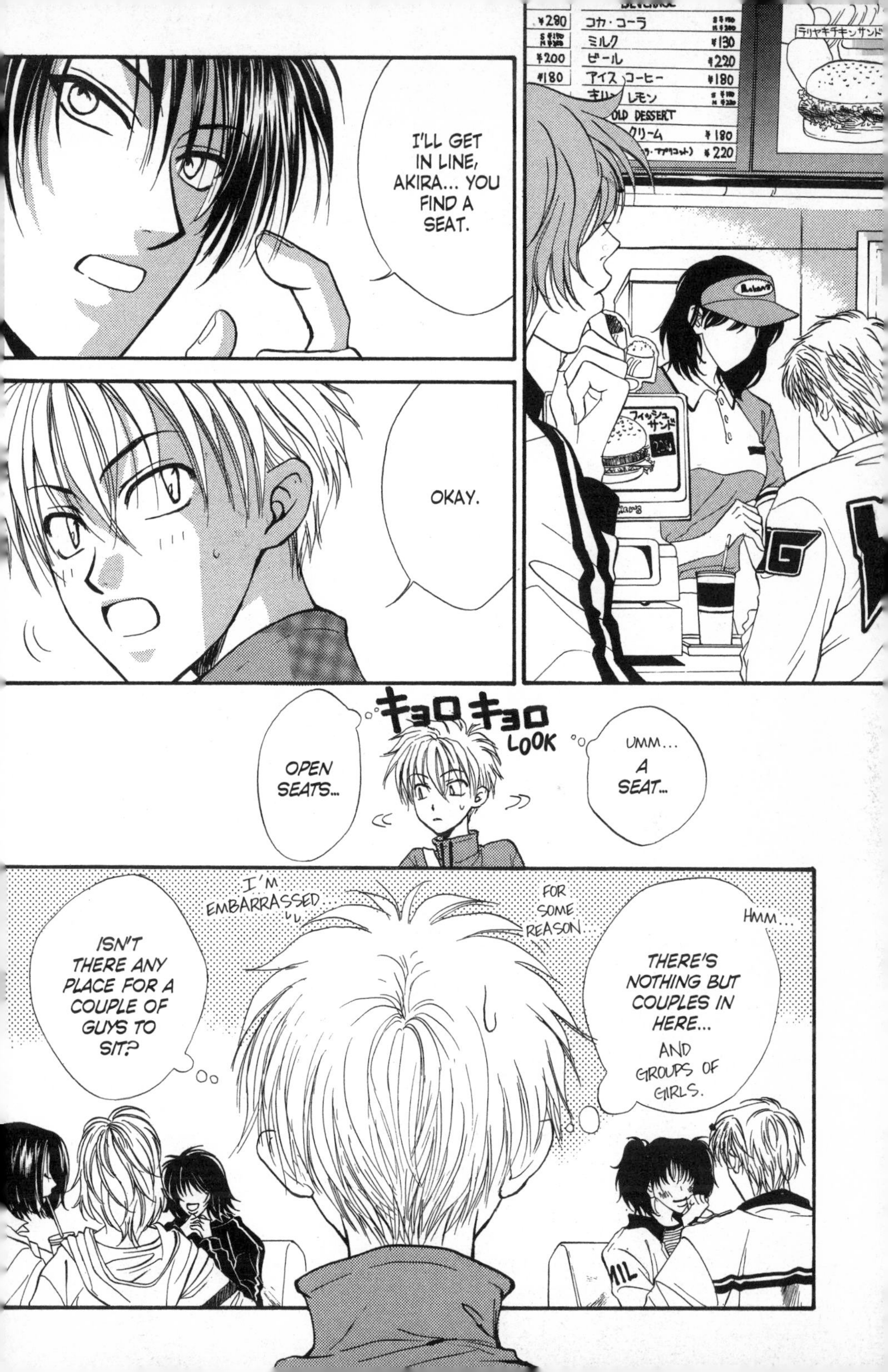
¥280 コカ・コーラ
ミルク ¥130
¥200 ビール ¥220
¥180 アイス コーヒー ¥180
OLD DESSERT
クリーム ¥180
¥220
テリヤキチキンサンド
フィッシュサンド
I'LL GET IN LINE, AKIRA... YOU FIND A SEAT.
OKAY.
キョロキョロ
LOOK
UMM... A SEAT...
OPEN SEATS...
HMM...
THERE'S NOTHING BUT COUPLES IN HERE...
AND GROUPS OF GIRLS.
FOR SOME REASON
I'M EMBARRASSED
ISN'T THERE ANY PLACE FOR A COUPLE OF GUYS TO SIT?

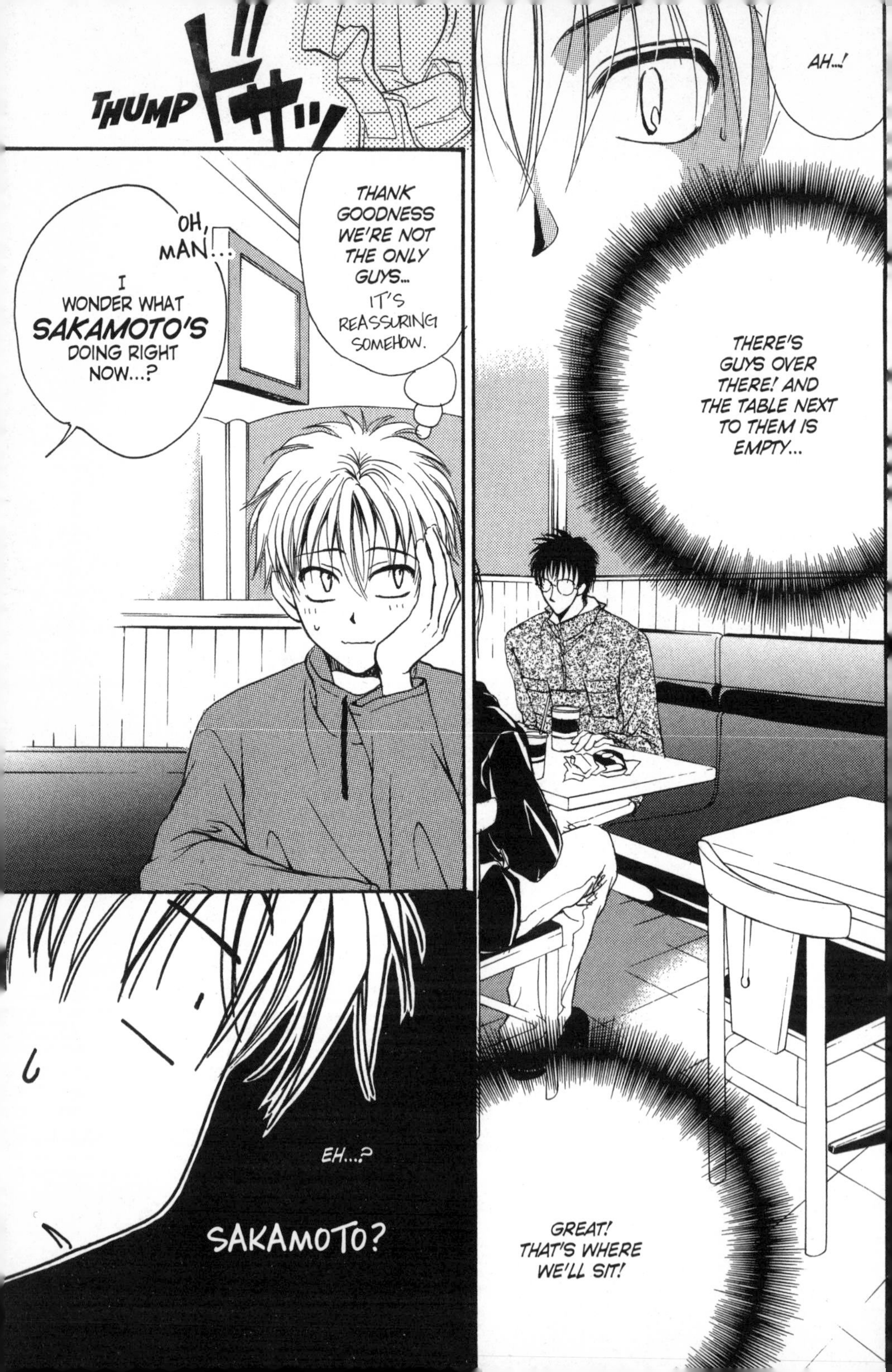
AH...!
THERE'S GUYS OVER THERE! AND THE TABLE NEXT TO THEM IS EMPTY...
GREAT! THAT'S WHERE WE'LL SIT!
THUMP ドギャッ
THANK GOODNESS WE'RE NOT THE ONLY GUYS...
IT'S REASSURING SOMEHOW.
OH, MAN...
I WONDER WHAT SAKAMOTO'S DOING RIGHT NOW...?
EH...?
SAKAMOTO?

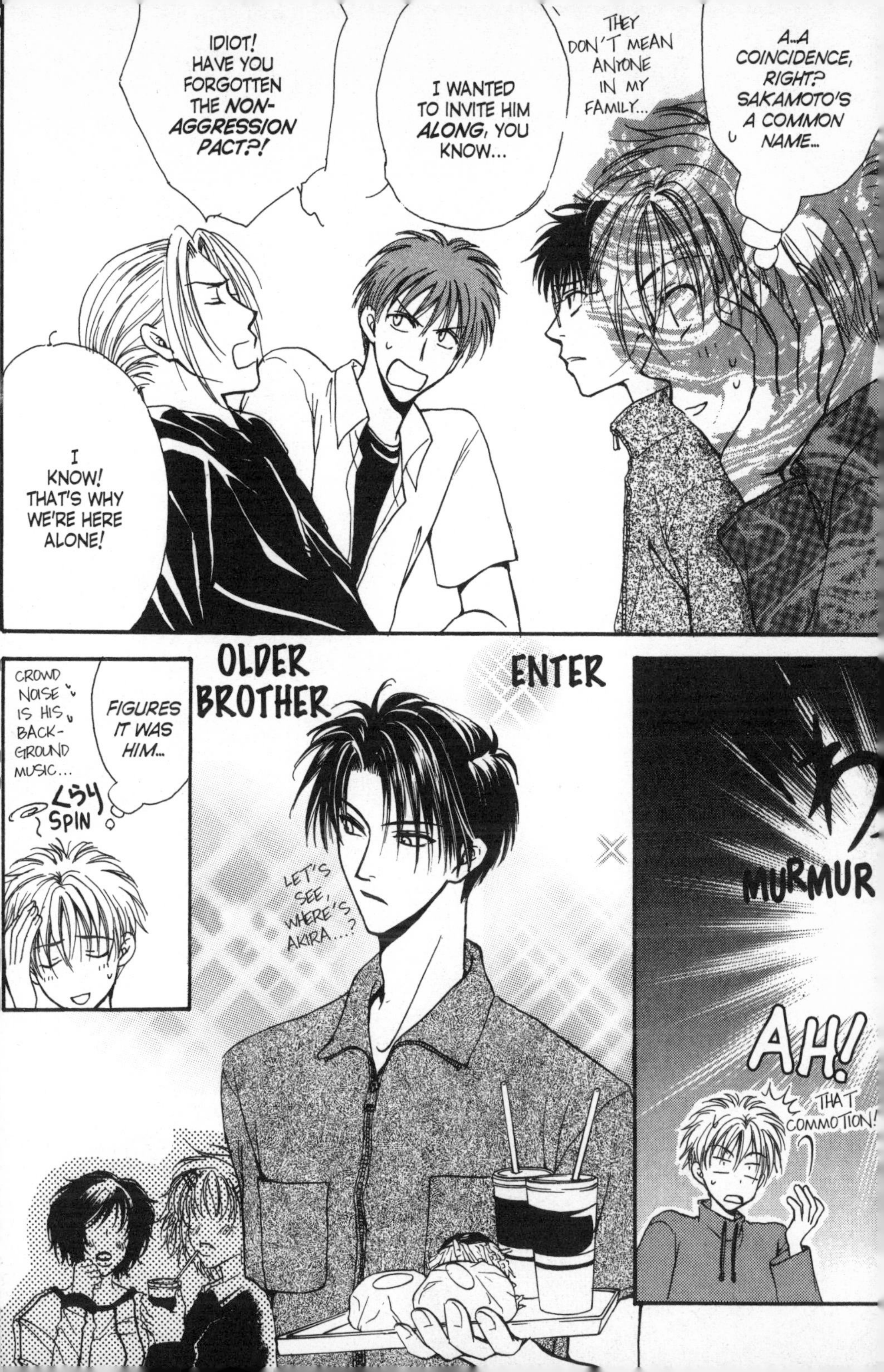
A...A COINCIDENCE, RIGHT? SAKAMOTO'S A COMMON NAME...
THEY DON'T MEAN ANYONE IN MY FAMILY...
I WANTED TO INVITE HIM ALONG, YOU KNOW...
IDIOT! HAVE YOU FORGOTTEN THE NON-AGGRESSION PACT?!
I KNOW! THAT'S WHY WE'RE HERE ALONE!
MURMUR
AH!
THAT COMMOTION!
ENTER
OLDER BROTHER
LET'S SEE, WHERE'S AKIRA...?
FIGURES IT WAS HIM...
CROWD NOISE IS HIS BACKGROUND MUSIC...
くらり SPIN

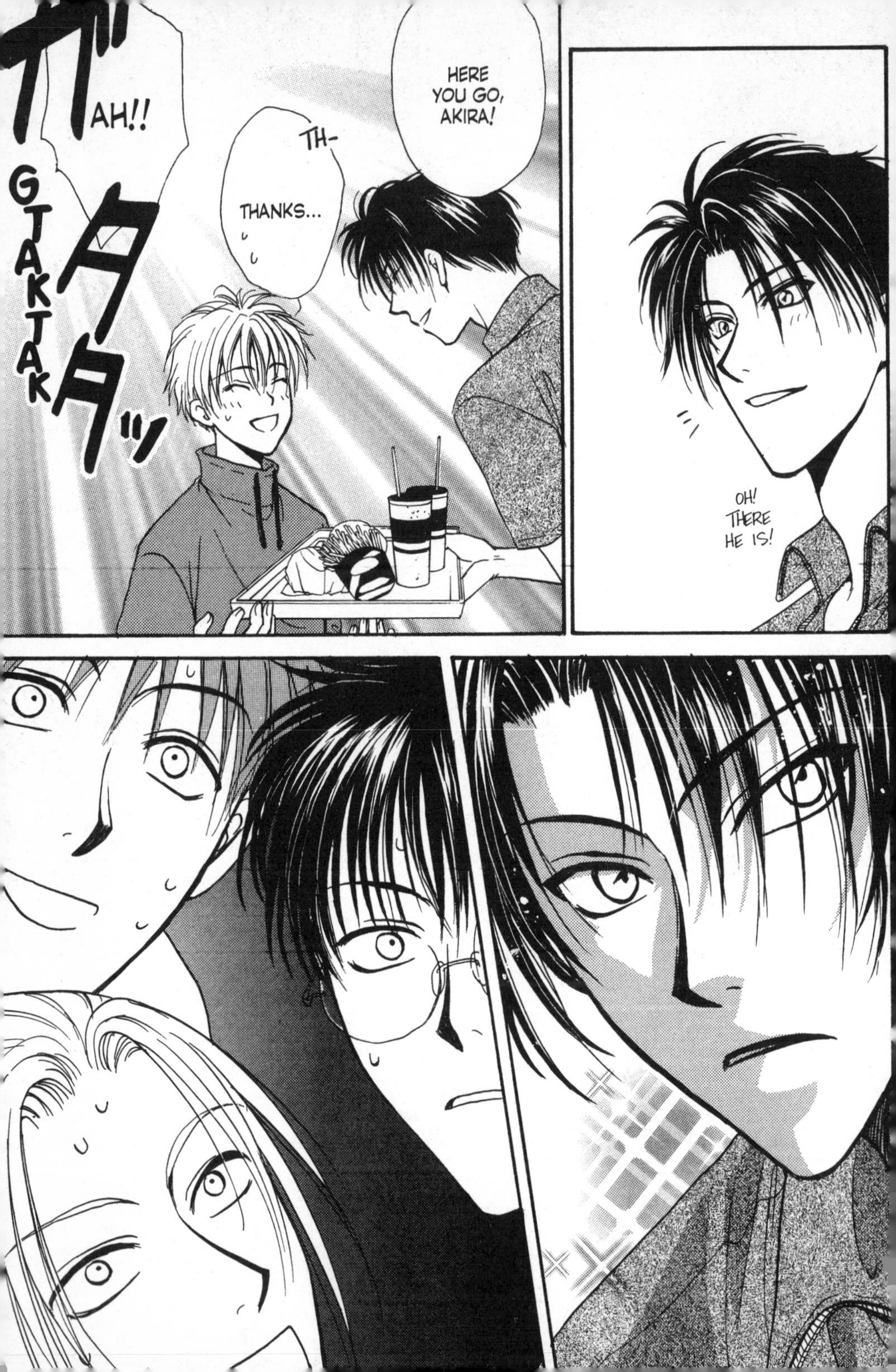
OH! THERE HE IS!
HERE YOU GO, AKIRA!
TH-
THANKS...
AH!!
ガタタッ
GTAKTAK

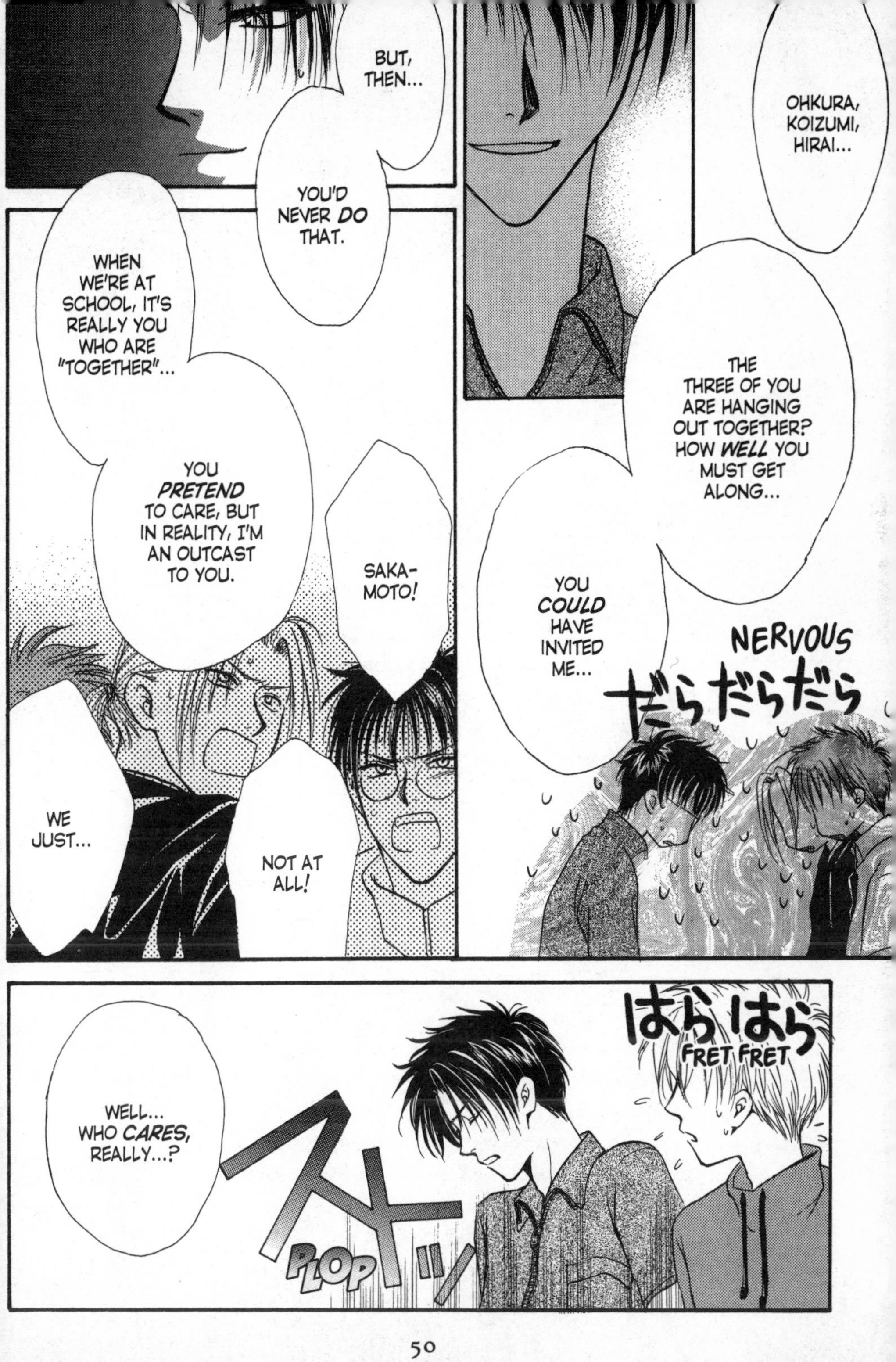
OHKURA, KOIZUMI, HIRAI...
THE THREE OF YOU ARE HANGING OUT TOGETHER? HOW *WELL* YOU MUST GET ALONG...
YOU *COULD* HAVE INVITED ME...
NERVOUS
だらだらだら
BUT, THEN...
YOU'D NEVER *DO* THAT.
WHEN WE'RE AT SCHOOL, IT'S REALLY YOU WHO ARE "TOGETHER"...
YOU *PRETEND* TO CARE, BUT IN REALITY, I'M AN OUTCAST TO YOU.
SAKA-MOTO!
NOT AT ALL!
WE JUST...
はらはら
FRET FRET
WELL... WHO *CARES*, REALLY...?
PLOP

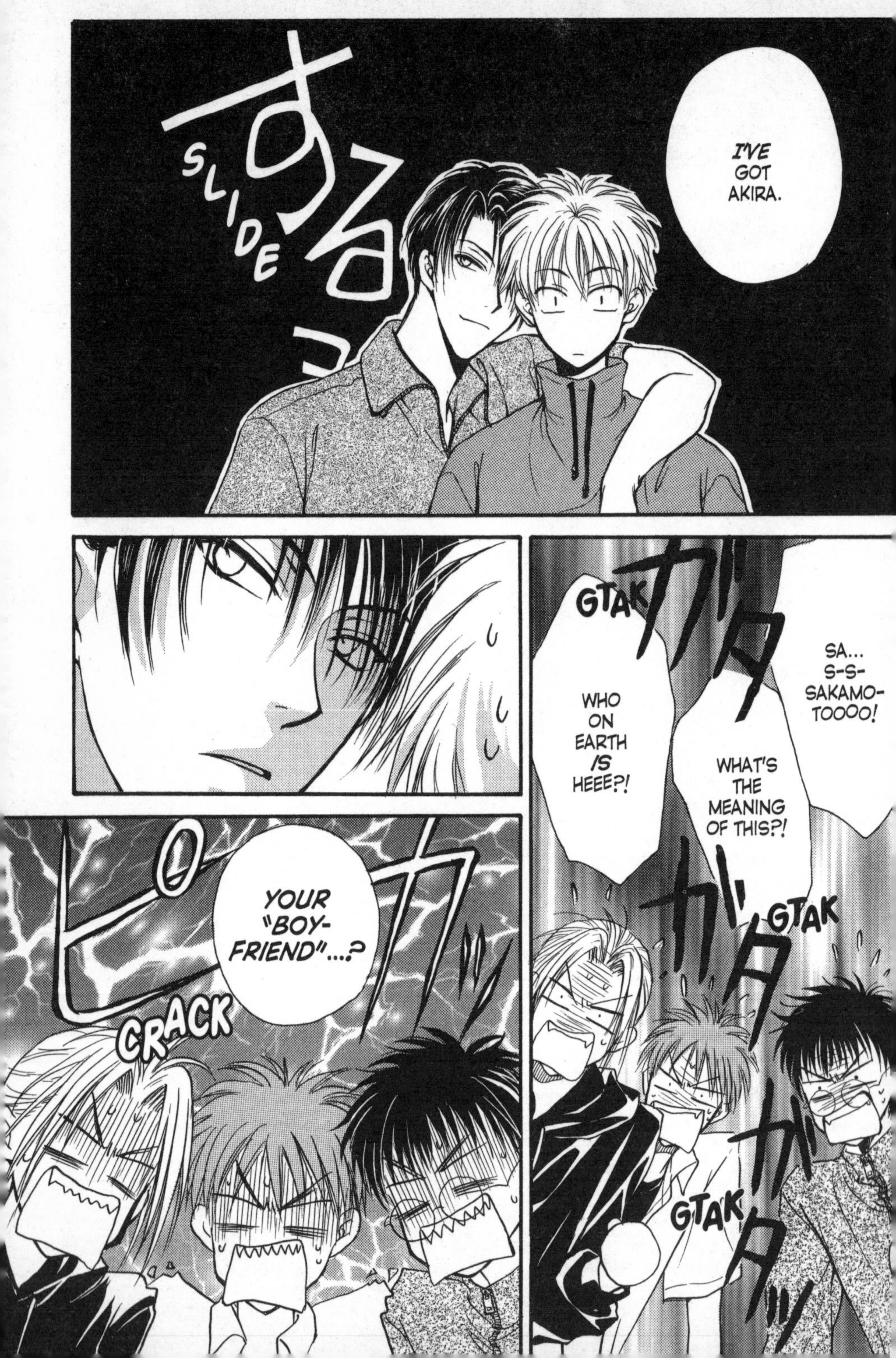
SLIDE
I'VE GOT AKIRA.
GTAK
SA... S-S-SAKAMO-TOOOO!
WHAT'S THE MEANING OF THIS?!
WHO ON EARTH *IS* HEEE?!
GTAK
GTAK
YOUR "BOY-FRIEND"...?
CRACK

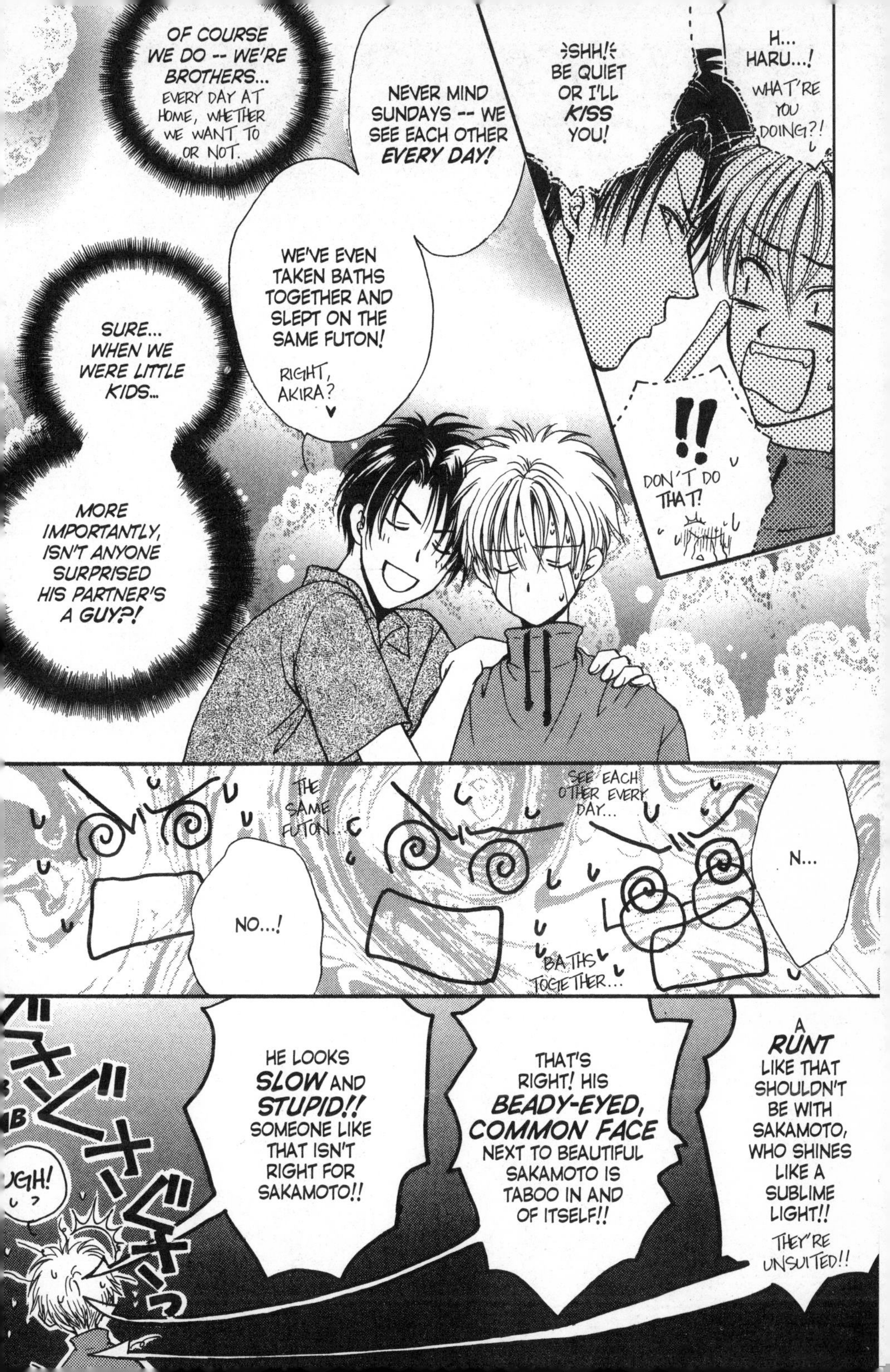
H... HARU...! WHAT'RE YOU DOING?!
SHH! BE QUIET OR I'LL KISS YOU!
!! DON'T DO THAT!
NEVER MIND SUNDAYS -- WE SEE EACH OTHER EVERY DAY!
OF COURSE WE DO -- WE'RE BROTHERS... EVERY DAY AT HOME, WHETHER WE WANT TO OR NOT.
WE'VE EVEN TAKEN BATHS TOGETHER AND SLEPT ON THE SAME FUTON! RIGHT, AKIRA?
SURE... WHEN WE WERE LITTLE KIDS...
MORE IMPORTANTLY, ISN'T ANYONE SURPRISED HIS PARTNER'S A GUY?!
N...
SEE EACH OTHER EVERY DAY...
BATHS TOGETHER...
THE SAME FUTON...
NO...!
A RUNT LIKE THAT SHOULDN'T BE WITH SAKAMOTO, WHO SHINES LIKE A SUBLIME LIGHT!! THEY'RE UNSUITED!!
THAT'S RIGHT! HIS BEADY-EYED, COMMON FACE NEXT TO BEAUTIFUL SAKAMOTO IS TABOO IN AND OF ITSELF!!
HE LOOKS SLOW AND STUPID!! SOMEONE LIKE THAT ISN'T RIGHT FOR SAKAMOTO!!
GH!

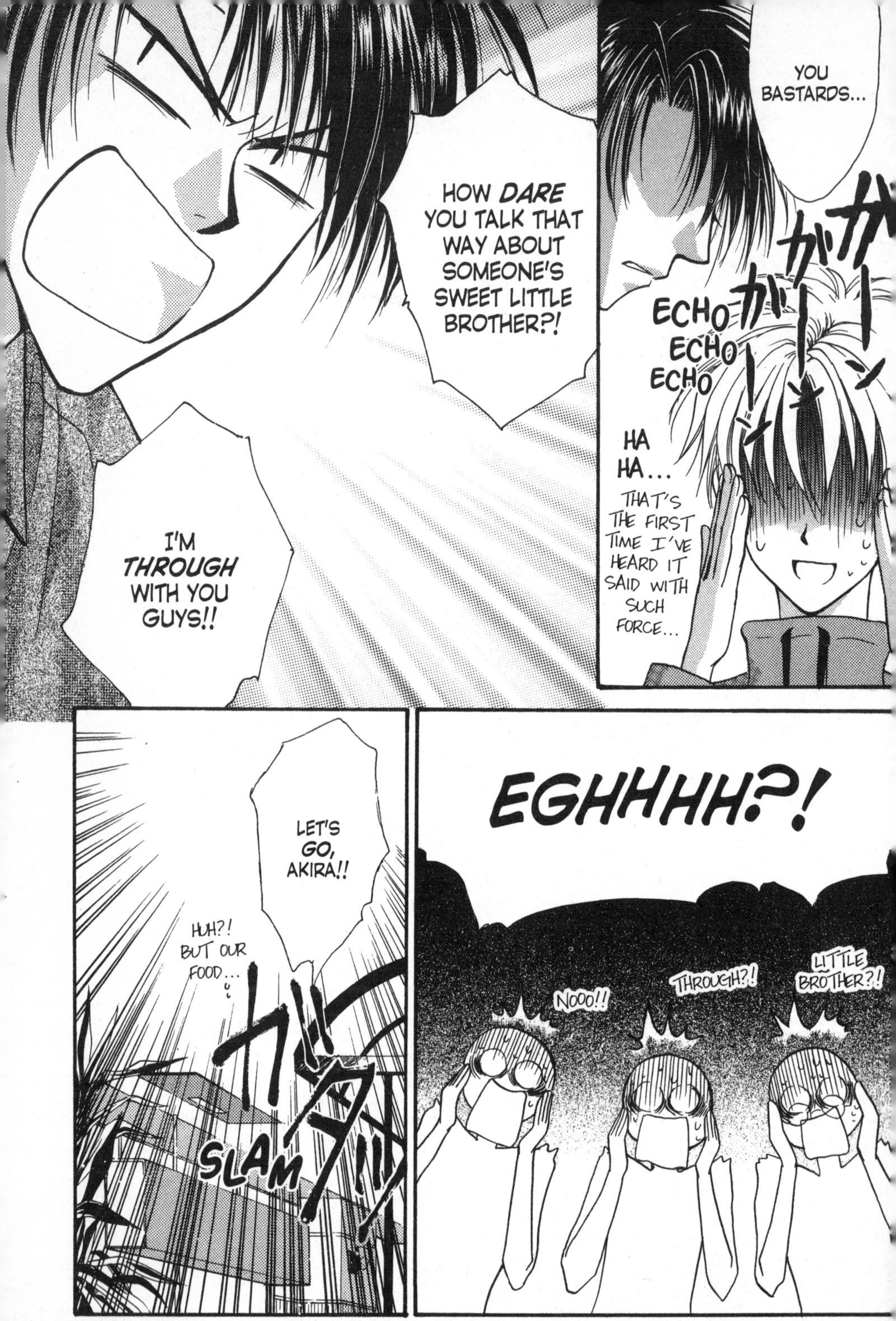
YOU BASTARDS...
ECHO ECHO ECHO
HA HA...
THAT'S THE FIRST TIME I'VE HEARD IT SAID WITH SUCH FORCE...
HOW *DARE* YOU TALK THAT WAY ABOUT SOMEONE'S SWEET LITTLE BROTHER?!
I'M *THROUGH* WITH YOU GUYS!!
EGHHHH?!
LITTLE BROTHER?!
THROUGH?!
NOOO!!
LET'S *GO*, AKIRA!!
HUH?! BUT OUR FOOD...
SLAM!!

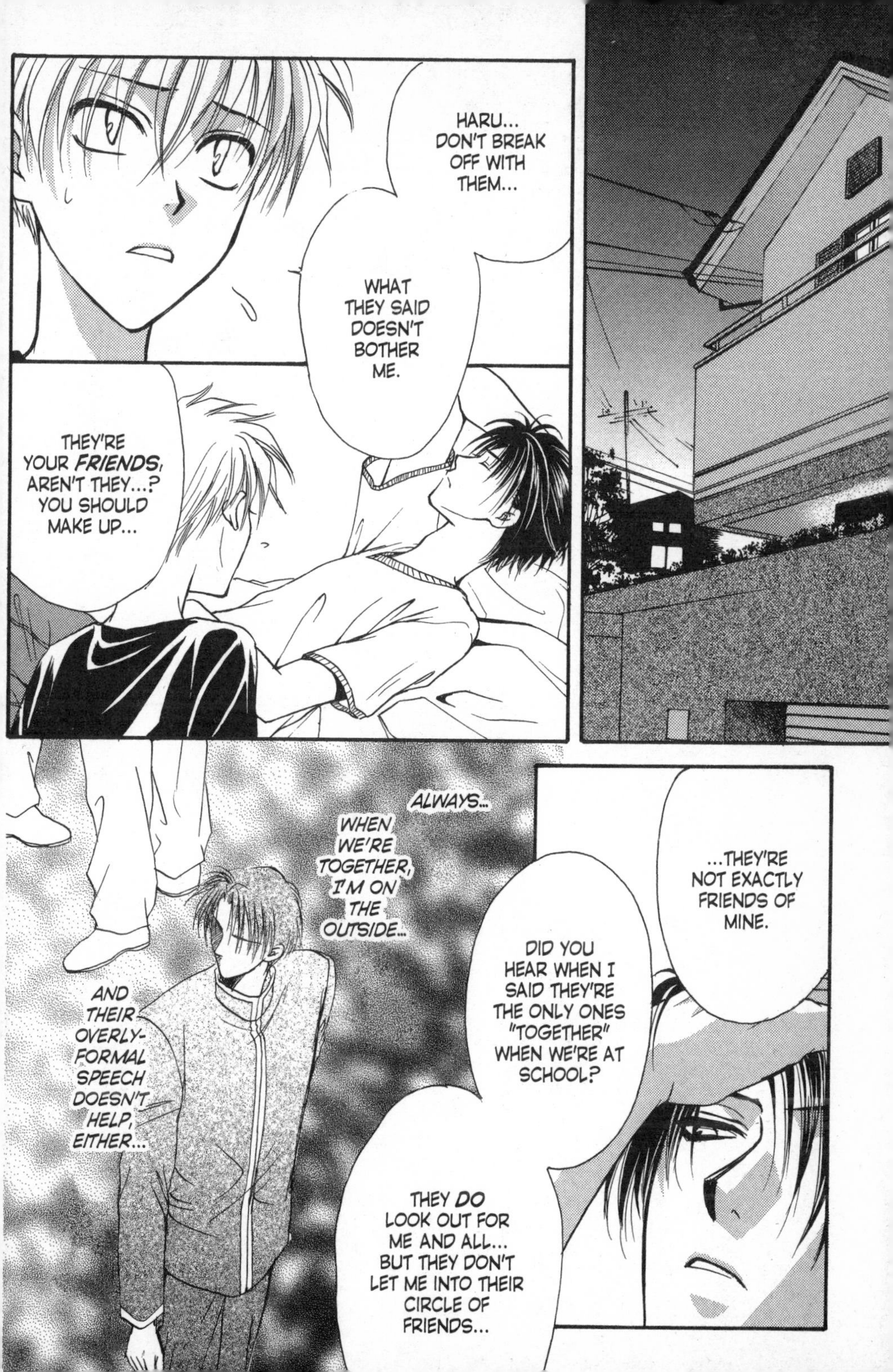

HARU... DON'T BREAK OFF WITH THEM...
WHAT THEY SAID DOESN'T BOTHER ME.
THEY'RE YOUR *FRIENDS*, AREN'T THEY...? YOU SHOULD MAKE UP...
...THEY'RE NOT EXACTLY FRIENDS OF MINE.
DID YOU HEAR WHEN I SAID THEY'RE THE ONLY ONES "TOGETHER" WHEN WE'RE AT SCHOOL?
THEY *DO* LOOK OUT FOR ME AND ALL... BUT THEY DON'T LET ME INTO THEIR CIRCLE OF FRIENDS...
ALWAYS...
WHEN WE'RE TOGETHER, I'M ON THE OUTSIDE...
AND THEIR OVERLY-FORMAL SPEECH DOESN'T HELP, EITHER...

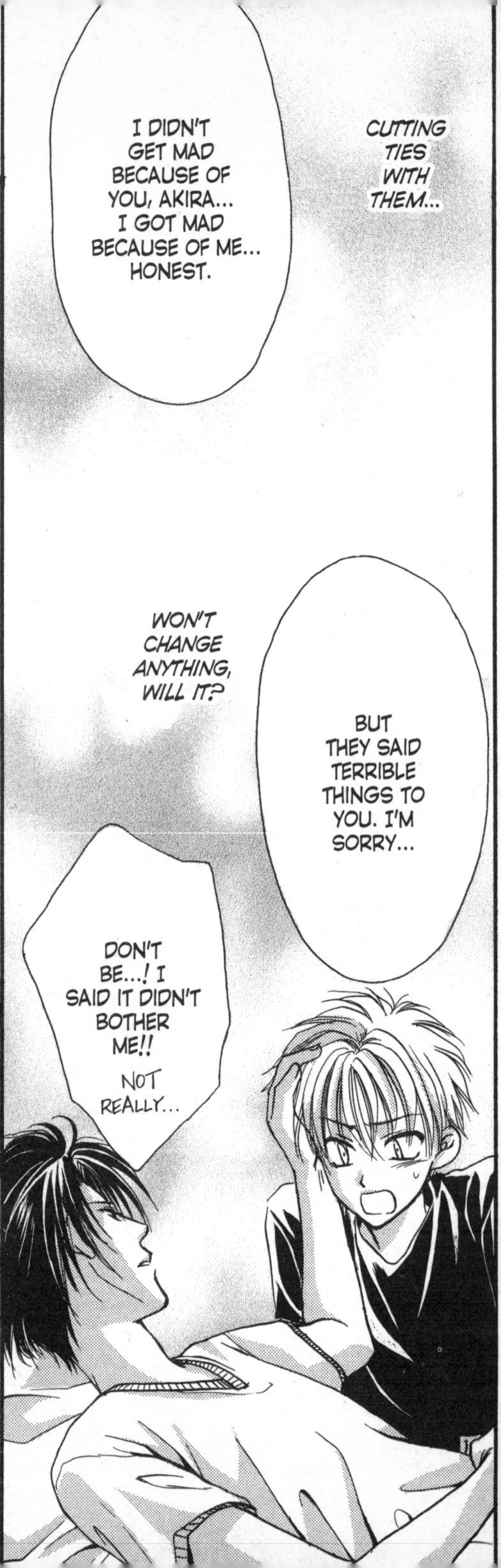
CUTTING TIES WITH THEM...
I DIDN'T GET MAD BECAUSE OF YOU, AKIRA... I GOT MAD BECAUSE OF ME... HONEST.
WON'T CHANGE ANYTHING, WILL IT?
BUT THEY SAID TERRIBLE THINGS TO YOU. I'M SORRY...
DON'T BE...! I SAID IT DIDN'T BOTHER ME!!
NOT REALLY...
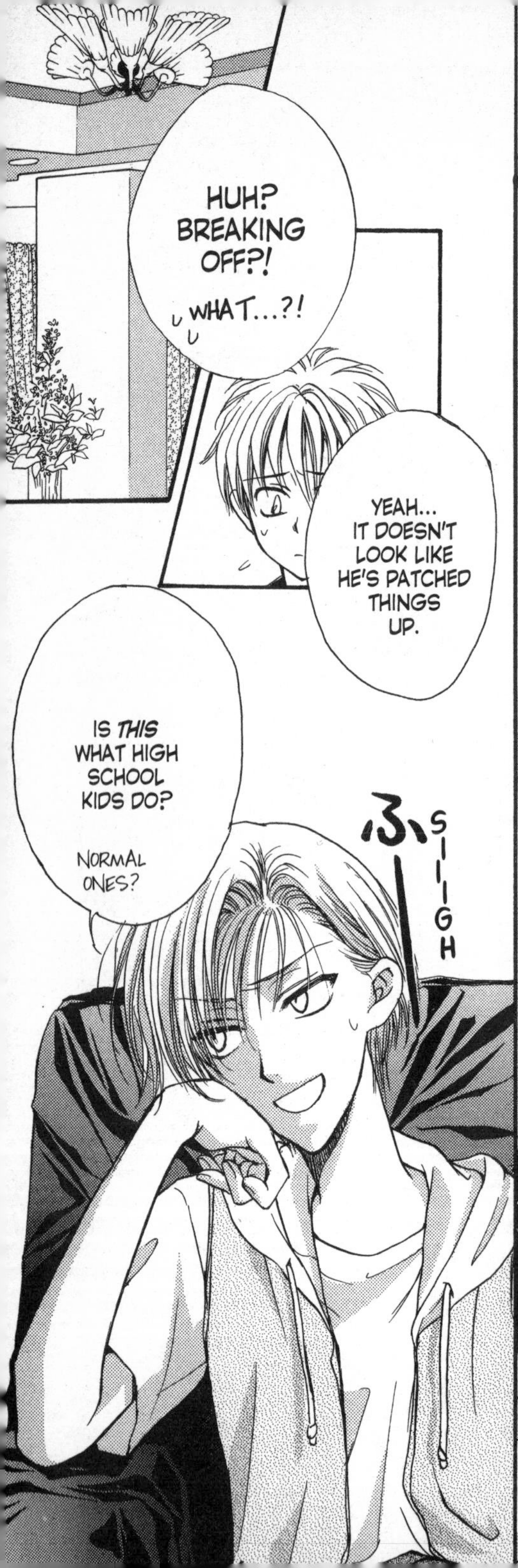
HUH? BREAKING OFF?!
WHAT...?!
YEAH... IT DOESN'T LOOK LIKE HE'S PATCHED THINGS UP.
IS THIS WHAT HIGH SCHOOL KIDS DO?
NORMAL ONES?
ふ SIIIGH

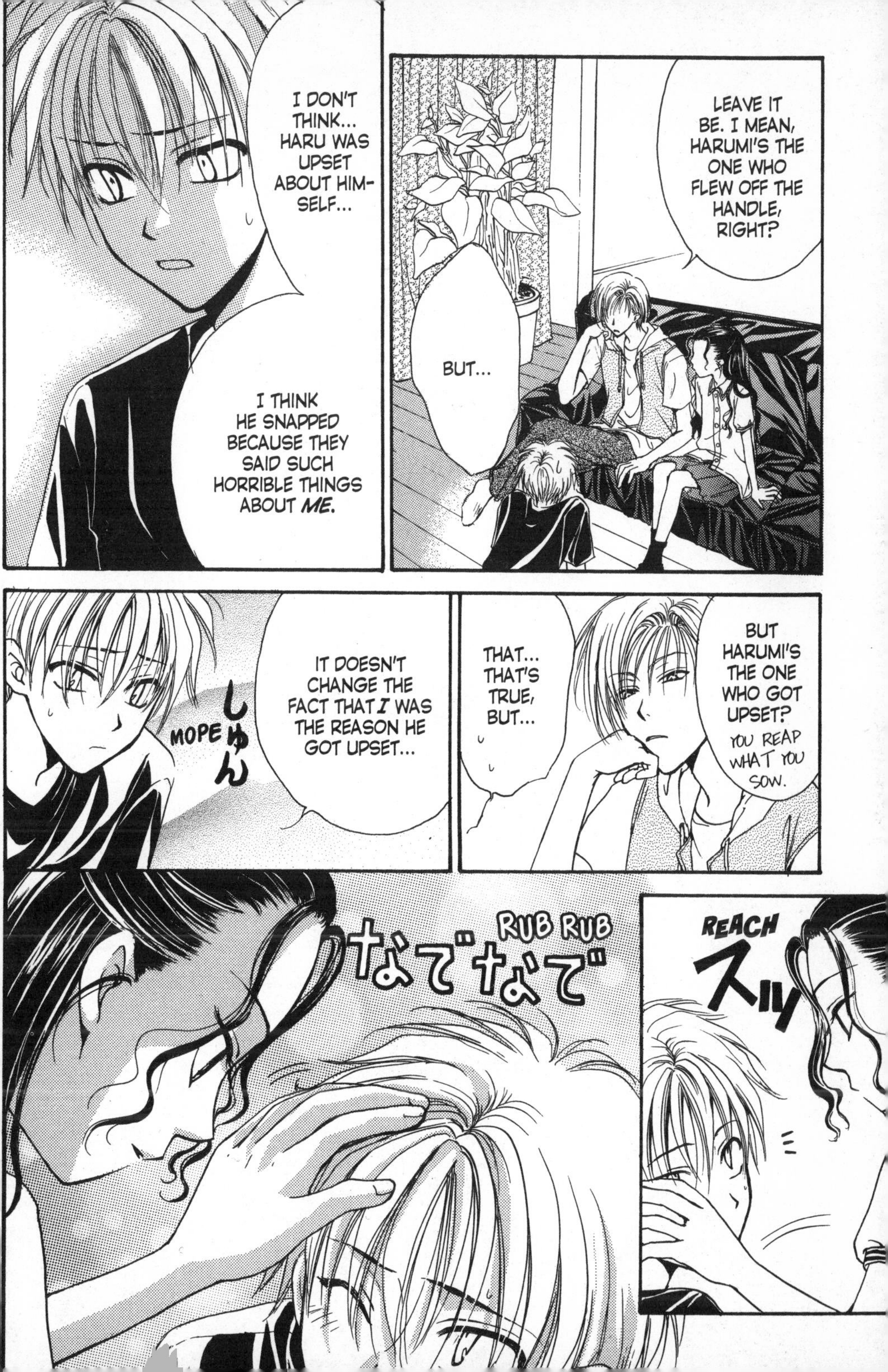
LEAVE IT BE. I MEAN, HARUMI'S THE ONE WHO FLEW OFF THE HANDLE, RIGHT?
BUT...
I DON'T THINK... HARU WAS UPSET ABOUT HIM-SELF...
I THINK HE SNAPPED BECAUSE THEY SAID SUCH HORRIBLE THINGS ABOUT *ME.*
BUT HARUMI'S THE ONE WHO GOT UPSET?
YOU REAP WHAT YOU SOW.
THAT... THAT'S TRUE, BUT...
IT DOESN'T CHANGE THE FACT THAT *I* WAS THE REASON HE GOT UPSET...
MOPE
しゅん
REACH
スッ
RUB RUB
なでなで

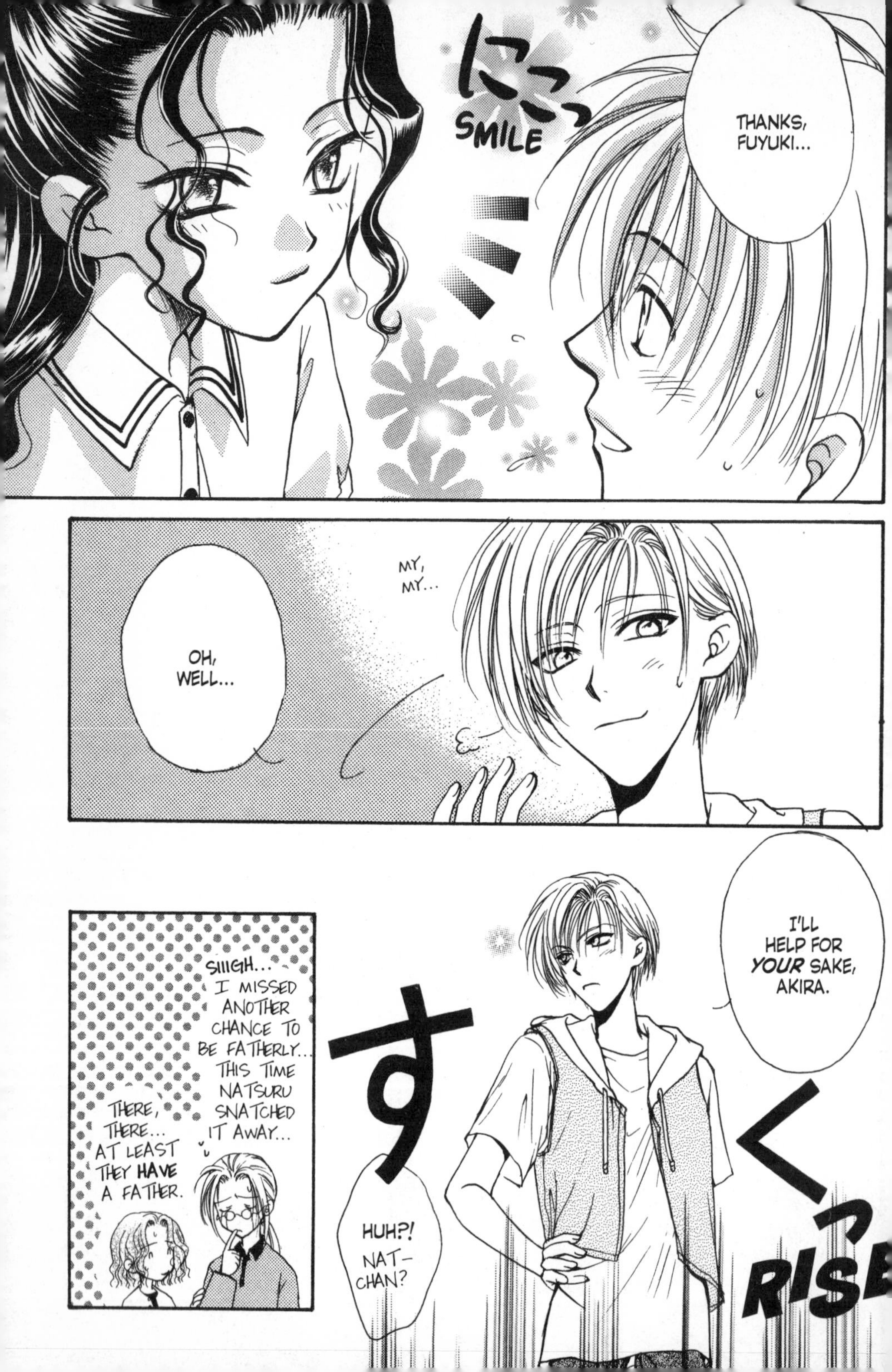
THANKS, FUYUKI...
にこっ
SMILE
MY, MY...
OH, WELL...
I'LL HELP FOR **YOUR** SAKE, AKIRA.
すくっ
RISE
HUH?! NAT-CHAN?
SIIGH... I MISSED ANOTHER CHANCE TO BE FATHERLY... THIS TIME NATSURU SNATCHED IT AWAY...
THERE, THERE... AT LEAST THEY **HAVE** A FATHER.

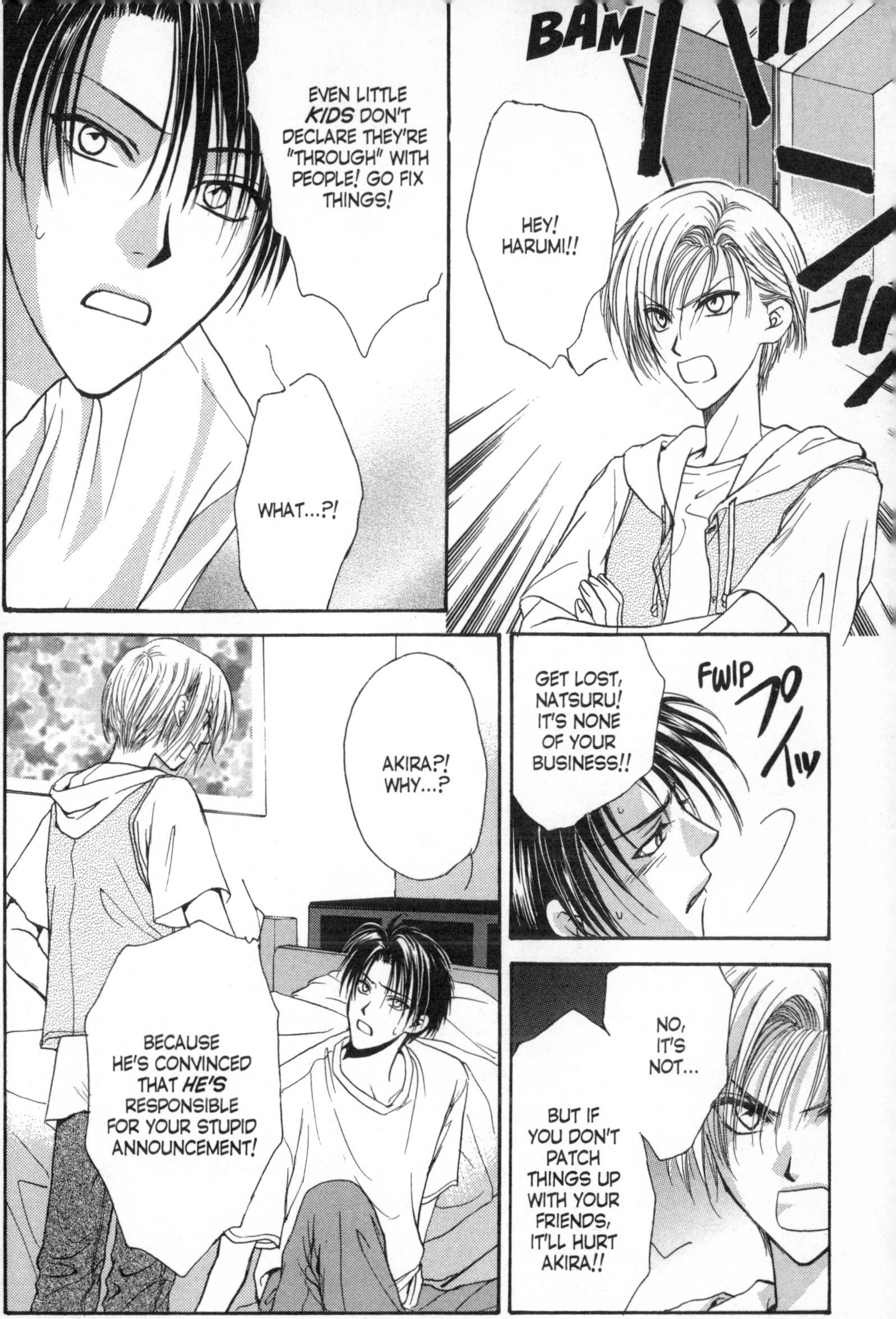
BAM
HEY! HARUMI!!
EVEN LITTLE *KIDS* DON'T DECLARE THEY'RE "THROUGH" WITH PEOPLE! GO FIX THINGS!
WHAT...?!
GET LOST, NATSURU! IT'S NONE OF YOUR BUSINESS!!
FWIP
NO, IT'S NOT...
BUT IF YOU DON'T PATCH THINGS UP WITH YOUR FRIENDS, IT'LL HURT AKIRA!!
AKIRA?! WHY...?
BECAUSE HE'S CONVINCED THAT *HE'S* RESPONSIBLE FOR YOUR STUPID ANNOUNCEMENT!

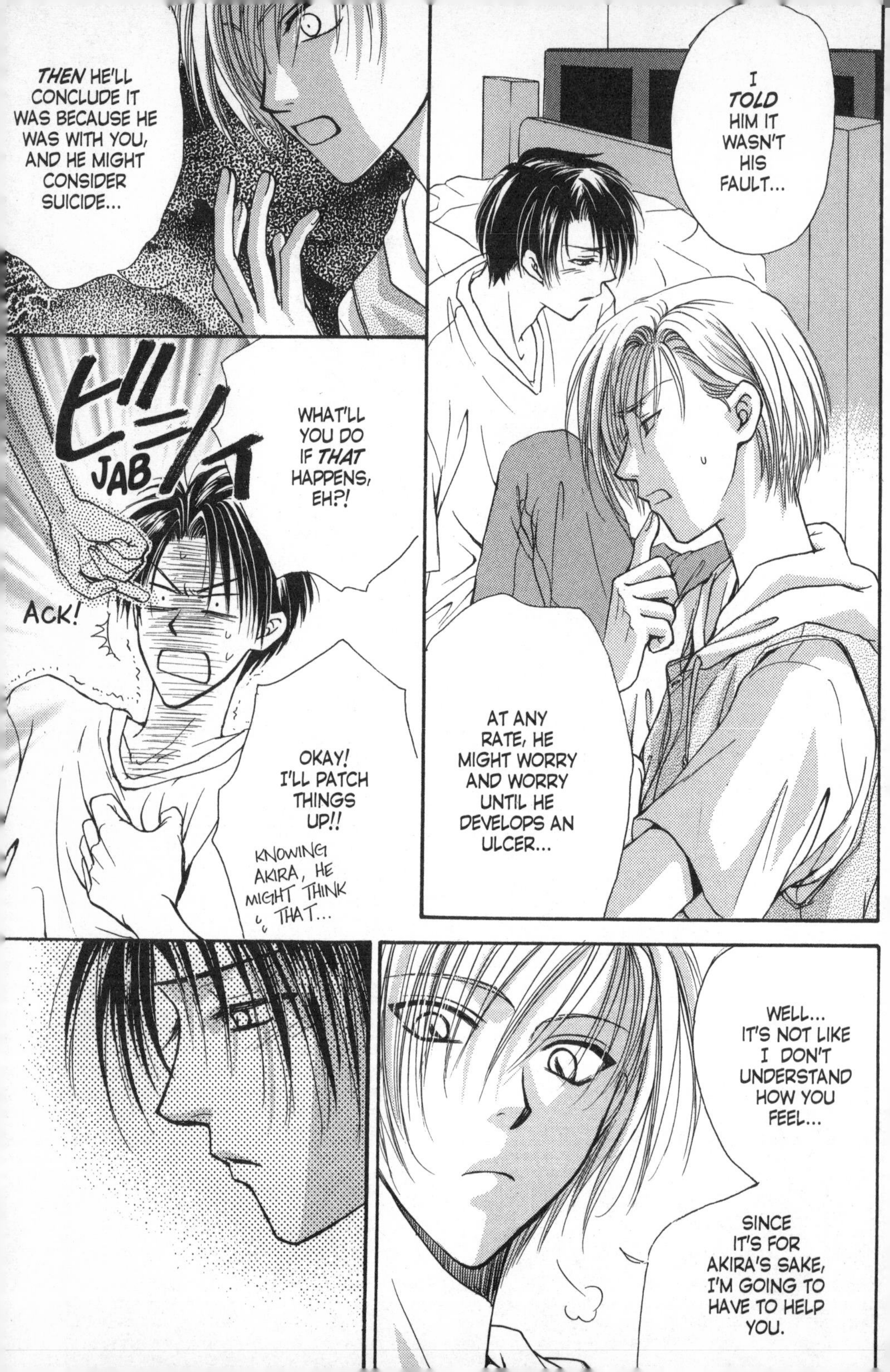
I TOLD HIM IT WASN'T HIS FAULT...
AT ANY RATE, HE MIGHT WORRY AND WORRY UNTIL HE DEVELOPS AN ULCER...
THEN HE'LL CONCLUDE IT WAS BECAUSE HE WAS WITH YOU, AND HE MIGHT CONSIDER SUICIDE...
WHAT'LL YOU DO IF THAT HAPPENS, EH?!
JAB
ACK!
OKAY! I'LL PATCH THINGS UP!!
KNOWING AKIRA, HE MIGHT THINK THAT...
WELL... IT'S NOT LIKE I DON'T UNDERSTAND HOW YOU FEEL...
SINCE IT'S FOR AKIRA'S SAKE, I'M GOING TO HAVE TO HELP YOU.

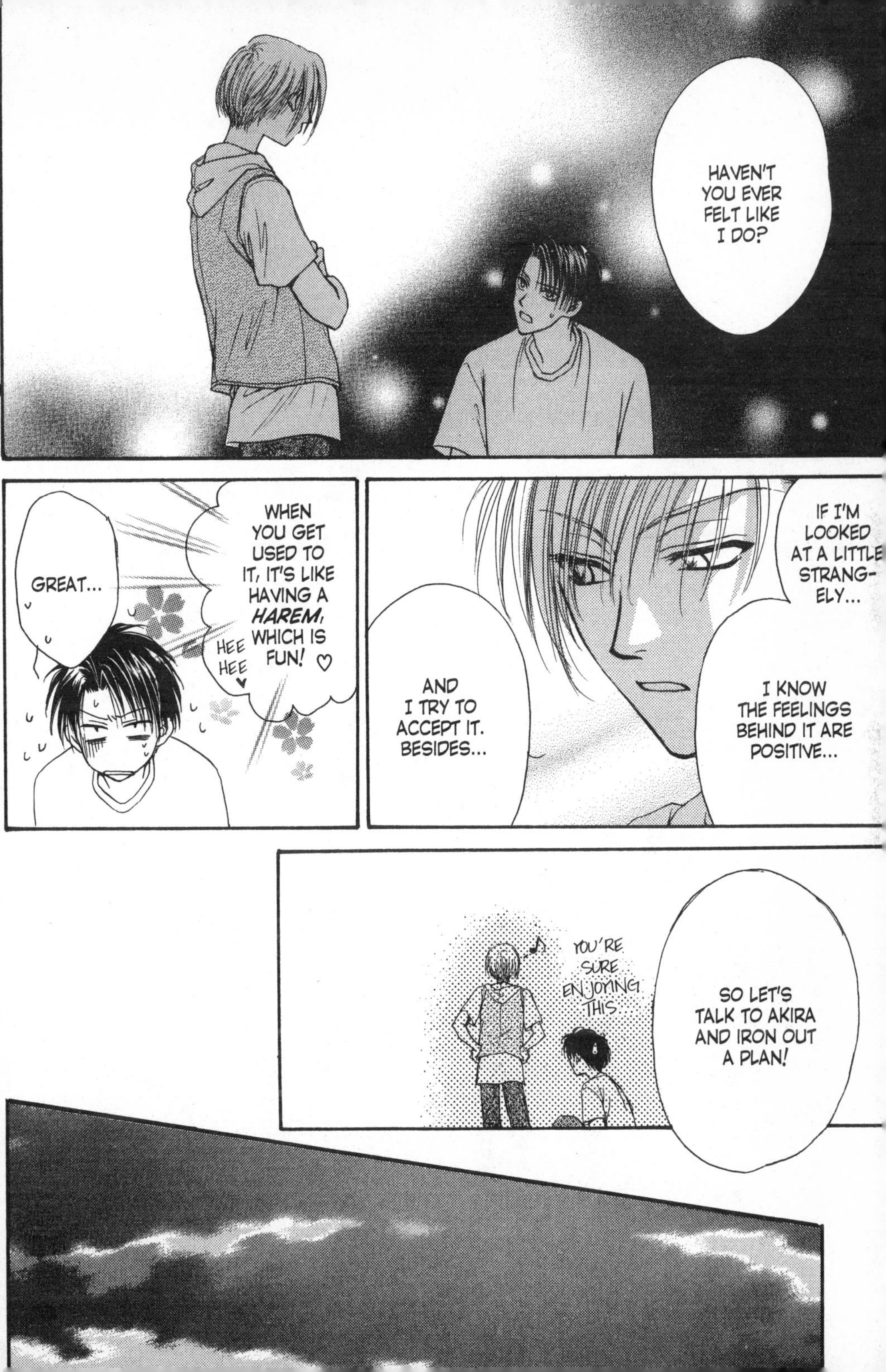
HAVEN'T YOU EVER FELT LIKE I DO?
IF I'M LOOKED AT A LITTLE STRANG-ELY...
I KNOW THE FEELINGS BEHIND IT ARE POSITIVE...
AND I TRY TO ACCEPT IT. BESIDES...
WHEN YOU GET USED TO IT, IT'S LIKE HAVING A *HAREM*, WHICH IS FUN! ♡
HEE HEE ♥
GREAT...
SO LET'S TALK TO AKIRA AND IRON OUT A PLAN!
YOU'RE SURE ENJOYING THIS

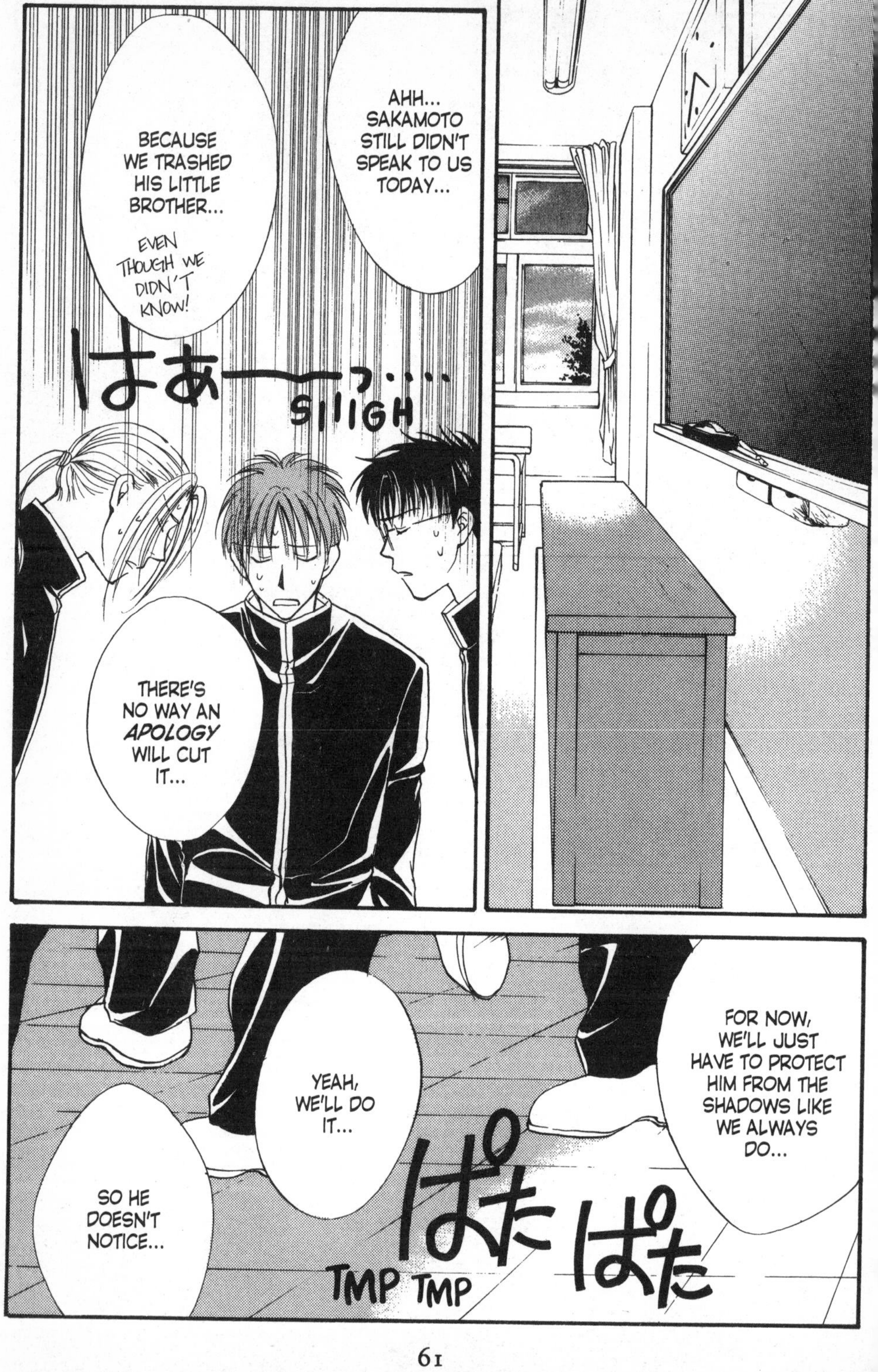
AHH... SAKAMOTO STILL DIDN'T SPEAK TO US TODAY...
BECAUSE WE TRASHED HIS LITTLE BROTHER...
EVEN THOUGH WE DIDN'T KNOW!
はあーーっ……
SIIIGH
THERE'S NO WAY AN *APOLOGY* WILL CUT IT...
FOR NOW, WE'LL JUST HAVE TO PROTECT HIM FROM THE SHADOWS LIKE WE ALWAYS DO...
ぱたぱた
TMP TMP
YEAH, WE'LL DO IT...
SO HE DOESN'T NOTICE...

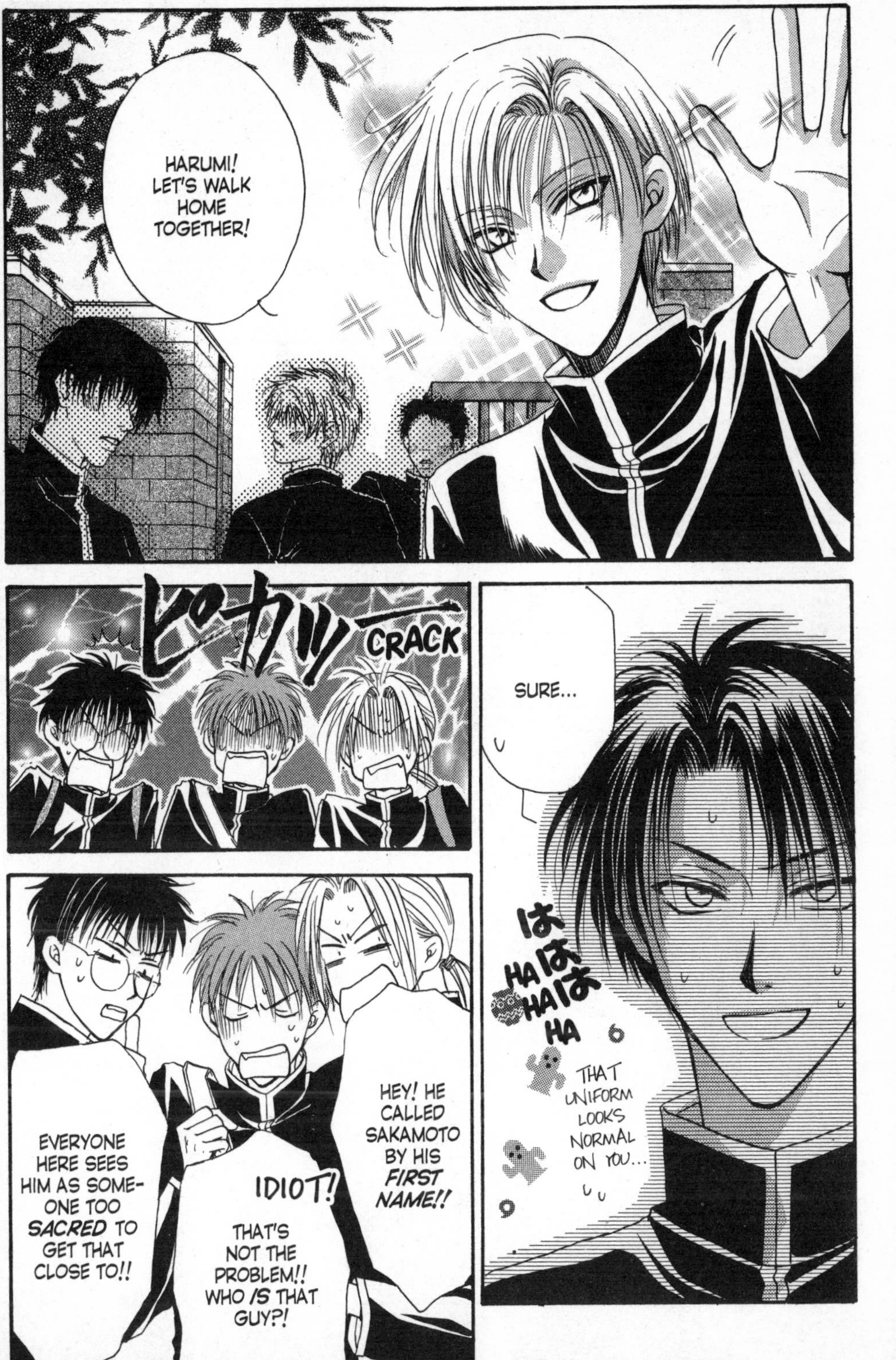
HARUMI! LET'S WALK HOME TOGETHER!
SURE...
ははは
HA HA HA
THAT UNIFORM LOOKS NORMAL ON YOU...
ピカッ
CRACK
HEY! HE CALLED SAKAMOTO BY HIS FIRST NAME!!
IDIOT!
THAT'S NOT THE PROBLEM!! WHO IS THAT GUY?!
EVERYONE HERE SEES HIM AS SOMEONE TOO SACRED TO GET THAT CLOSE TO!!

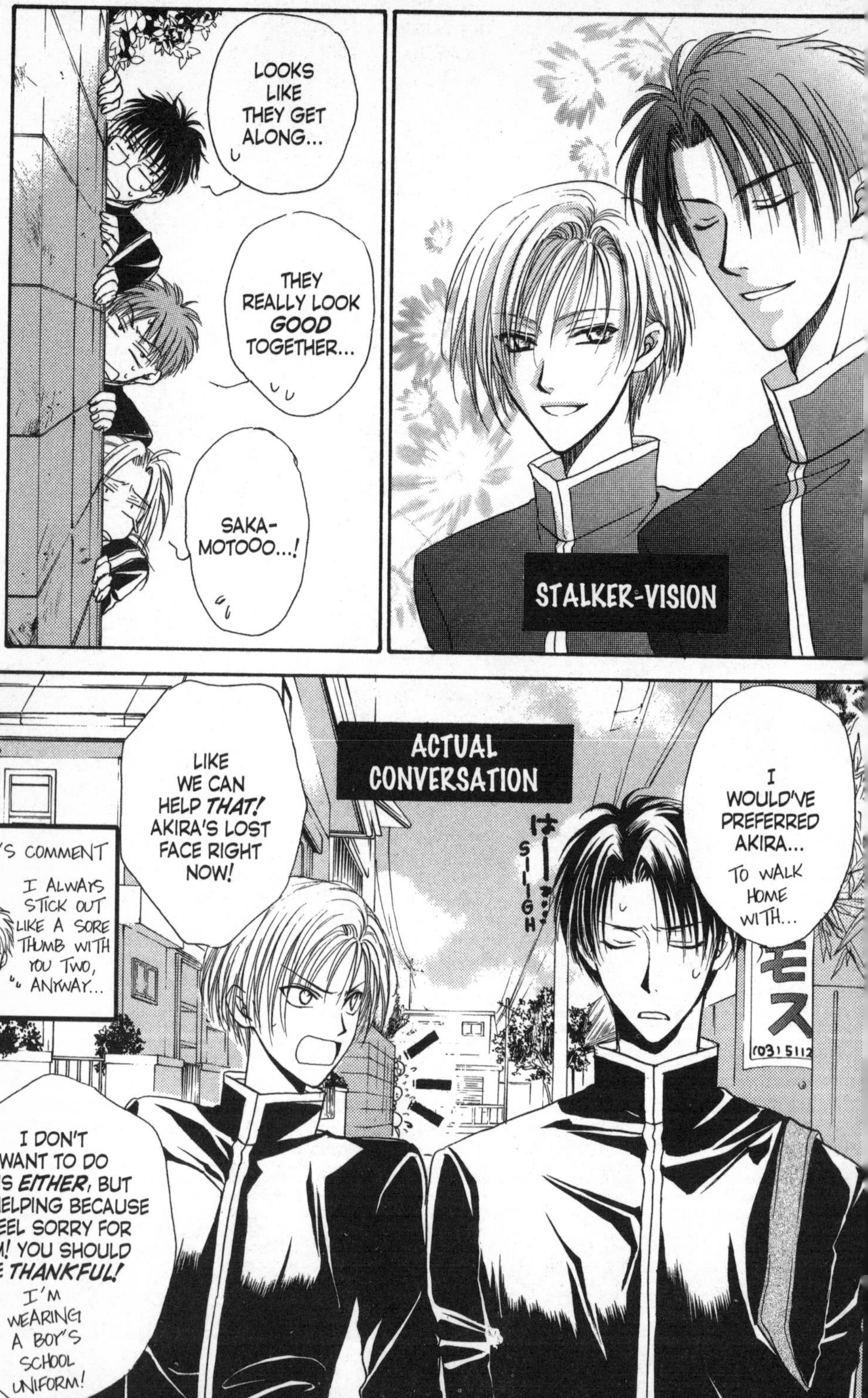

STALKER-VISION
LOOKS LIKE THEY GET ALONG...
THEY REALLY LOOK *GOOD* TOGETHER...
SAKA-MOTOOO...!
ACTUAL CONVERSATION
I WOULD'VE PREFERRED AKIRA... TO WALK HOME WITH...
はーっ SIIIGH
LIKE WE CAN HELP *THAT!* AKIRA'S LOST FACE RIGHT NOW!
AKIRA'S COMMENT
I ALWAYS STICK OUT LIKE A SORE THUMB WITH YOU TWO, ANYWAY...
I DON'T WANT TO DO THIS *EITHER*, BUT I'M HELPING BECAUSE I FEEL SORRY FOR HIM! YOU SHOULD BE *THANKFUL!*
I'M WEARING A BOY'S SCHOOL UNIFORM!

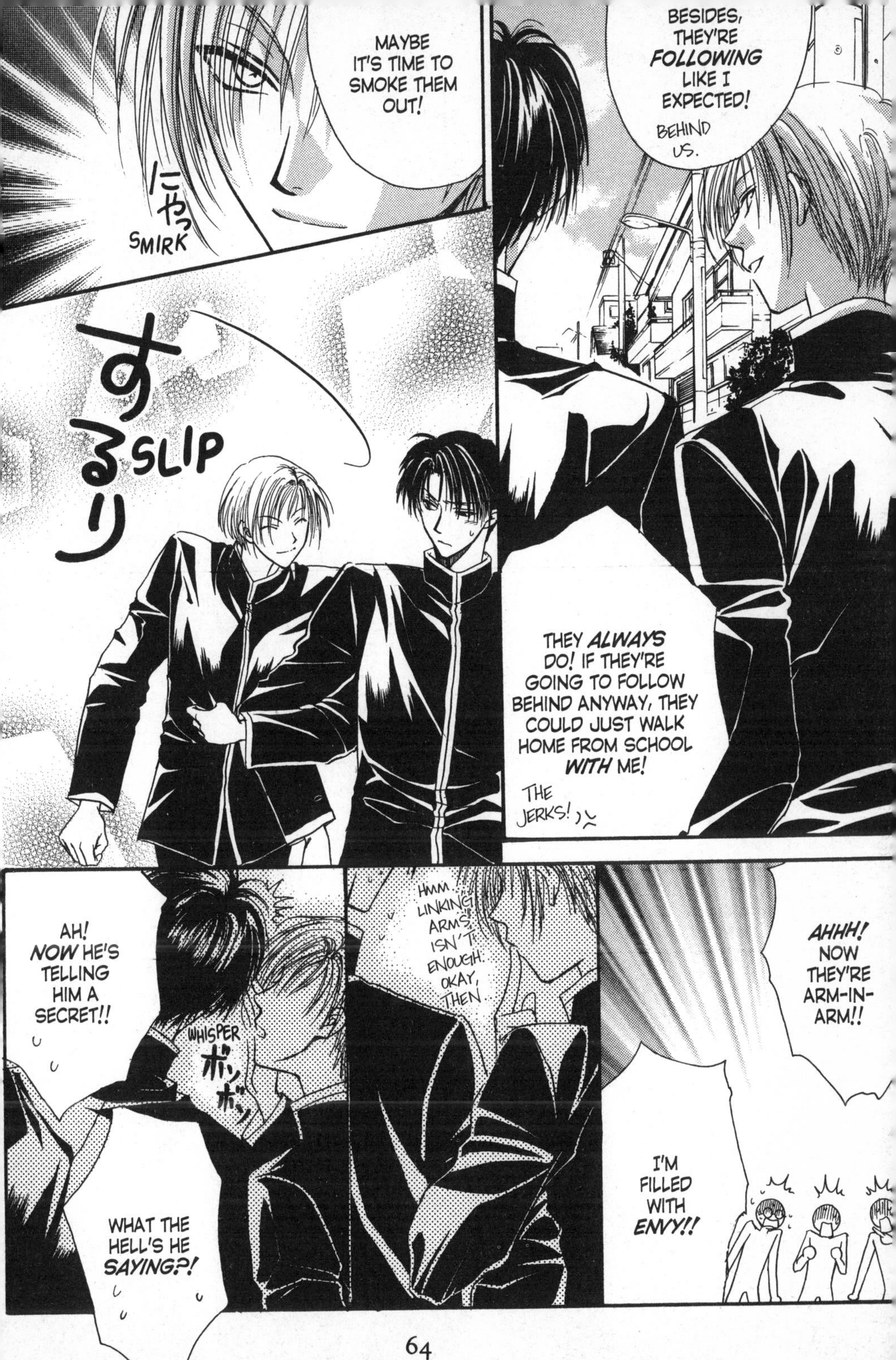
BESIDES, THEY'RE *FOLLOWING* LIKE I EXPECTED!
BEHIND US.
THEY *ALWAYS* DO! IF THEY'RE GOING TO FOLLOW BEHIND ANYWAY, THEY COULD JUST WALK HOME FROM SCHOOL *WITH* ME!
THE JERKS!
MAYBE IT'S TIME TO SMOKE THEM OUT!
にやっ
SMIRK
するり
SLIP
AHHH! NOW THEY'RE ARM-IN-ARM!!
I'M FILLED WITH *ENVY!!*
HMM LINKING ARMS ISN'T ENOUGH OKAY, THEN
AH! *NOW* HE'S TELLING HIM A SECRET!!
WHISPER
ボソボソ
WHAT THE HELL'S HE *SAYING?!*

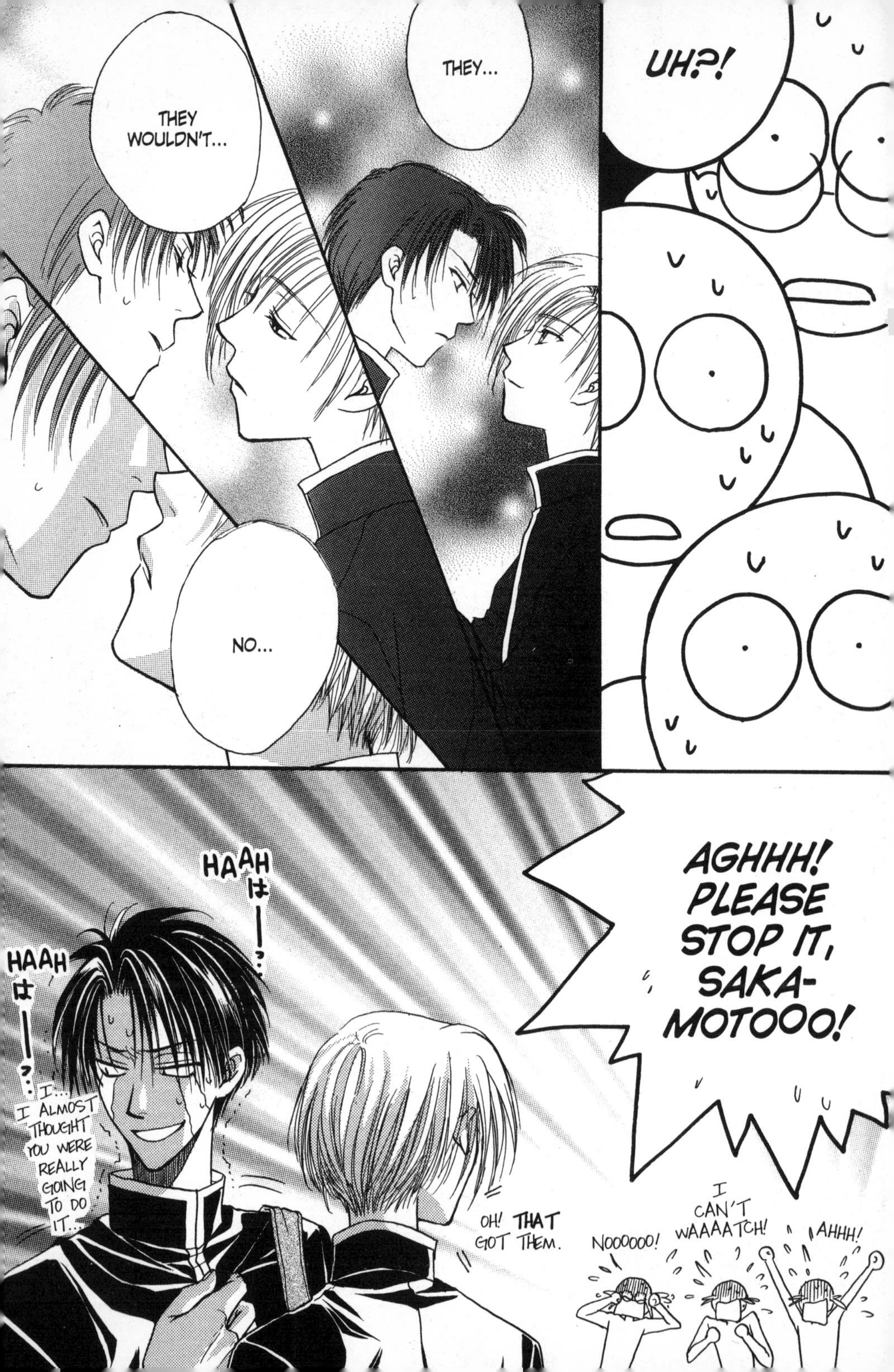
UH?!
THEY...
THEY WOULDN'T...
NO...
AGHHH! PLEASE STOP IT, SAKA-MOTOOO!
HAAH はー っ
HAAH はー っ...
I... I ALMOST THOUGHT YOU WERE REALLY GOING TO DO IT...
OH! THAT GOT THEM.
AHHH!
I CAN'T WAAAATCH!
NOOOOOO!

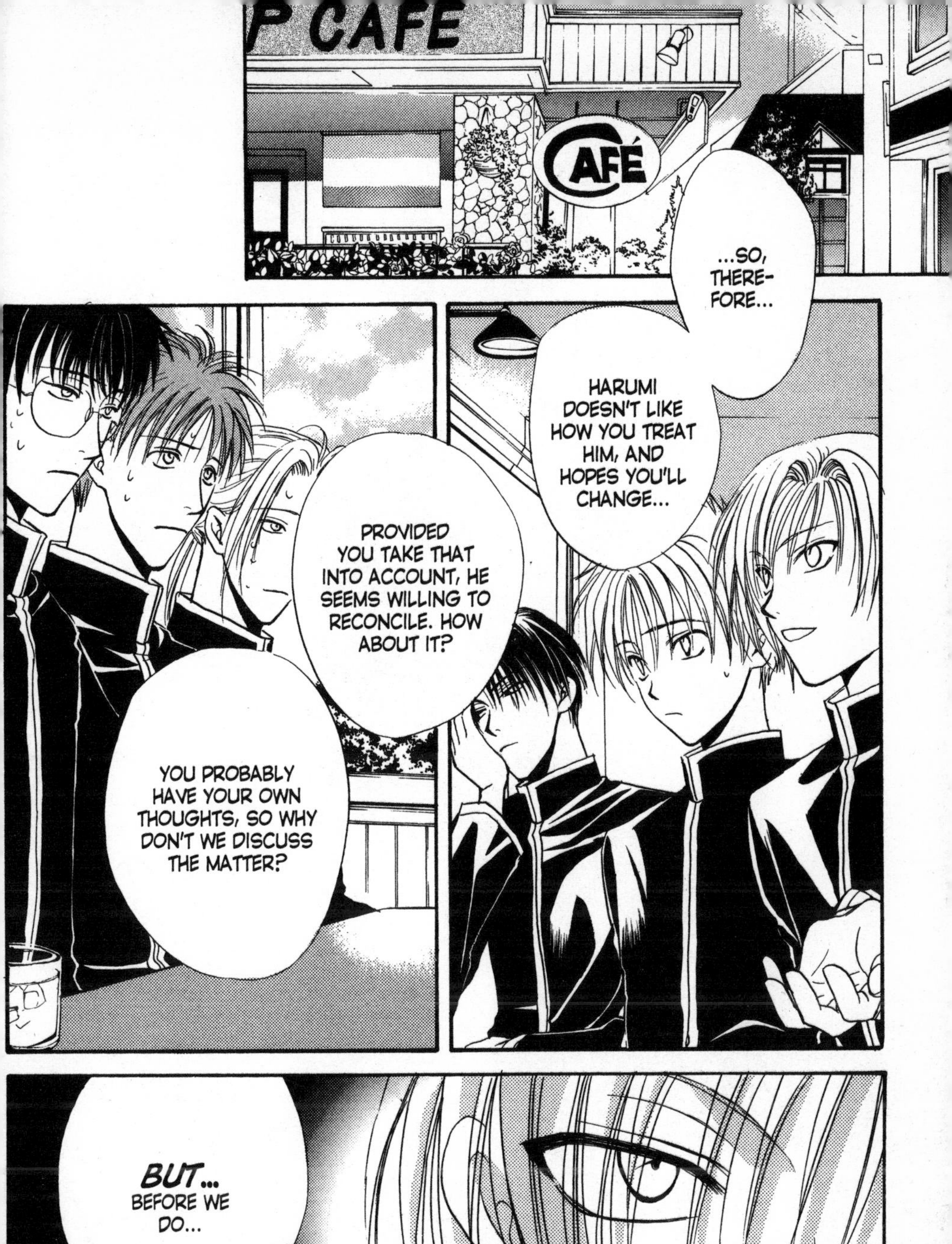
P CAFE
CAFÉ
...SO, THEREFORE...
HARUMI DOESN'T LIKE HOW YOU TREAT HIM, AND HOPES YOU'LL CHANGE...
PROVIDED YOU TAKE THAT INTO ACCOUNT, HE SEEMS WILLING TO RECONCILE. HOW ABOUT IT?
YOU PROBABLY HAVE YOUR OWN THOUGHTS, SO WHY DON'T WE DISCUSS THE MATTER?
BUT... BEFORE WE DO...

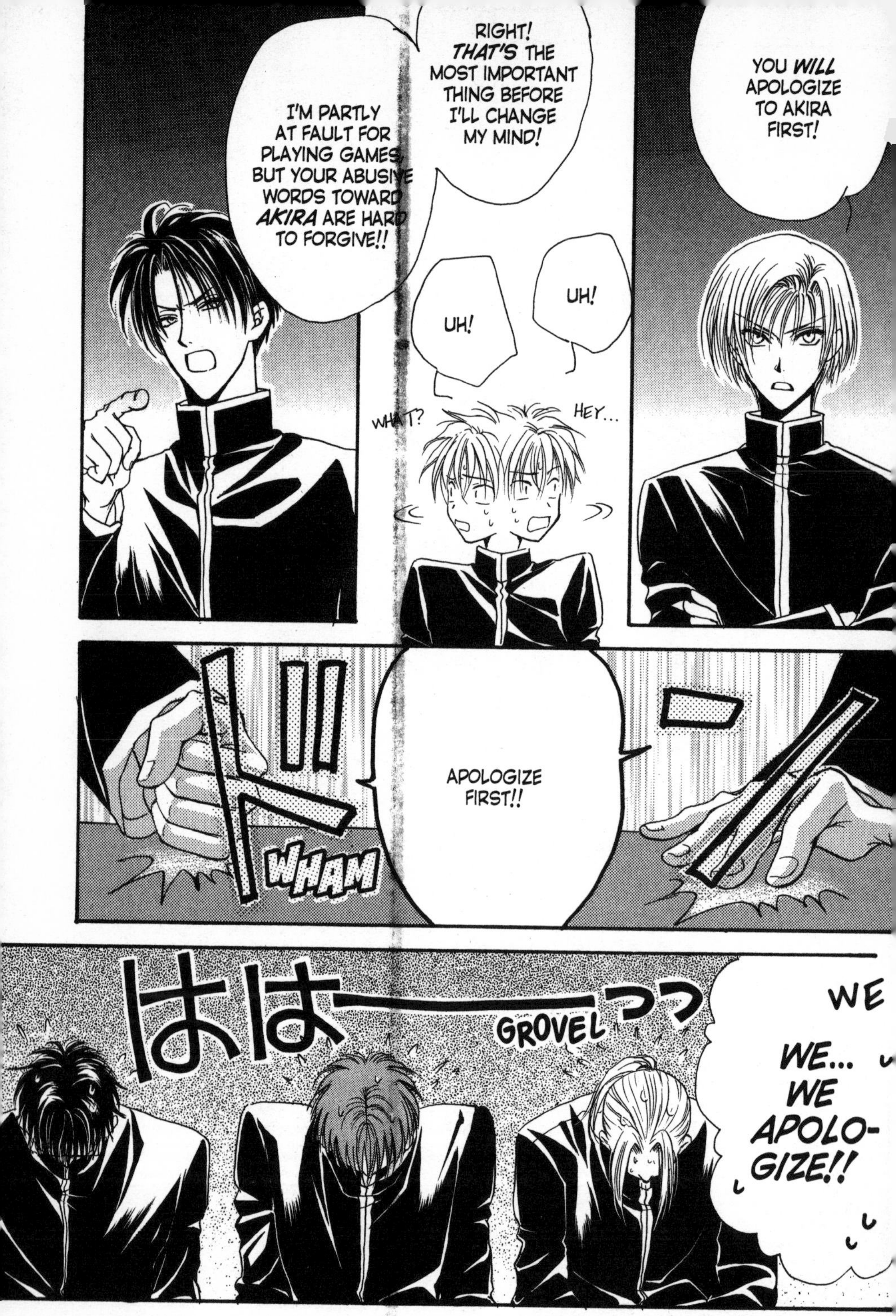
YOU WILL APOLOGIZE TO AKIRA FIRST!
RIGHT! THAT'S THE MOST IMPORTANT THING BEFORE I'LL CHANGE MY MIND!
UH!
UH!
HEY...
WHAT?
I'M PARTLY AT FAULT FOR PLAYING GAMES, BUT YOUR ABUSIVE WORDS TOWARD AKIRA ARE HARD TO FORGIVE!!
APOLOGIZE FIRST!!
WHAM
WE
WE... WE APOLOGIZE!!
ははーーっっ
GROVEL

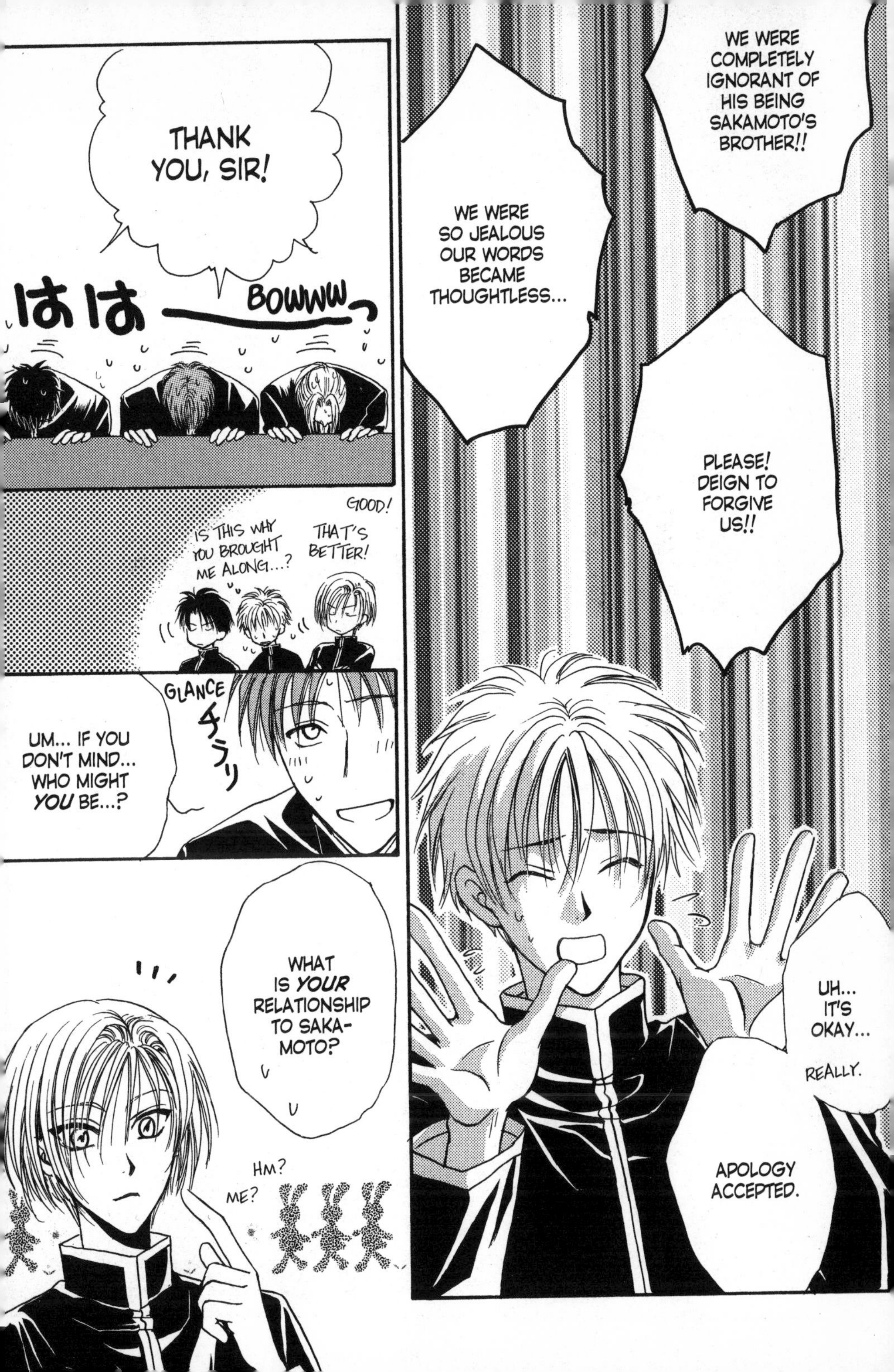
WE WERE COMPLETELY IGNORANT OF HIS BEING SAKAMOTO'S BROTHER!!
WE WERE SO JEALOUS OUR WORDS BECAME THOUGHTLESS...
PLEASE! DEIGN TO FORGIVE US!!
UH... IT'S OKAY... REALLY.
APOLOGY ACCEPTED.
THANK YOU, SIR!
ははー
BOWWW
GOOD!
THAT'S BETTER!
IS THIS WHY YOU BROUGHT ME ALONG...?
GLANCE
チラリ
UM... IF YOU DON'T MIND... WHO MIGHT YOU BE...?
WHAT IS YOUR RELATIONSHIP TO SAKA-MOTO?
HM?
ME?

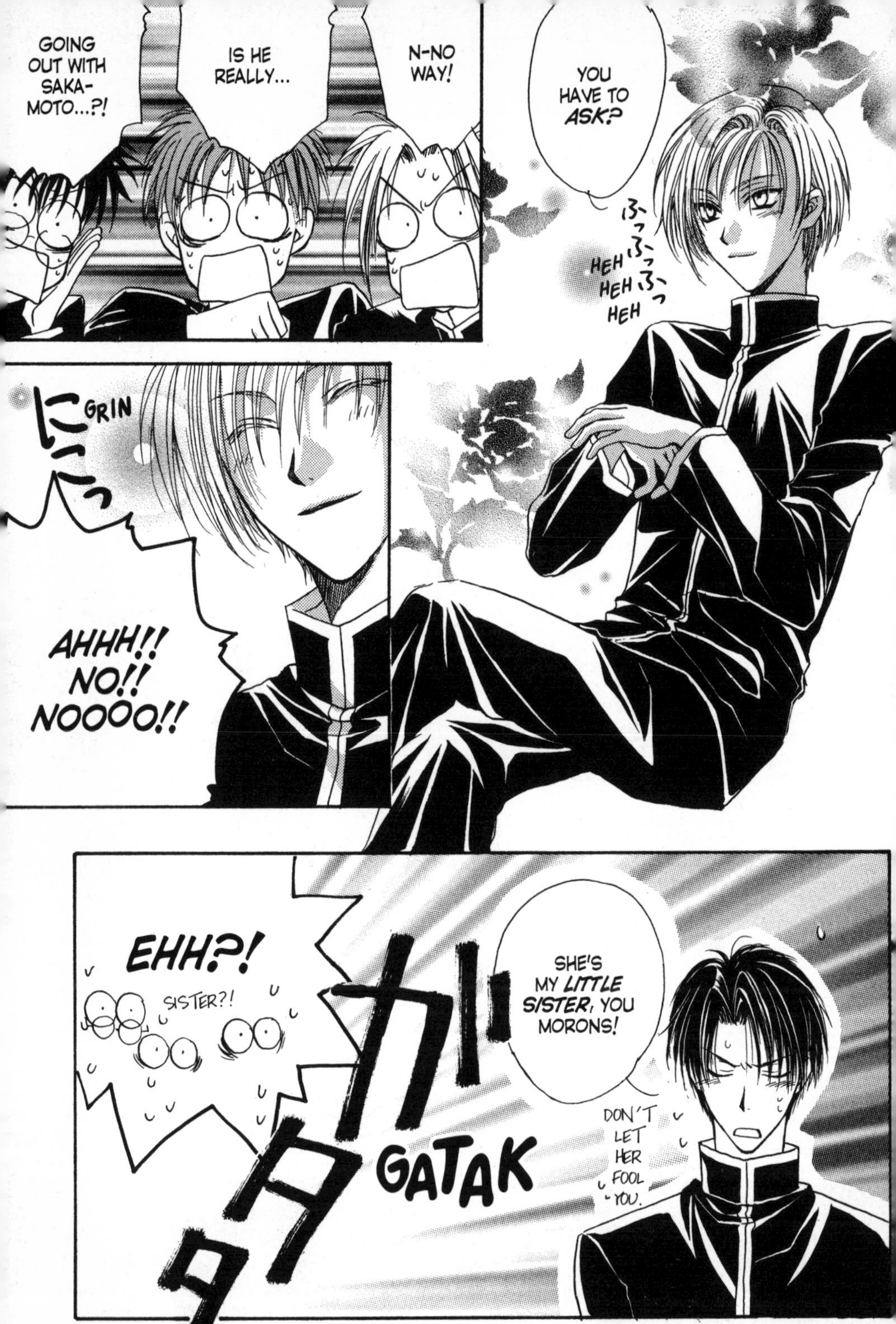
YOU HAVE TO *ASK?*
ふっふっふっ
HEH HEH HEH
N-NO WAY!
IS HE REALLY...
GOING OUT WITH SAKA-MOTO...?!
にこっ
GRIN
AHHH!! NO!! NOOOO!!
SHE'S MY *LITTLE SISTER*, YOU MORONS!
DON'T LET HER FOOL YOU.
ガタタ
GATAK
EHH?!
SISTER?!

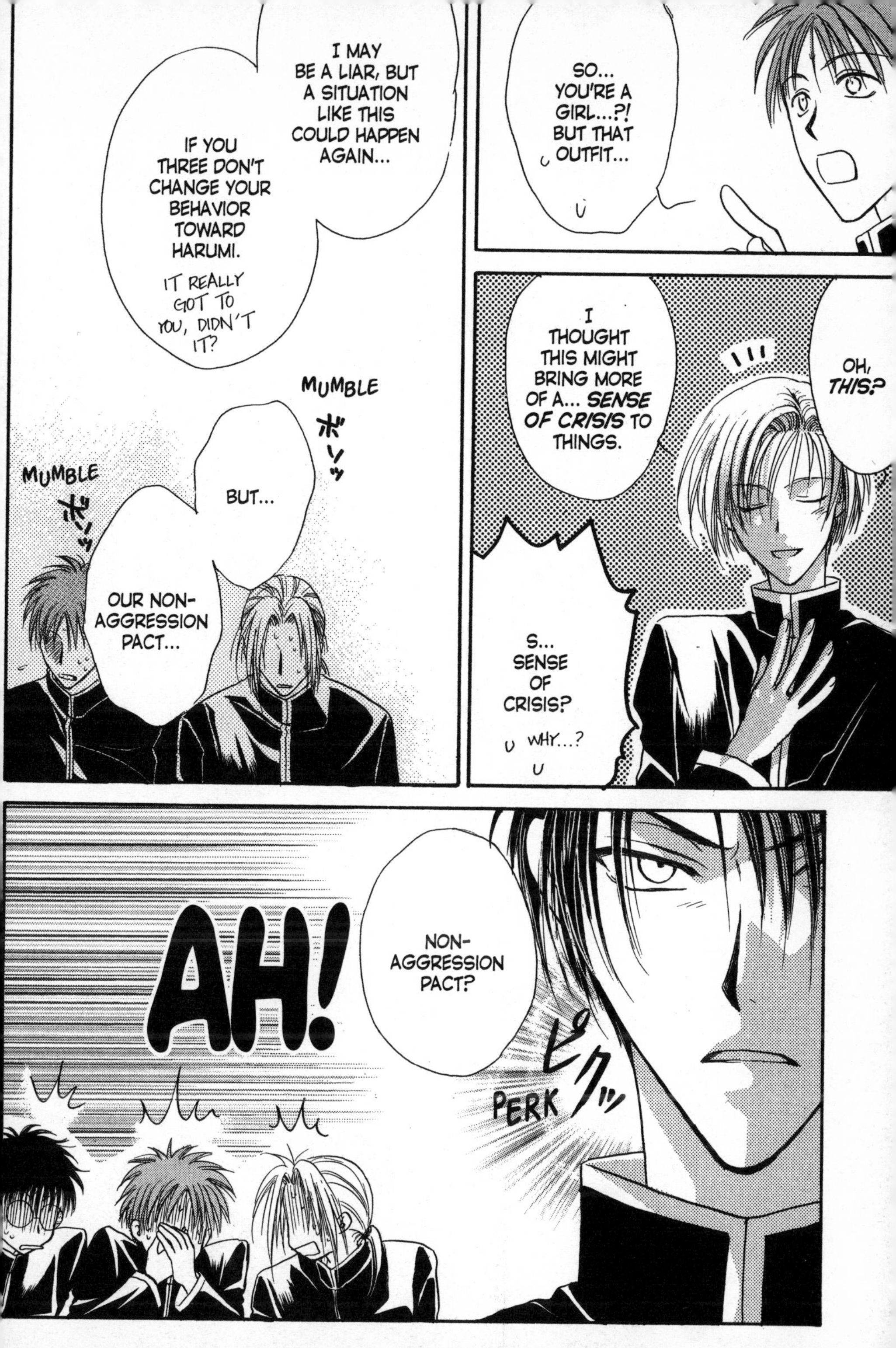
SO... YOU'RE A GIRL...?! BUT THAT OUTFIT...
OH, THIS?
I THOUGHT THIS MIGHT BRING MORE OF A... SENSE OF CRISIS TO THINGS.
S... SENSE OF CRISIS?
WHY...?
I MAY BE A LIAR, BUT A SITUATION LIKE THIS COULD HAPPEN AGAIN...
IF YOU THREE DON'T CHANGE YOUR BEHAVIOR TOWARD HARUMI.
IT REALLY GOT TO YOU, DIDN'T IT?
MUMBLE
ボソッ
BUT...
MUMBLE
ボソッ
OUR NON-AGGRESSION PACT...
NON-AGGRESSION PACT?
PERK
ピクッ
AH!

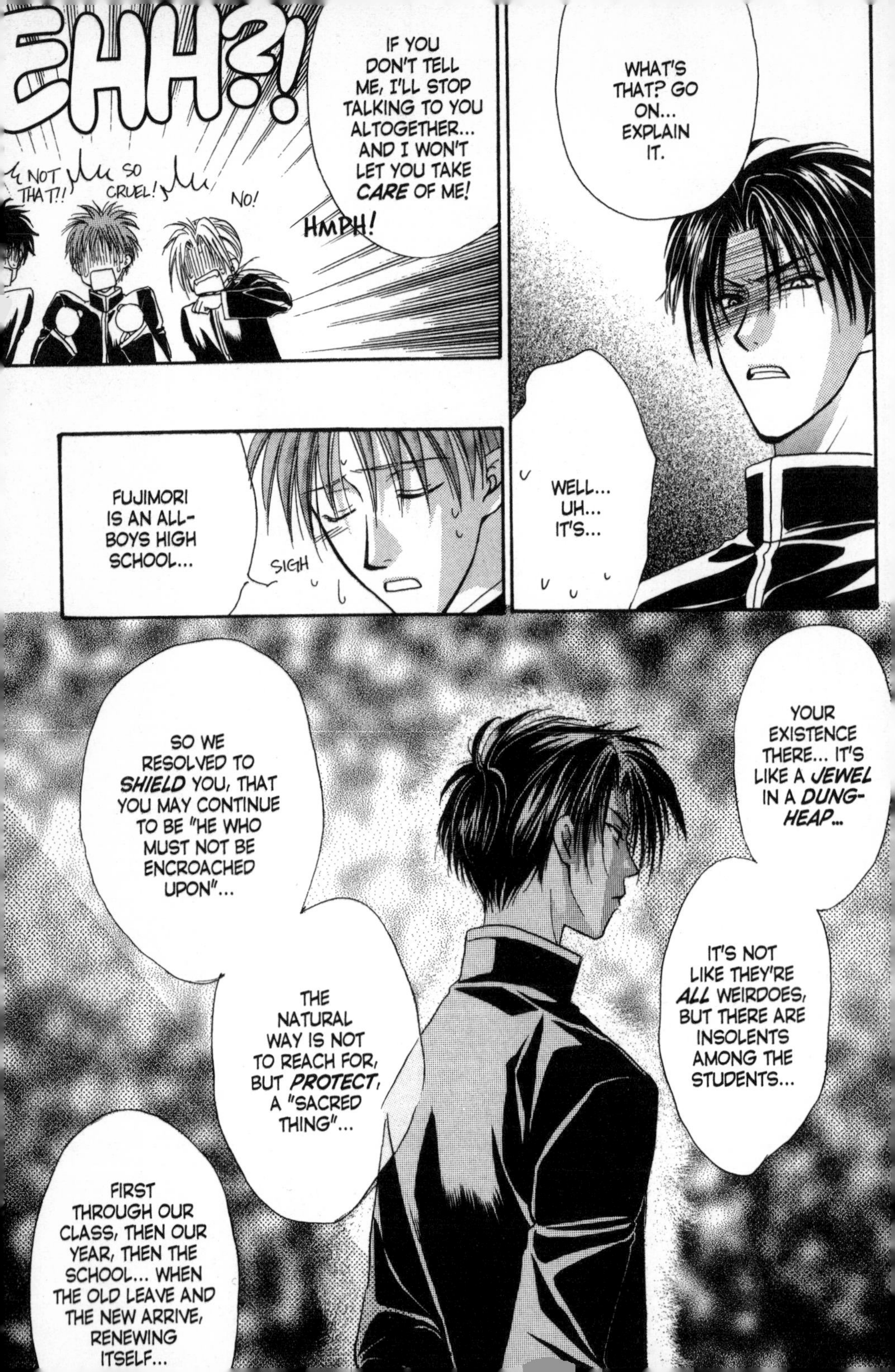

WHAT'S THAT? GO ON... EXPLAIN IT.
WELL... UH... IT'S...
IF YOU DON'T TELL ME, I'LL STOP TALKING TO YOU ALTOGETHER... AND I WON'T LET YOU TAKE CARE OF ME!
HMPH!
EHH?!
NOT THAT?!
SO CRUEL!
NO!
FUJIMORI IS AN ALL-BOYS HIGH SCHOOL...
SIGH
YOUR EXISTENCE THERE... IT'S LIKE A JEWEL IN A DUNG-HEAP...
IT'S NOT LIKE THEY'RE ALL WEIRDOES, BUT THERE ARE INSOLENTS AMONG THE STUDENTS...
SO WE RESOLVED TO SHIELD YOU, THAT YOU MAY CONTINUE TO BE "HE WHO MUST NOT BE ENCROACHED UPON"...
THE NATURAL WAY IS NOT TO REACH FOR, BUT PROTECT, A "SACRED THING"...
FIRST THROUGH OUR CLASS, THEN OUR YEAR, THEN THE SCHOOL... WHEN THE OLD LEAVE AND THE NEW ARRIVE, RENEWING ITSELF...

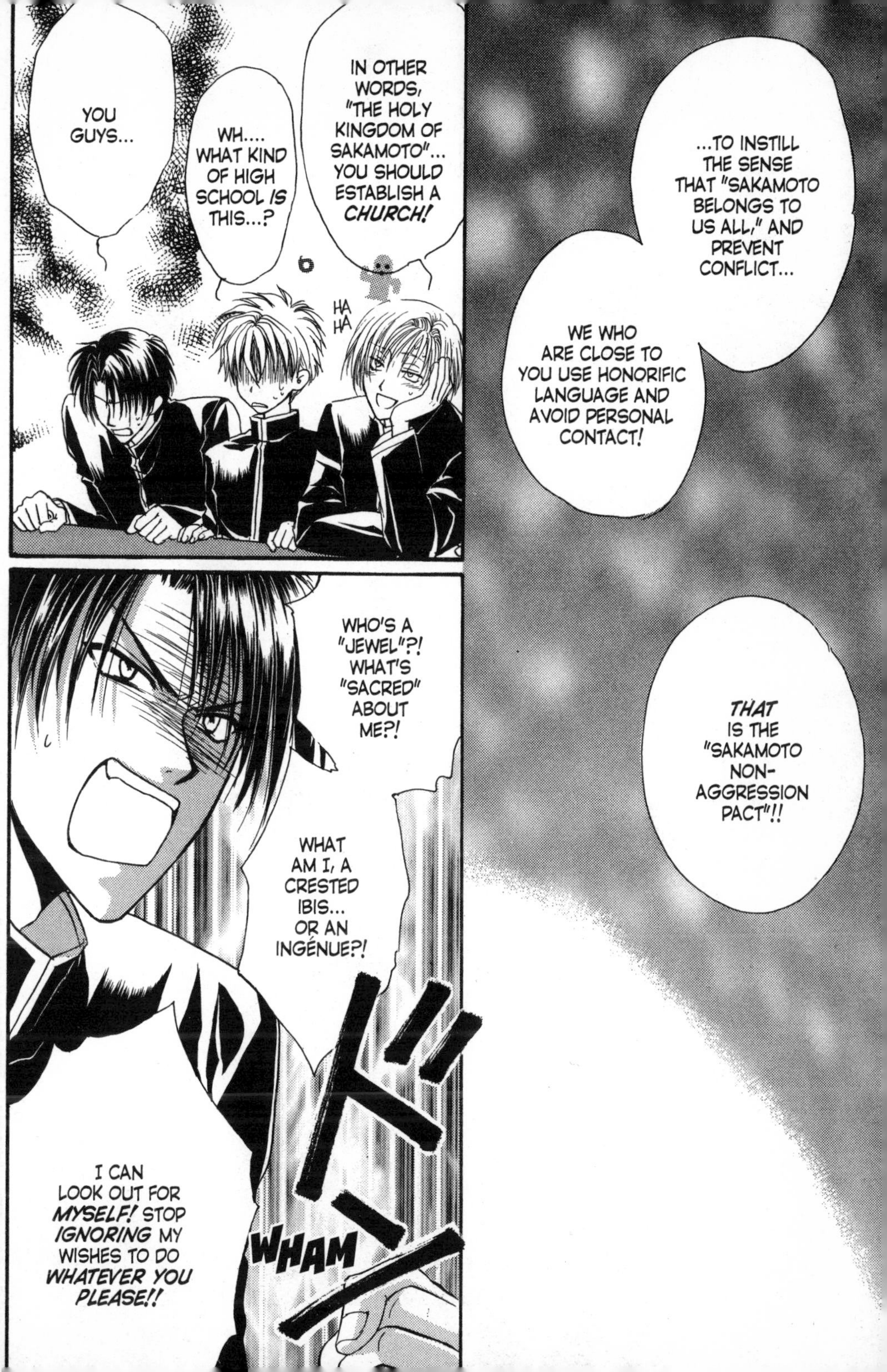
...TO INSTILL THE SENSE THAT "SAKAMOTO BELONGS TO US ALL," AND PREVENT CONFLICT...
WE WHO ARE CLOSE TO YOU USE HONORIFIC LANGUAGE AND AVOID PERSONAL CONTACT!
THAT IS THE "SAKAMOTO NON-AGGRESSION PACT"!!
IN OTHER WORDS, "THE HOLY KINGDOM OF SAKAMOTO"... YOU SHOULD ESTABLISH A ***CHURCH!***
WH.... WHAT KIND OF HIGH SCHOOL *IS* THIS...?
YOU GUYS...
HA HA
WHO'S A "JEWEL"?! WHAT'S "SACRED" ABOUT ME?!
WHAT AM I, A CRESTED IBIS... OR AN INGÉNUE?!
WHAM
I CAN LOOK OUT FOR ***MYSELF!*** STOP ***IGNORING*** MY WISHES TO DO ***WHATEVER YOU PLEASE!!***

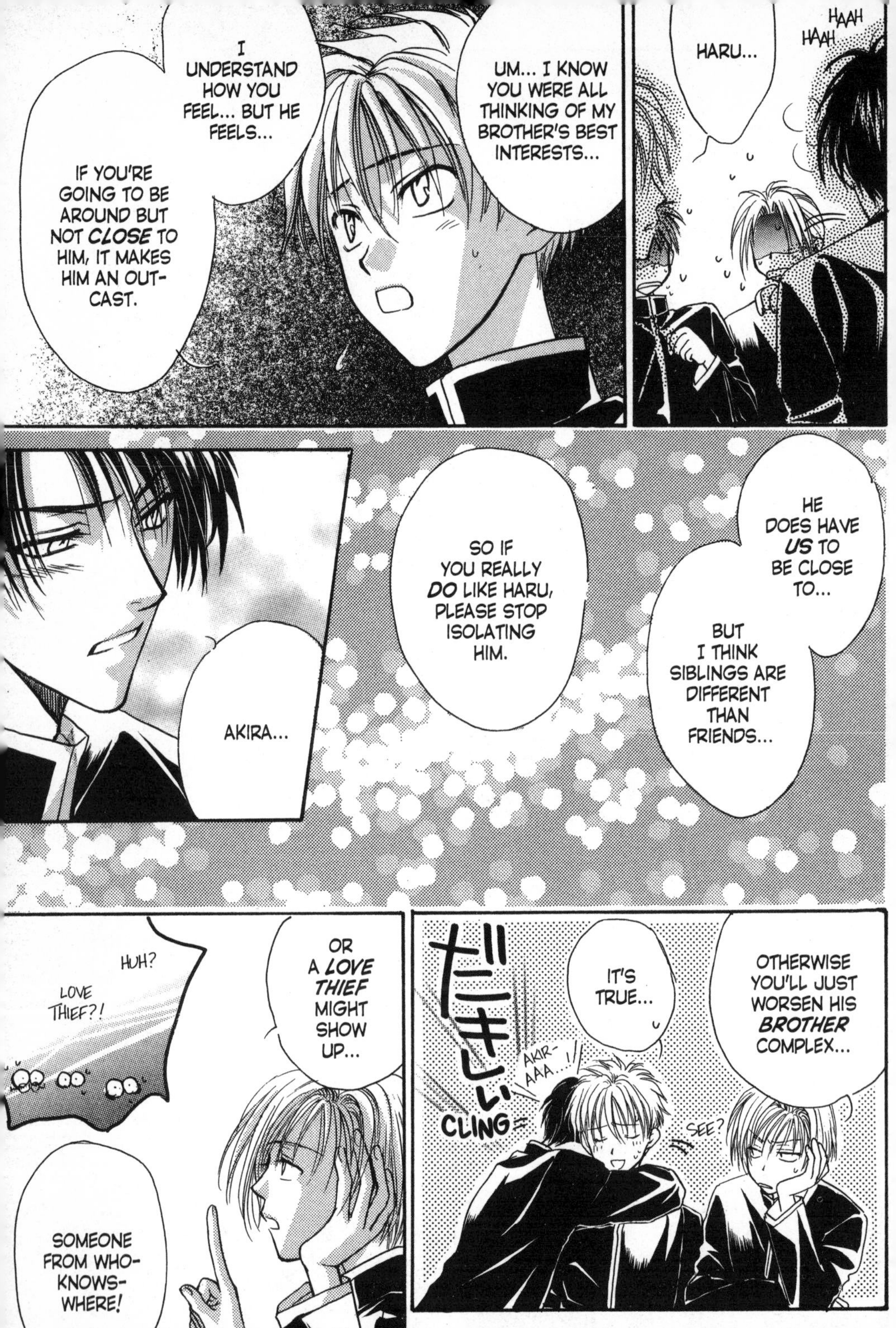
HAAH HAAH
HARU...
UM... I KNOW YOU WERE ALL THINKING OF MY BROTHER'S BEST INTERESTS...
I UNDERSTAND HOW YOU FEEL... BUT HE FEELS...
IF YOU'RE GOING TO BE AROUND BUT NOT *CLOSE* TO HIM, IT MAKES HIM AN OUT-CAST.
HE DOES HAVE *US* TO BE CLOSE TO...
BUT I THINK SIBLINGS ARE DIFFERENT THAN FRIENDS...
SO IF YOU REALLY *DO* LIKE HARU, PLEASE STOP ISOLATING HIM.
AKIRA...
OTHERWISE YOU'LL JUST WORSEN HIS *BROTHER* COMPLEX...
IT'S TRUE...
SEE?
AKIR-AAA...!
CLING
OR A *LOVE THIEF* MIGHT SHOW UP...
HUH?
LOVE THIEF?!
SOMEONE FROM WHO-KNOWS-WHERE!

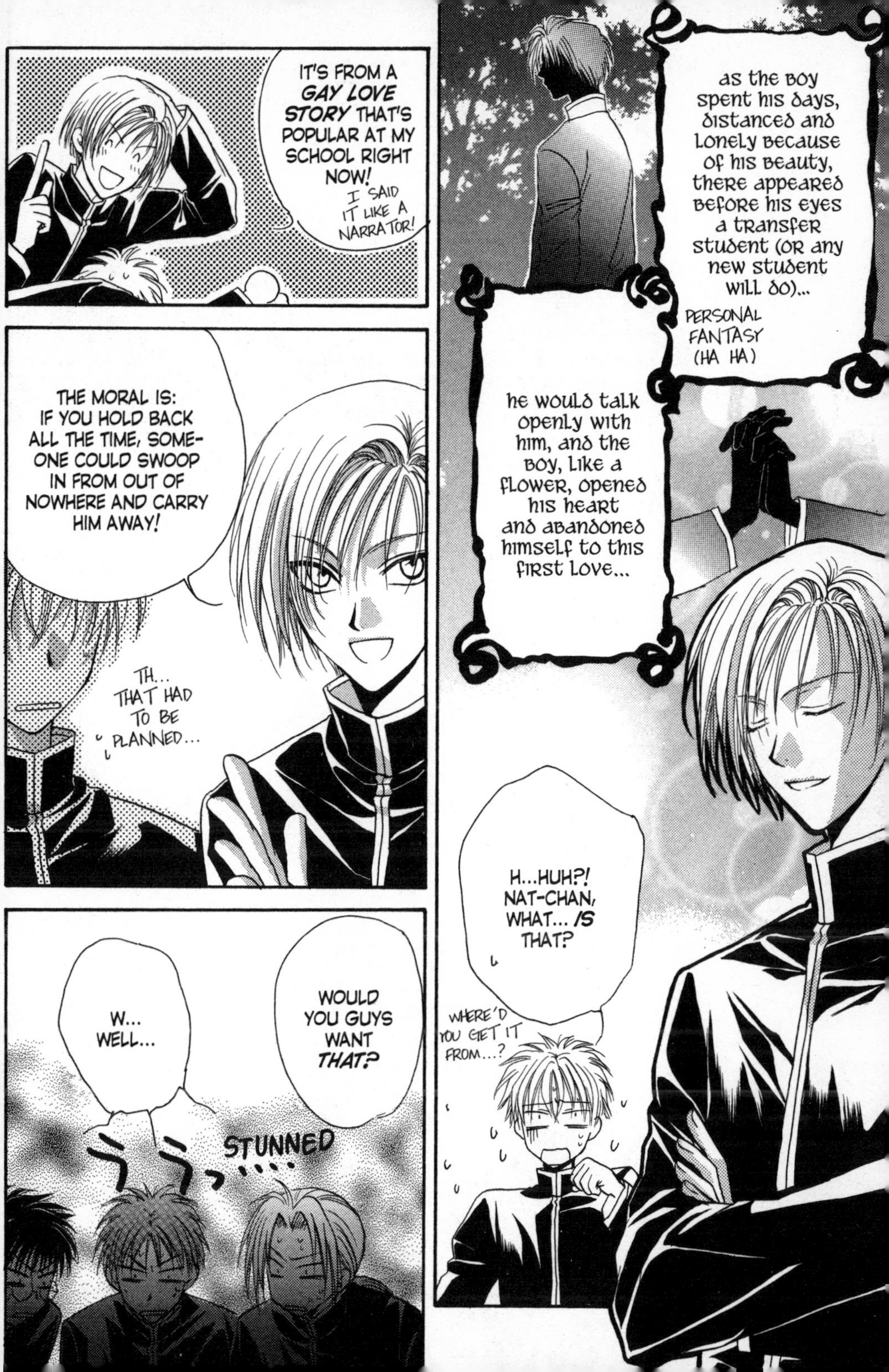
as the boy spent his days, distanced and lonely because of his beauty, there appeared before his eyes a transfer student (or any new student will do)...
PERSONAL FANTASY (HA HA)
he would talk openly with him, and the boy, like a flower, opened his heart and abandoned himself to this first love...
H...HUH?! NAT-CHAN, WHAT... *IS* THAT?
WHERE'D YOU GET IT FROM...?
IT'S FROM A ***GAY LOVE STORY*** THAT'S POPULAR AT MY SCHOOL RIGHT NOW!
I SAID IT LIKE A NARRATOR!
THE MORAL IS: IF YOU HOLD BACK ALL THE TIME, SOME-ONE COULD SWOOP IN FROM OUT OF NOWHERE AND CARRY HIM AWAY!
TH... THAT HAD TO BE PLANNED...
WOULD YOU GUYS WANT ***THAT?***
W... WELL...
STUNNED

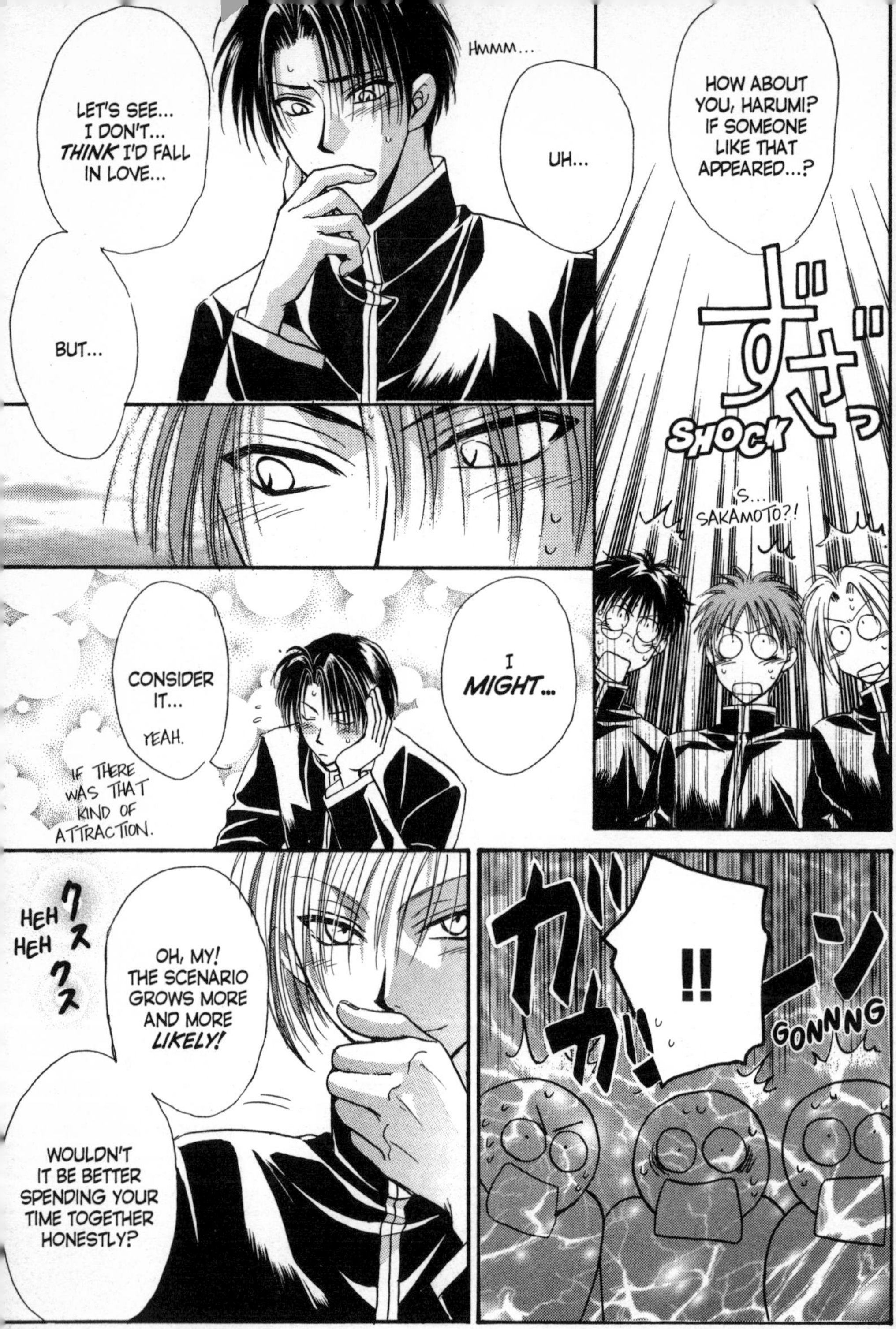
HOW ABOUT YOU, HARUMI? IF SOMEONE LIKE THAT APPEARED...?
ずざっ
SHOCK
IS... SAKAMOTO?!
HMMM...
UH...
LET'S SEE... I DON'T... *THINK* I'D FALL IN LOVE...
BUT...
I *MIGHT*...
CONSIDER IT... YEAH.
IF THERE WAS THAT KIND OF ATTRACTION.
があーン
GONNNG
!!
クスクス
HEH HEH
OH, MY! THE SCENARIO GROWS MORE AND MORE *LIKELY!*
WOULDN'T IT BE BETTER SPENDING YOUR TIME TOGETHER HONESTLY?

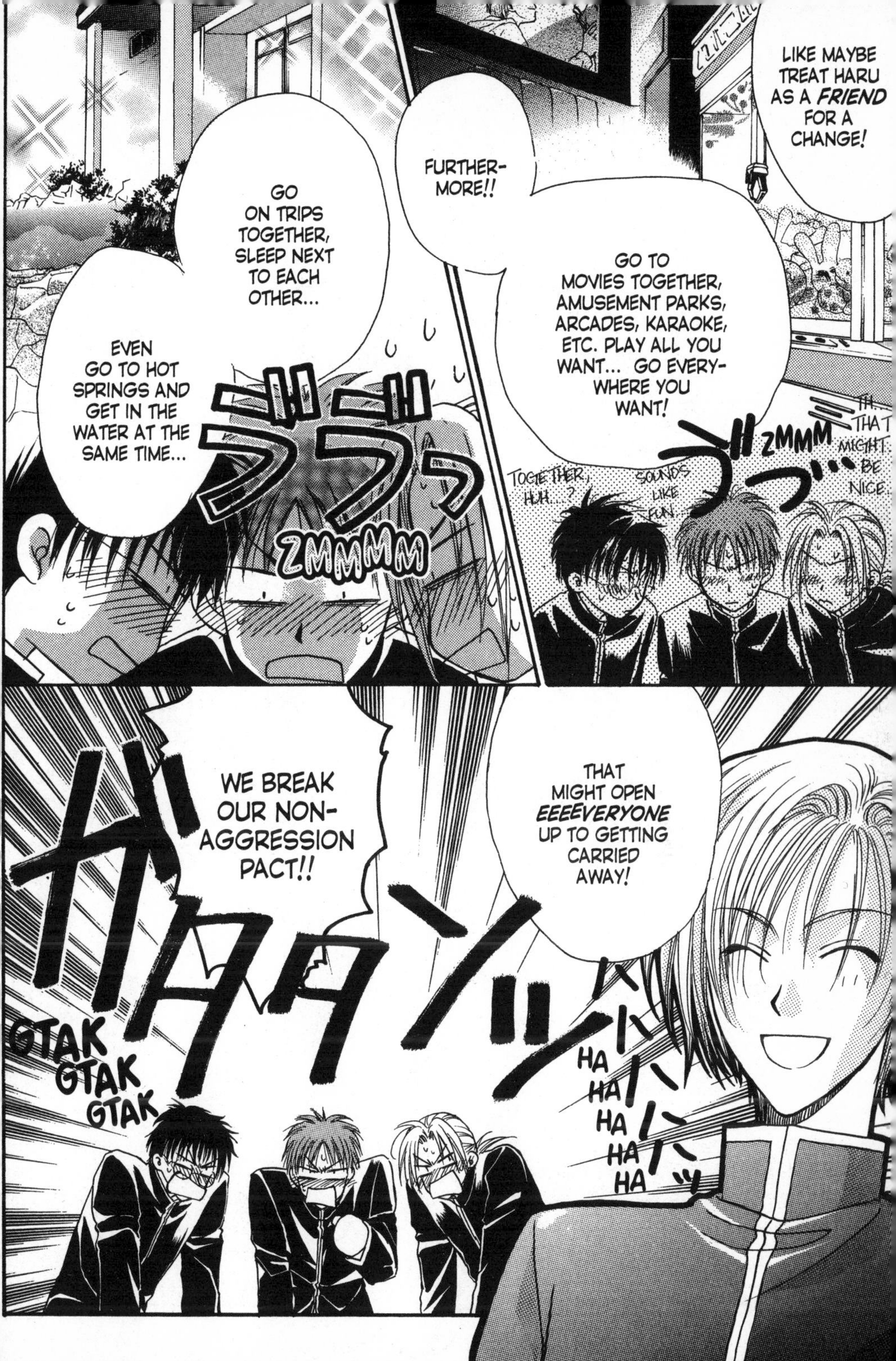
LIKE MAYBE TREAT HARU AS A *FRIEND* FOR A CHANGE!
FURTHER-MORE!!
GO TO MOVIES TOGETHER, AMUSEMENT PARKS, ARCADES, KARAOKE, ETC. PLAY ALL YOU WANT... GO EVERY-WHERE YOU WANT!
ZMMM
TH... THAT MIGHT BE NICE
SOUNDS LIKE FUN
TOGETHER, HUH...?
GO ON TRIPS TOGETHER, SLEEP NEXT TO EACH OTHER...
EVEN GO TO HOT SPRINGS AND GET IN THE WATER AT THE SAME TIME...
ZMMMMM
THAT MIGHT OPEN *EEEEVERYONE* UP TO GETTING CARRIED AWAY!
WE BREAK OUR NON-AGGRESSION PACT!!
HA HA HA HA HA HA
GTAK GTAK GTAK

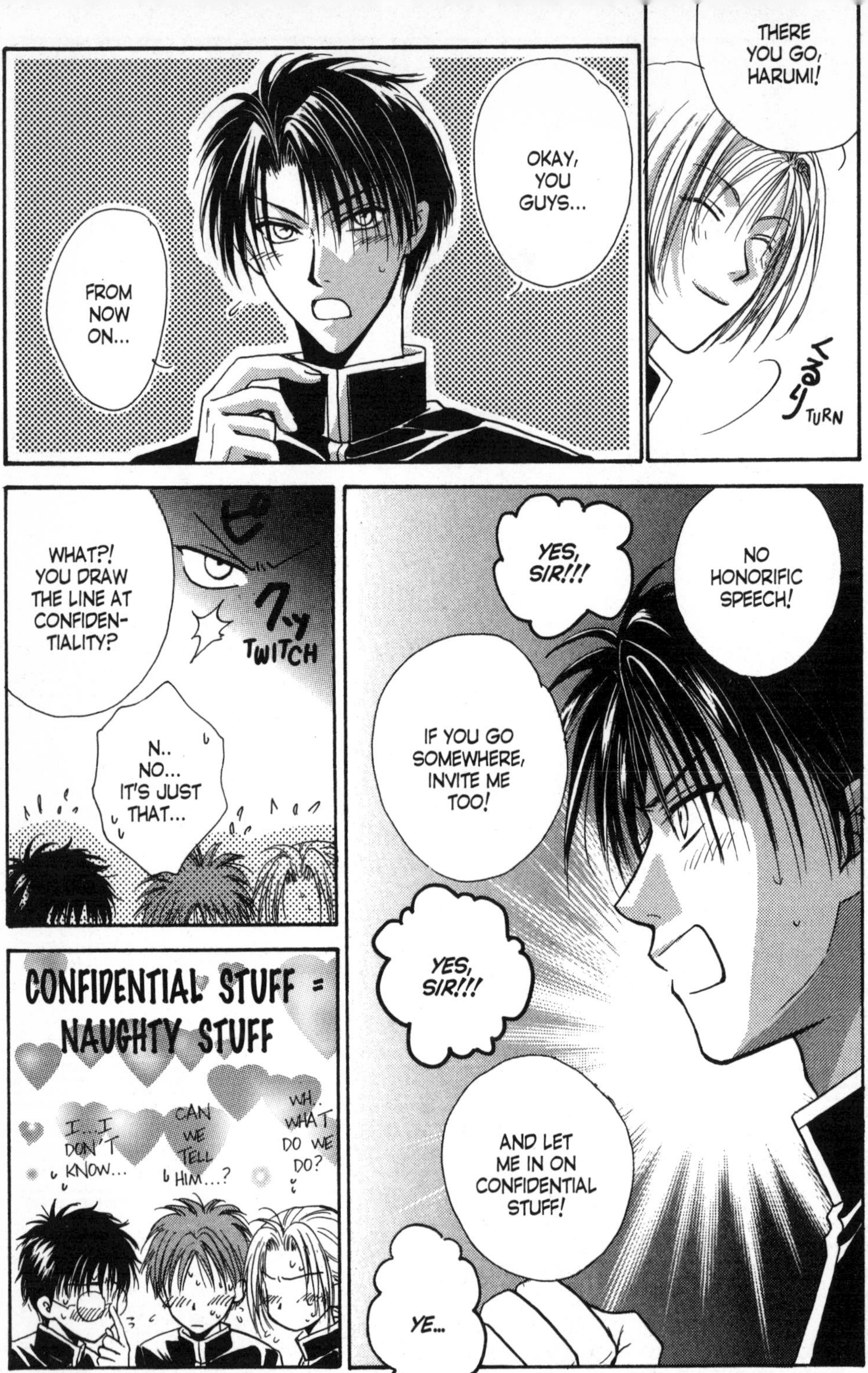
THERE YOU GO, HARUMI!
TURN
OKAY, YOU GUYS...
FROM NOW ON...
NO HONORIFIC SPEECH!
YES, SIR!!!
IF YOU GO SOMEWHERE, INVITE ME TOO!
YES, SIR!!!
AND LET ME IN ON CONFIDENTIAL STUFF!
YE...
WHAT?! YOU DRAW THE LINE AT CONFIDEN-TIALITY?
TWITCH
N.. NO... IT'S JUST THAT...
CONFIDENTIAL STUFF = NAUGHTY STUFF
WH. WHAT DO WE DO?
CAN WE TELL HIM...?
I...I DON'T KNOW...

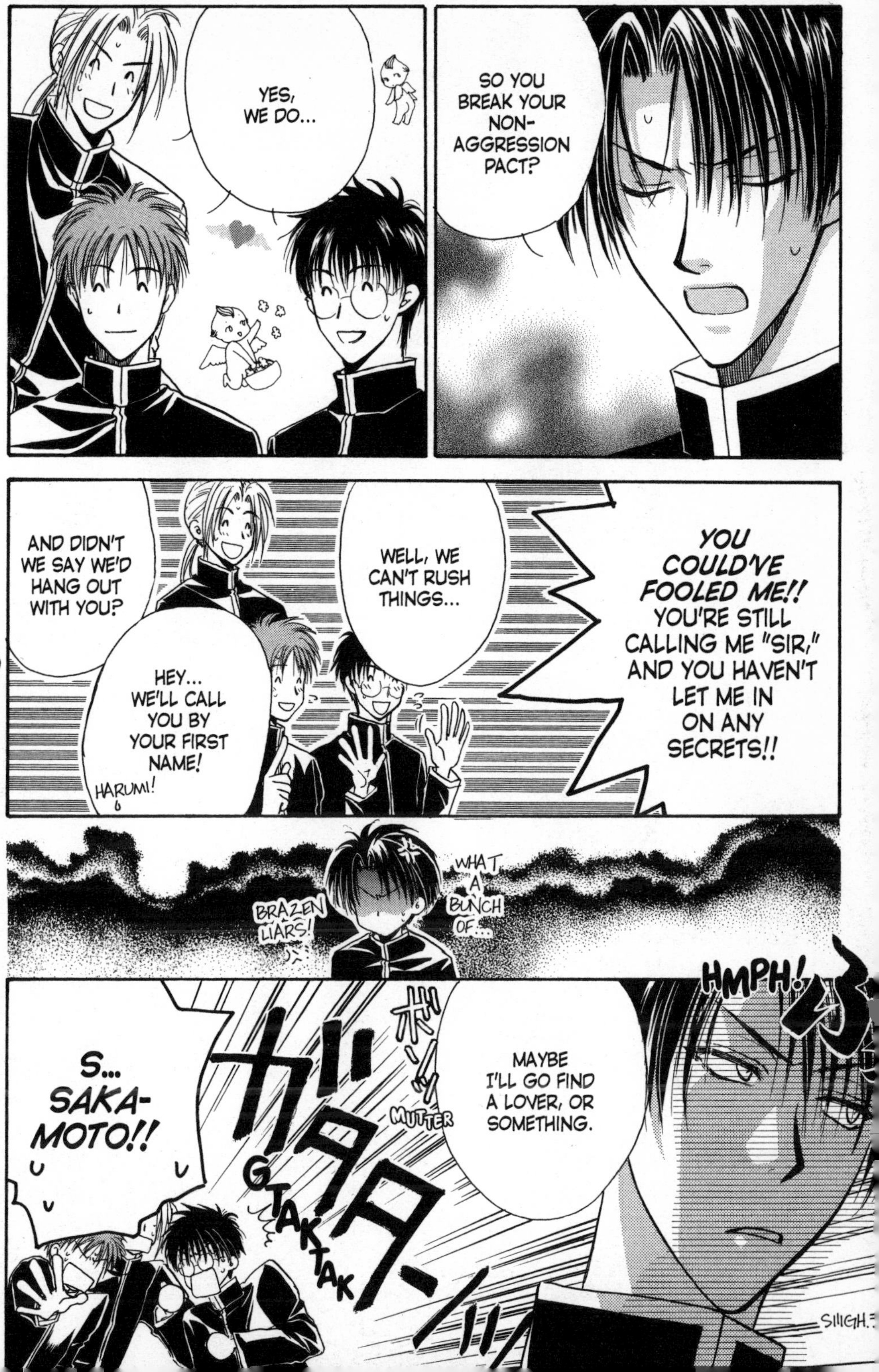
SO YOU BREAK YOUR NON-AGGRESSION PACT?
YES, WE DO...
YOU COULD'VE FOOLED ME!! YOU'RE STILL CALLING ME "SIR," AND YOU HAVEN'T LET ME IN ON ANY SECRETS!!
WELL, WE CAN'T RUSH THINGS...
AND DIDN'T WE SAY WE'D HANG OUT WITH YOU?
HEY... WE'LL CALL YOU BY YOUR FIRST NAME!
HARUMI!
WHAT A BUNCH OF...
BRAZEN LIARS!
HMPH!
SIIIGH.
MAYBE I'LL GO FIND A LOVER, OR SOMETHING.
MUTTER
GTAKTAK
S... SAKA-MOTO!!

FAMILY COMPLEX
ファミリー・コンプレックス

FIRST DAUGHTER • NATSURU

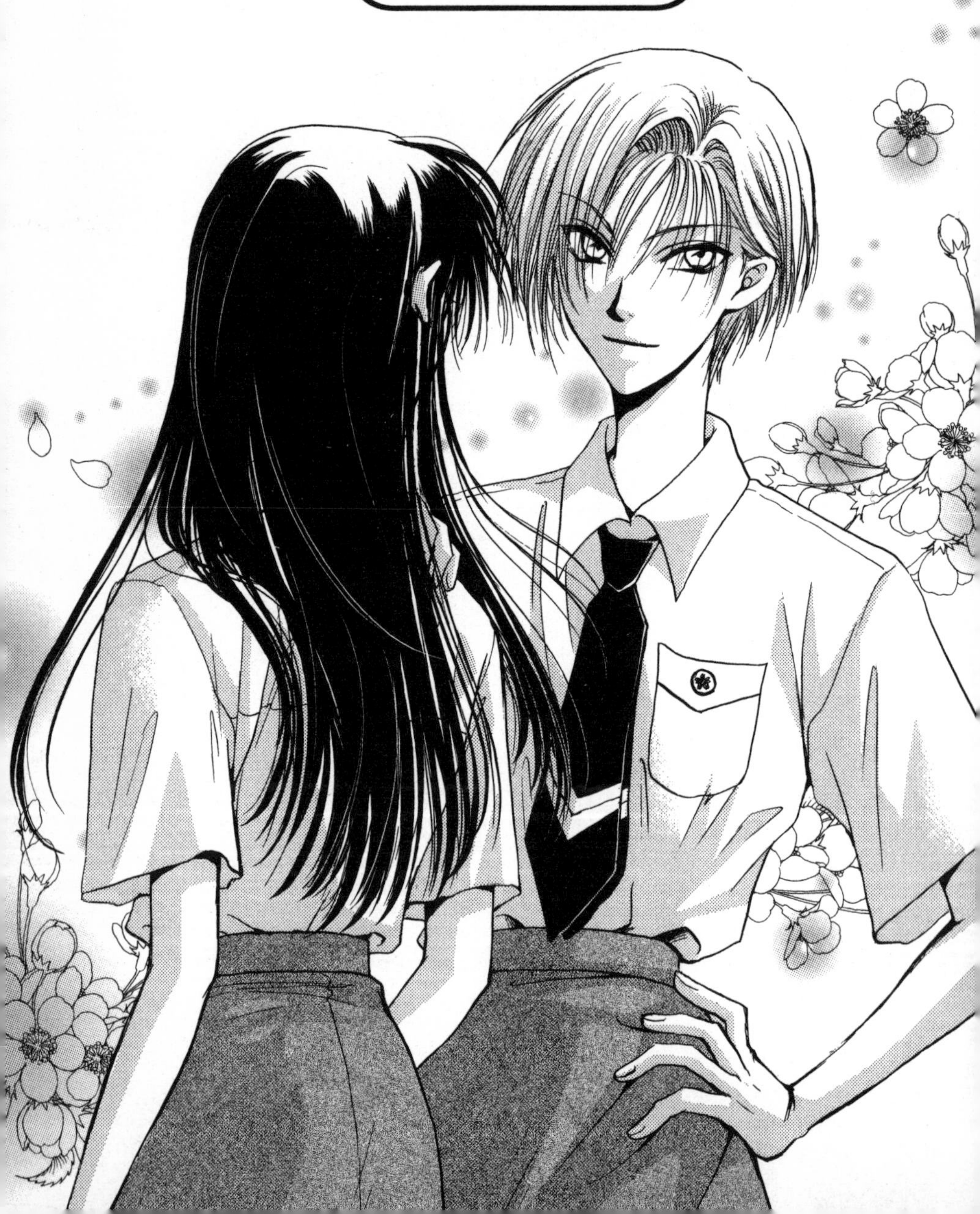

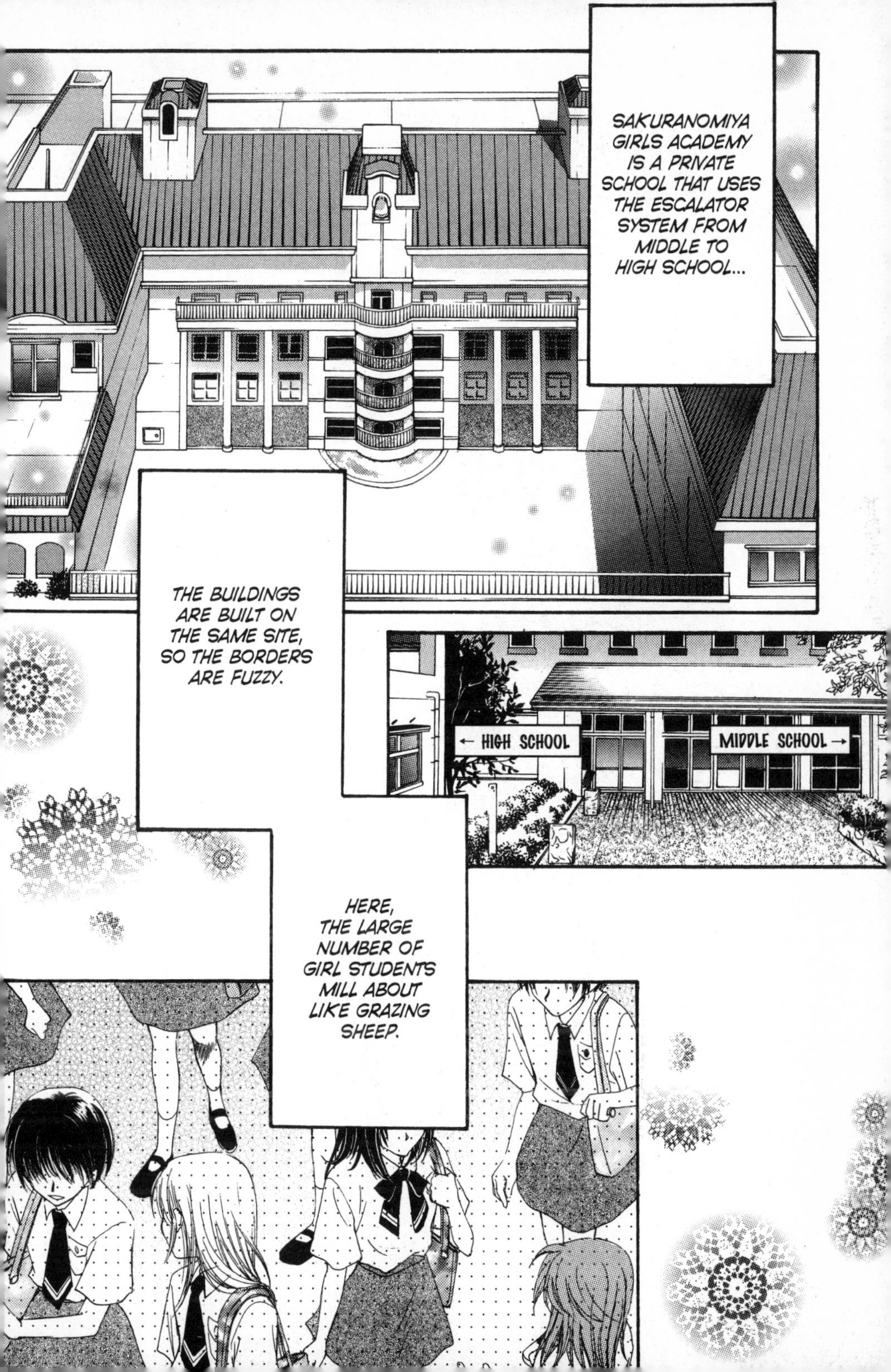
SAKURANOMIYA GIRLS ACADEMY IS A PRIVATE SCHOOL THAT USES THE ESCALATOR SYSTEM FROM MIDDLE TO HIGH SCHOOL...
THE BUILDINGS ARE BUILT ON THE SAME SITE, SO THE BORDERS ARE FUZZY.
← HIGH SCHOOL
MIDDLE SCHOOL →
HERE, THE LARGE NUMBER OF GIRL STUDENTS MILL ABOUT LIKE GRAZING SHEEP.

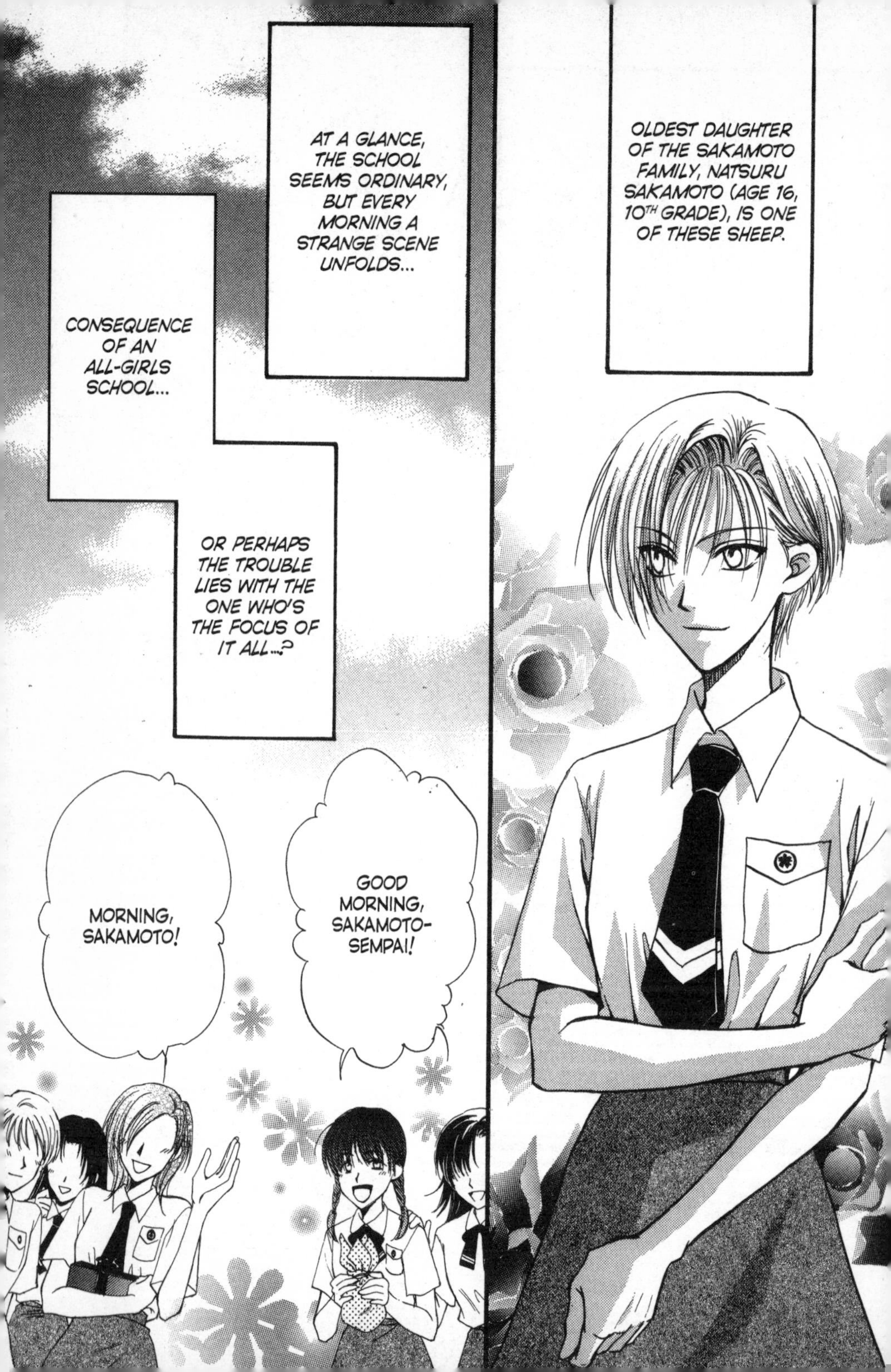
OLDEST DAUGHTER OF THE SAKAMOTO FAMILY, NATSURU SAKAMOTO (AGE 16, 10TH GRADE), IS ONE OF THESE SHEEP.
AT A GLANCE, THE SCHOOL SEEMS ORDINARY, BUT EVERY MORNING A STRANGE SCENE UNFOLDS...
CONSEQUENCE OF AN ALL-GIRLS SCHOOL...
OR PERHAPS THE TROUBLE LIES WITH THE ONE WHO'S THE FOCUS OF IT ALL...?
GOOD MORNING, SAKAMOTO-SEMPAI!
MORNING, SAKAMOTO!

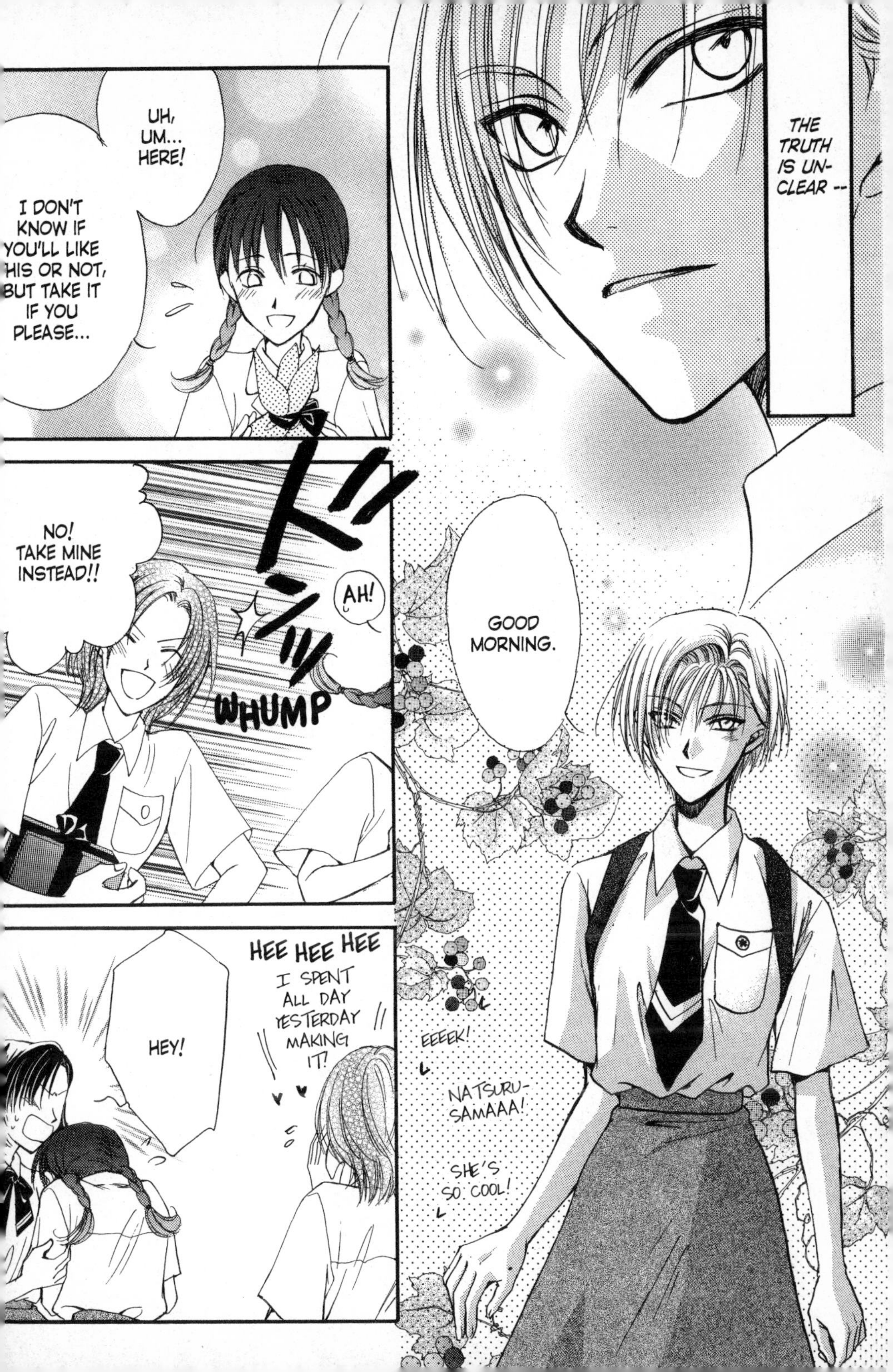
THE TRUTH IS UN-CLEAR --
GOOD MORNING.
EEEEK!
NATSURU-SAMAAA!
SHE'S SO COOL!
UH, UM... HERE!
I DON'T KNOW IF YOU'LL LIKE HIS OR NOT, BUT TAKE IT IF YOU PLEASE...
AH!
NO! TAKE MINE INSTEAD!!
WHUMP
HEE HEE HEE
I SPENT ALL DAY YESTERDAY MAKING IT!
HEY!

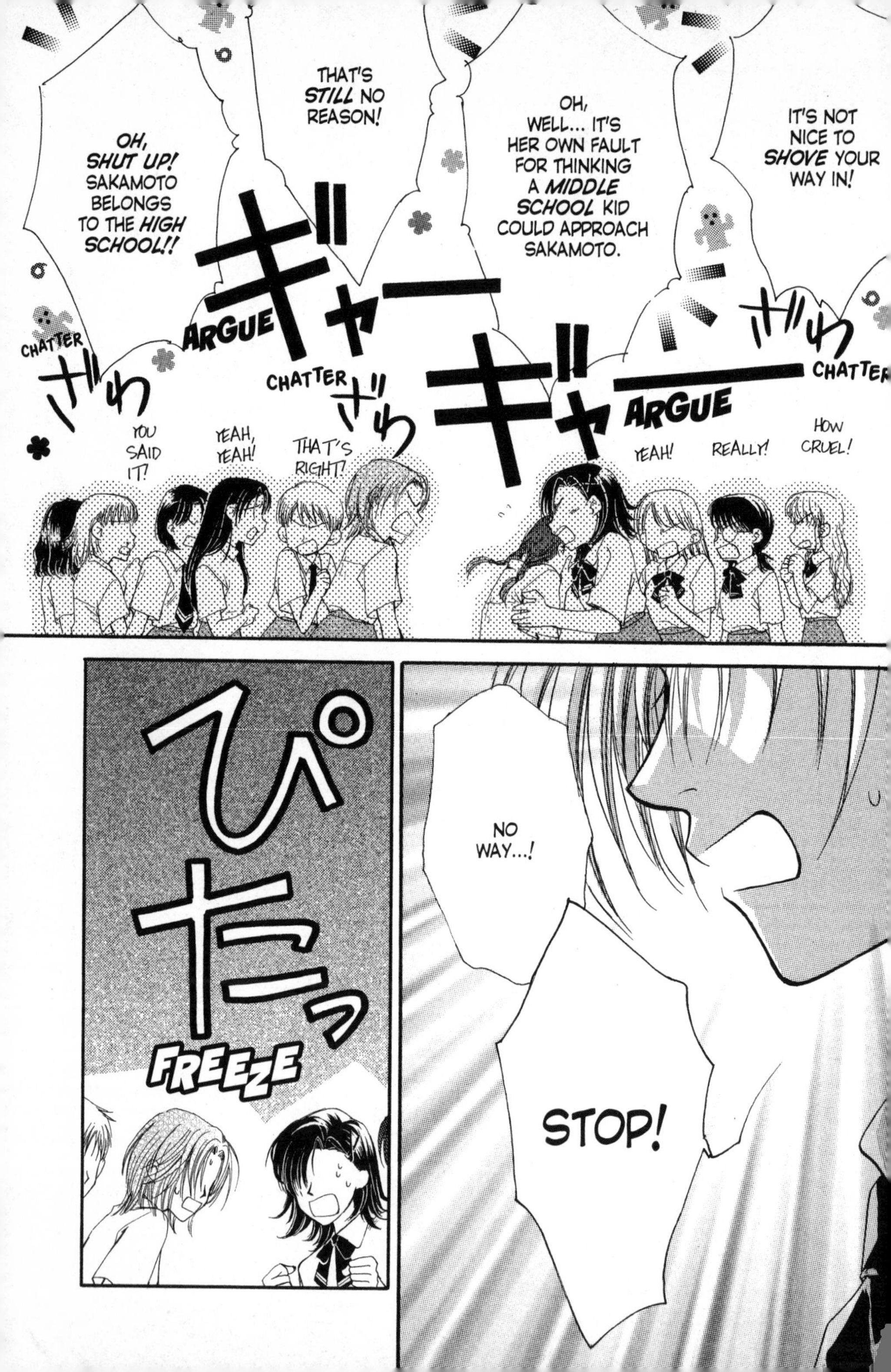
IT'S NOT NICE TO SHOVE YOUR WAY IN!
OH, WELL... IT'S HER OWN FAULT FOR THINKING A MIDDLE SCHOOL KID COULD APPROACH SAKAMOTO.
THAT'S STILL NO REASON!
OH, SHUT UP! SAKAMOTO BELONGS TO THE HIGH SCHOOL!!
ざわ
CHATTER
ギャー
ARGUE
ざわ
CHATTER
ギャー
ARGUE
ざわ
CHATTER
HOW CRUEL!
REALLY!
YEAH!
THAT'S RIGHT!
YEAH, YEAH!
YOU SAID IT!
NO WAY...!
STOP!
ぴたっ
FREEZE

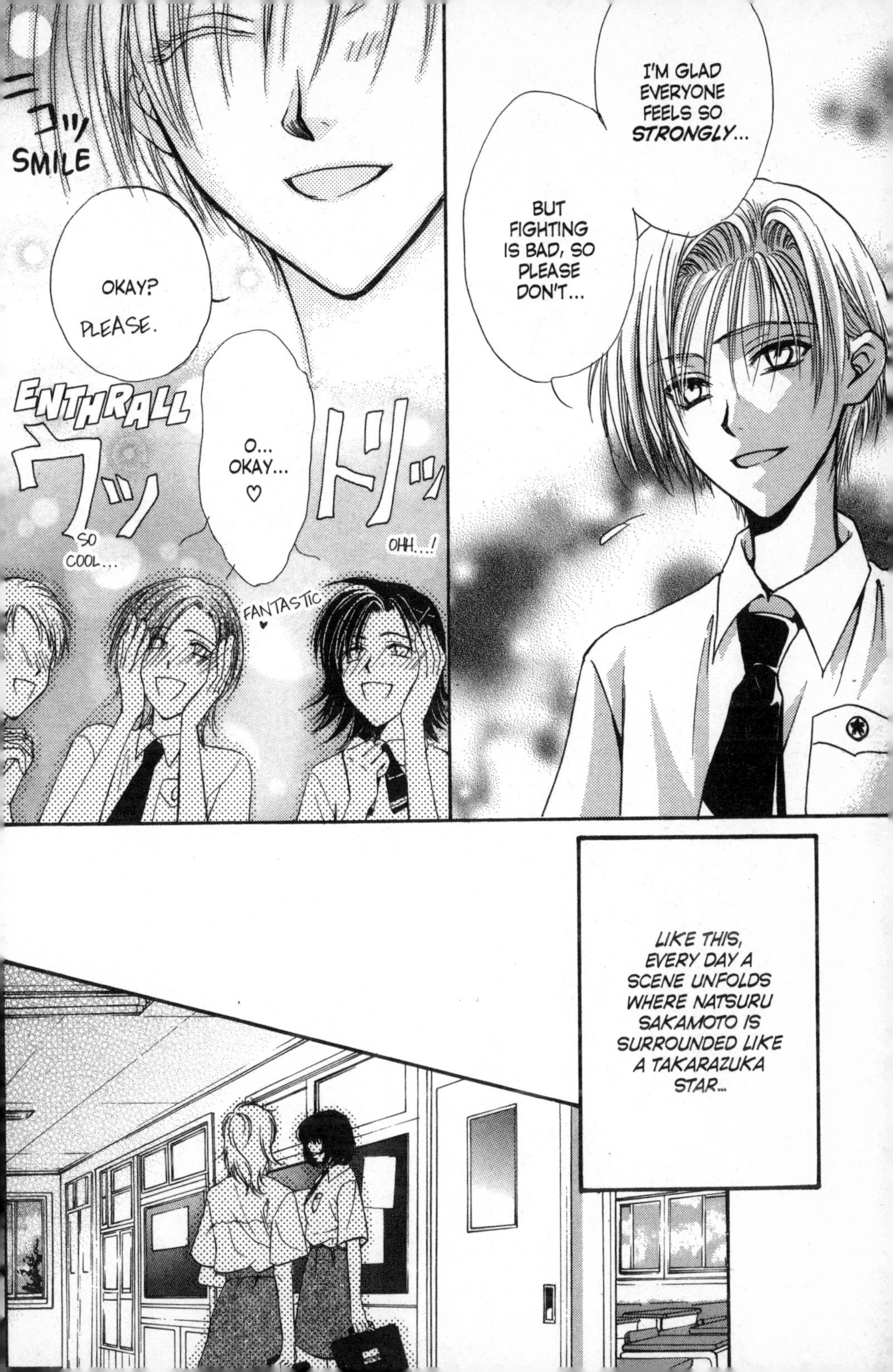
I'M GLAD EVERYONE FEELS SO STRONGLY...
BUT FIGHTING IS BAD, SO PLEASE DON'T...
ニコッ
SMILE
OKAY? PLEASE.
ENTHRALL
ウットリッ
O... OKAY... ♡
OHH...!
SO COOL...
FANTASTIC ♥
LIKE THIS, EVERY DAY A SCENE UNFOLDS WHERE NATSURU SAKAMOTO IS SURROUNDED LIKE A TAKARAZUKA STAR...

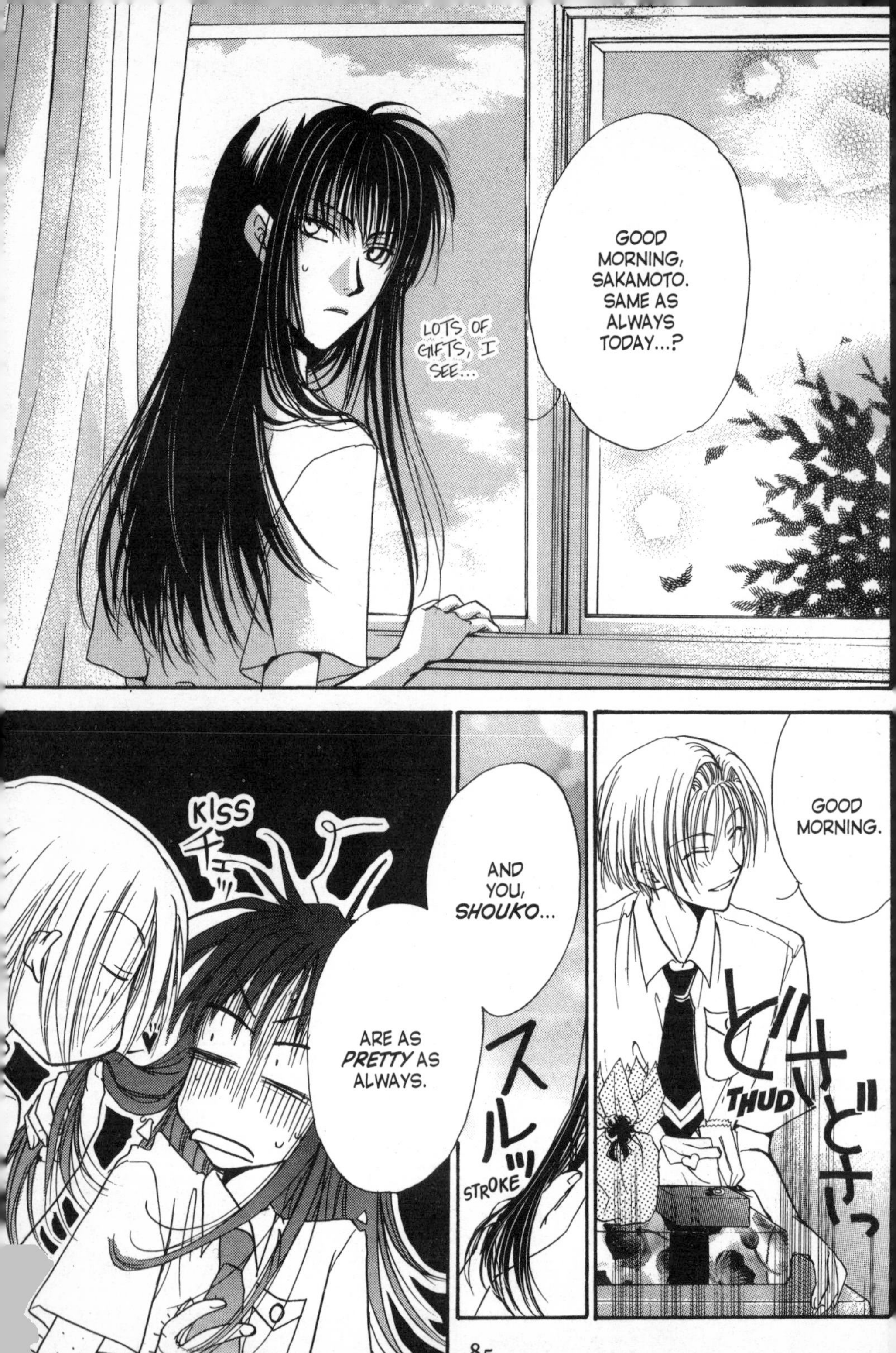
GOOD MORNING, SAKAMOTO. SAME AS ALWAYS TODAY...?
LOTS OF GIFTS, I SEE...
GOOD MORNING.
どさどさっ
THUD
AND YOU, SHOUKO...
ARE AS PRETTY AS ALWAYS.
スルッ
STROKE
チュッ
KISS

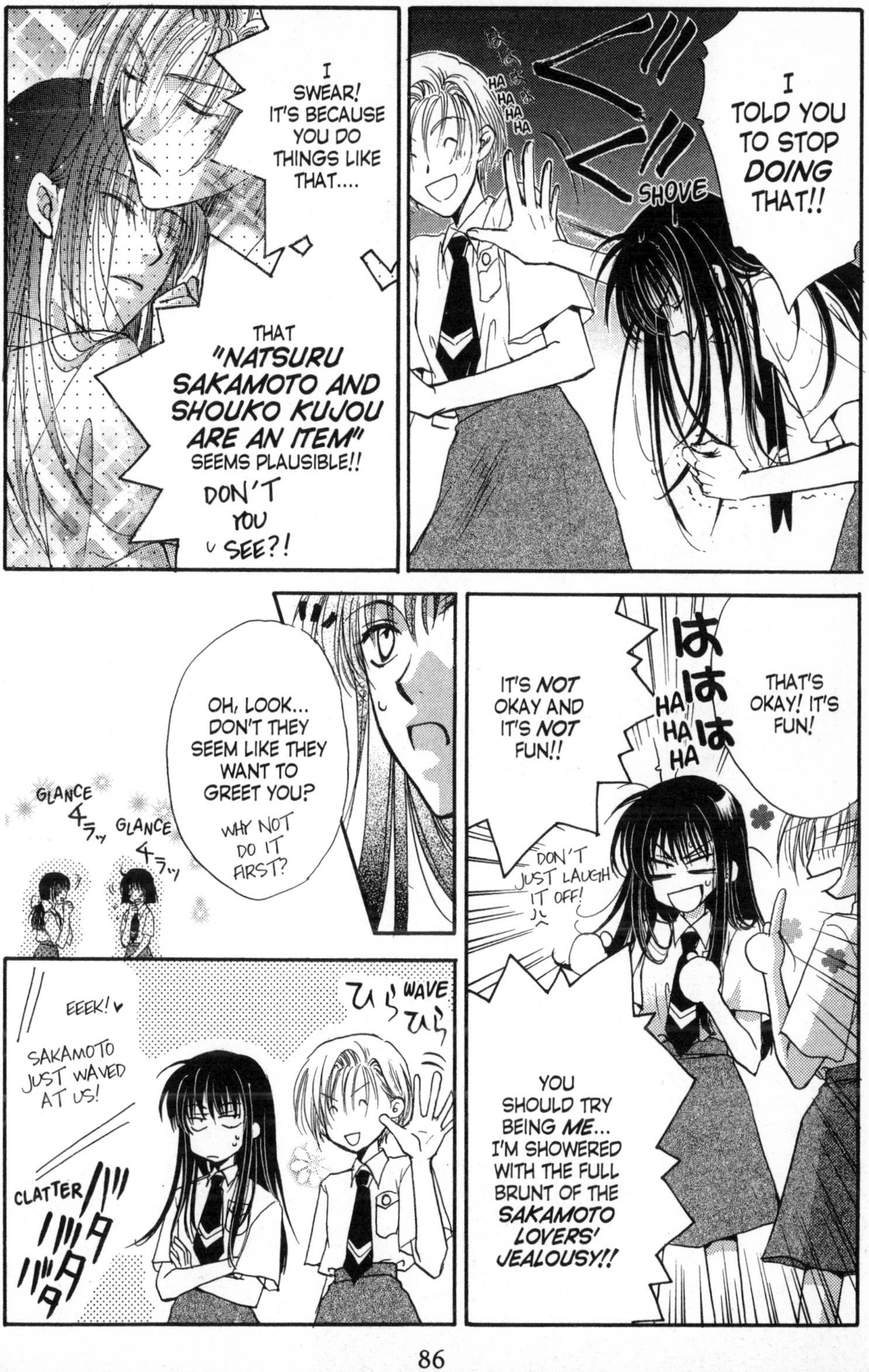
HA HA HA HA
I TOLD YOU TO STOP *DOING* THAT!!
SHOVE
I SWEAR! IT'S BECAUSE YOU DO THINGS LIKE THAT....
THAT ***"NATSURU SAKAMOTO AND SHOUKO KUJOU ARE AN ITEM"*** SEEMS PLAUSIBLE!!
DON'T YOU SEE?!
ははは
HA HA HA
THAT'S OKAY! IT'S FUN!
IT'S *NOT* OKAY AND IT'S *NOT* FUN!!
DON'T JUST LAUGH IT OFF!
YOU SHOULD TRY BEING *ME*... I'M SHOWERED WITH THE FULL BRUNT OF THE ***SAKAMOTO LOVERS' JEALOUSY!!***
OH, LOOK... DON'T THEY SEEM LIKE THEY WANT TO GREET YOU?
WHY NOT DO IT FIRST?
GLANCE
GLANCE
ひら WAVE ひら
EEEK!
SAKAMOTO JUST WAVED AT US!
CLATTER

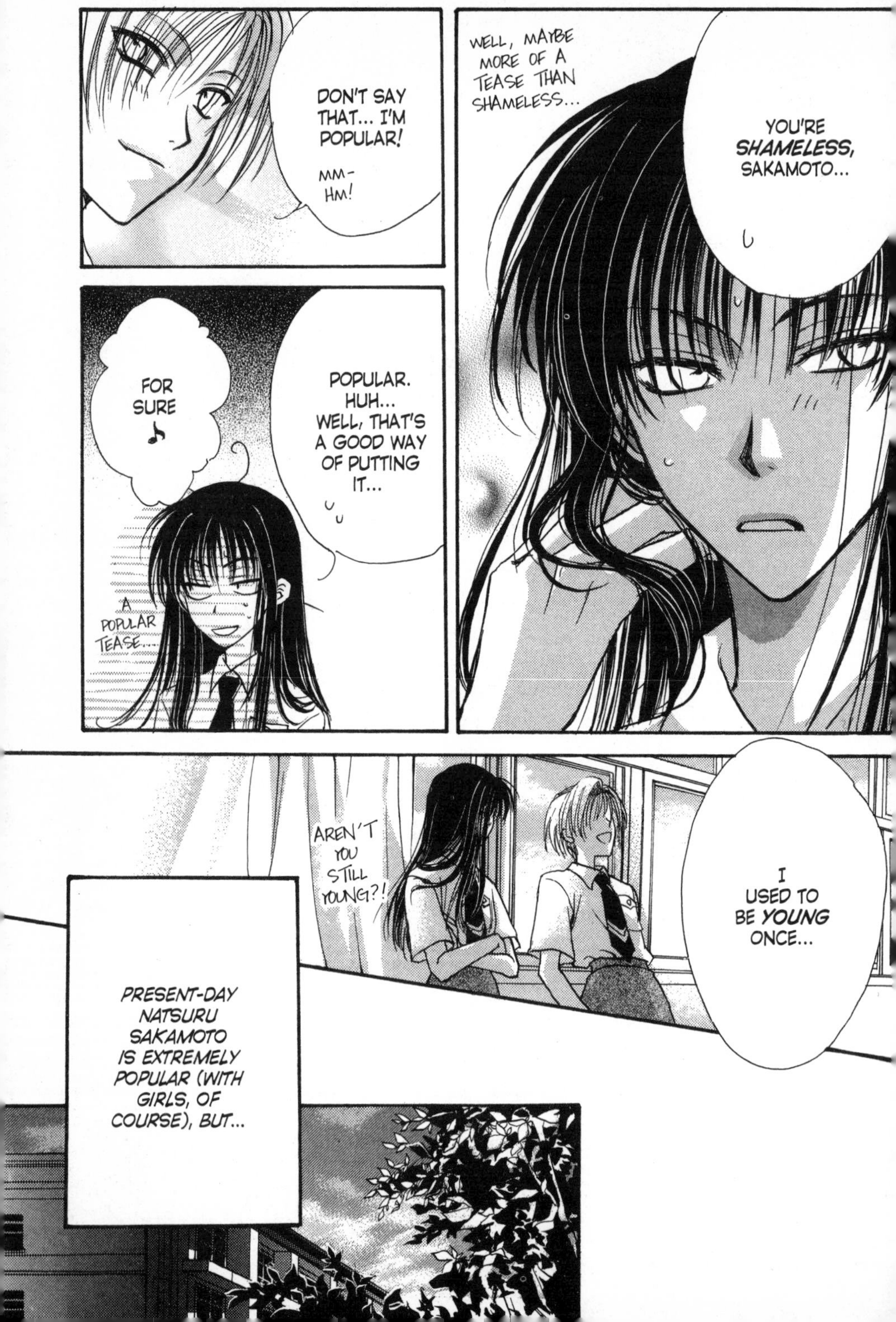
YOU'RE SHAMELESS, SAKAMOTO...
WELL, MAYBE MORE OF A TEASE THAN SHAMELESS...
DON'T SAY THAT... I'M POPULAR!
MM-HM!
POPULAR. HUH... WELL, THAT'S A GOOD WAY OF PUTTING IT...
FOR SURE ♪
A POPULAR TEASE...
I USED TO BE YOUNG ONCE...
AREN'T YOU STILL YOUNG?!
PRESENT-DAY NATSURU SAKAMOTO IS EXTREMELY POPULAR (WITH GIRLS, OF COURSE), BUT...

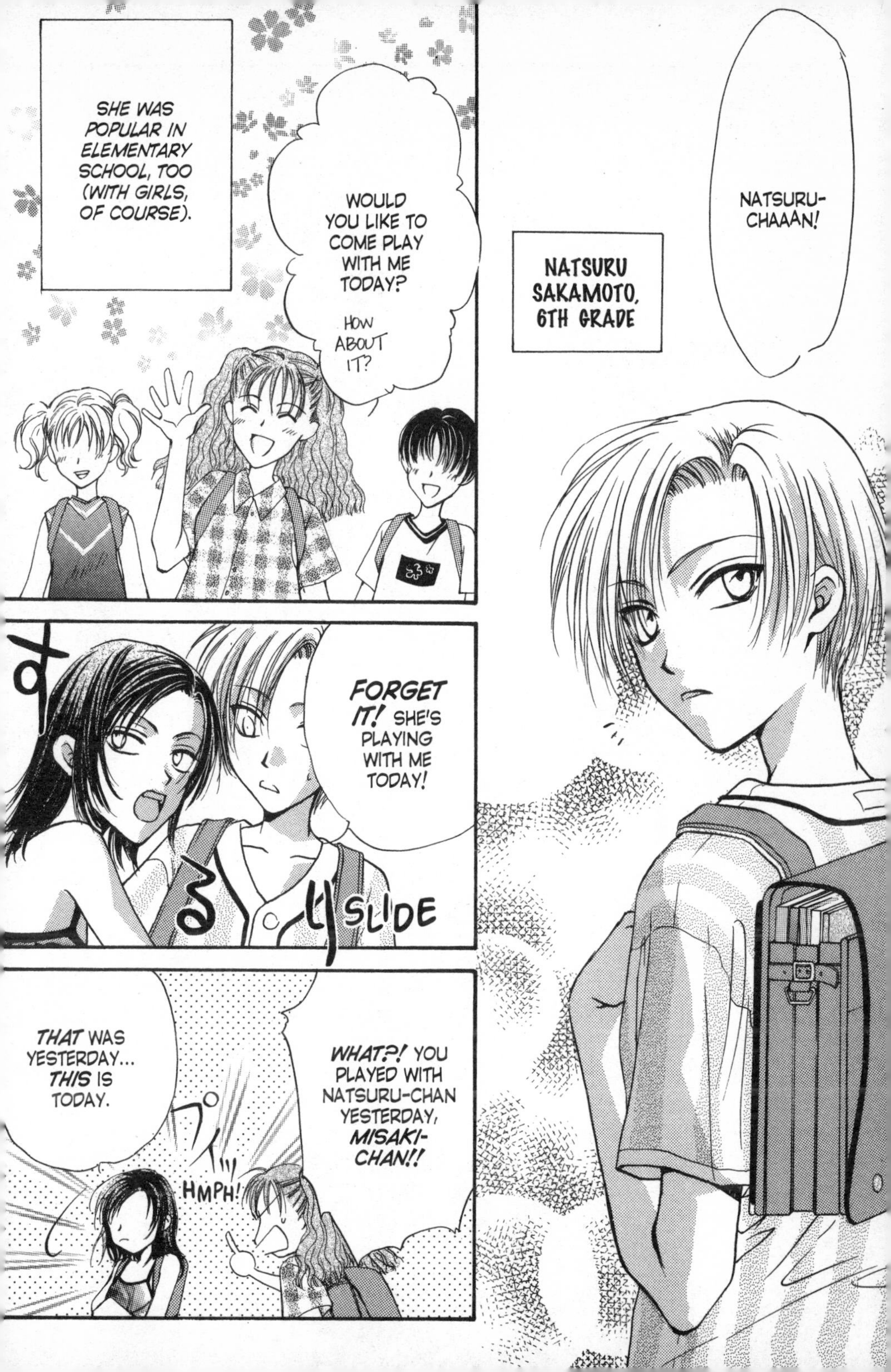
NATSURU-CHAAAN!
NATSURU SAKAMOTO, 6TH GRADE
WOULD YOU LIKE TO COME PLAY WITH ME TODAY?
HOW ABOUT IT?
SHE WAS POPULAR IN ELEMENTARY SCHOOL, TOO (WITH GIRLS, OF COURSE).
FORGET IT! SHE'S PLAYING WITH ME TODAY!
SLIDE
WHAT?! YOU PLAYED WITH NATSURU-CHAN YESTERDAY, MISAKI-CHAN!!
THAT WAS YESTERDAY... THIS IS TODAY.
HMPH!

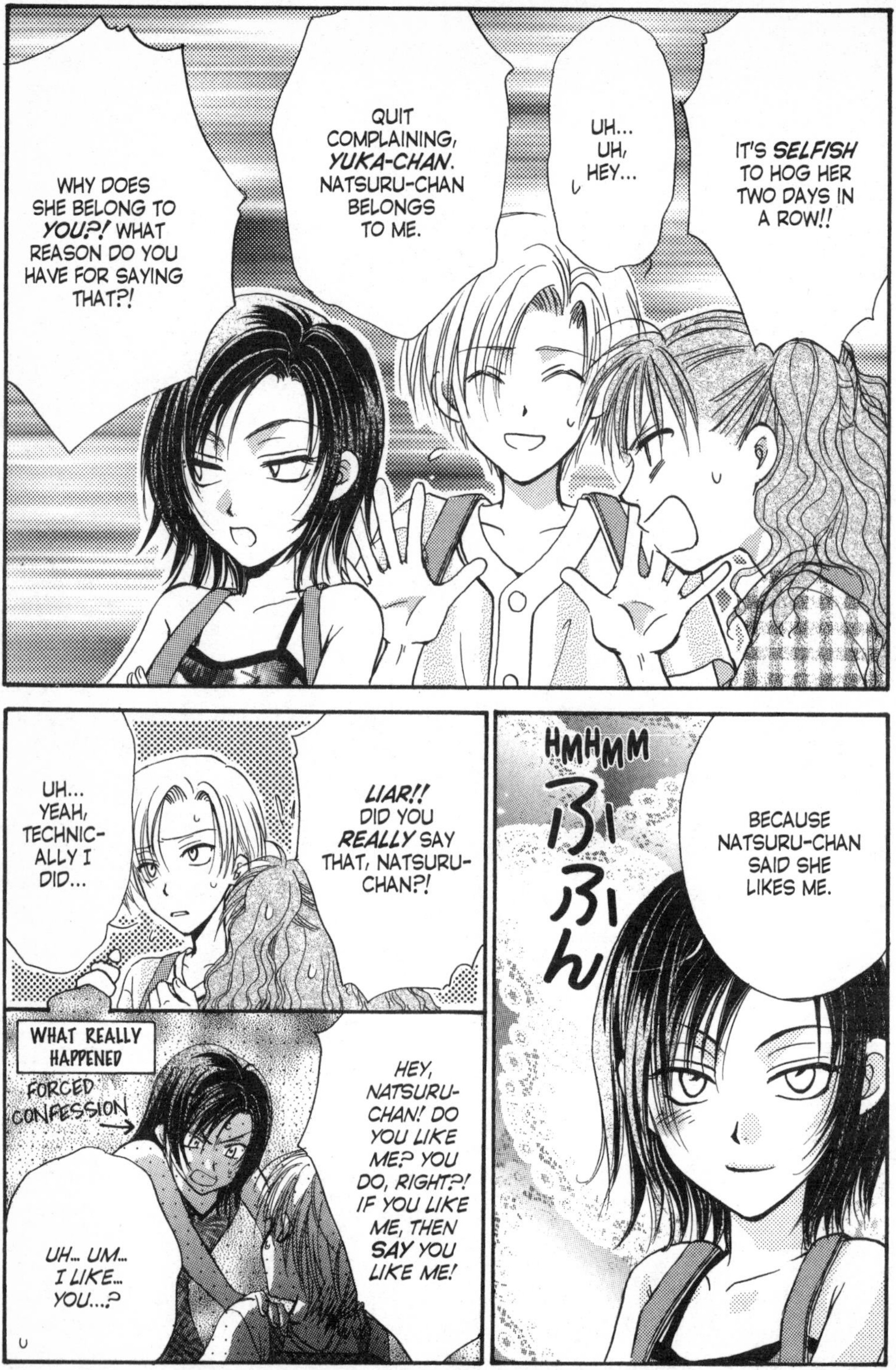
IT'S SELFISH TO HOG HER TWO DAYS IN A ROW!!
UH... UH, HEY...
QUIT COMPLAINING, YUKA-CHAN. NATSURU-CHAN BELONGS TO ME.
WHY DOES SHE BELONG TO YOU?! WHAT REASON DO YOU HAVE FOR SAYING THAT?!
HMHMM
ふふん
BECAUSE NATSURU-CHAN SAID SHE LIKES ME.
LIAR!! DID YOU REALLY SAY THAT, NATSURU-CHAN?!
UH... YEAH, TECHNIC-ALLY I DID...
WHAT REALLY HAPPENED
FORCED CONFESSION
HEY, NATSURU-CHAN! DO YOU LIKE ME? YOU DO, RIGHT?! IF YOU LIKE ME, THEN SAY YOU LIKE ME!
UH... UM... I LIKE... YOU...?

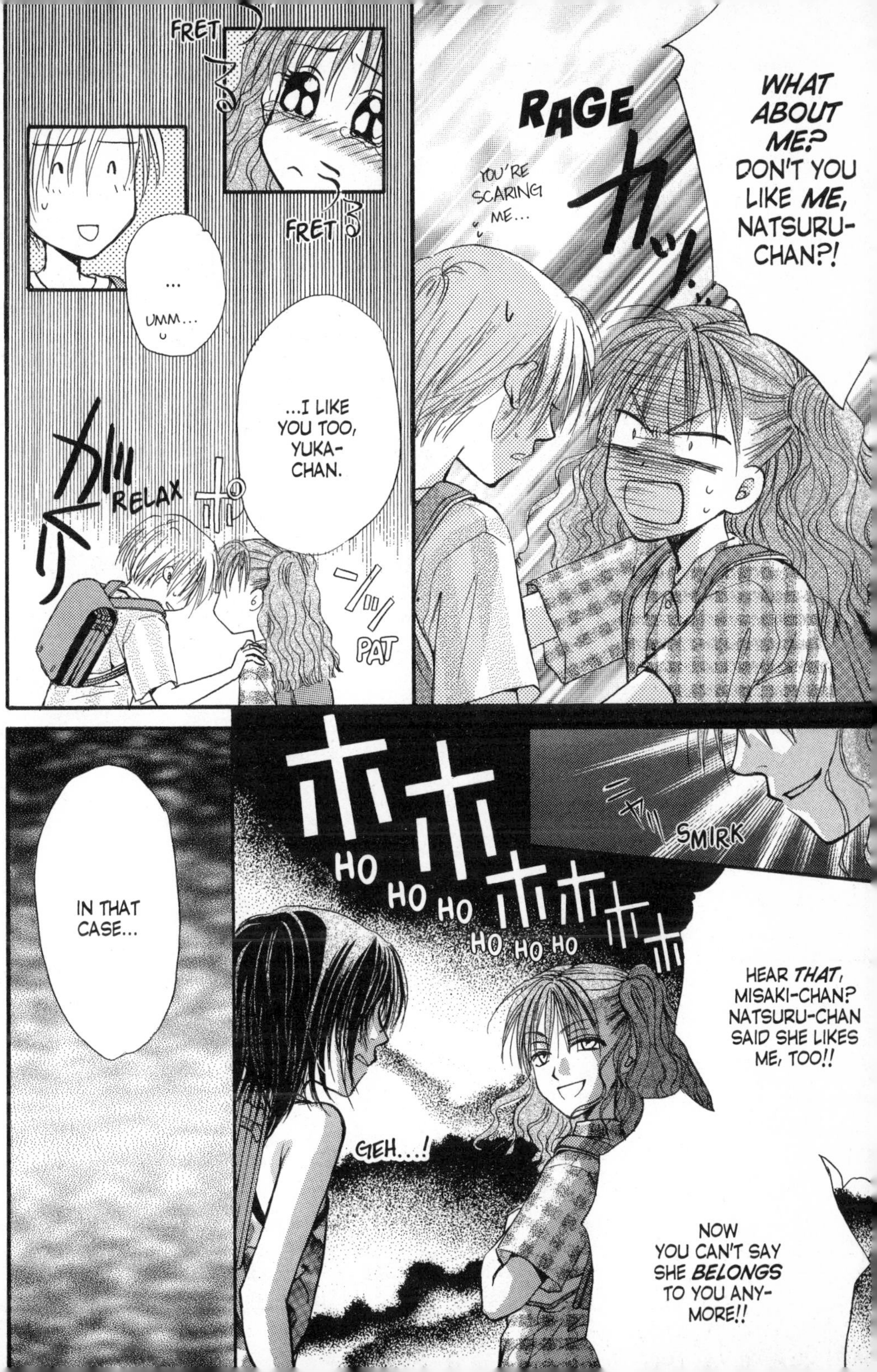
WHAT ABOUT ME? DON'T YOU LIKE ME, NATSURU-CHAN?!
RAGE
YOU'RE SCARING ME...
FRET
FRET
...
UMM...
...I LIKE YOU TOO, YUKA-CHAN.
RELAX
PAT
SMIRK
ホホ
HO HO HO
ホホホホ
HO HO HO
HEAR THAT, MISAKI-CHAN? NATSURU-CHAN SAID SHE LIKES ME, TOO!!
NOW YOU CAN'T SAY SHE BELONGS TO YOU ANYMORE!!
GEH...!
IN THAT CASE...

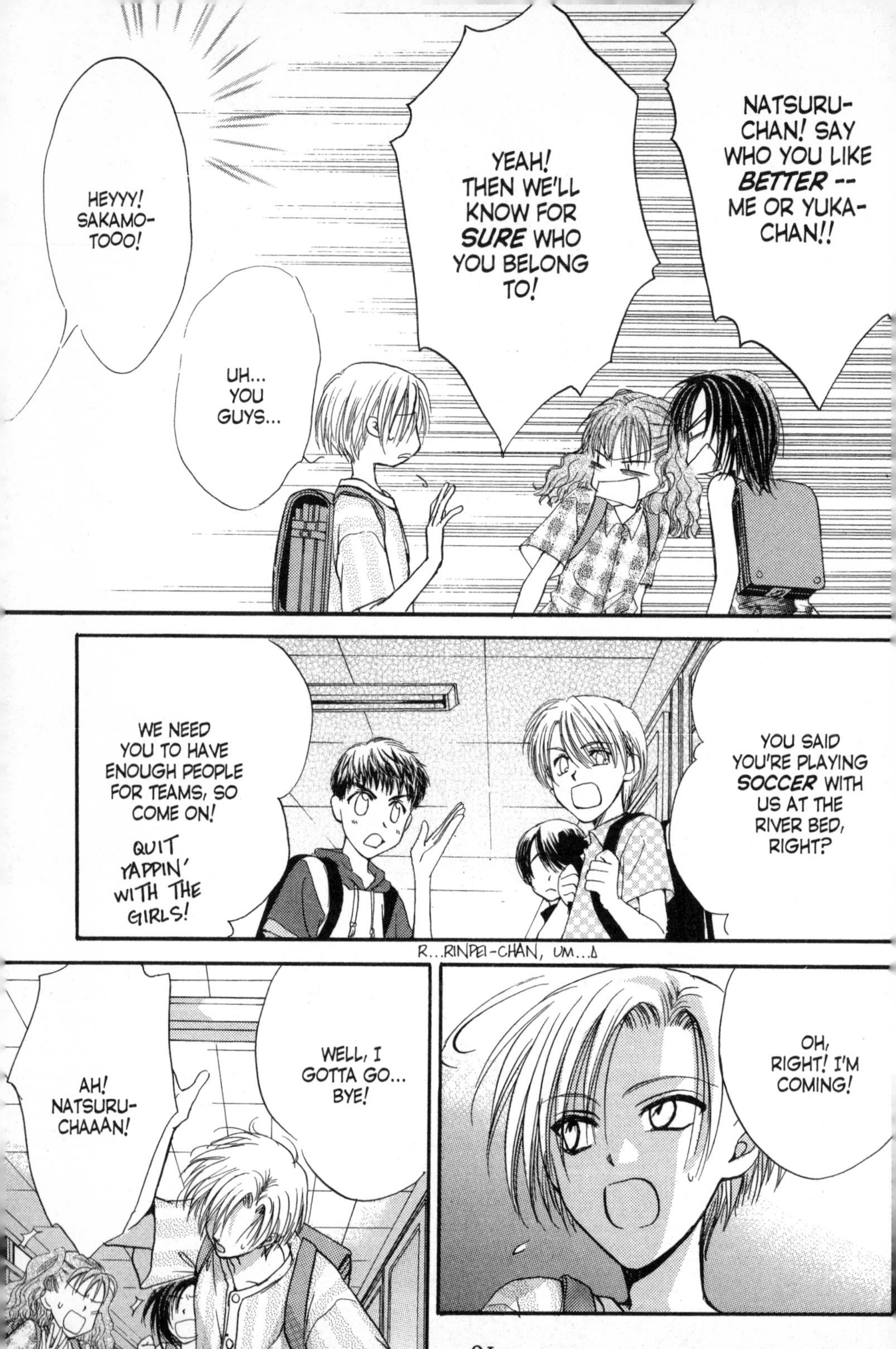
NATSURU-CHAN! SAY WHO YOU LIKE BETTER -- ME OR YUKA-CHAN!!
YEAH! THEN WE'LL KNOW FOR SURE WHO YOU BELONG TO!
HEYYY! SAKAMO-TOOO!
UH... YOU GUYS...
YOU SAID YOU'RE PLAYING SOCCER WITH US AT THE RIVER BED, RIGHT?
WE NEED YOU TO HAVE ENOUGH PEOPLE FOR TEAMS, SO COME ON!
QUIT YAPPIN' WITH THE GIRLS!
R...RINPEI-CHAN, UM...
OH, RIGHT! I'M COMING!
WELL, I GOTTA GO... BYE!
AH! NATSURU-CHAAAN!

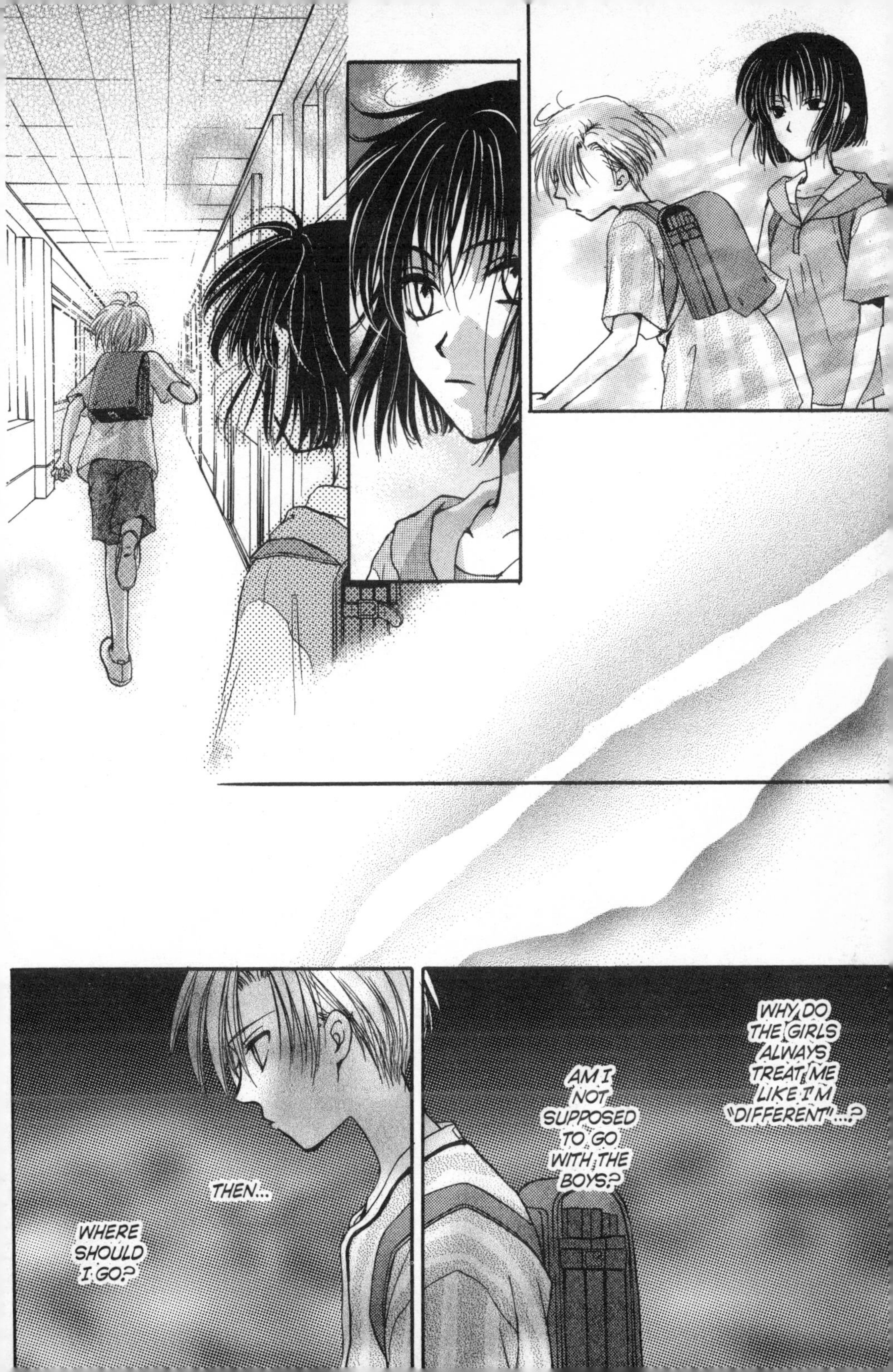
WHY DO THE GIRLS ALWAYS TREAT ME LIKE I'M "DIFFERENT"...?
AM I NOT SUPPOSED TO GO WITH THE BOYS?
THEN...
WHERE SHOULD I GO?

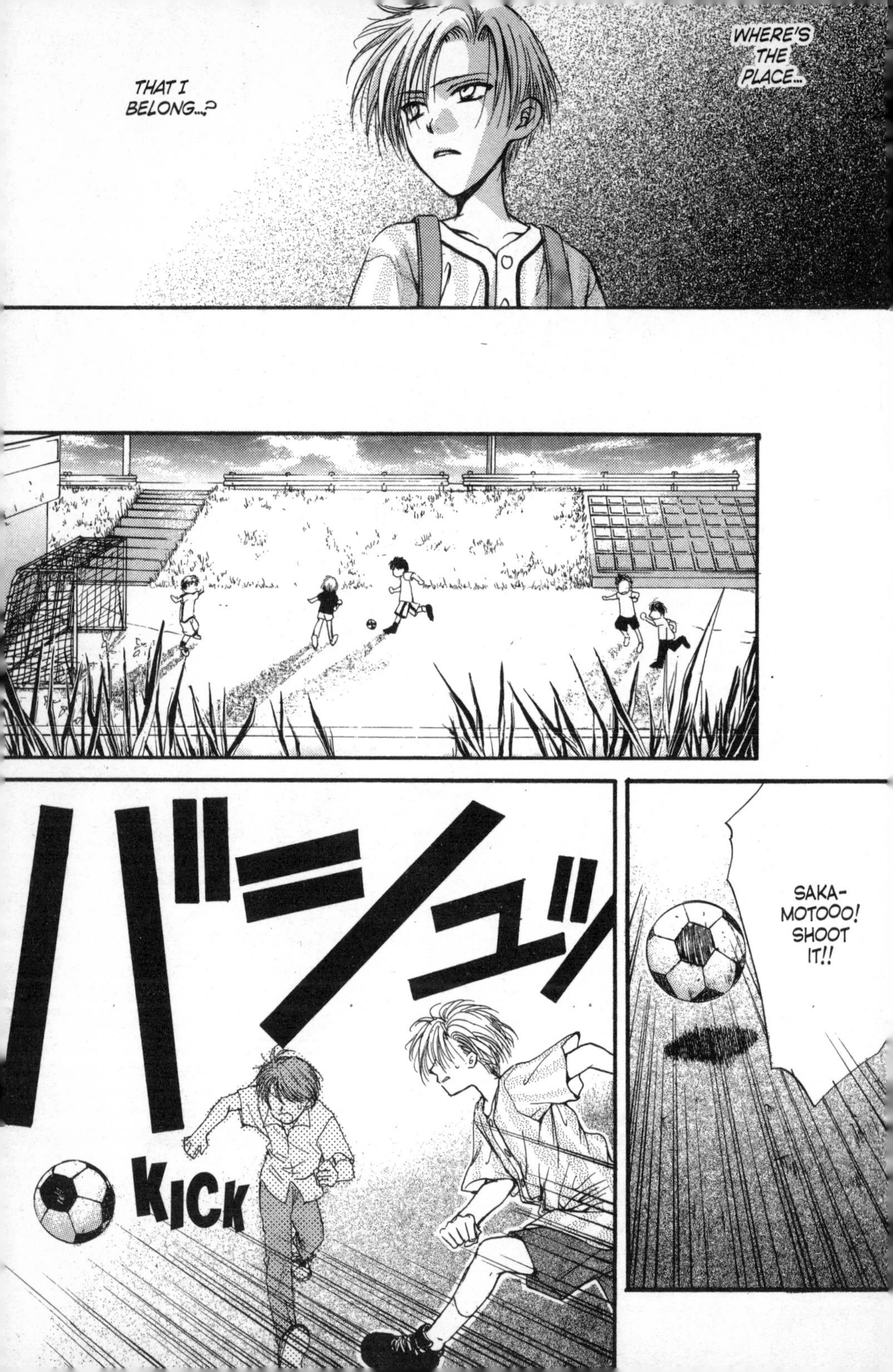
WHERE'S THE PLACE...
THAT I BELONG...?
SAKA-MOTOOO! SHOOT IT!!
KICK

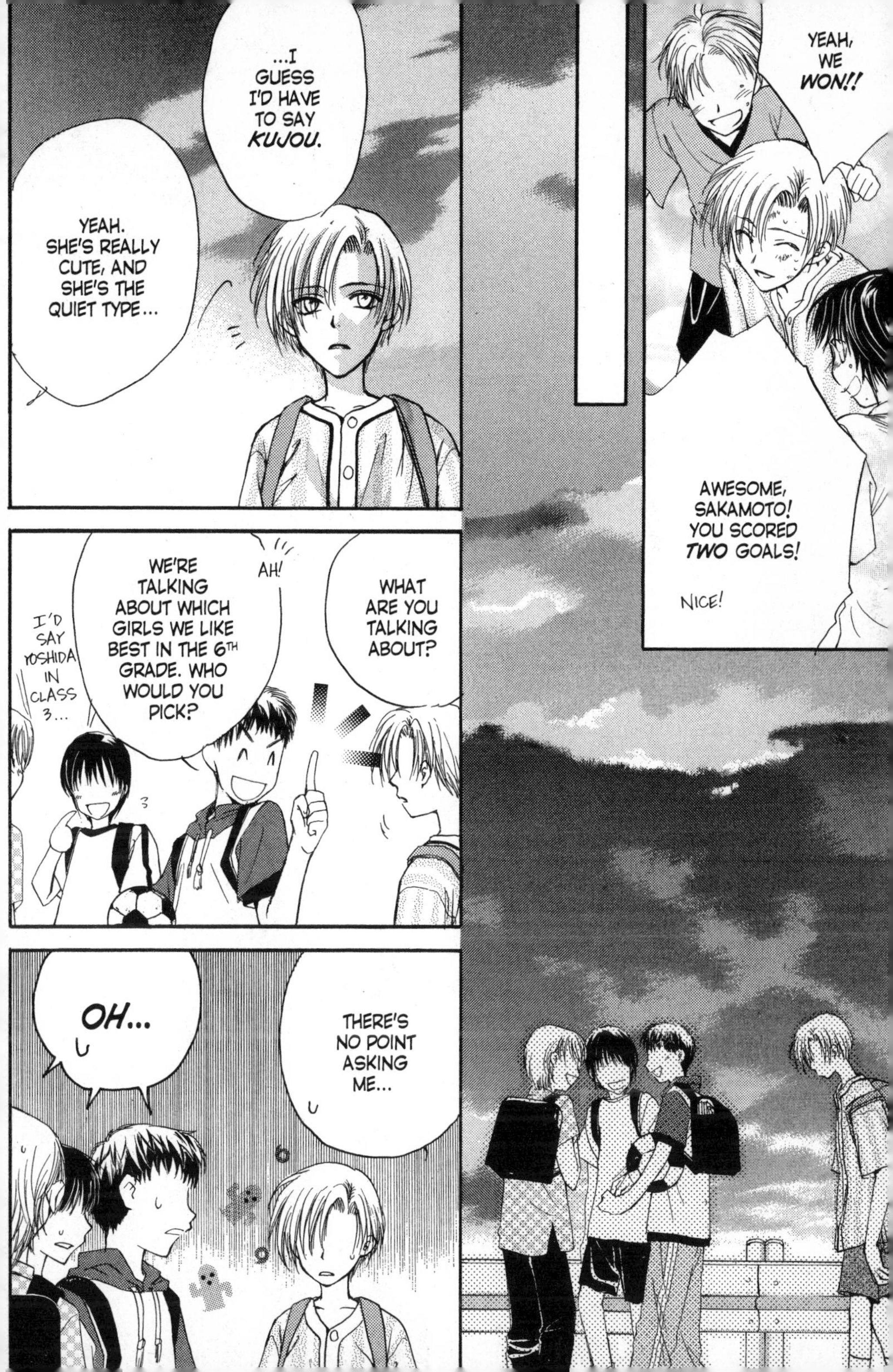

YEAH, WE WON!!
AWESOME, SAKAMOTO! YOU SCORED TWO GOALS!
NICE!
...I GUESS I'D HAVE TO SAY KUJOU.
YEAH. SHE'S REALLY CUTE, AND SHE'S THE QUIET TYPE...
WHAT ARE YOU TALKING ABOUT?
AH!
WE'RE TALKING ABOUT WHICH GIRLS WE LIKE BEST IN THE 6TH GRADE. WHO WOULD YOU PICK?
I'D SAY YOSHIDA IN CLASS 3...
THERE'S NO POINT ASKING ME...
OH...

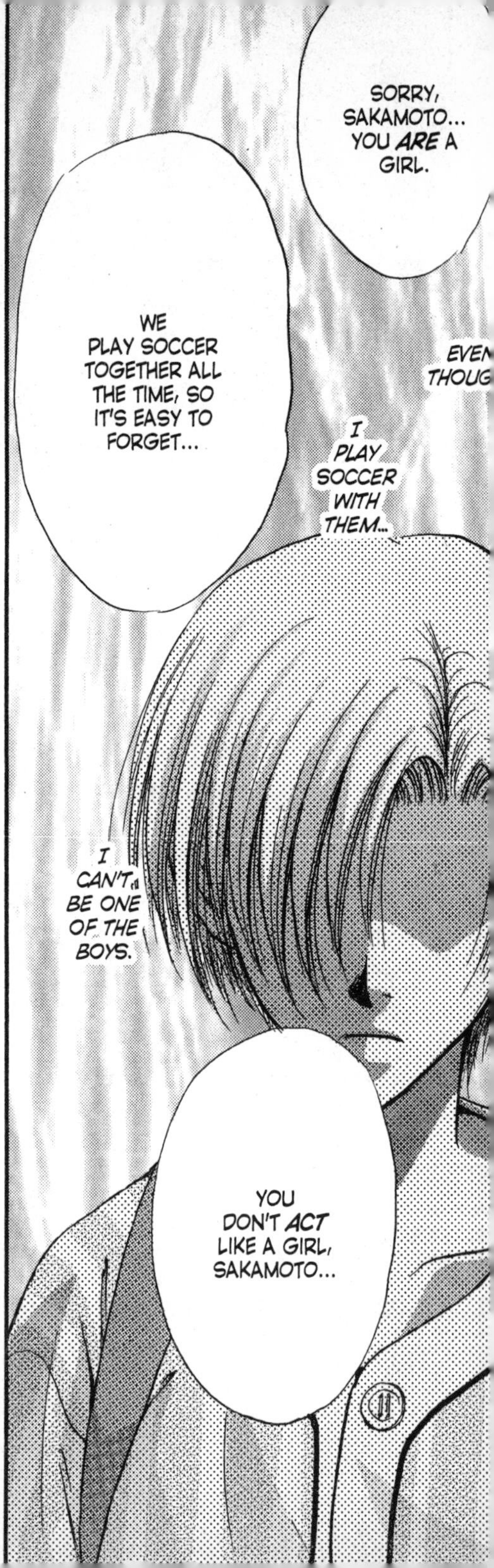
SORRY, SAKAMOTO... YOU **ARE** A GIRL.
EVEN THOUG
WE PLAY SOCCER TOGETHER ALL THE TIME, SO IT'S EASY TO FORGET...
I PLAY SOCCER WITH THEM...
I CAN'T BE ONE OF THE BOYS.
YOU DON'T **ACT** LIKE A GIRL, SAKAMOTO...

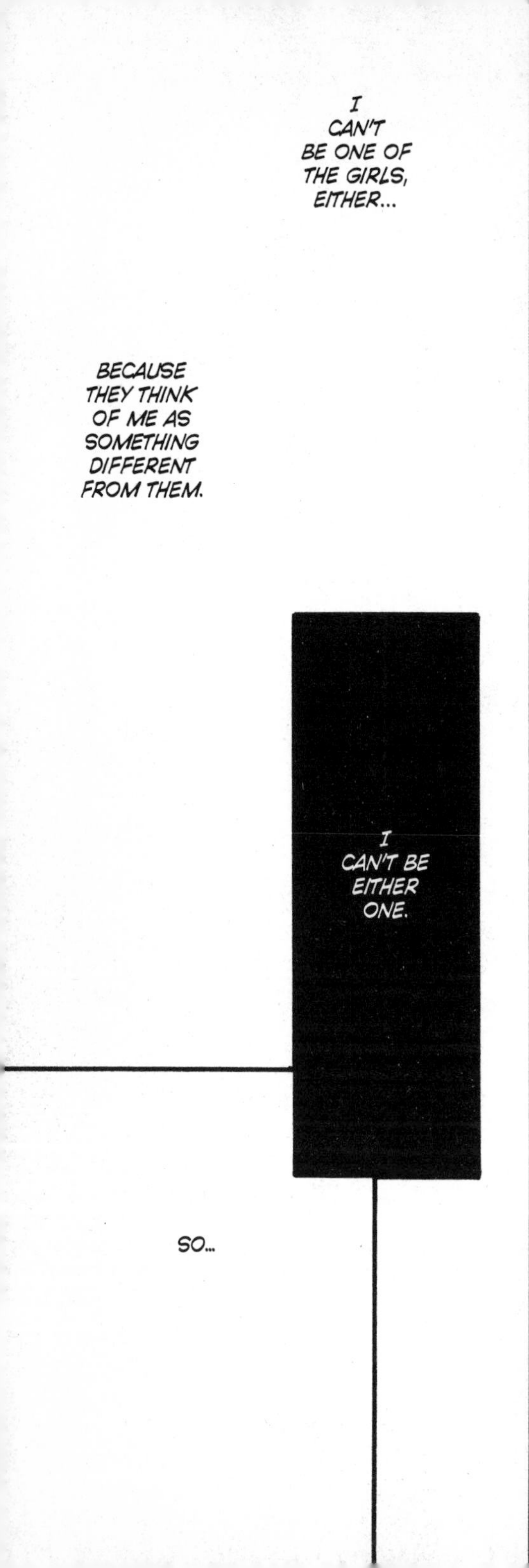
I CAN'T BE ONE OF THE GIRLS, EITHER...
BECAUSE THEY THINK OF ME AS SOMETHING DIFFERENT FROM THEM.
I CAN'T BE EITHER ONE.
SO...

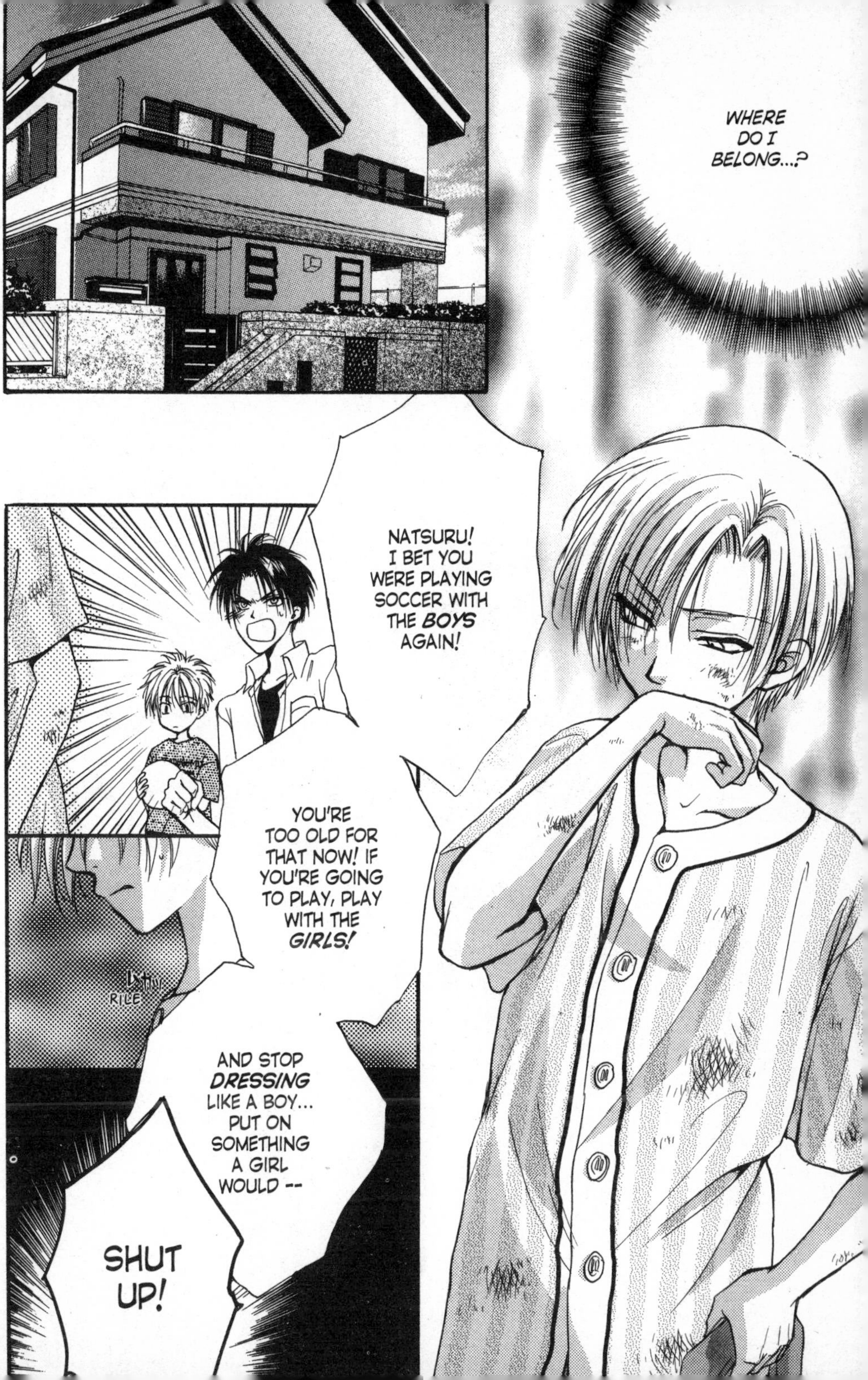
WHERE DO I BELONG...?
NATSURU! I BET YOU WERE PLAYING SOCCER WITH THE *BOYS* AGAIN!
YOU'RE TOO OLD FOR THAT NOW! IF YOU'RE GOING TO PLAY, PLAY WITH THE *GIRLS!*
RILE
AND STOP *DRESSING* LIKE A BOY... PUT ON SOMETHING A GIRL WOULD --
SHUT UP!

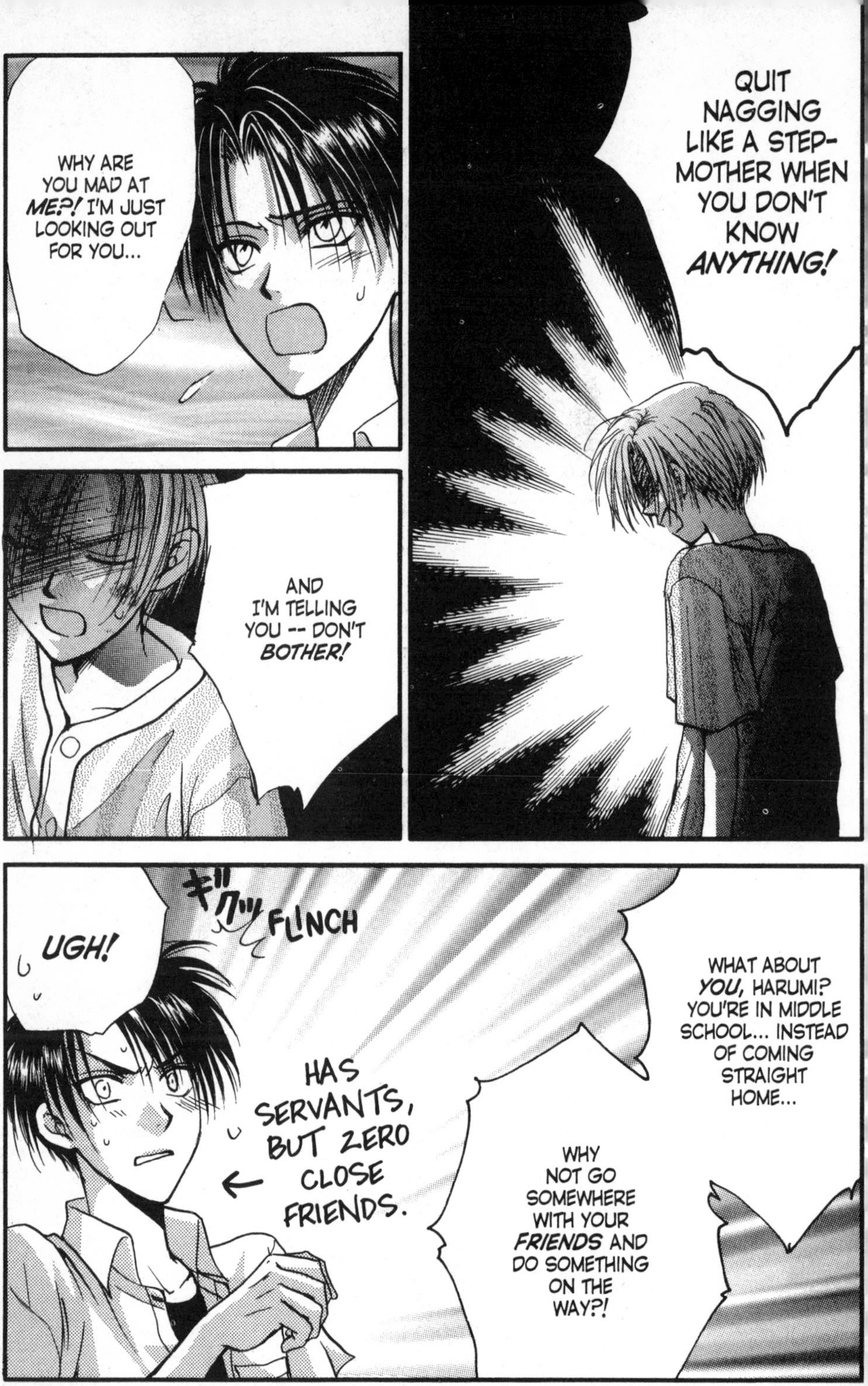
QUIT NAGGING LIKE A STEP-MOTHER WHEN YOU DON'T KNOW *ANYTHING!*
WHY ARE YOU MAD AT *ME?!* I'M JUST LOOKING OUT FOR YOU...
AND I'M TELLING YOU -- DON'T *BOTHER!*
WHAT ABOUT *YOU*, HARUMI? YOU'RE IN MIDDLE SCHOOL... INSTEAD OF COMING STRAIGHT HOME...
ギクッ FLINCH
UGH!
WHY NOT GO SOMEWHERE WITH YOUR *FRIENDS* AND DO SOMETHING ON THE WAY?!
HAS SERVANTS, BUT ZERO CLOSE FRIENDS.

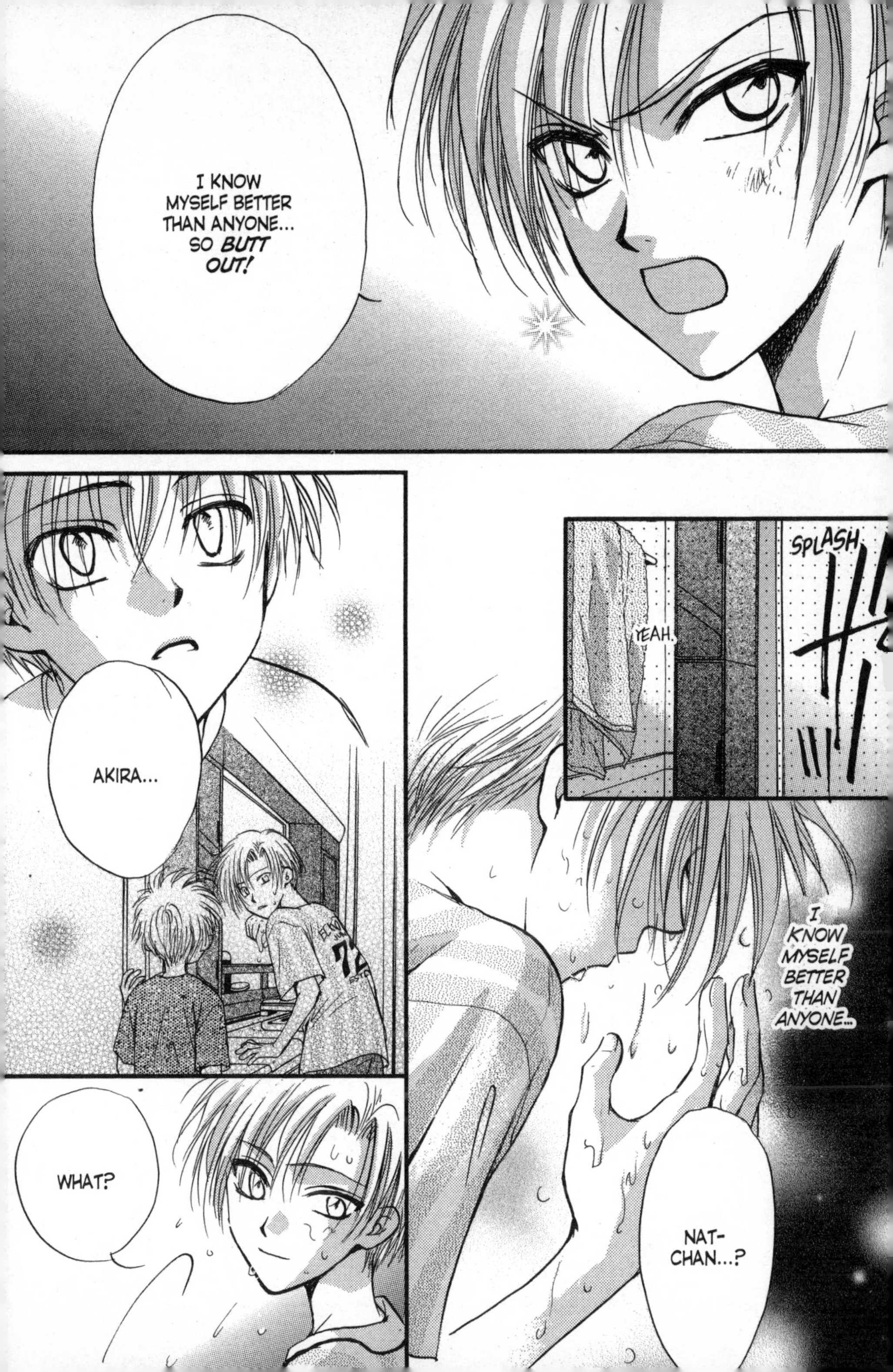
I KNOW MYSELF BETTER THAN ANYONE... SO *BUTT OUT!*
SPLASH
YEAH.
I KNOW MYSELF BETTER THAN ANYONE...
NAT-CHAN...?
AKIRA...
WHAT?

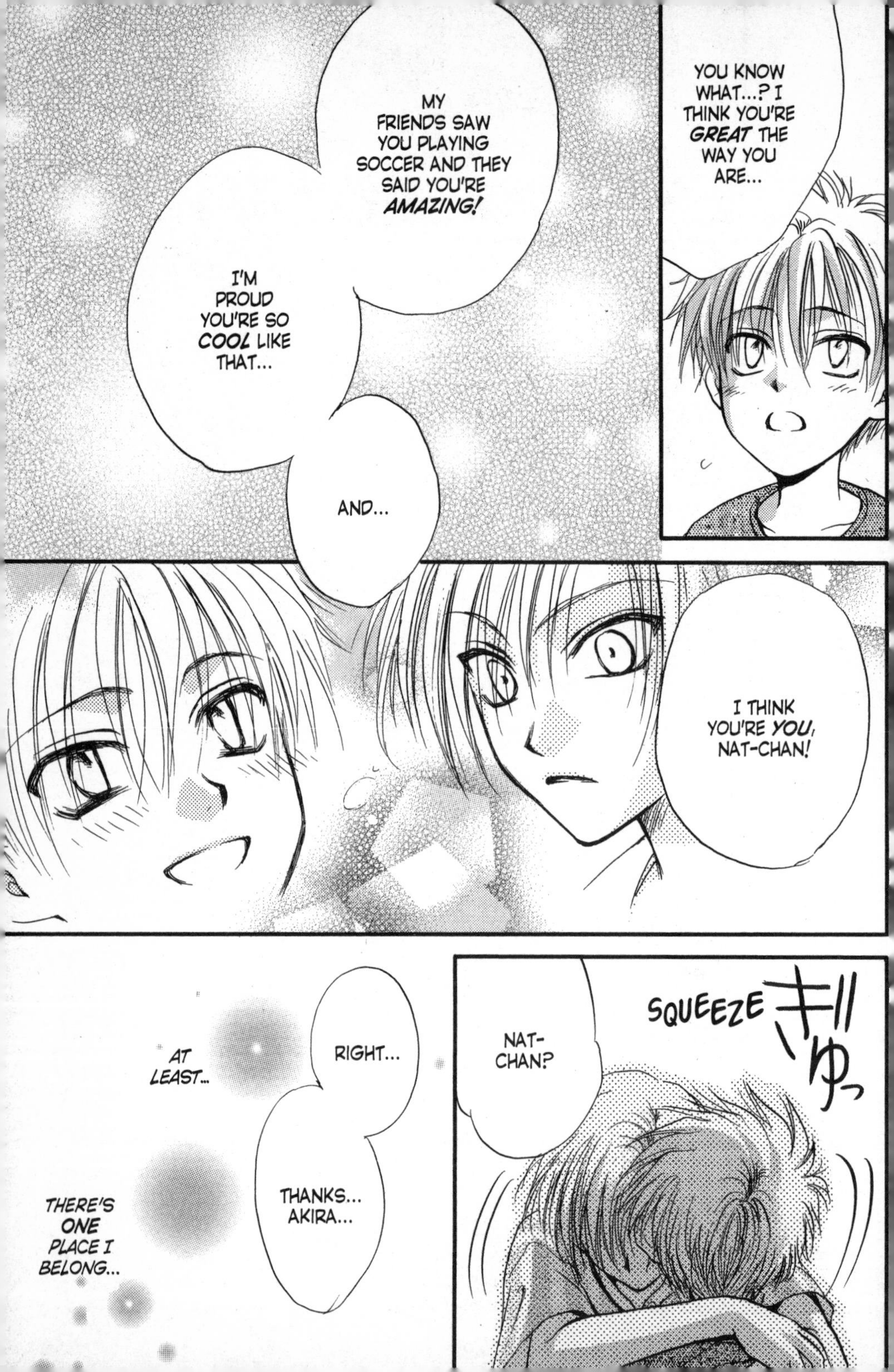
YOU KNOW WHAT...? I THINK YOU'RE *GREAT* THE WAY YOU ARE...
MY FRIENDS SAW YOU PLAYING SOCCER AND THEY SAID YOU'RE *AMAZING!*
I'M PROUD YOU'RE SO *COOL* LIKE THAT...
AND...
I THINK YOU'RE *YOU*, NAT-CHAN!
SQUEEZE
ぎゅっ
NAT-CHAN?
RIGHT...
THANKS... AKIRA...
AT LEAST...
THERE'S ONE PLACE I BELONG...

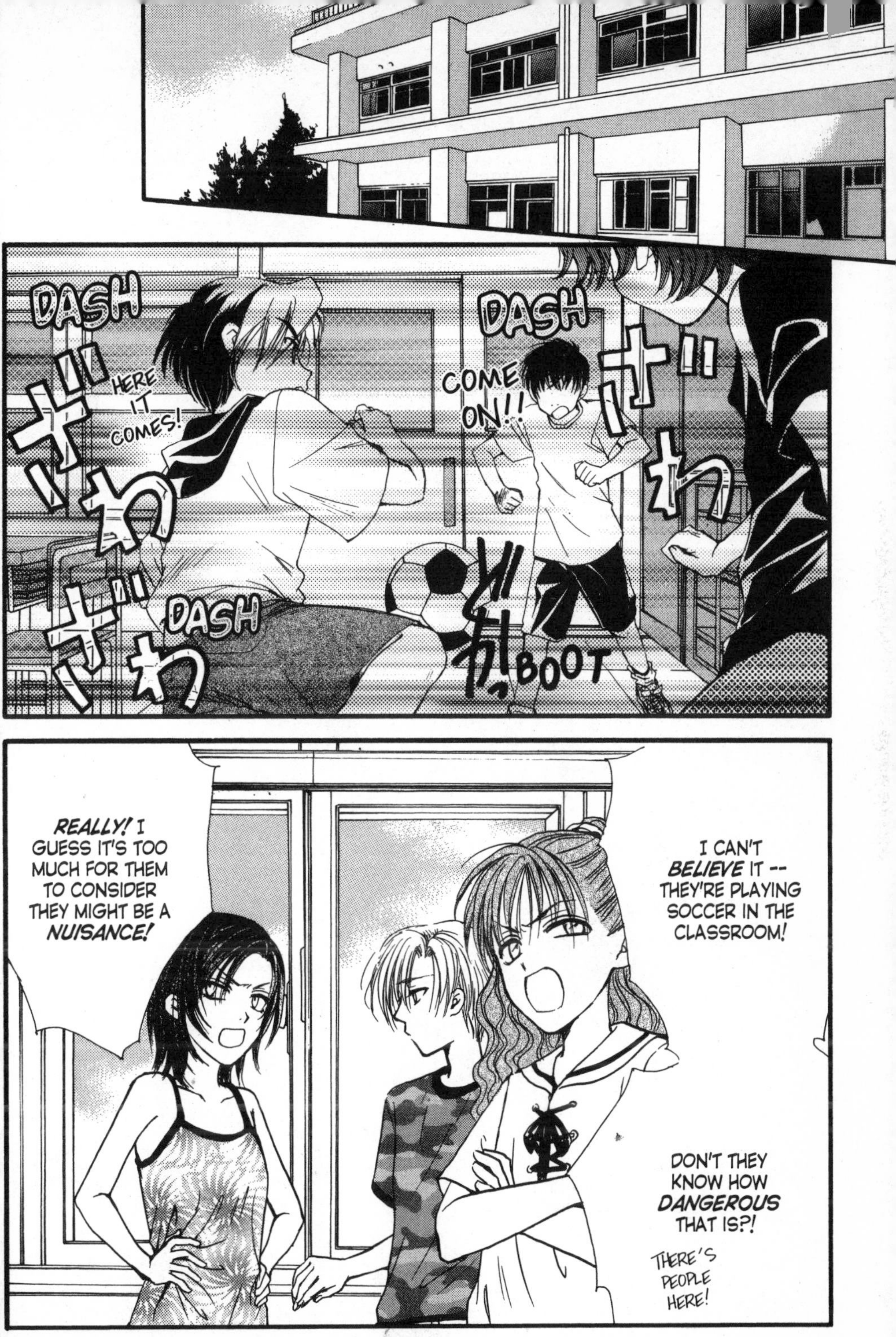

ざわ
DASH
COME ON!!
DASH
HERE IT COMES!
ざわ
ざわ
DASH
ガッ
BOOT
I CAN'T *BELIEVE* IT -- THEY'RE PLAYING SOCCER IN THE CLASSROOM!
DON'T THEY KNOW HOW *DANGEROUS* THAT IS?!
THERE'S PEOPLE HERE!
REALLY! I GUESS IT'S TOO MUCH FOR THEM TO CONSIDER THEY MIGHT BE A *NUISANCE!*

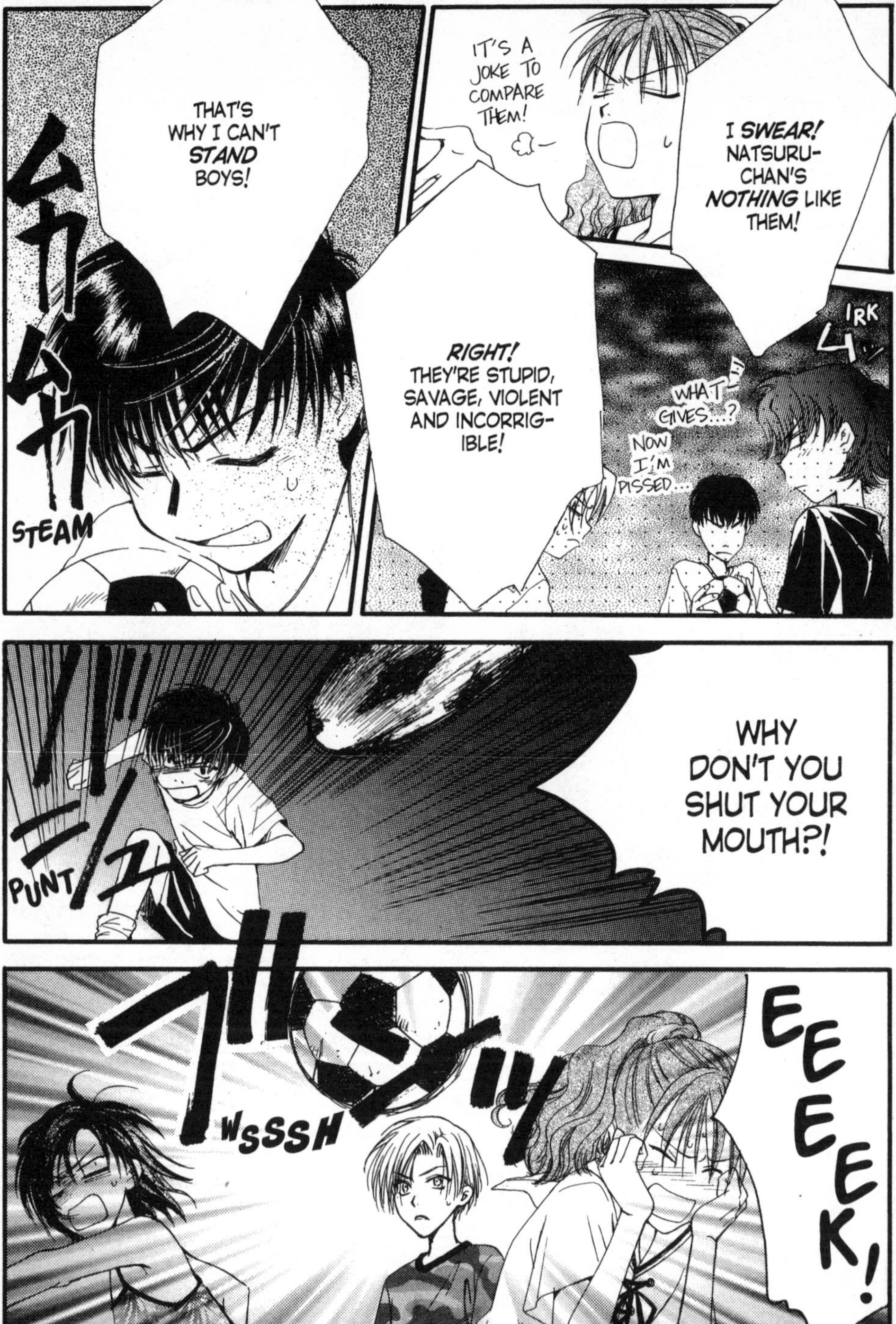
IT'S A JOKE TO COMPARE THEM!
I SWEAR! NATSURU-CHAN'S NOTHING LIKE THEM!
RIGHT! THEY'RE STUPID, SAVAGE, VIOLENT AND INCORRIG-IBLE!
IRK
WHAT GIVES...?
NOW I'M PISSED...
THAT'S WHY I CAN'T STAND BOYS!
STEAM
WHY DON'T YOU SHUT YOUR MOUTH?!
PUNT
EEEEK!
WSSSH

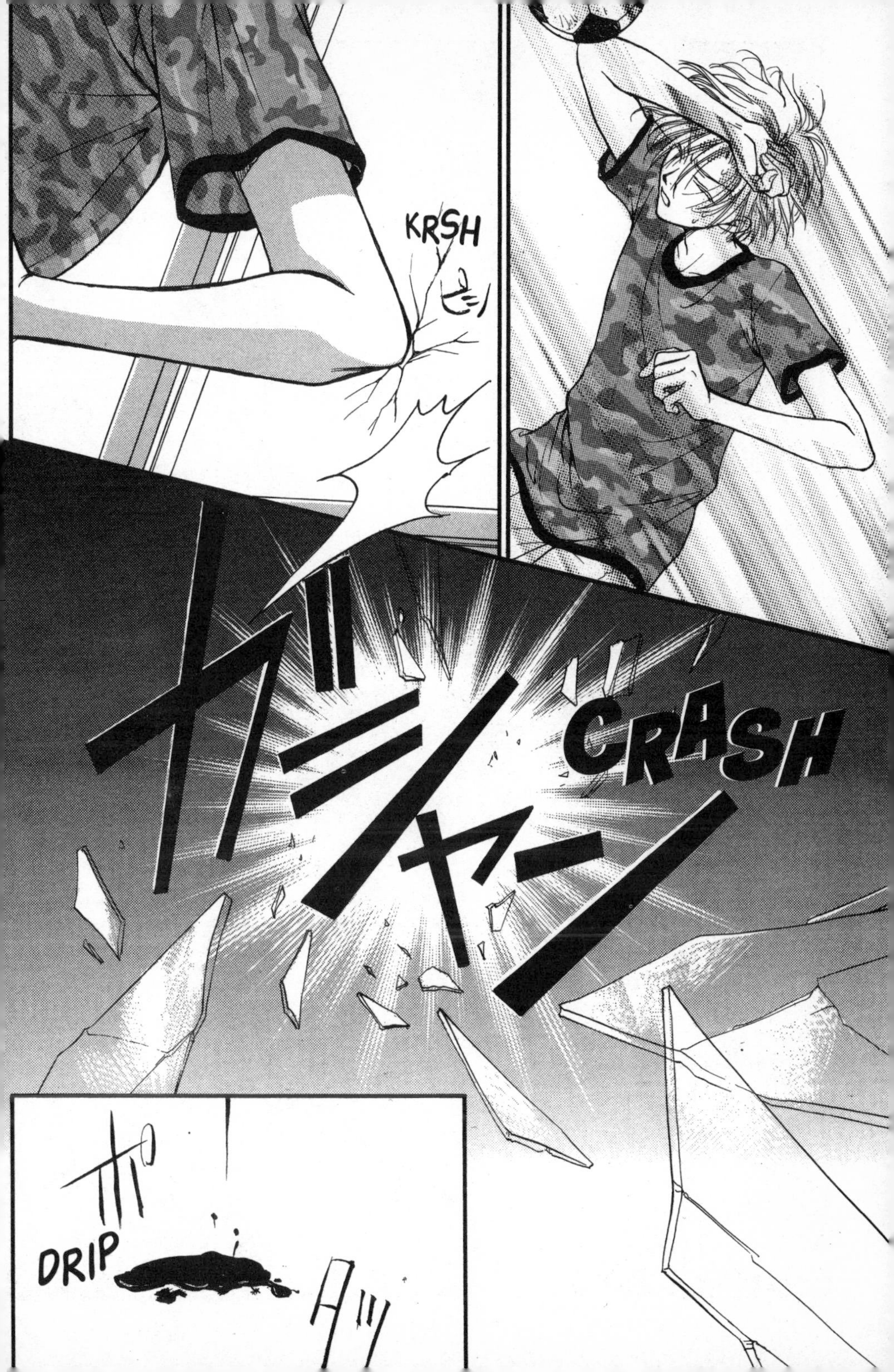
KRSH
CRASH
DRIP

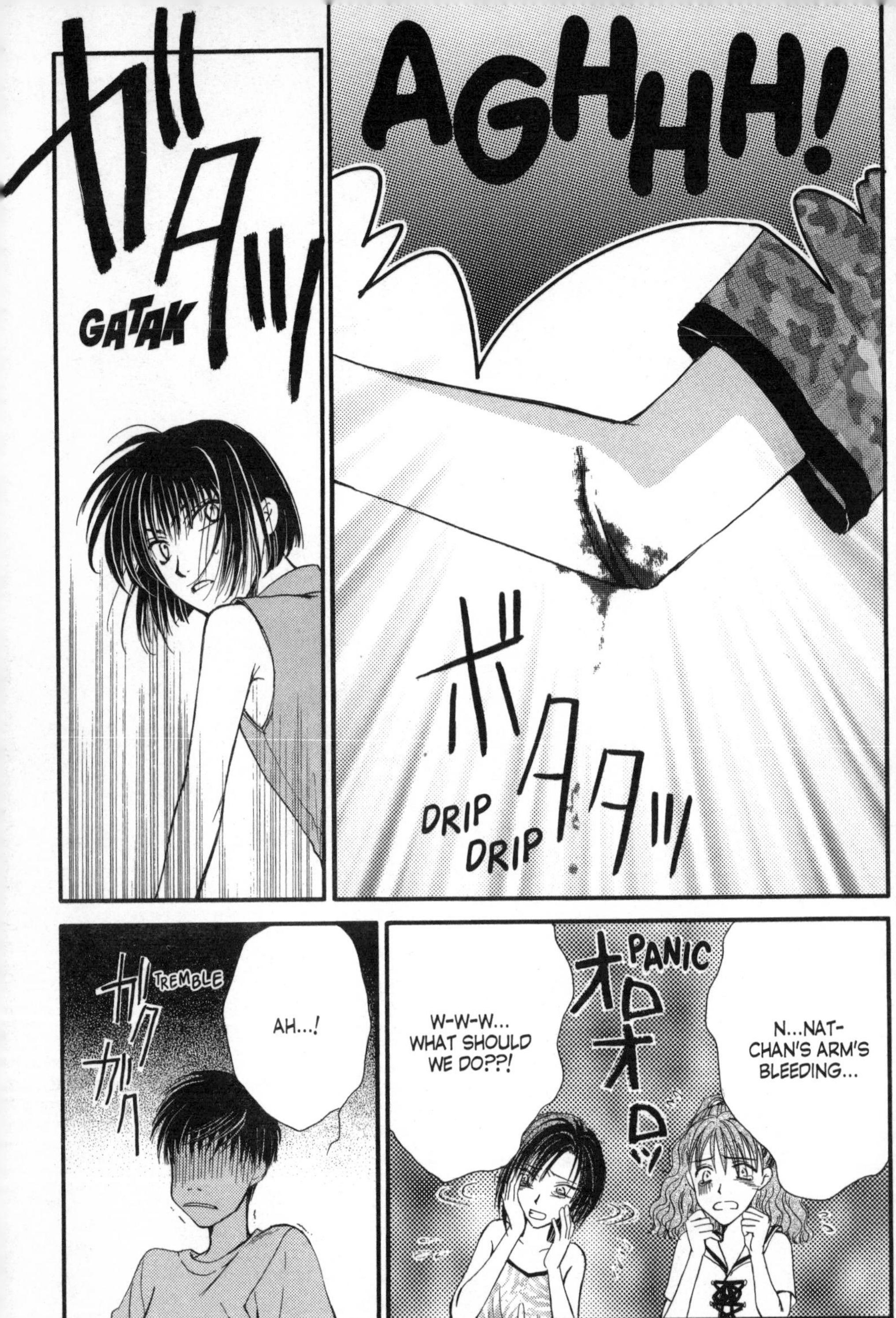
AGHHH!
ボタタッ
DRIP DRIP
ガタッ
GATAK
N...NAT-CHAN'S ARM'S BLEEDING...
オロオロッ
PANIC
W-W-W... WHAT SHOULD WE DO??!
AH...!
TREMBLE

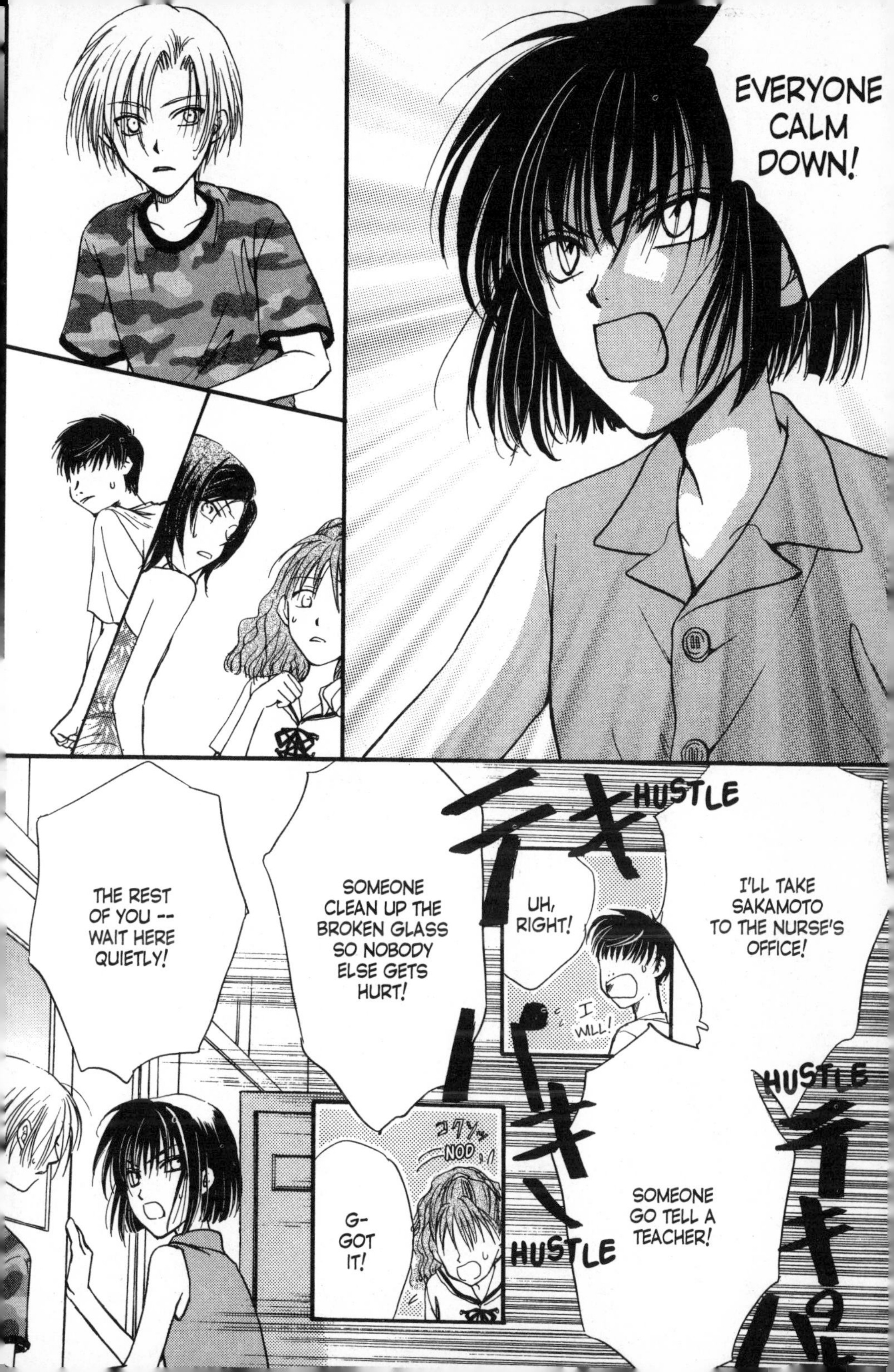
EVERYONE CALM DOWN!
HUSTLE
I'LL TAKE SAKAMOTO TO THE NURSE'S OFFICE!
UH, RIGHT!
I WILL!
HUSTLE
SOMEONE GO TELL A TEACHER!
HUSTLE
SOMEONE CLEAN UP THE BROKEN GLASS SO NOBODY ELSE GETS HURT!
NOD
G-GOT IT!
THE REST OF YOU -- WAIT HERE QUIETLY!

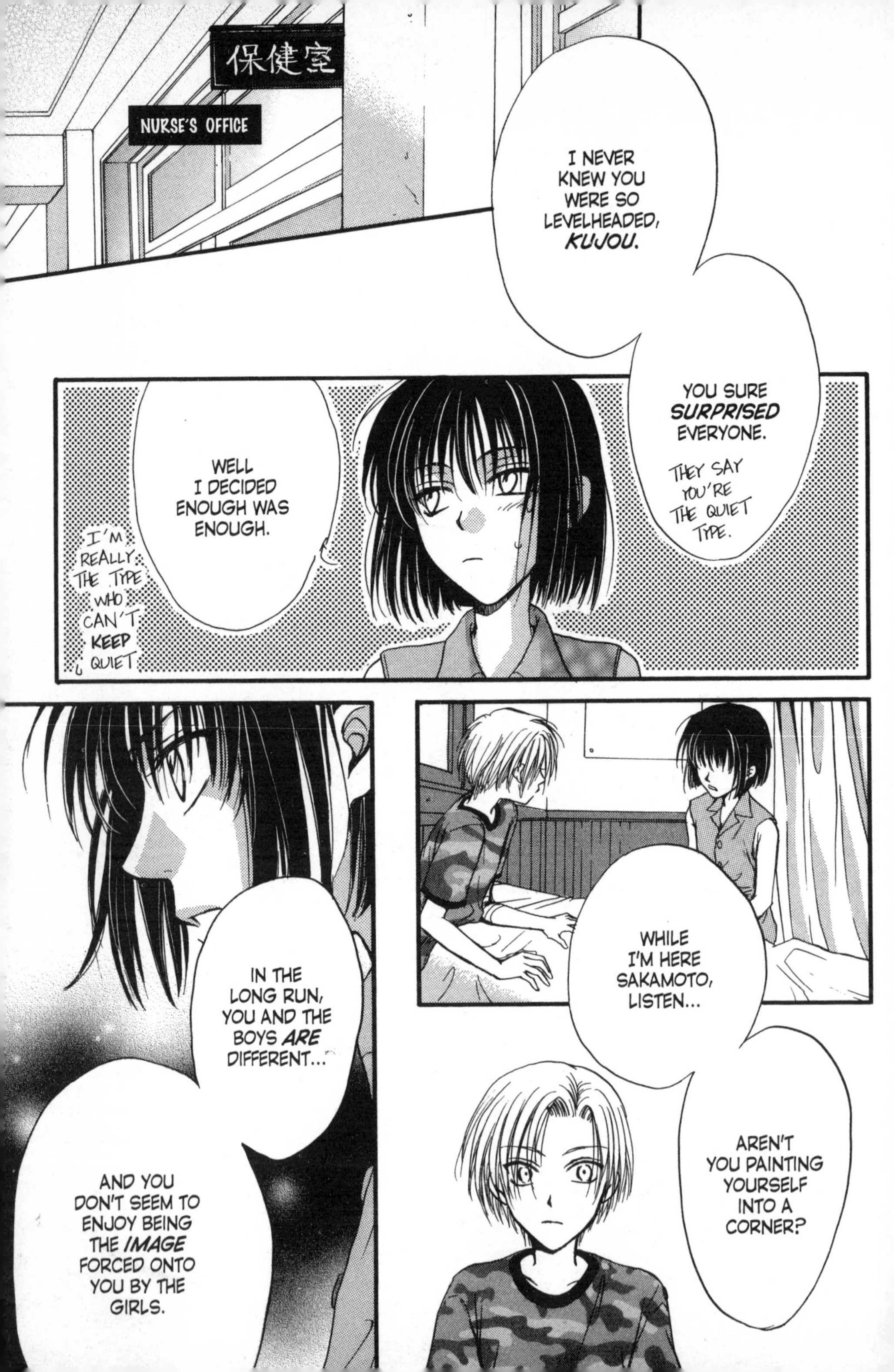

保健室
NURSE'S OFFICE
I NEVER KNEW YOU WERE SO LEVELHEADED, **KUJOU.**
YOU SURE **SURPRISED** EVERYONE.
THEY SAY YOU'RE THE QUIET TYPE.
WELL I DECIDED ENOUGH WAS ENOUGH.
I'M REALLY THE TYPE WHO CAN'T **KEEP** QUIET
WHILE I'M HERE SAKAMOTO, LISTEN...
AREN'T YOU PAINTING YOURSELF INTO A CORNER?
IN THE LONG RUN, YOU AND THE BOYS ***ARE*** DIFFERENT...
AND YOU DON'T SEEM TO ENJOY BEING THE ***IMAGE*** FORCED ONTO YOU BY THE GIRLS.

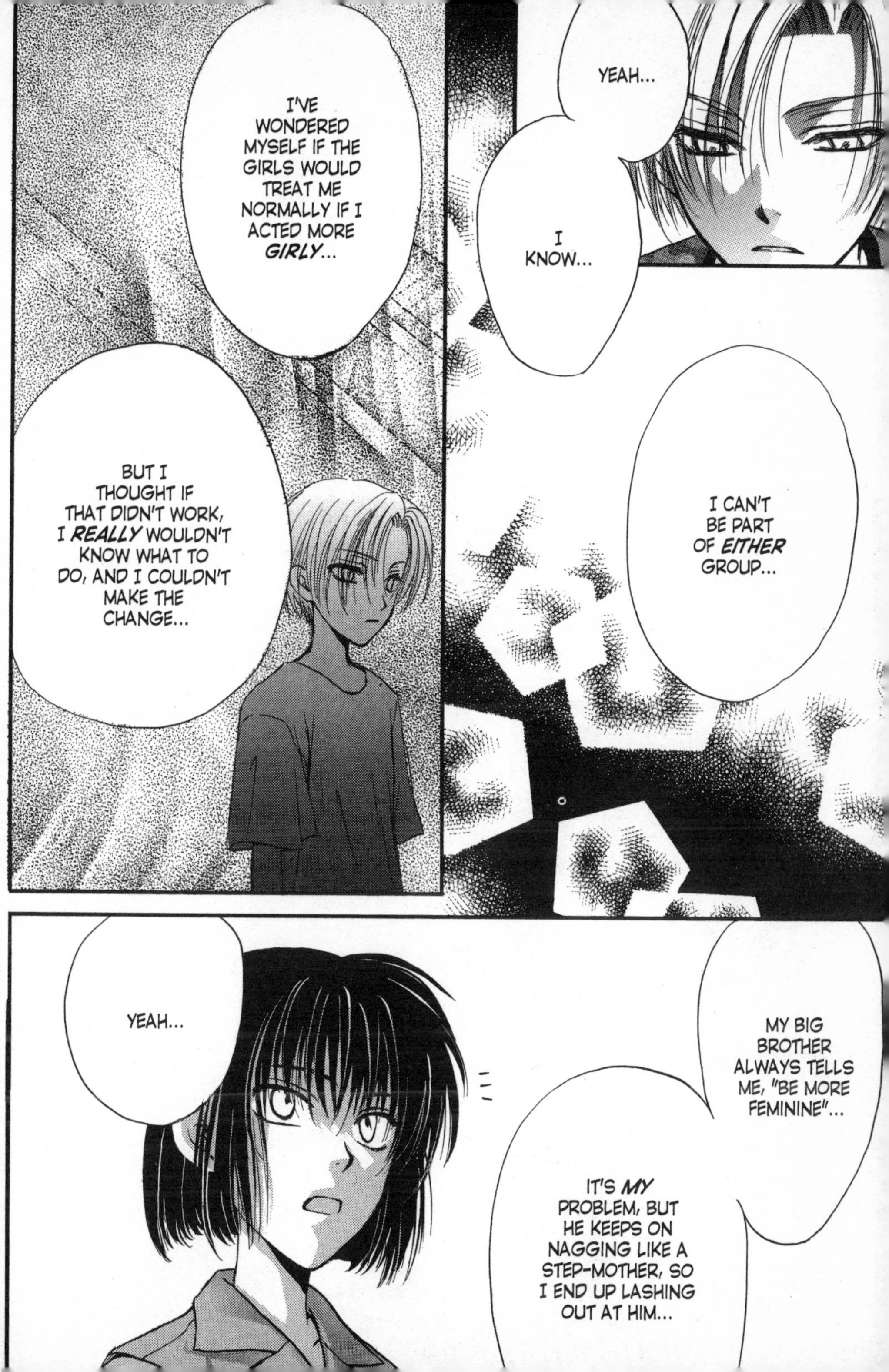
YEAH...
I KNOW...
I CAN'T BE PART OF *EITHER* GROUP...
I'VE WONDERED MYSELF IF THE GIRLS WOULD TREAT ME NORMALLY IF I ACTED MORE *GIRLY*...
BUT I THOUGHT IF THAT DIDN'T WORK, I *REALLY* WOULDN'T KNOW WHAT TO DO, AND I COULDN'T MAKE THE CHANGE...
MY BIG BROTHER ALWAYS TELLS ME, "BE MORE FEMININE"...
IT'S *MY* PROBLEM, BUT HE KEEPS ON NAGGING LIKE A STEP-MOTHER, SO I END UP LASHING OUT AT HIM...
YEAH...

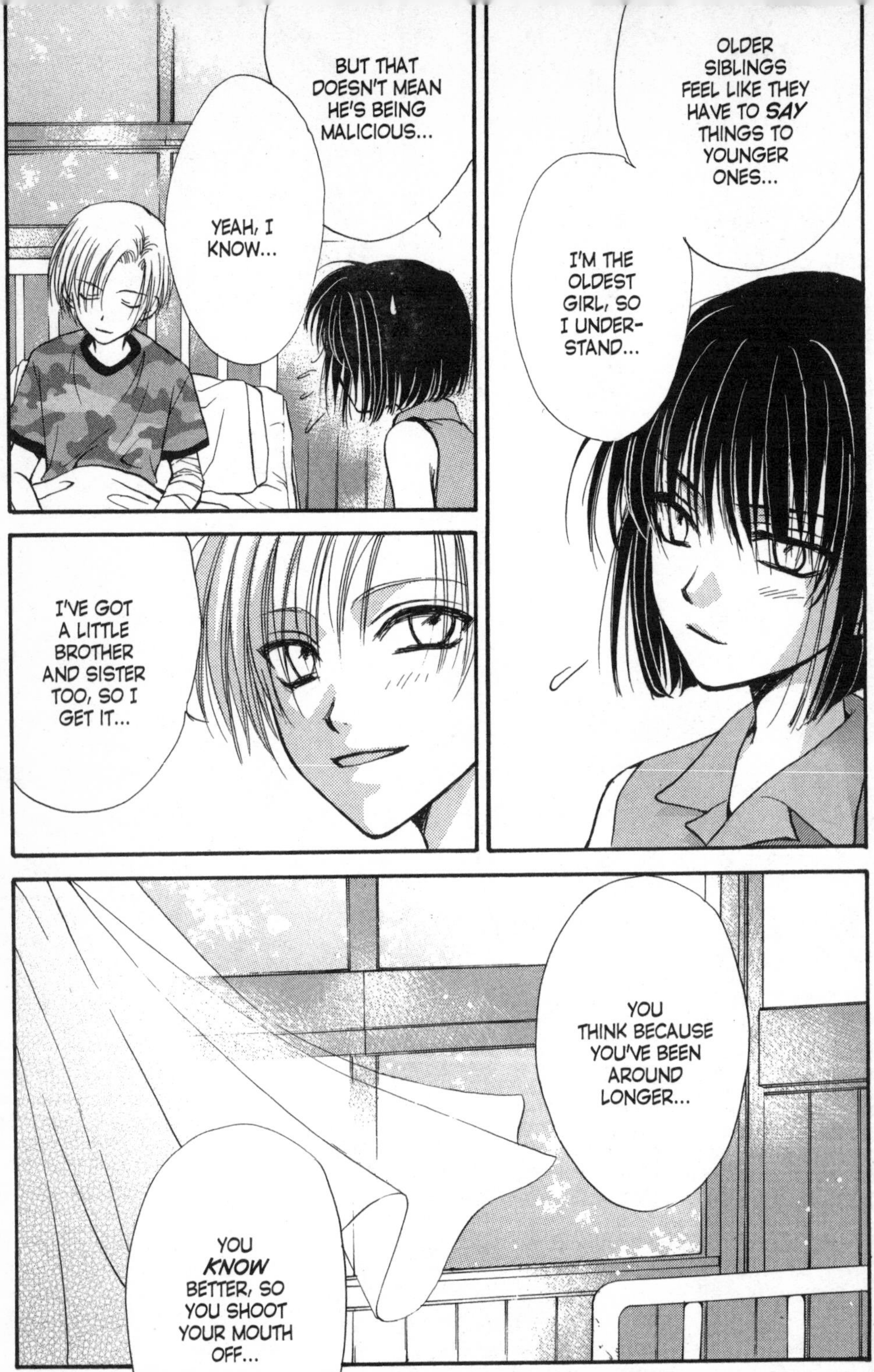
OLDER SIBLINGS FEEL LIKE THEY HAVE TO SAY THINGS TO YOUNGER ONES...
I'M THE OLDEST GIRL, SO I UNDER-STAND...
BUT THAT DOESN'T MEAN HE'S BEING MALICIOUS...
YEAH, I KNOW...
I'VE GOT A LITTLE BROTHER AND SISTER TOO, SO I GET IT...
YOU THINK BECAUSE YOU'VE BEEN AROUND LONGER...
YOU KNOW BETTER, SO YOU SHOOT YOUR MOUTH OFF...

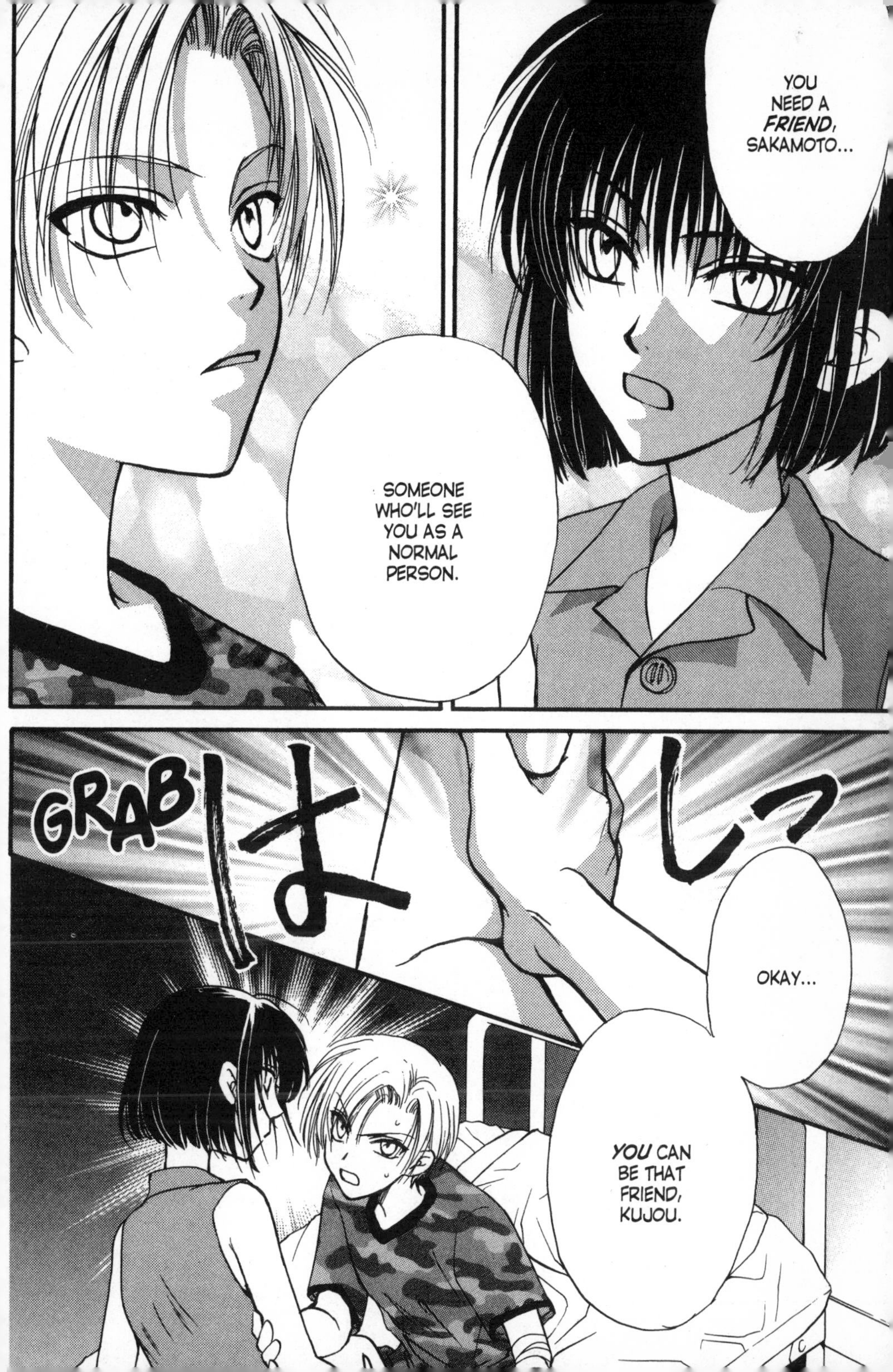

YOU NEED A *FRIEND*, SAKAMOTO...
SOMEONE WHO'LL SEE YOU AS A NORMAL PERSON.
はしっ
GRAB
OKAY...
YOU CAN BE THAT FRIEND, KUJOU.

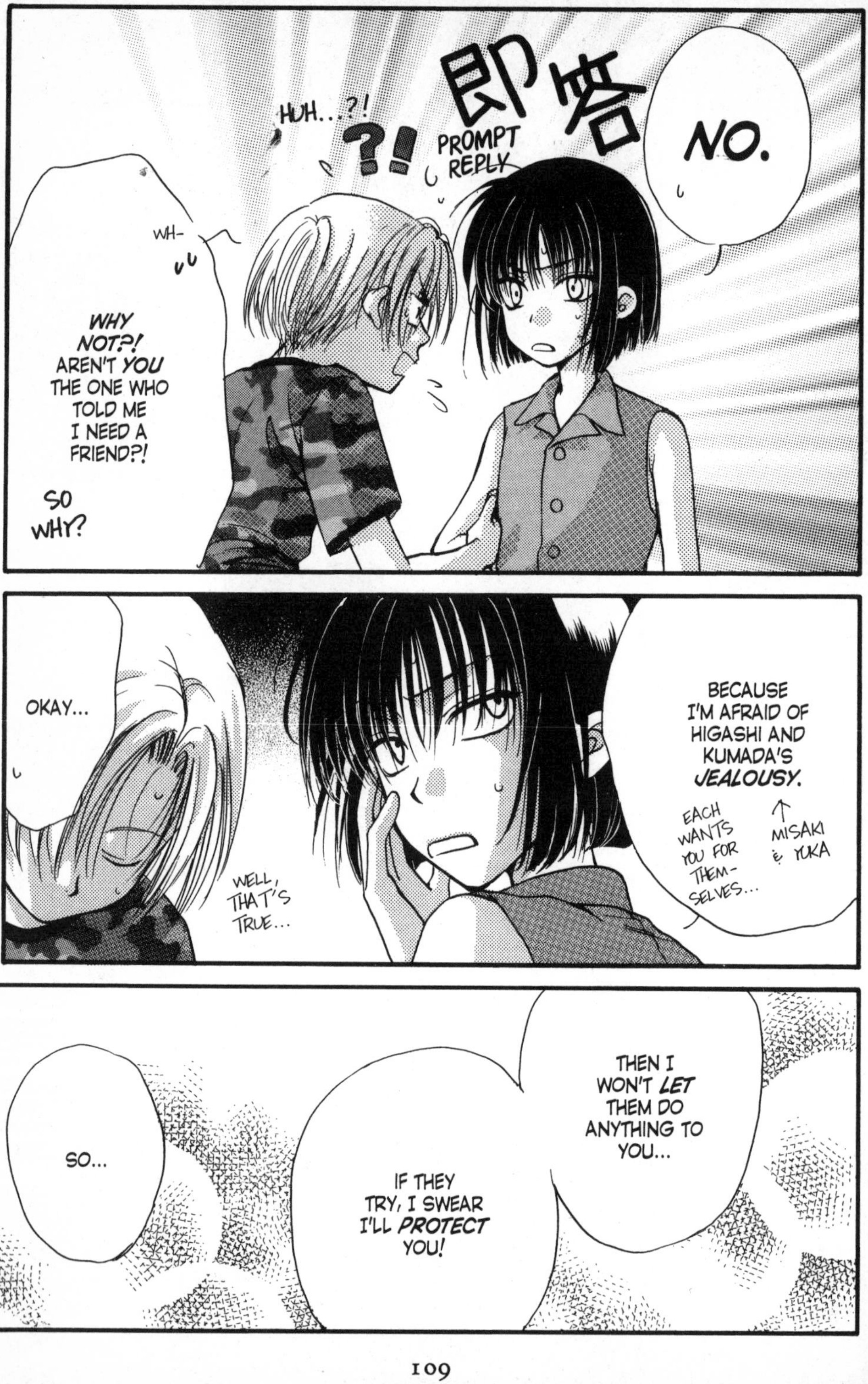
NO.
即答
PROMPT REPLY
?!
HUH...?!
WH-
WHY NOT?! AREN'T YOU THE ONE WHO TOLD ME I NEED A FRIEND?!
SO WHY?
BECAUSE I'M AFRAID OF HIGASHI AND KUMADA'S JEALOUSY.
MISAKI & YUKA
EACH WANTS YOU FOR THEMSELVES...
WELL, THAT'S TRUE...
OKAY...
THEN I WON'T LET THEM DO ANYTHING TO YOU...
IF THEY TRY, I SWEAR I'LL PROTECT YOU!
SO...

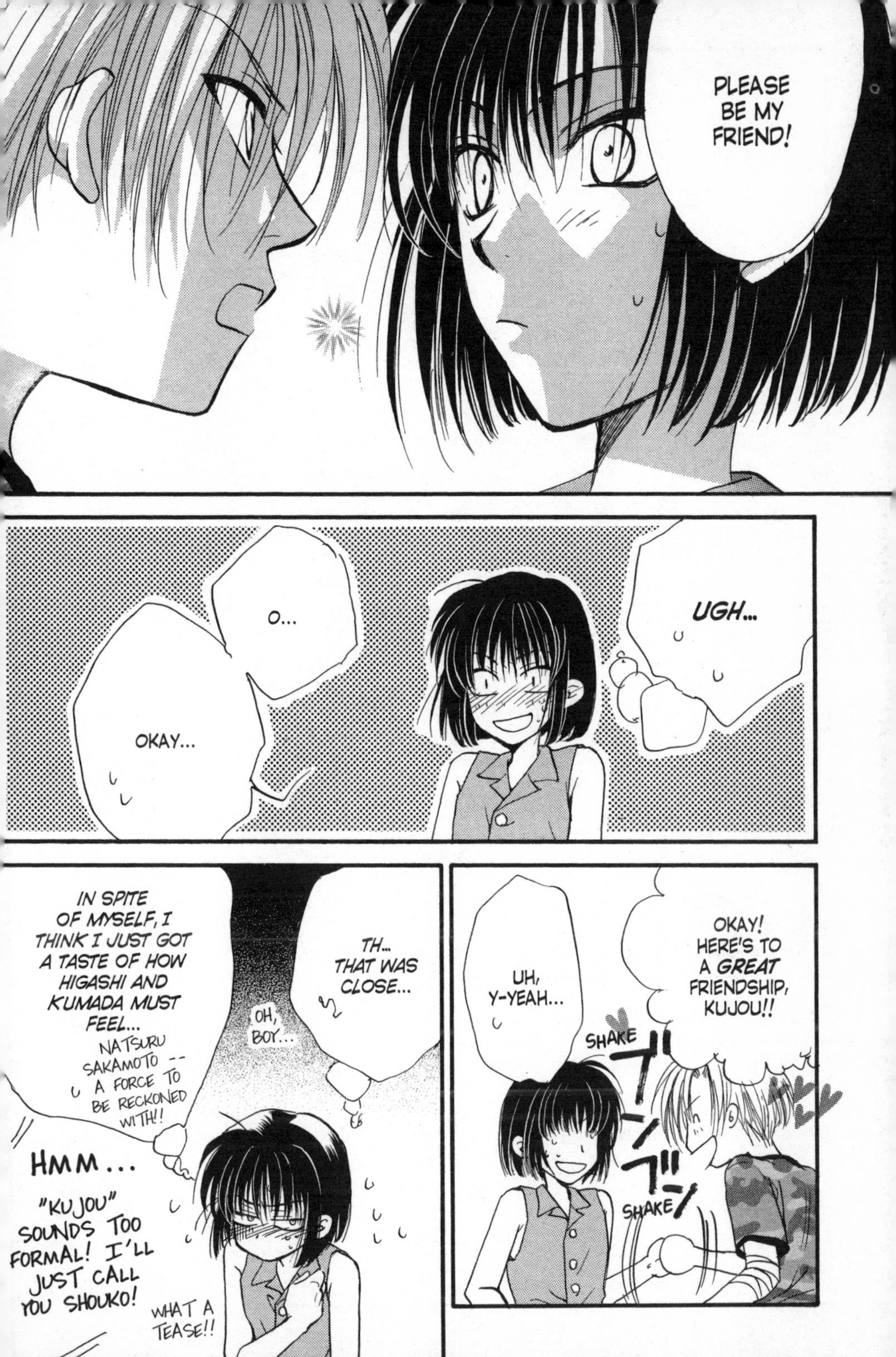
PLEASE BE MY FRIEND!
UGH...
O...
OKAY...
OKAY! HERE'S TO A GREAT FRIENDSHIP, KUJOU!!
UH, Y-YEAH...
SHAKE
SHAKE
TH... THAT WAS CLOSE...
OH, BOY...
IN SPITE OF MYSELF, I THINK I JUST GOT A TASTE OF HOW HIGASHI AND KUMADA MUST FEEL...
NATSURU SAKAMOTO -- A FORCE TO BE RECKONED WITH!!
HMM... "KUJOU" SOUNDS TOO FORMAL! I'LL JUST CALL YOU SHOUKO!
WHAT A TEASE!!

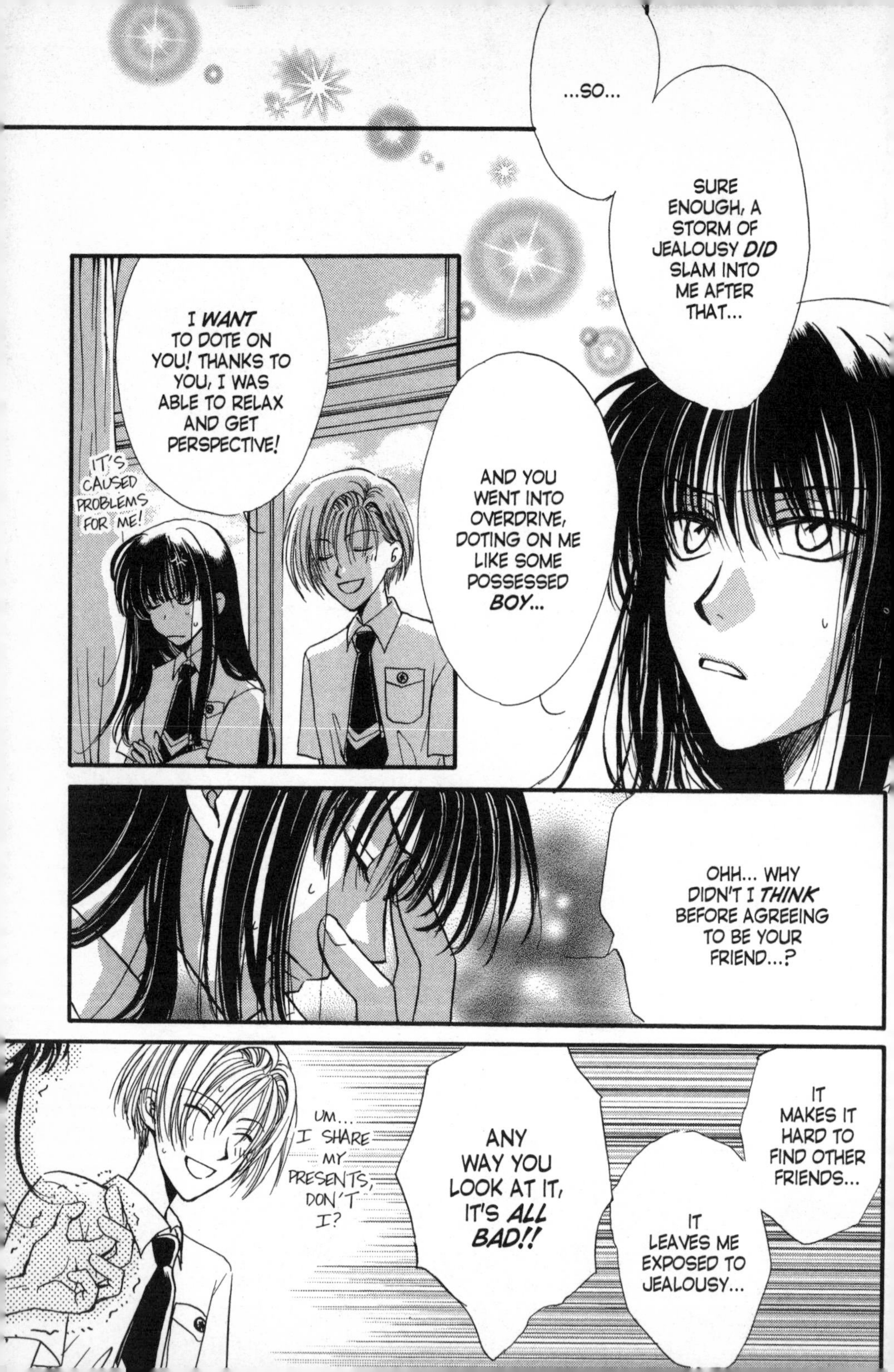
...SO...
SURE ENOUGH, A STORM OF JEALOUSY *DID* SLAM INTO ME AFTER THAT...
AND YOU WENT INTO OVERDRIVE, DOTING ON ME LIKE SOME POSSESSED *BOY*...
I *WANT* TO DOTE ON YOU! THANKS TO YOU, I WAS ABLE TO RELAX AND GET PERSPECTIVE!
IT'S CAUSED PROBLEMS FOR ME!
OHH... WHY DIDN'T I *THINK* BEFORE AGREEING TO BE YOUR FRIEND...?
IT MAKES IT HARD TO FIND OTHER FRIENDS...
IT LEAVES ME EXPOSED TO JEALOUSY...
ANY WAY YOU LOOK AT IT, IT'S *ALL BAD!!*
UM... I SHARE MY PRESENTS, DON'T I?

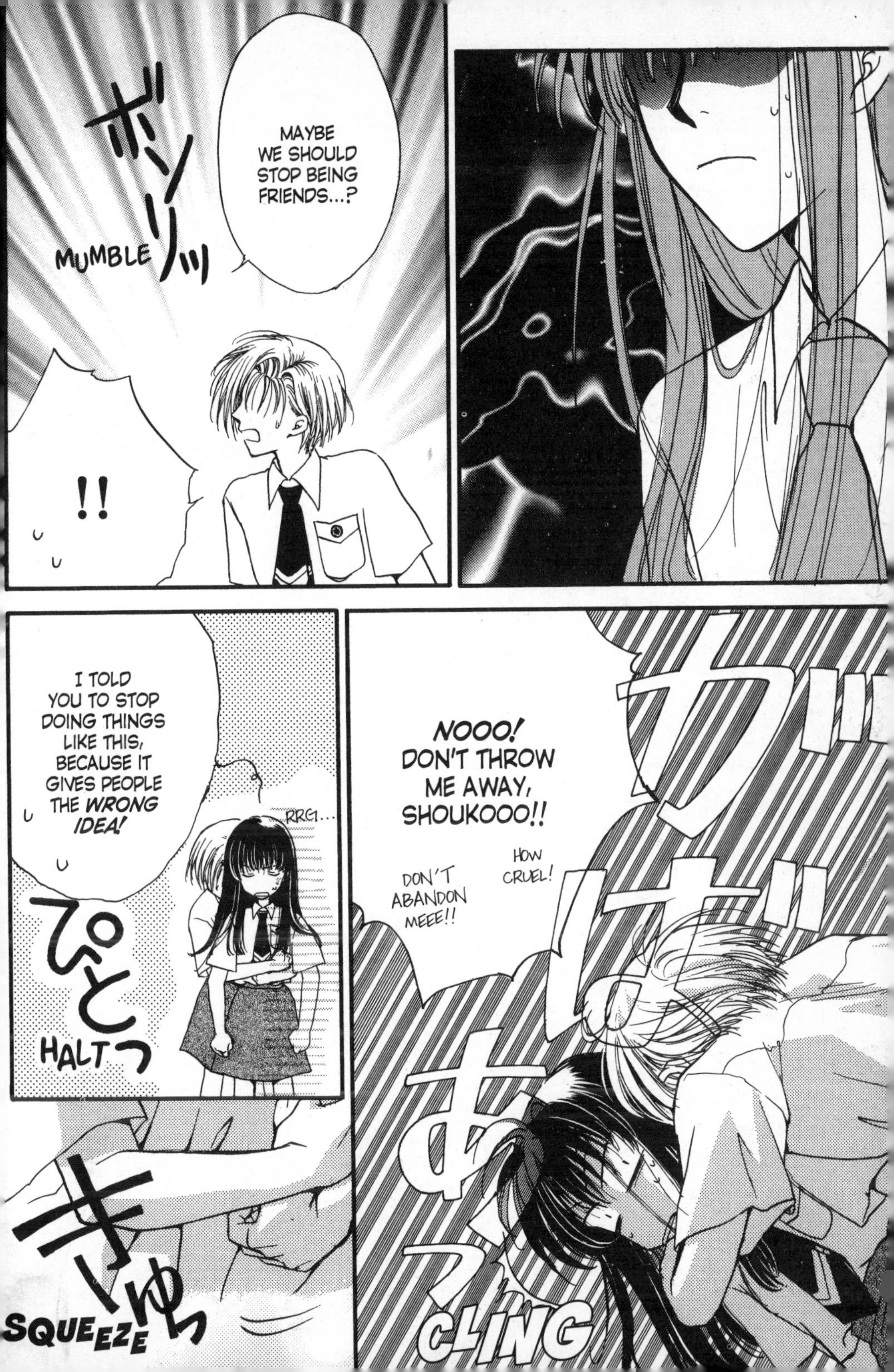
MAYBE WE SHOULD STOP BEING FRIENDS...?
MUMBLE
!!
NOOO! DON'T THROW ME AWAY, SHOUKOOO!!
HOW CRUEL!
DON'T ABANDON MEEE!!
CLING
I TOLD YOU TO STOP DOING THINGS LIKE THIS, BECAUSE IT GIVES PEOPLE THE WRONG IDEA!
RRG...
HALT
SQUEEZE

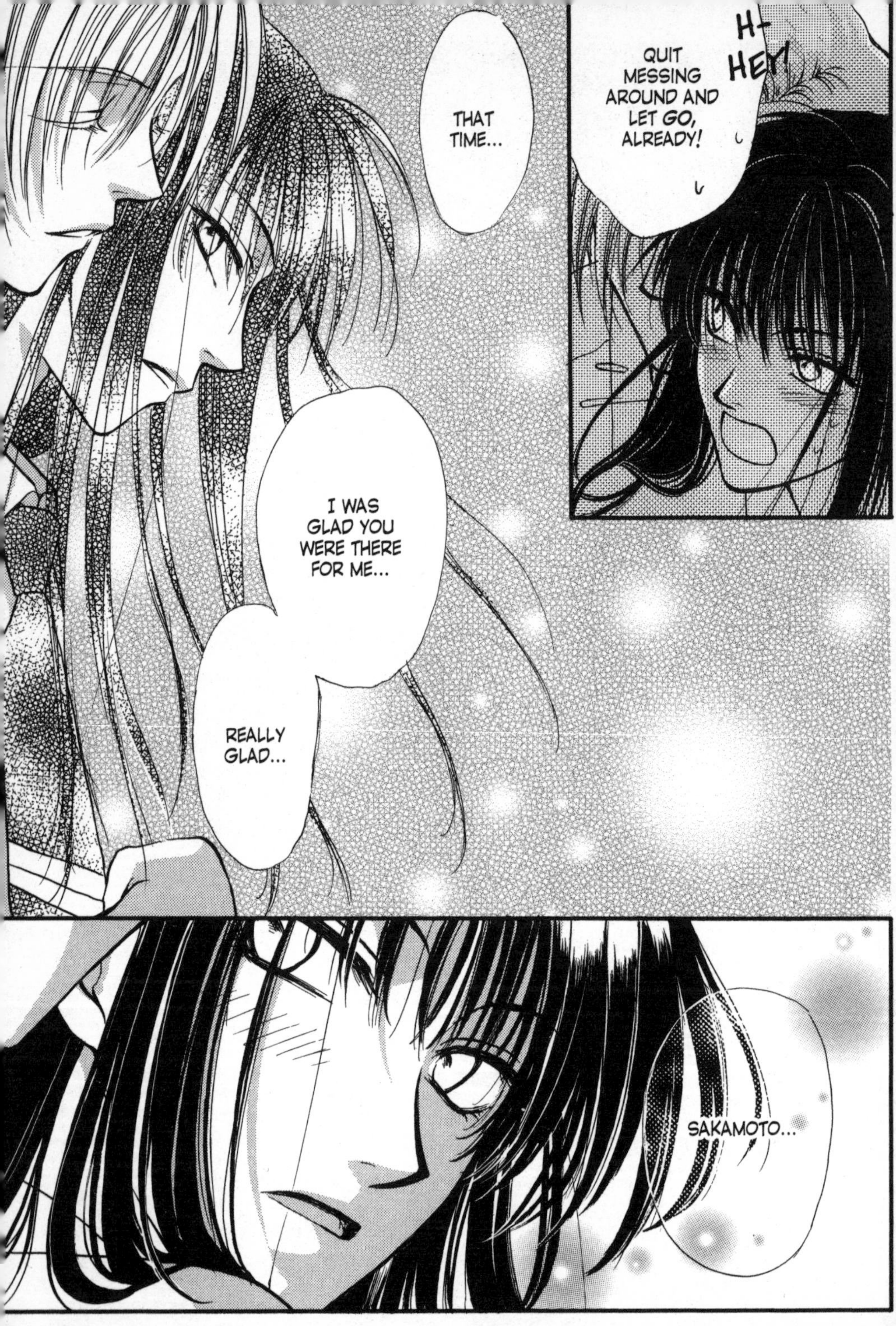
H-HEY!
QUIT MESSING AROUND AND LET GO, ALREADY!
THAT TIME...
I WAS GLAD YOU WERE THERE FOR ME...
REALLY GLAD...
SAKAMOTO...

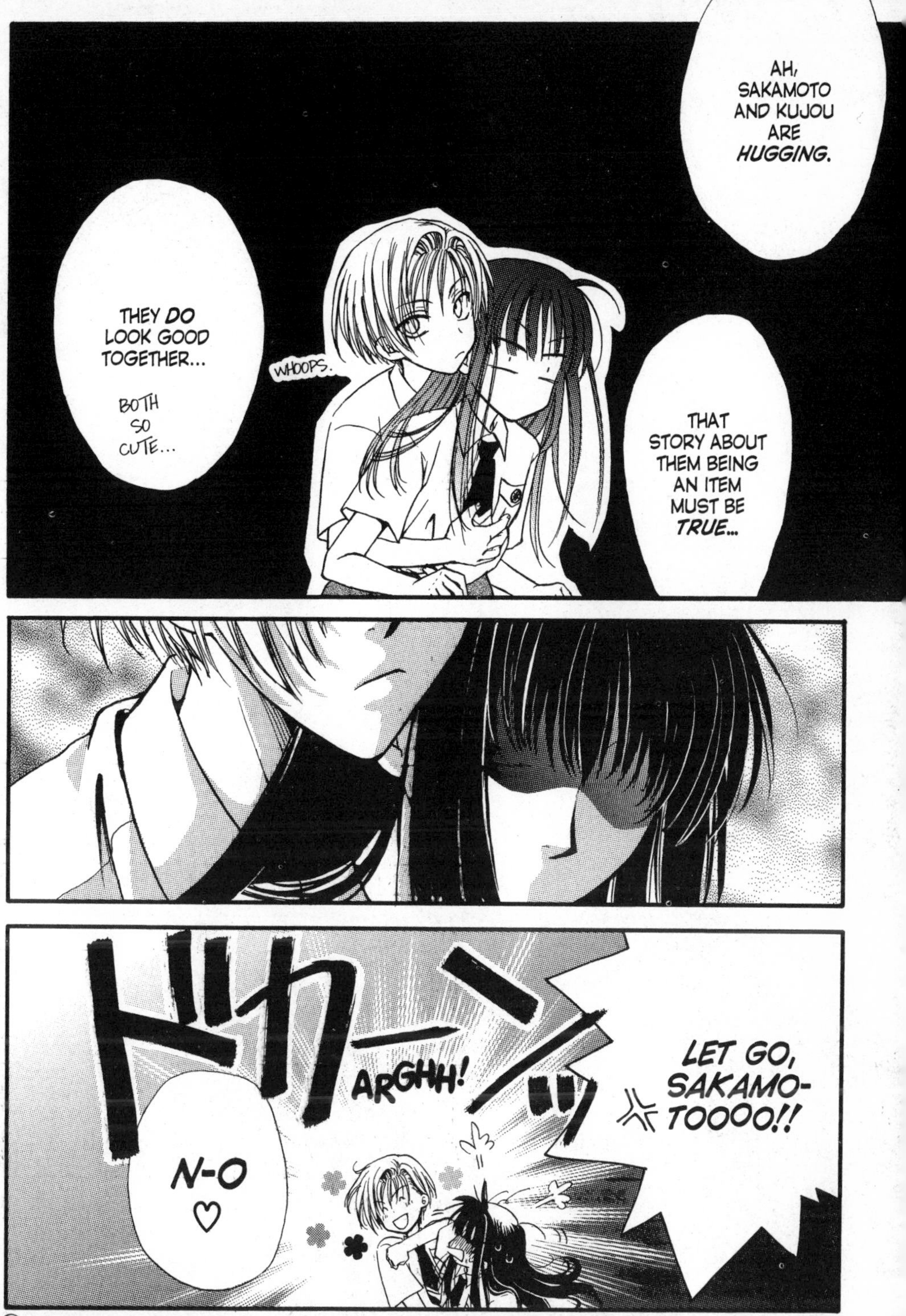
AH, SAKAMOTO AND KUJOU ARE *HUGGING*.
THAT STORY ABOUT THEM BEING AN ITEM MUST BE *TRUE*...
THEY *DO* LOOK GOOD TOGETHER...
BOTH SO CUTE...
WHOOPS.
ドカーンッ
LET GO, SAKAMO-TOOOO!!
ARGHH!
N-O ♡

FAMILY COMPLEX - FIRST DAUGHTER • NATSURU ✷ END

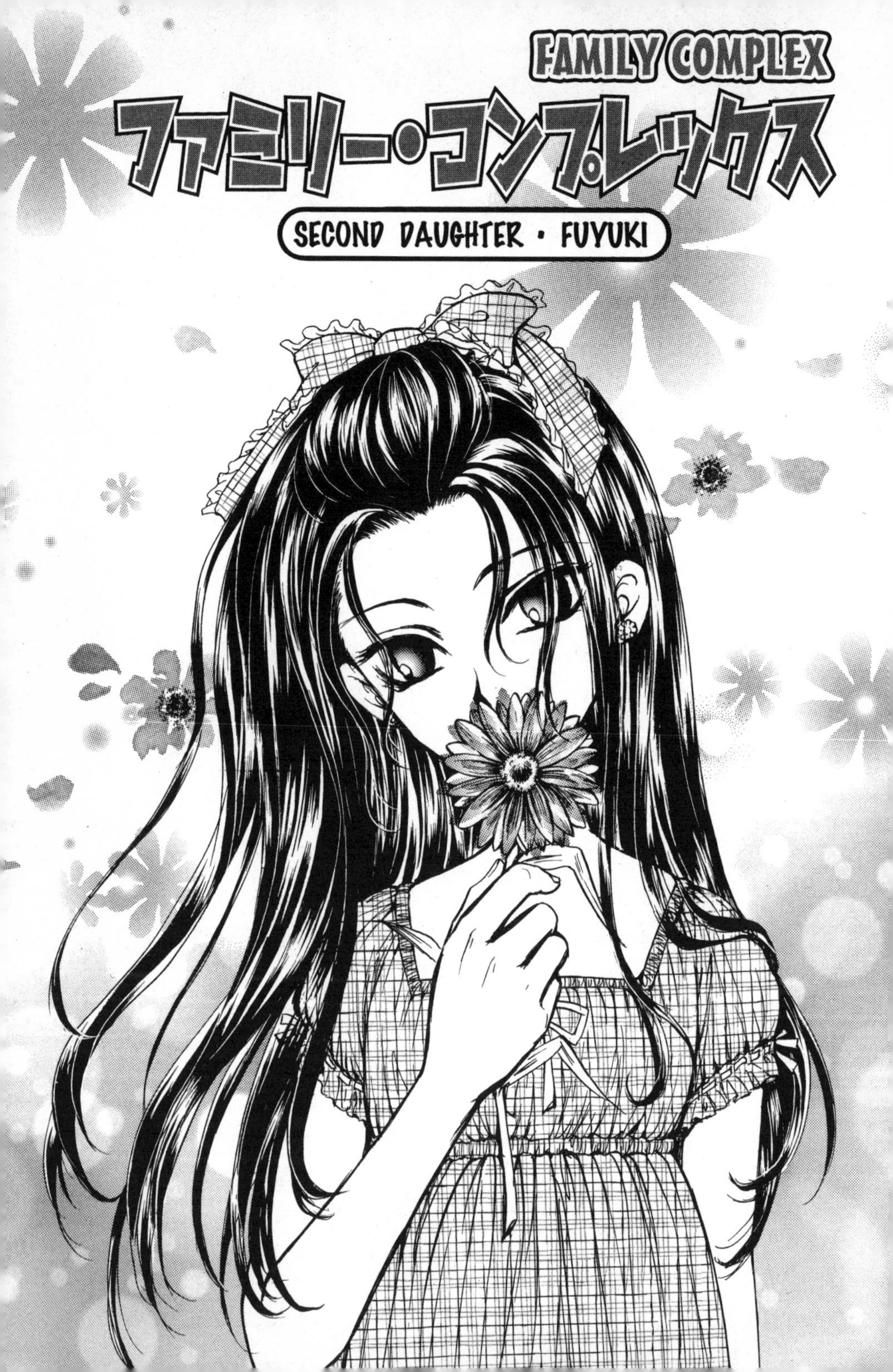
FAMILY COMPLEX
ファミリー・コンプレックス
SECOND DAUGHTER • FUYUKI

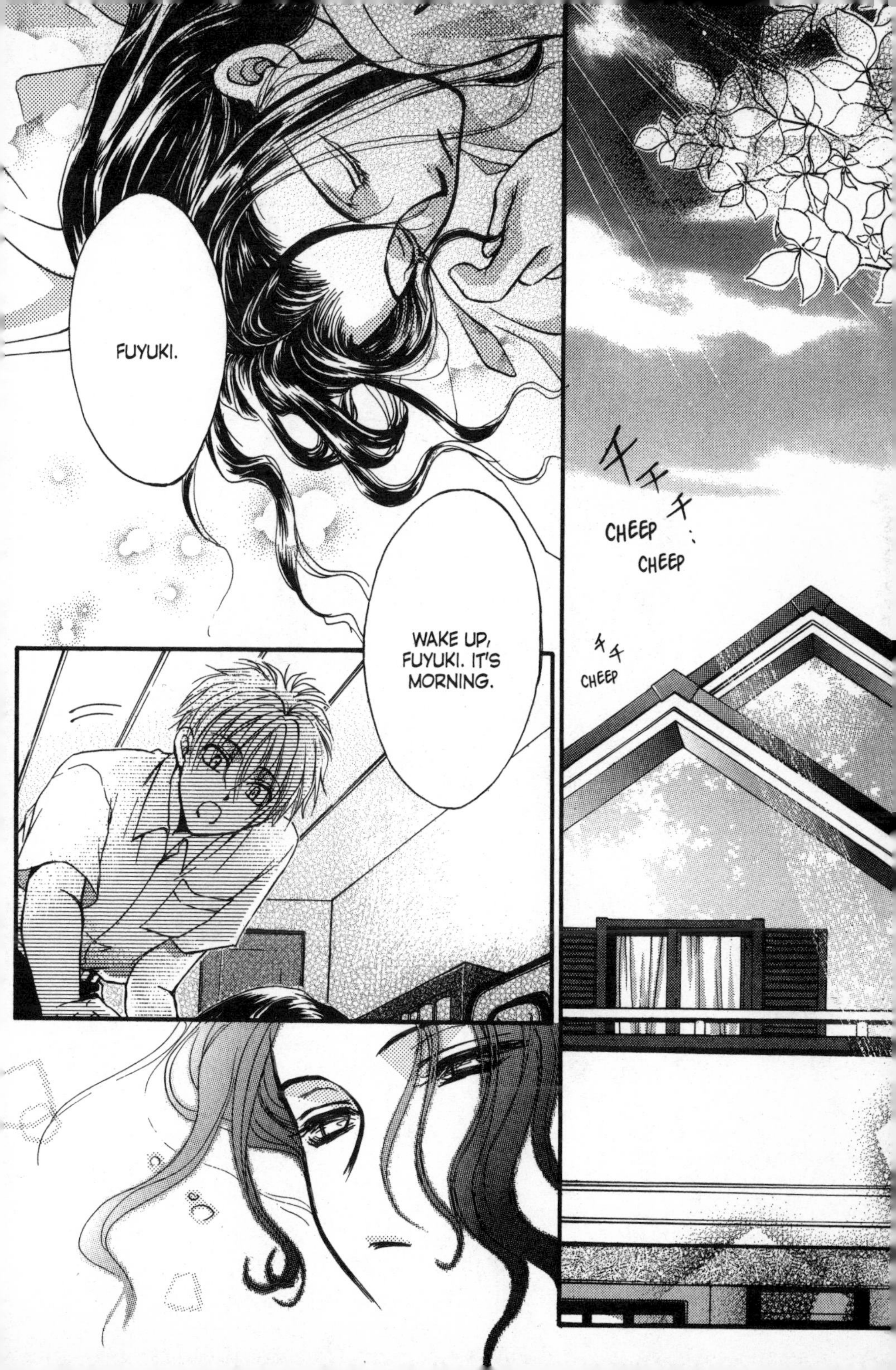

チチチ…
CHEEP
CHEEP
チチ
CHEEP
FUYUKI.
WAKE UP, FUYUKI. IT'S MORNING.

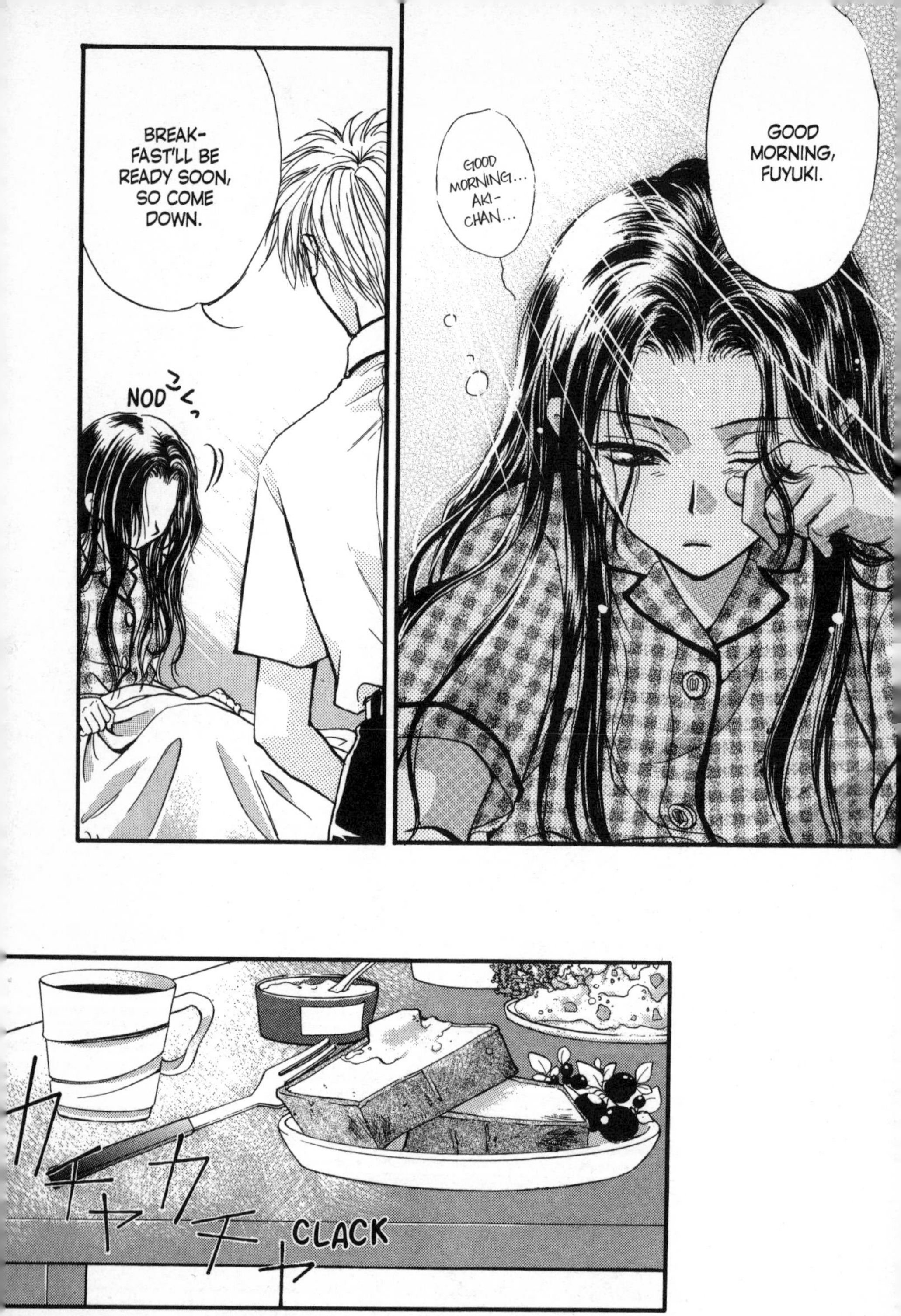
GOOD MORNING, FUYUKI.
GOOD MORNING... AKI-CHAN...
BREAK-FAST'LL BE READY SOON, SO COME DOWN.
NOD こくっ
カチャカチャ
CLACK

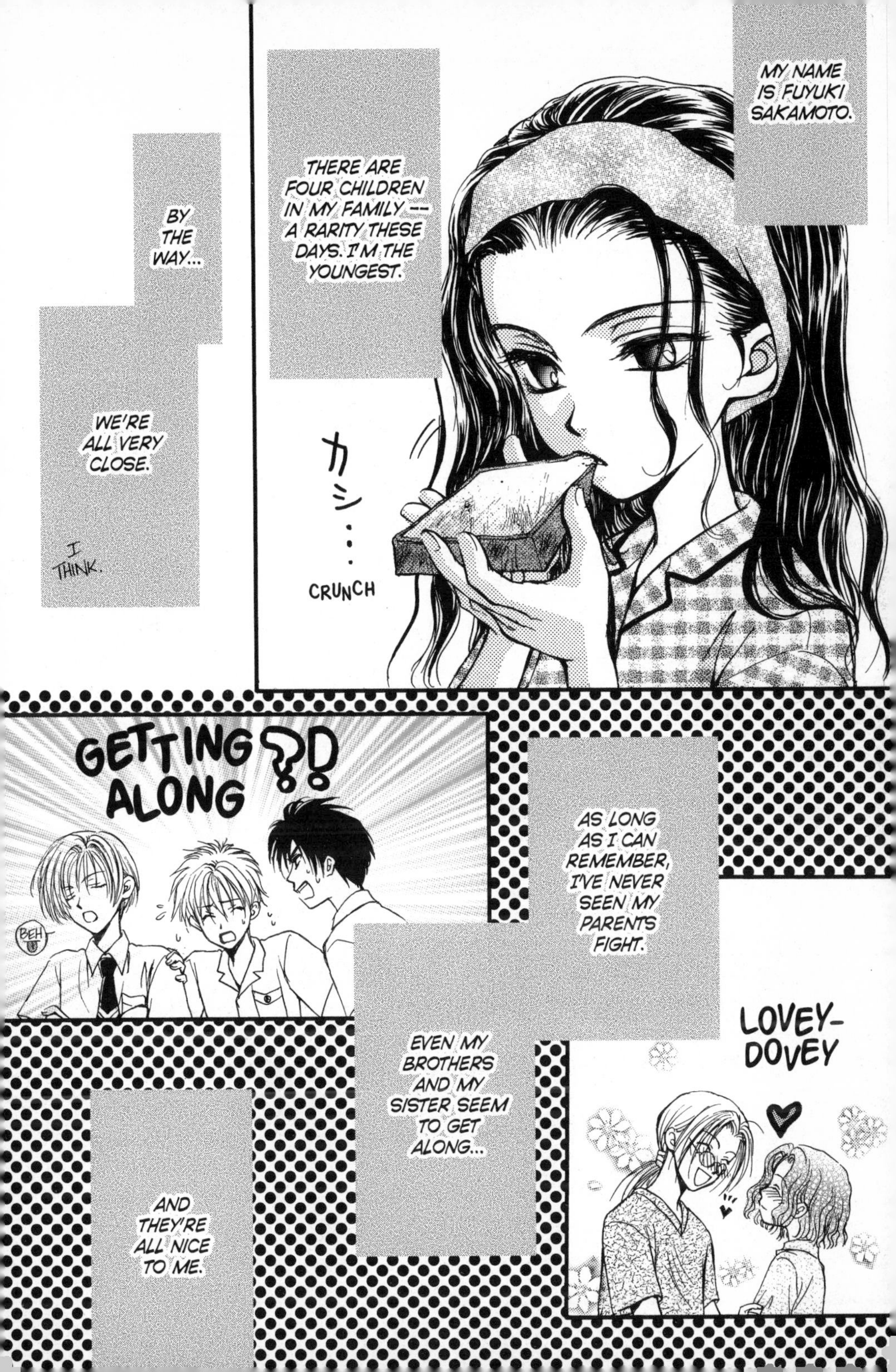

MY NAME IS FUYUKI SAKAMOTO.
THERE ARE FOUR CHILDREN IN MY FAMILY -- A RARITY THESE DAYS. I'M THE YOUNGEST.
カシ...
CRUNCH
BY THE WAY...
WE'RE ALL VERY CLOSE.
I THINK.
AS LONG AS I CAN REMEMBER, I'VE NEVER SEEN MY PARENTS FIGHT.
LOVEY-DOVEY
EVEN MY BROTHERS AND MY SISTER SEEM TO GET ALONG...
GETTING ALONG?!
BEH
AND THEY'RE ALL NICE TO ME.

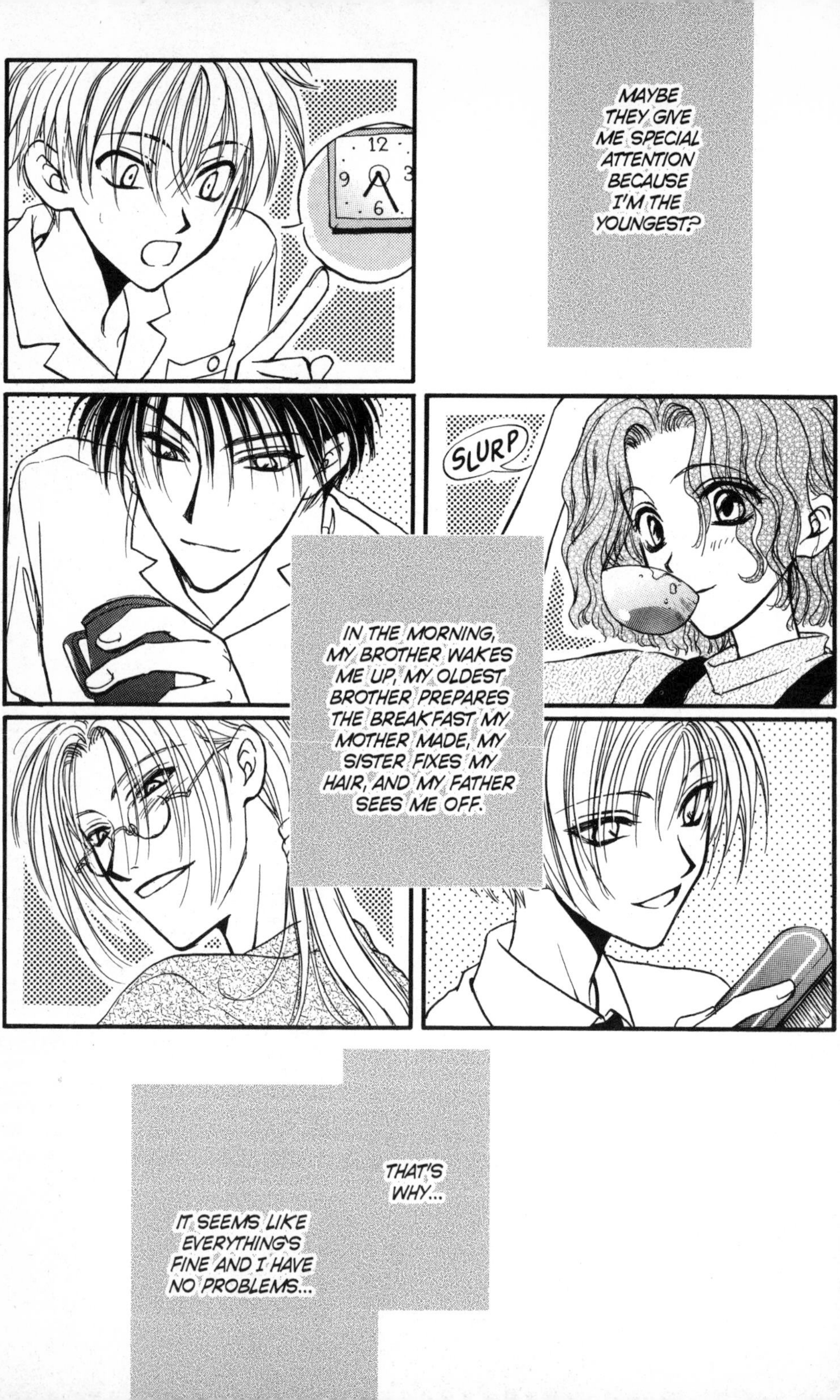
MAYBE THEY GIVE ME SPECIAL ATTENTION BECAUSE I'M THE YOUNGEST?
SLURP
IN THE MORNING, MY BROTHER WAKES ME UP, MY OLDEST BROTHER PREPARES THE BREAKFAST MY MOTHER MADE, MY SISTER FIXES MY HAIR, AND MY FATHER SEES ME OFF.
THAT'S WHY...
IT SEEMS LIKE EVERYTHING'S FINE AND I HAVE NO PROBLEMS...

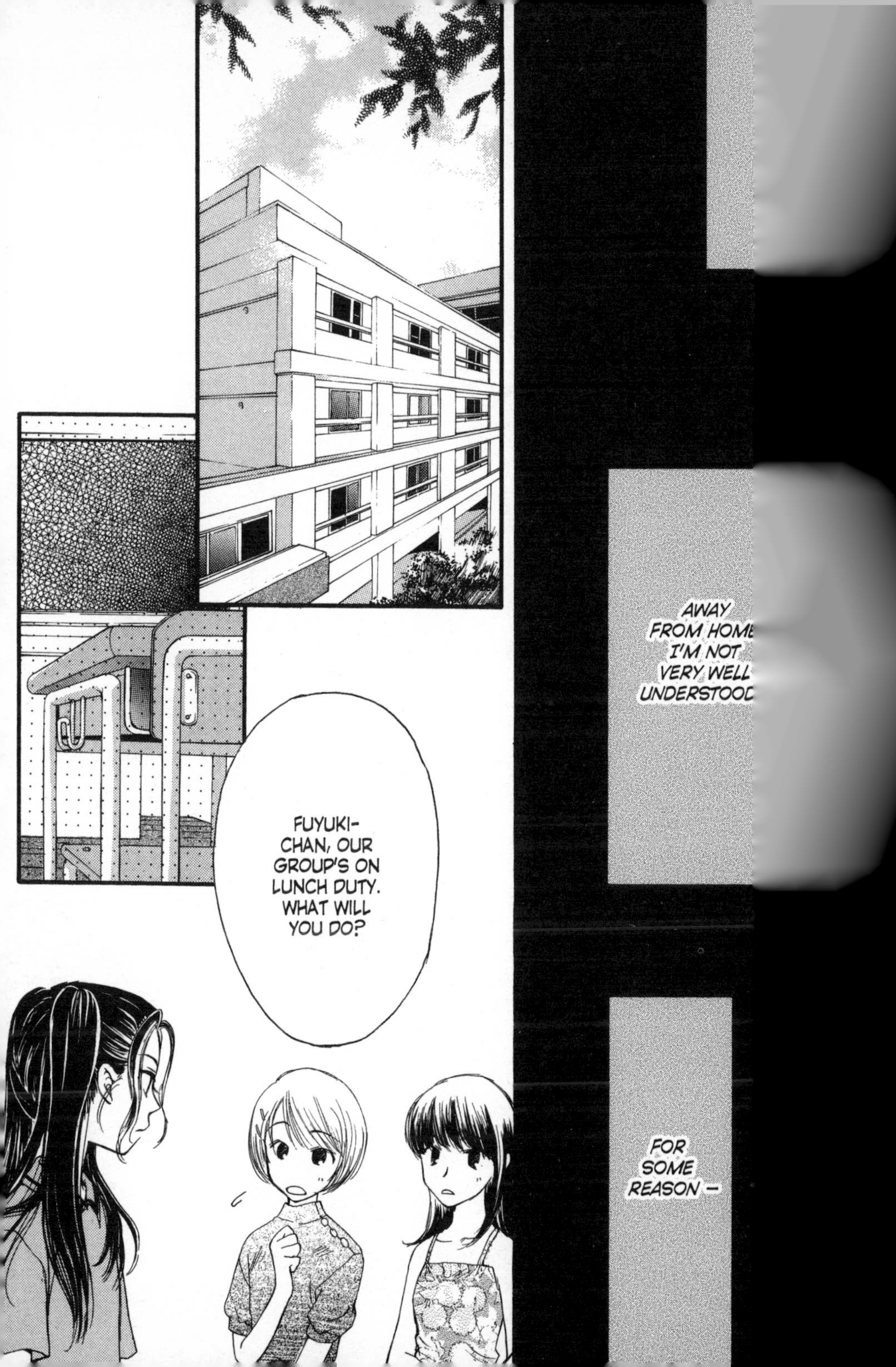
AWAY FROM HOME I'M NOT VERY WELL UNDERSTOOD
FOR SOME REASON –
FUYUKI-CHAN, OUR GROUP'S ON LUNCH DUTY. WHAT WILL YOU DO?

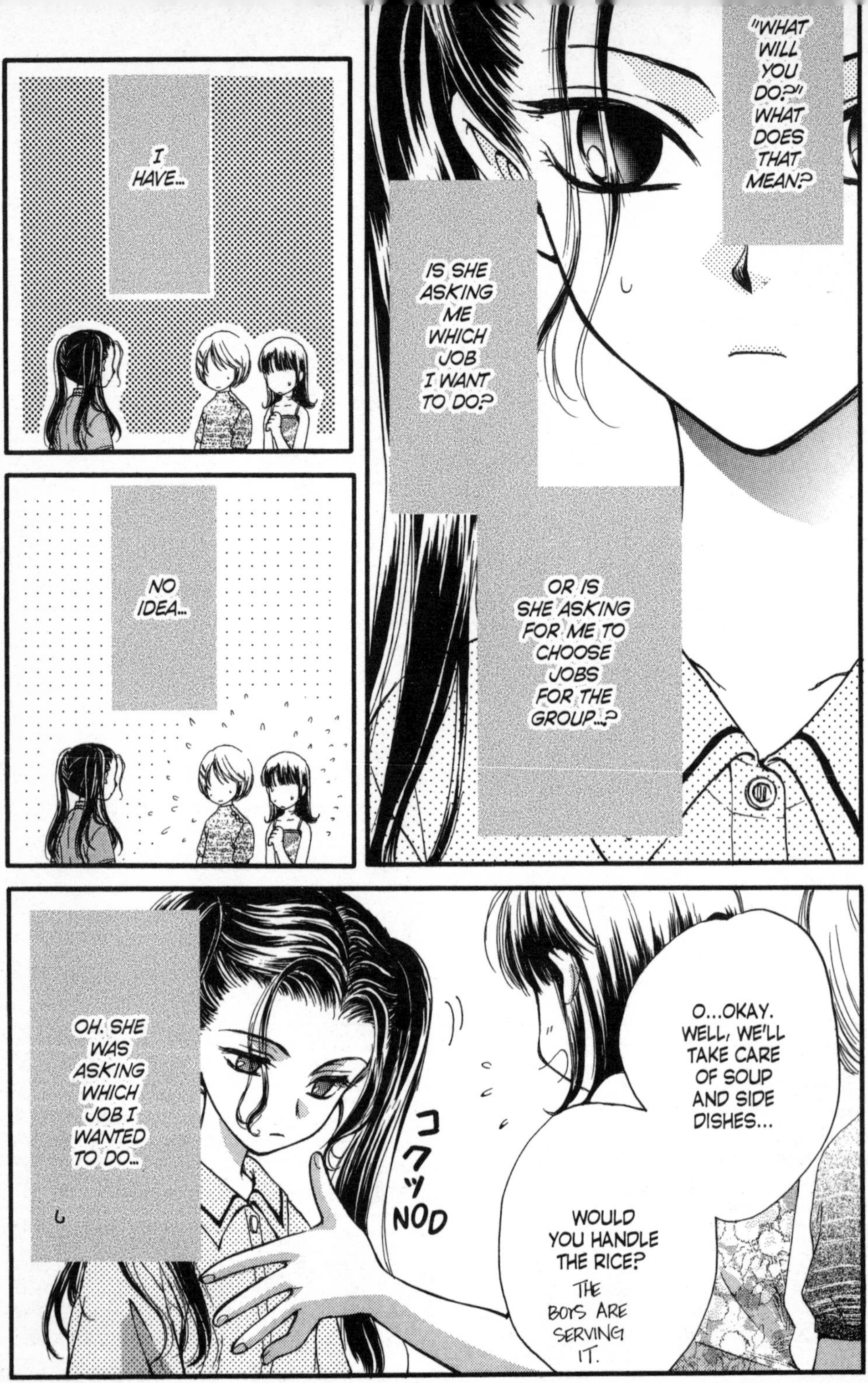
"WHAT WILL YOU DO?" WHAT DOES THAT MEAN?
IS SHE ASKING ME WHICH JOB I WANT TO DO?
OR IS SHE ASKING FOR ME TO CHOOSE JOBS FOR THE GROUP...?
I HAVE...
NO IDEA...
O...OKAY. WELL, WE'LL TAKE CARE OF SOUP AND SIDE DISHES...
WOULD YOU HANDLE THE RICE?
THE BOYS ARE SERVING IT.
コクッ
NOD
OH. SHE WAS ASKING WHICH JOB I WANTED TO DO...

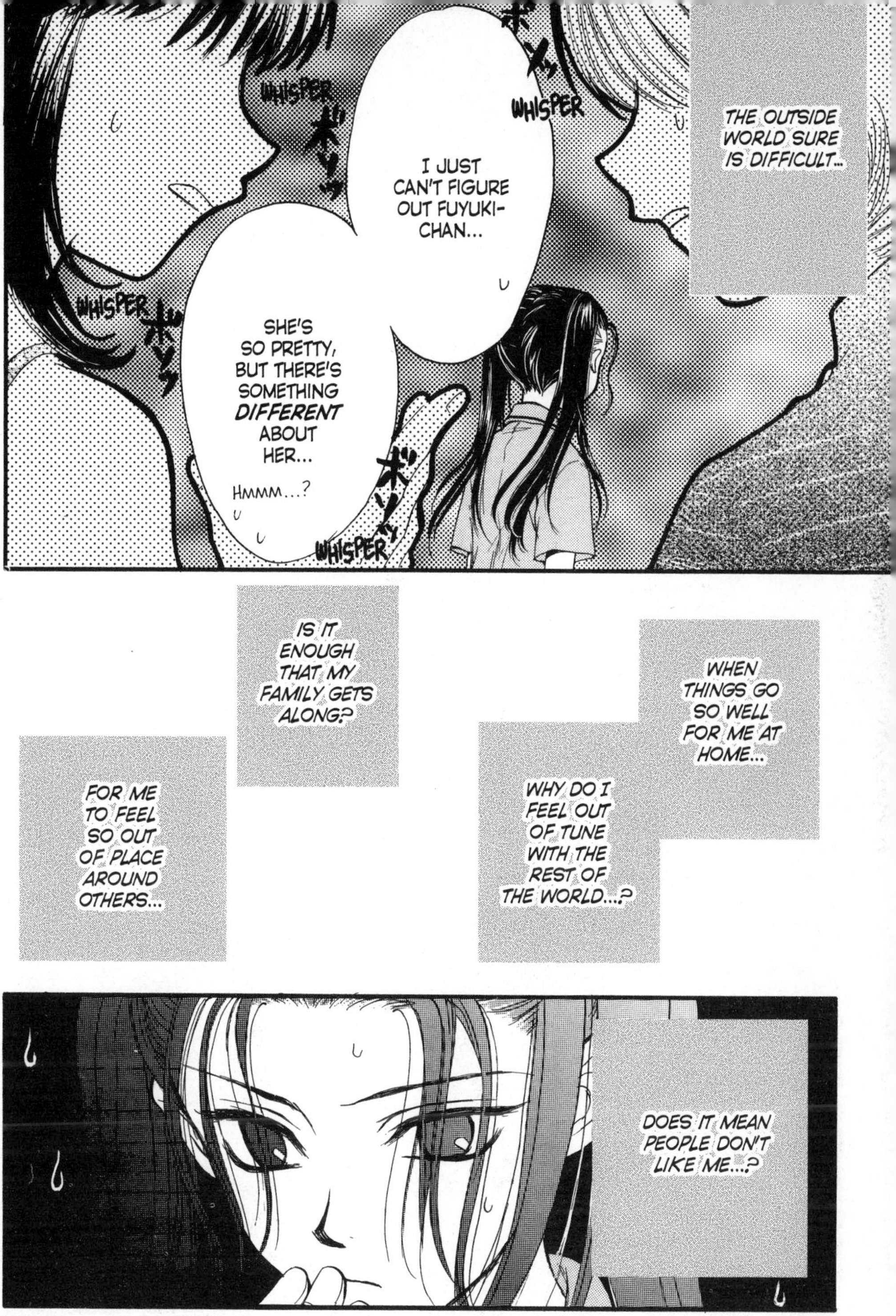
THE OUTSIDE WORLD SURE IS DIFFICULT...
WHISPER
WHISPER
I JUST CAN'T FIGURE OUT FUYUKI-CHAN...
WHISPER
SHE'S SO PRETTY, BUT THERE'S SOMETHING ***DIFFERENT*** ABOUT HER...
HMMM...?
WHISPER
WHEN THINGS GO SO WELL FOR ME AT HOME...
WHY DO I FEEL OUT OF TUNE WITH THE REST OF THE WORLD...?
IS IT ENOUGH THAT MY FAMILY GETS ALONG?
FOR ME TO FEEL SO OUT OF PLACE AROUND OTHERS...
DOES IT MEAN PEOPLE DON'T LIKE ME...?

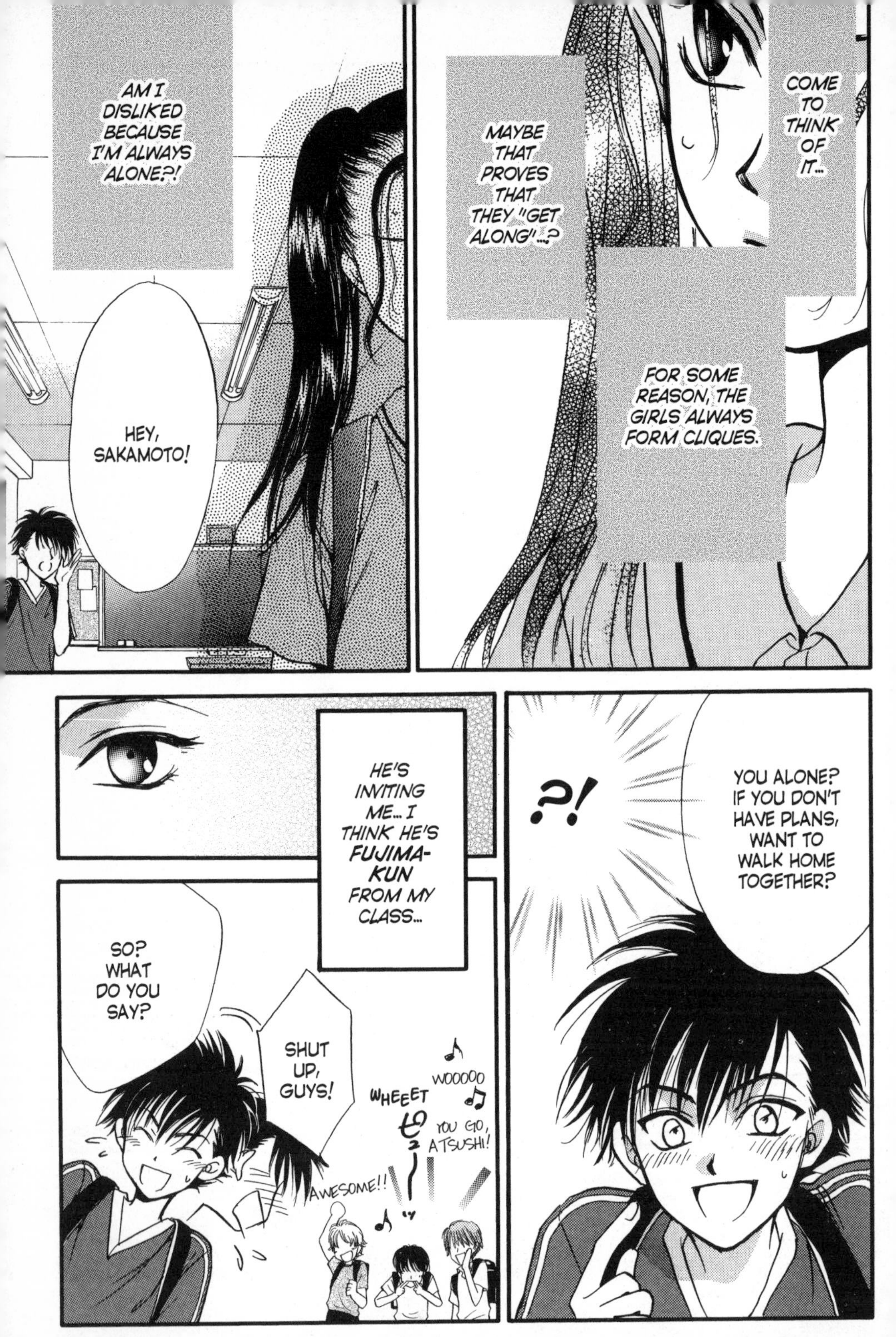
COME TO THINK OF IT...
FOR SOME REASON, THE GIRLS ALWAYS FORM CLIQUES.
MAYBE THAT PROVES THAT THEY "GET ALONG"...?
AM I DISLIKED BECAUSE I'M ALWAYS ALONE?!
HEY, SAKAMOTO!
?!
YOU ALONE? IF YOU DON'T HAVE PLANS, WANT TO WALK HOME TOGETHER?
HE'S INVITING ME... I THINK HE'S FUJIMA-KUN FROM MY CLASS...
SO? WHAT DO YOU SAY?
WOOOOO
WHEEET
YOU GO, ATSUSHI!
AWESOME!!
SHUT UP, GUYS!

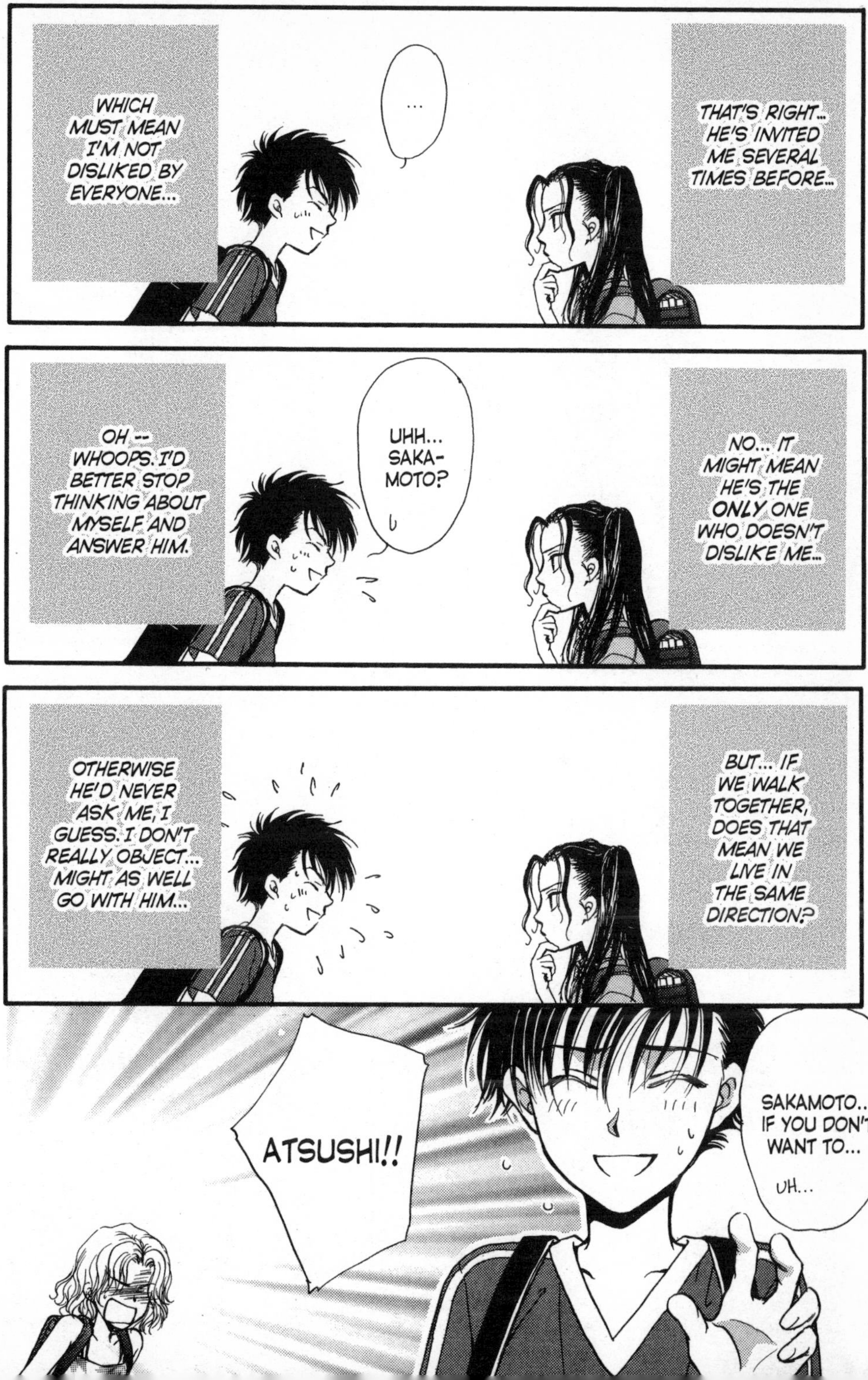

THAT'S RIGHT... HE'S INVITED ME SEVERAL TIMES BEFORE...
...
WHICH MUST MEAN I'M NOT DISLIKED BY EVERYONE...
NO... IT MIGHT MEAN HE'S THE ONLY ONE WHO DOESN'T DISLIKE ME...
UHH... SAKAMOTO?
OH -- WHOOPS. I'D BETTER STOP THINKING ABOUT MYSELF AND ANSWER HIM.
BUT... IF WE WALK TOGETHER, DOES THAT MEAN WE LIVE IN THE SAME DIRECTION?
OTHERWISE HE'D NEVER ASK ME, I GUESS. I DON'T REALLY OBJECT... MIGHT AS WELL GO WITH HIM...
SAKAMOTO... IF YOU DON'T WANT TO...
UH...
ATSUSHI!!

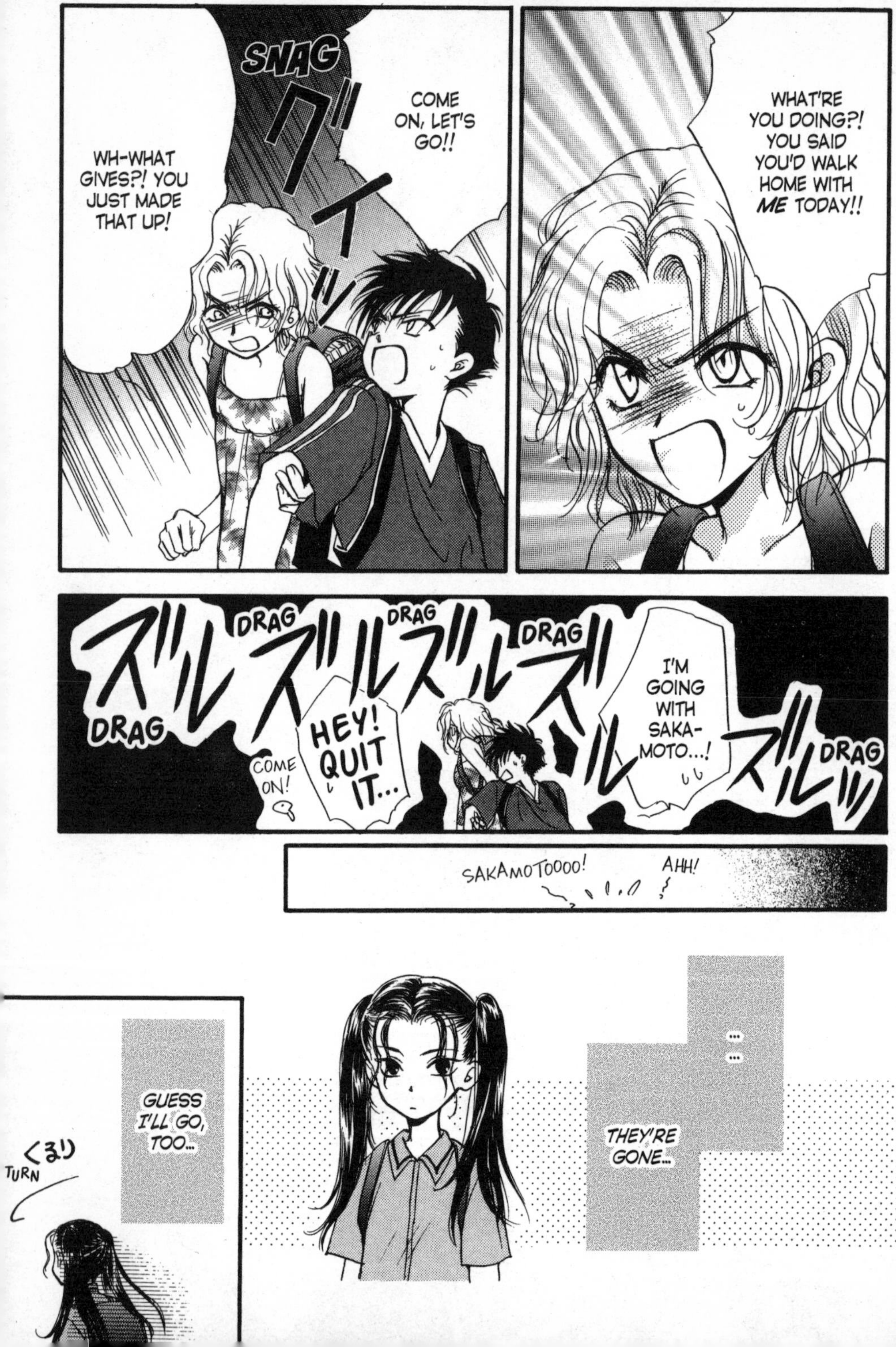

WHAT'RE YOU DOING?! YOU SAID YOU'D WALK HOME WITH ME TODAY!!
SNAG
COME ON, LET'S GO!!
WH-WHAT GIVES?! YOU JUST MADE THAT UP!
DRAG
I'M GOING WITH SAKA-MOTO...!
DRAG
DRAG
HEY! QUIT IT...
COME ON!
DRAG
AHH!
SAKAMOTOOOO!
...
...
THEY'RE GONE...
くるり
TURN
GUESS I'LL GO, TOO...

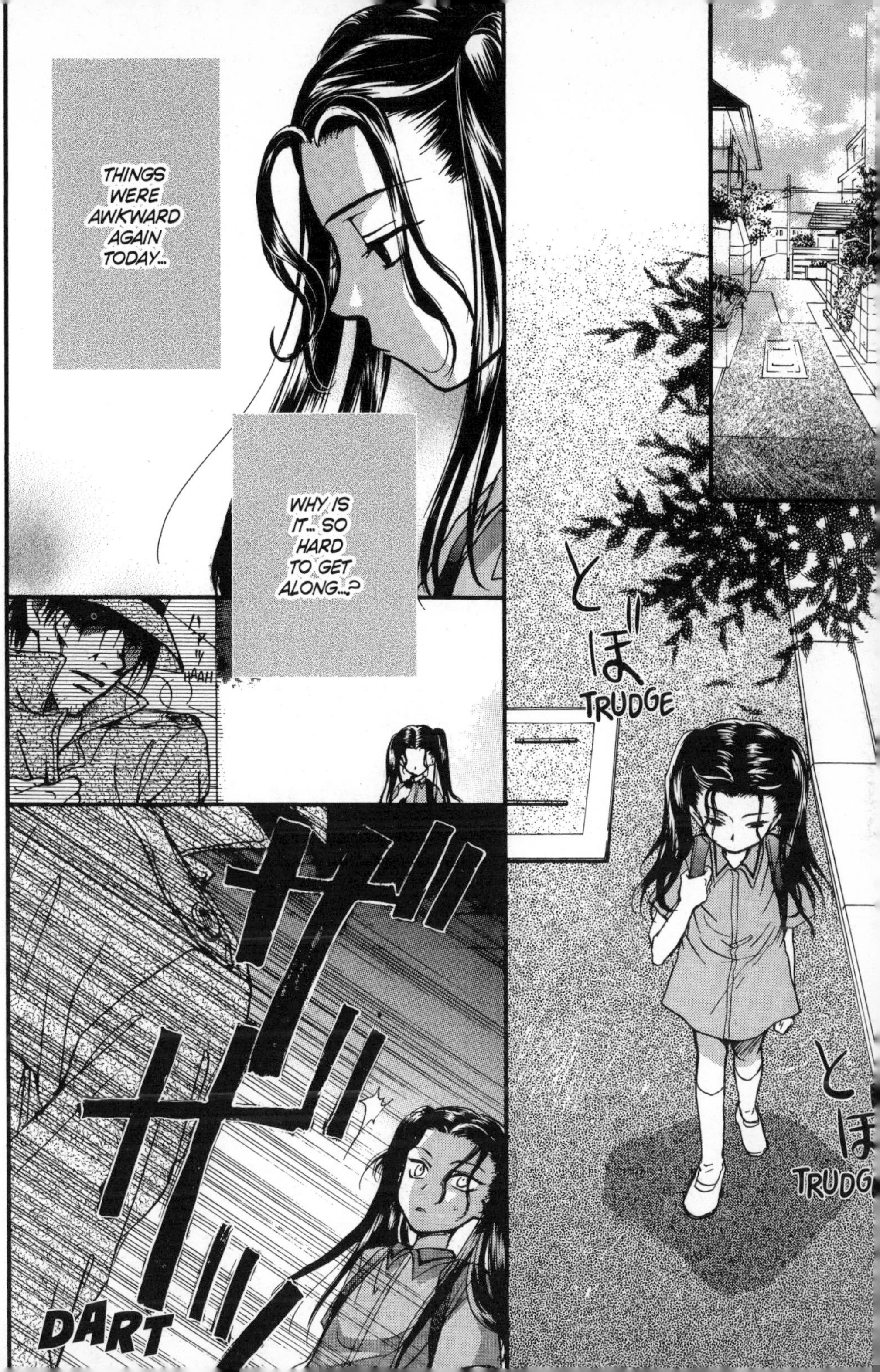

とぼ
TRUDGE
とほ
TRUDG
THINGS WERE AWKWARD AGAIN TODAY...
WHY IS IT... SO HARD TO GET ALONG...?
ハァッ
HAAH
ザザッ
DART

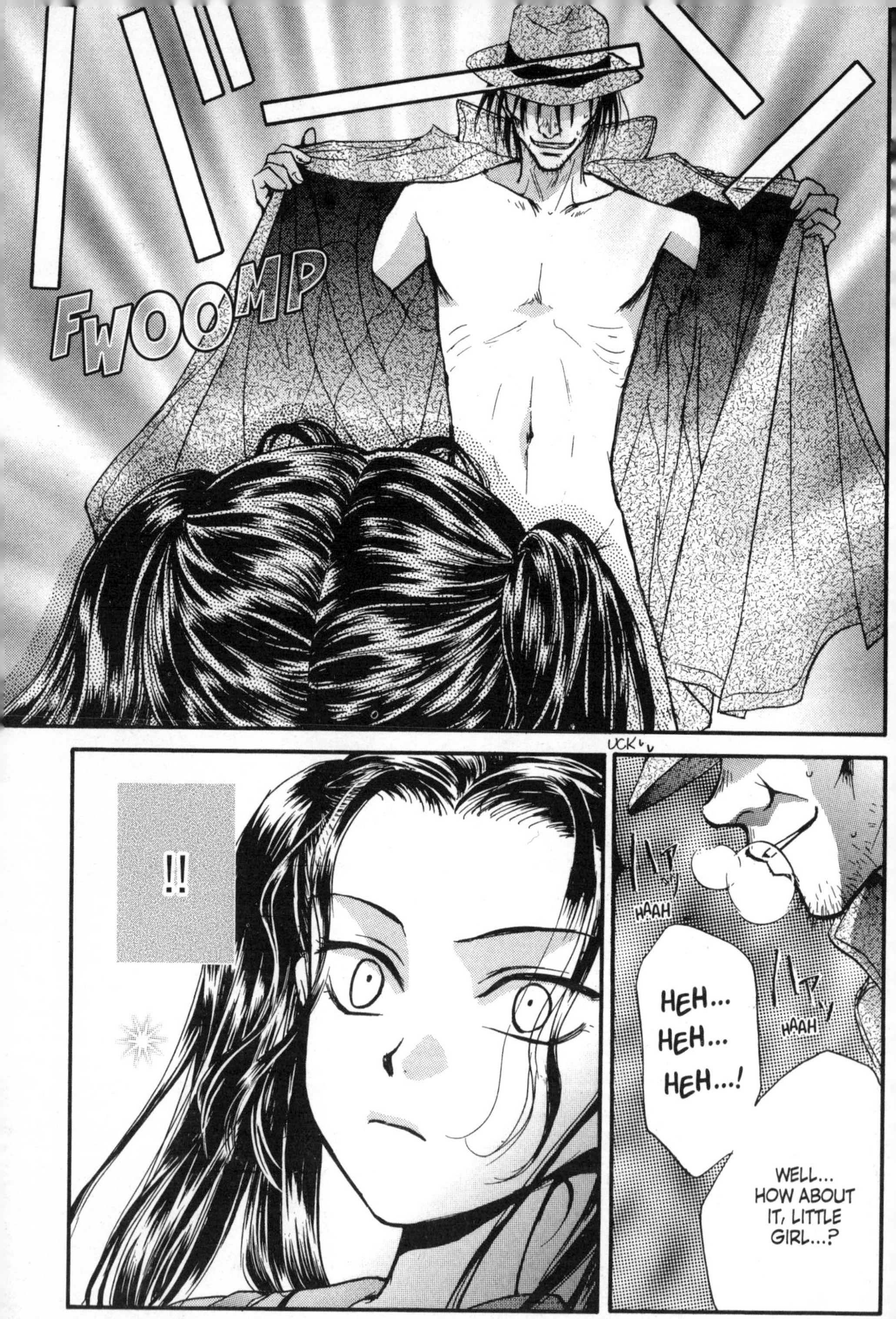
FWOOMP
UCK
HAAH
HAAH
HEH... HEH... HEH...!
WELL... HOW ABOUT IT, LITTLE GIRL...?
!!

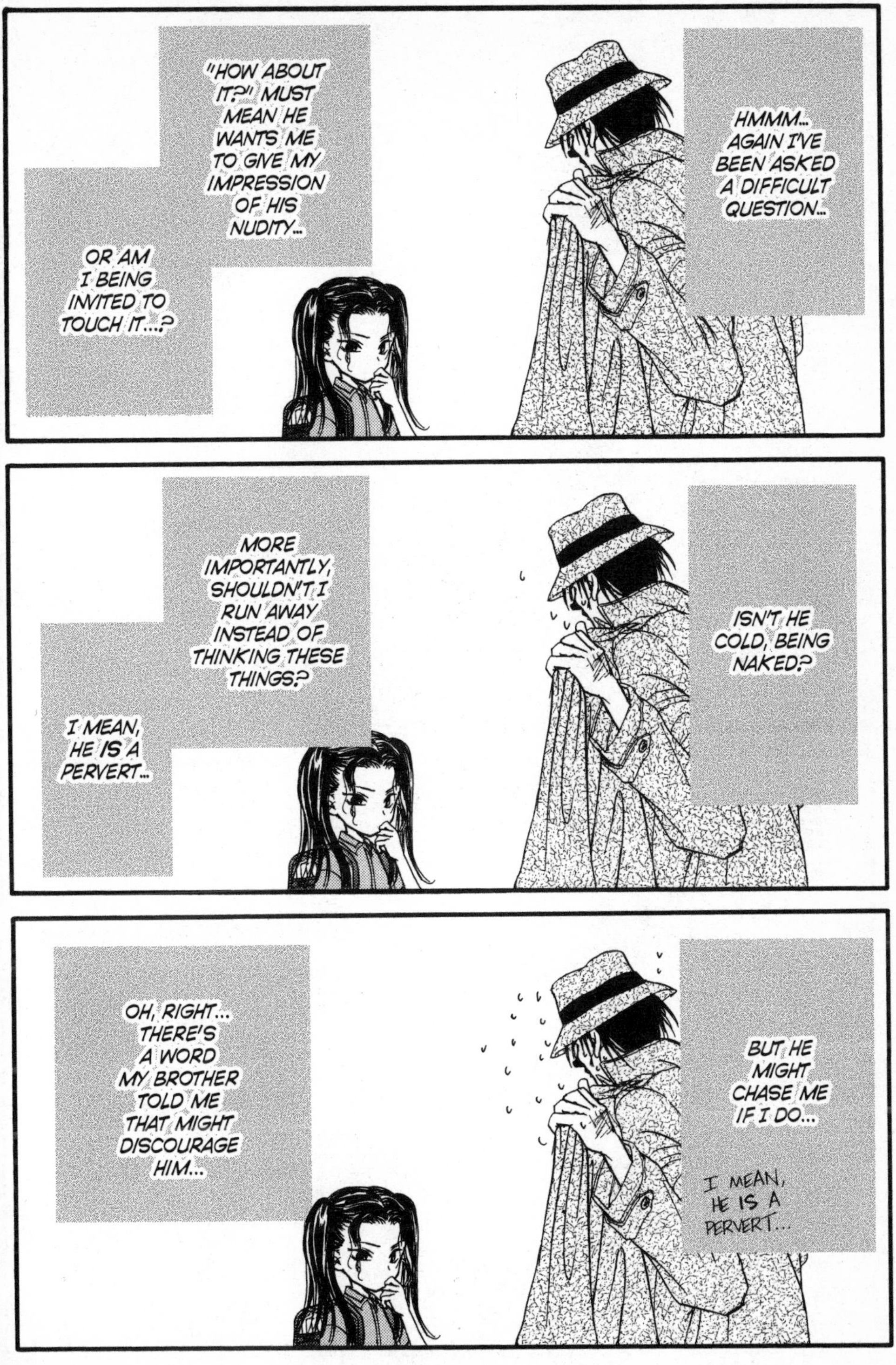
HMMM... AGAIN I'VE BEEN ASKED A DIFFICULT QUESTION...
"HOW ABOUT IT?" MUST MEAN HE WANTS ME TO GIVE MY IMPRESSION OF HIS NUDITY...
OR AM I BEING INVITED TO TOUCH IT...?
ISN'T HE COLD, BEING NAKED?
MORE IMPORTANTLY, SHOULDN'T I RUN AWAY INSTEAD OF THINKING THESE THINGS?
I MEAN, HE IS A PERVERT...
BUT HE MIGHT CHASE ME IF I DO...
I MEAN, HE IS A PERVERT...
OH, RIGHT... THERE'S A WORD MY BROTHER TOLD ME THAT MIGHT DISCOURAGE HIM...

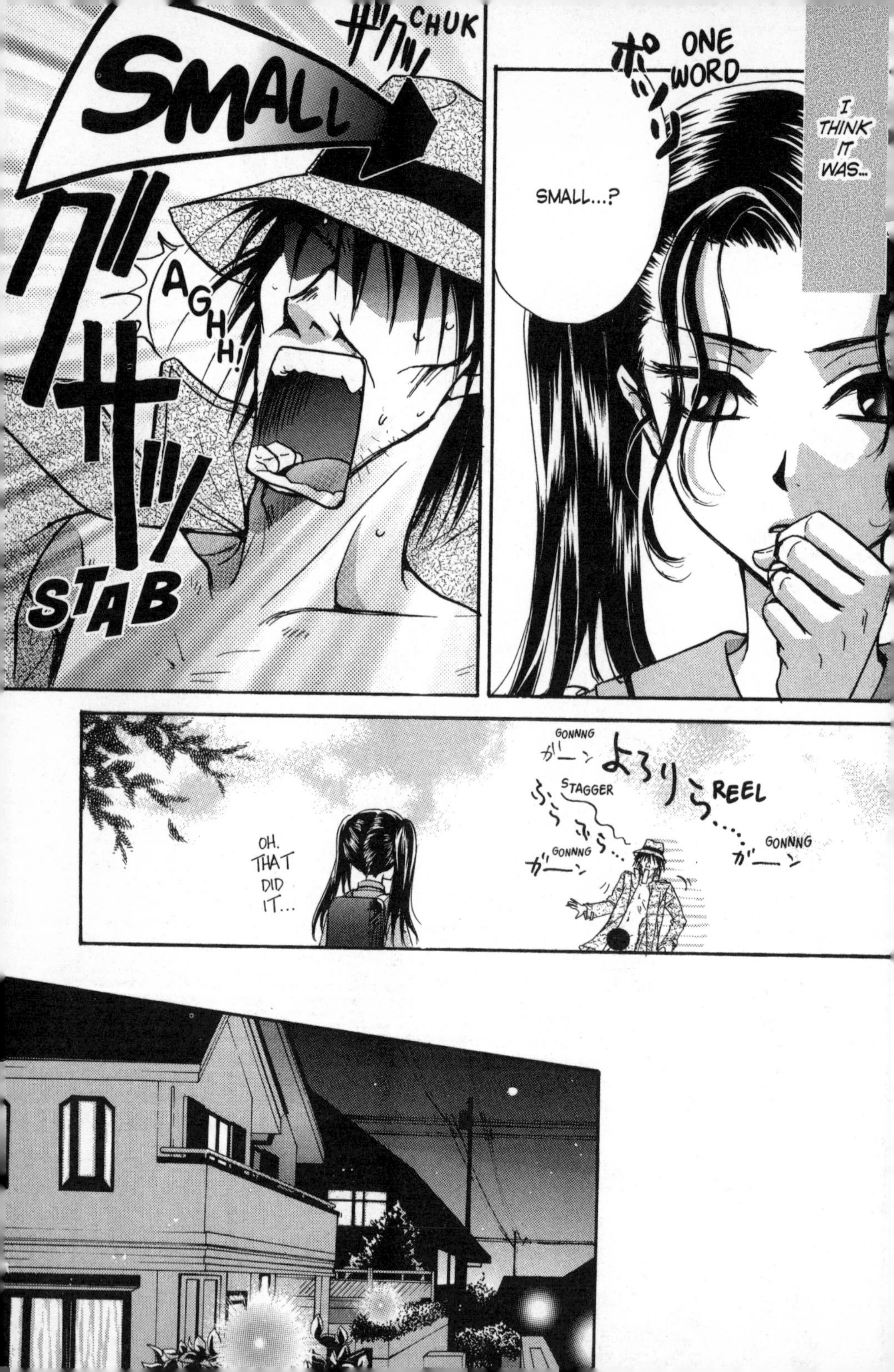
I THINK IT WAS...
ONE WORD
SMALL...?
SMALL
CHUK
AGHHH!
STAB
GONNNG
ガーン
よろり
REEL
GONNNG
ガーン
STAGGER
GONNNG
ガーン
OH. THAT DID IT...

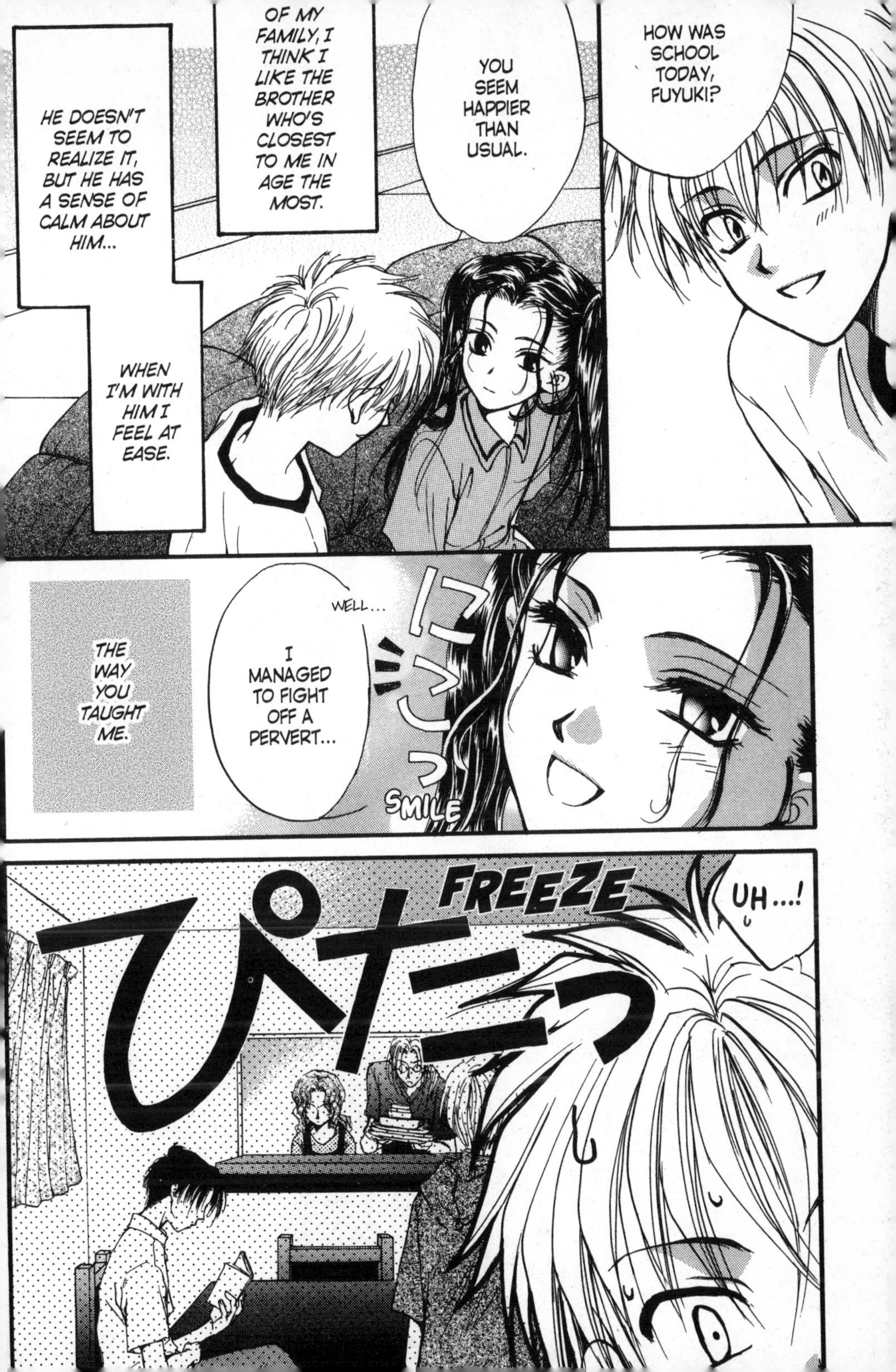
HOW WAS SCHOOL TODAY, FUYUKI?
YOU SEEM HAPPIER THAN USUAL.
OF MY FAMILY, I THINK I LIKE THE BROTHER WHO'S CLOSEST TO ME IN AGE THE MOST.
HE DOESN'T SEEM TO REALIZE IT, BUT HE HAS A SENSE OF CALM ABOUT HIM...
WHEN I'M WITH HIM I FEEL AT EASE.
WELL...
I MANAGED TO FIGHT OFF A PERVERT...
SMILE
THE WAY YOU TAUGHT ME.
UH...!
FREEZE

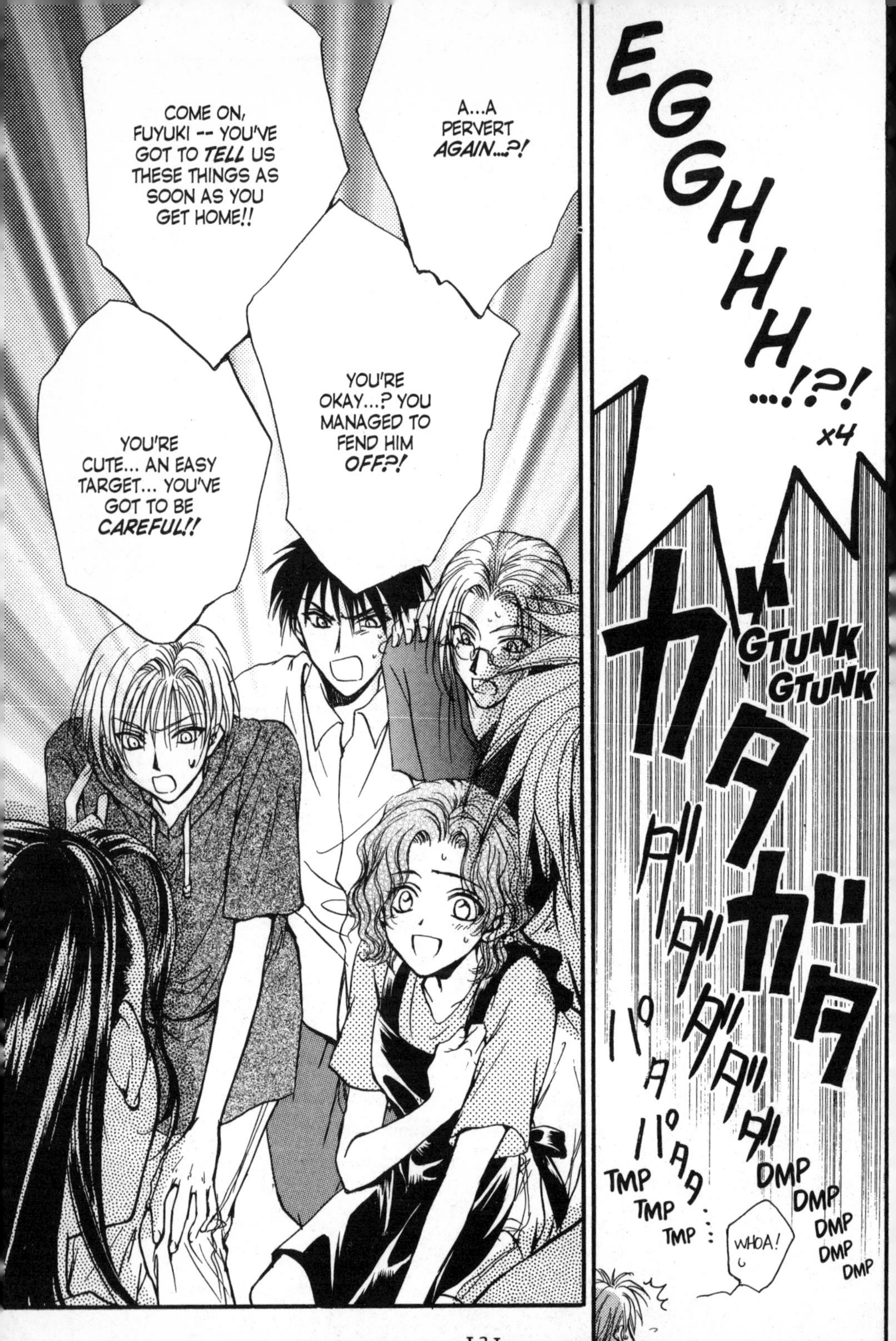
EGGHHHH....!?!
x4
ガタガタ
GTUNK GTUNK
ダダダダダダ
パタパタ
TMP TMP TMP
DMP DMP DMP DMP DMP
WHOA!
A...A PERVERT AGAIN...?!
COME ON, FUYUKI -- YOU'VE GOT TO TELL US THESE THINGS AS SOON AS YOU GET HOME!!
YOU'RE OKAY...? YOU MANAGED TO FEND HIM OFF?!
YOU'RE CUTE... AN EASY TARGET... YOU'VE GOT TO BE CAREFUL!!

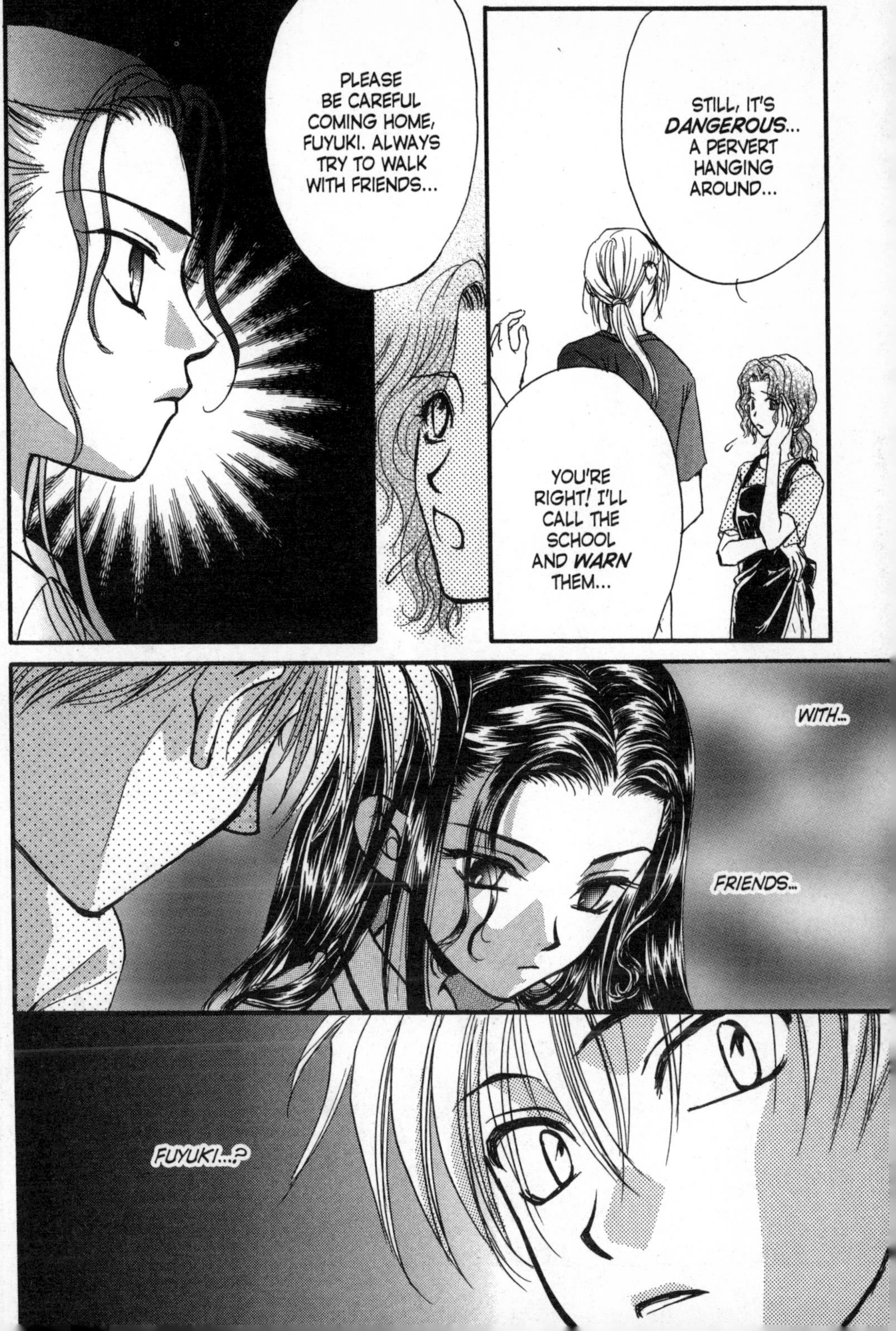
STILL, IT'S *DANGEROUS*... A PERVERT HANGING AROUND...
YOU'RE RIGHT! I'LL CALL THE SCHOOL AND *WARN* THEM...
PLEASE BE CAREFUL COMING HOME, FUYUKI. ALWAYS TRY TO WALK WITH FRIENDS...
WITH...
FRIENDS...
FUYUKI...?

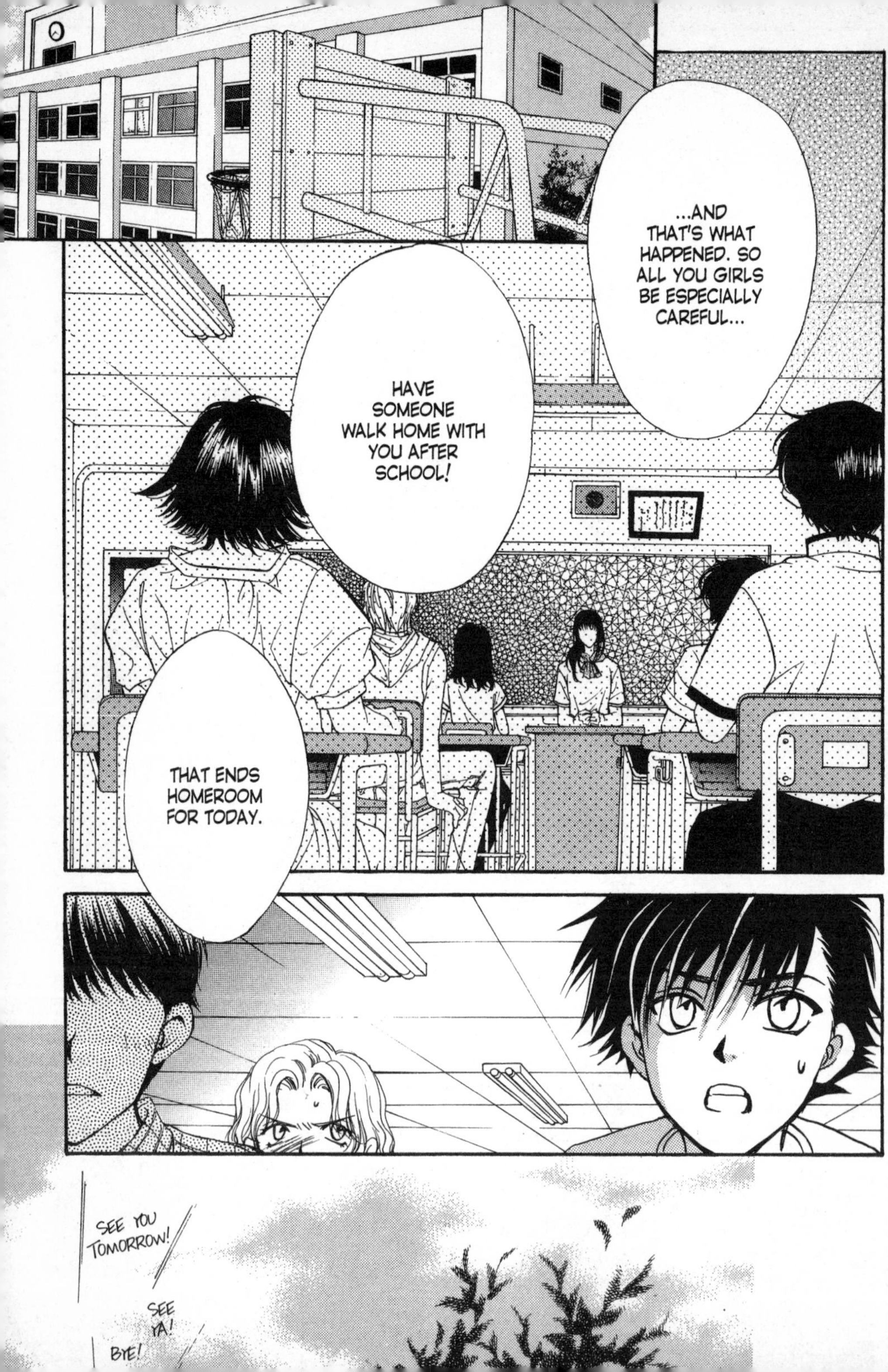
...AND THAT'S WHAT HAPPENED. SO ALL YOU GIRLS BE ESPECIALLY CAREFUL...
HAVE SOMEONE WALK HOME WITH YOU AFTER SCHOOL!
THAT ENDS HOMEROOM FOR TODAY.
SEE YOU TOMORROW!
SEE YA!
BYE!

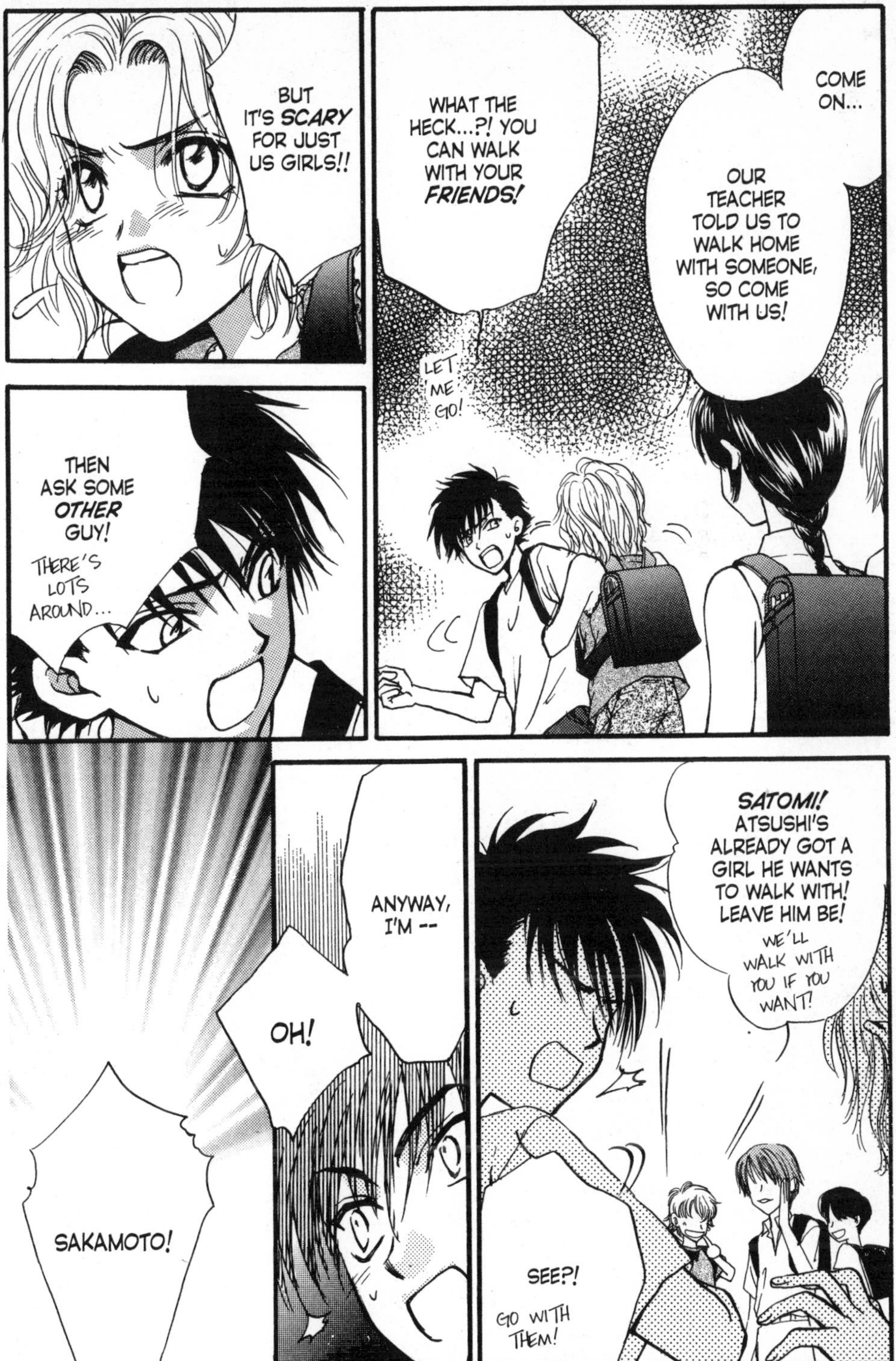
COME ON...
OUR TEACHER TOLD US TO WALK HOME WITH SOMEONE, SO COME WITH US!
WHAT THE HECK...?! YOU CAN WALK WITH YOUR FRIENDS!
LET ME GO!
BUT IT'S SCARY FOR JUST US GIRLS!!
THEN ASK SOME OTHER GUY!
THERE'S LOTS AROUND...
SATOMI! ATSUSHI'S ALREADY GOT A GIRL HE WANTS TO WALK WITH! LEAVE HIM BE!
WE'LL WALK WITH YOU IF YOU WANT!
SEE?!
GO WITH THEM!
ANYWAY, I'M --
OH!
SAKAMOTO!

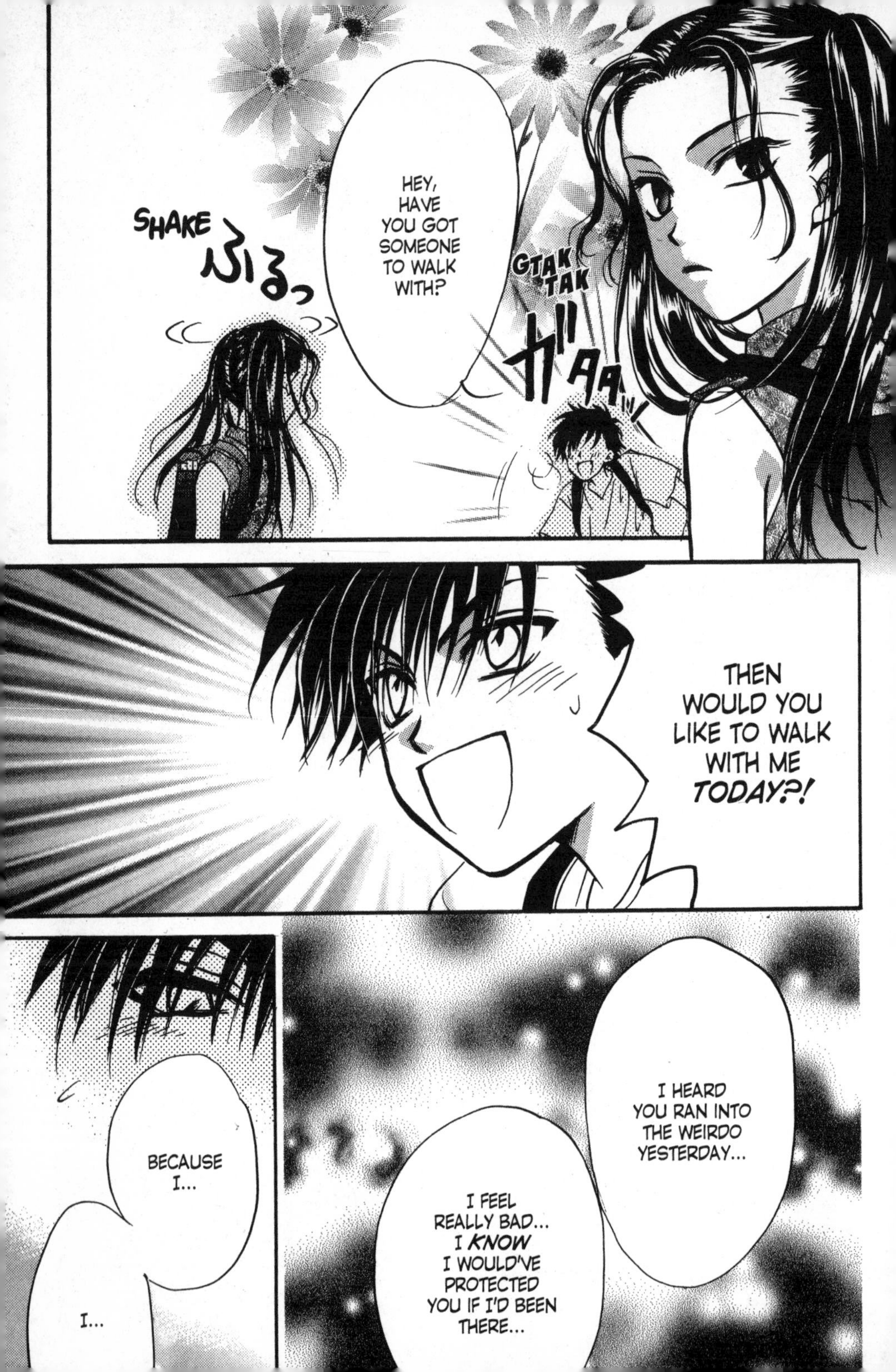
GTAK TAK
ガ
HEY, HAVE YOU GOT SOMEONE TO WALK WITH?
SHAKE ぶるっ
THEN WOULD YOU LIKE TO WALK WITH ME TODAY?!
I HEARD YOU RAN INTO THE WEIRDO YESTERDAY...
I FEEL REALLY BAD... I KNOW I WOULD'VE PROTECTED YOU IF I'D BEEN THERE...
BECAUSE I...
I...

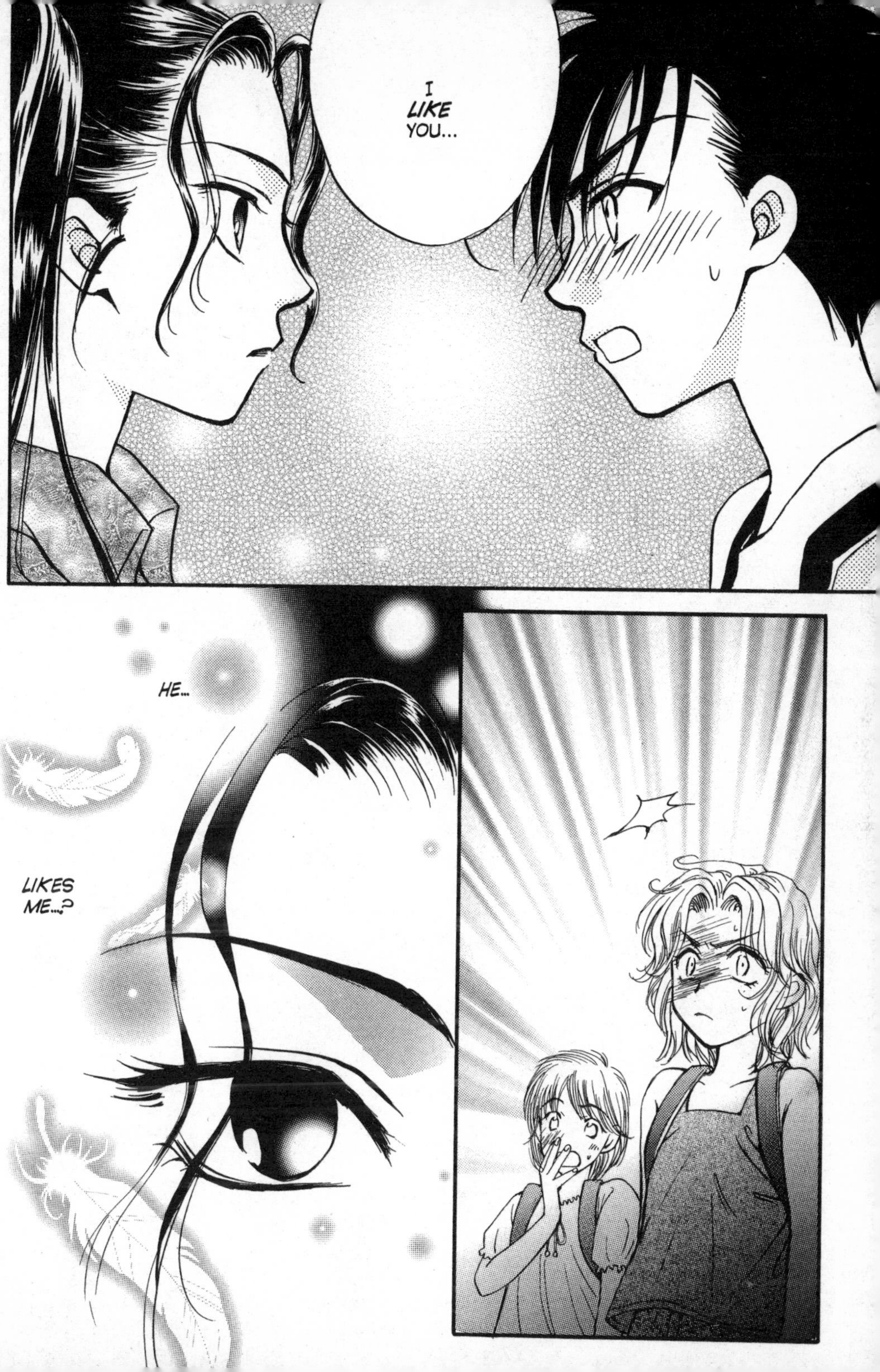
I LIKE YOU...
HE...
LIKES ME...?

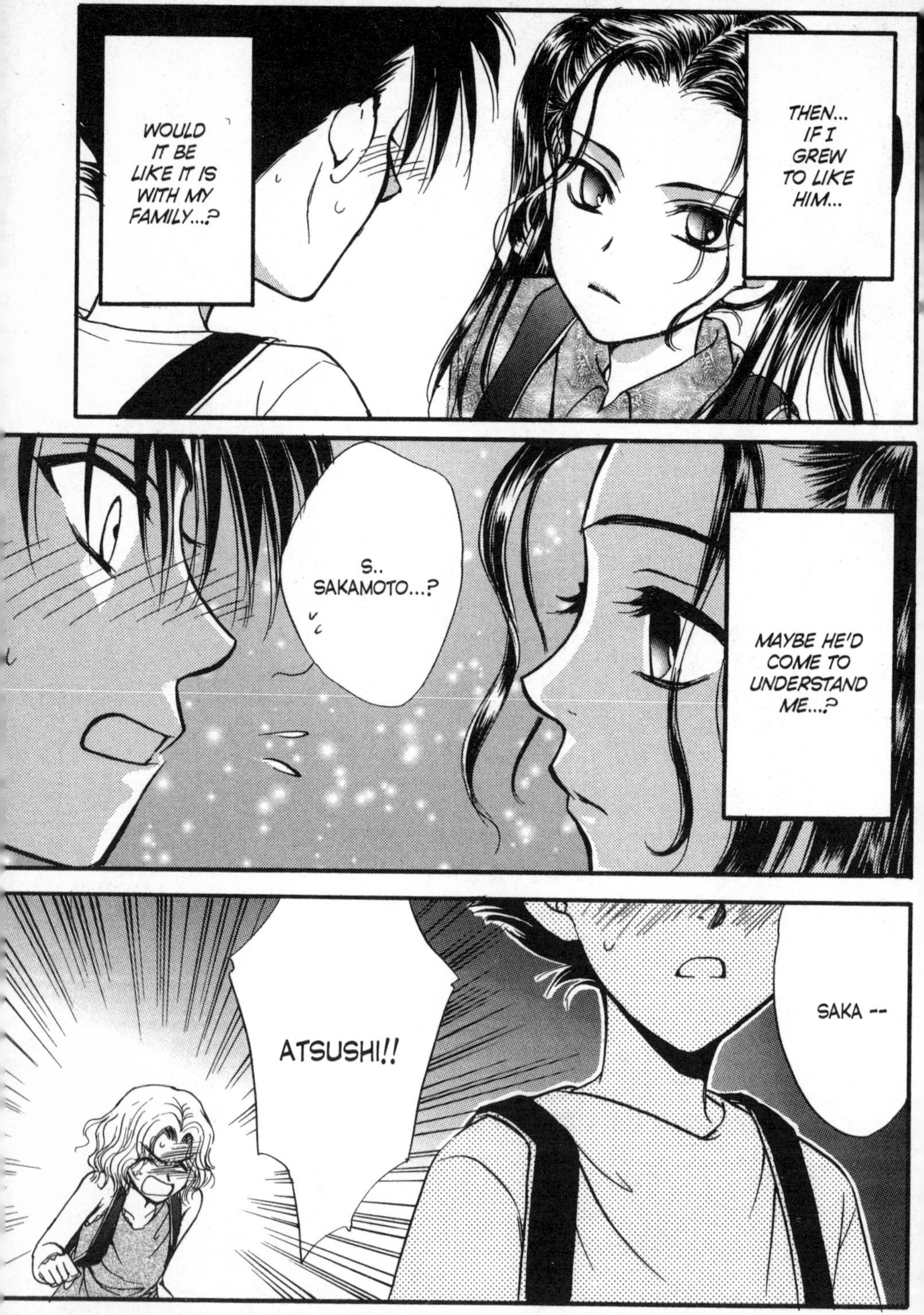
THEN... IF I GREW TO LIKE HIM...
WOULD IT BE LIKE IT IS WITH MY FAMILY...?
MAYBE HE'D COME TO UNDERSTAND ME...?
S.. SAKAMOTO...?
SAKA --
ATSUSHI!!

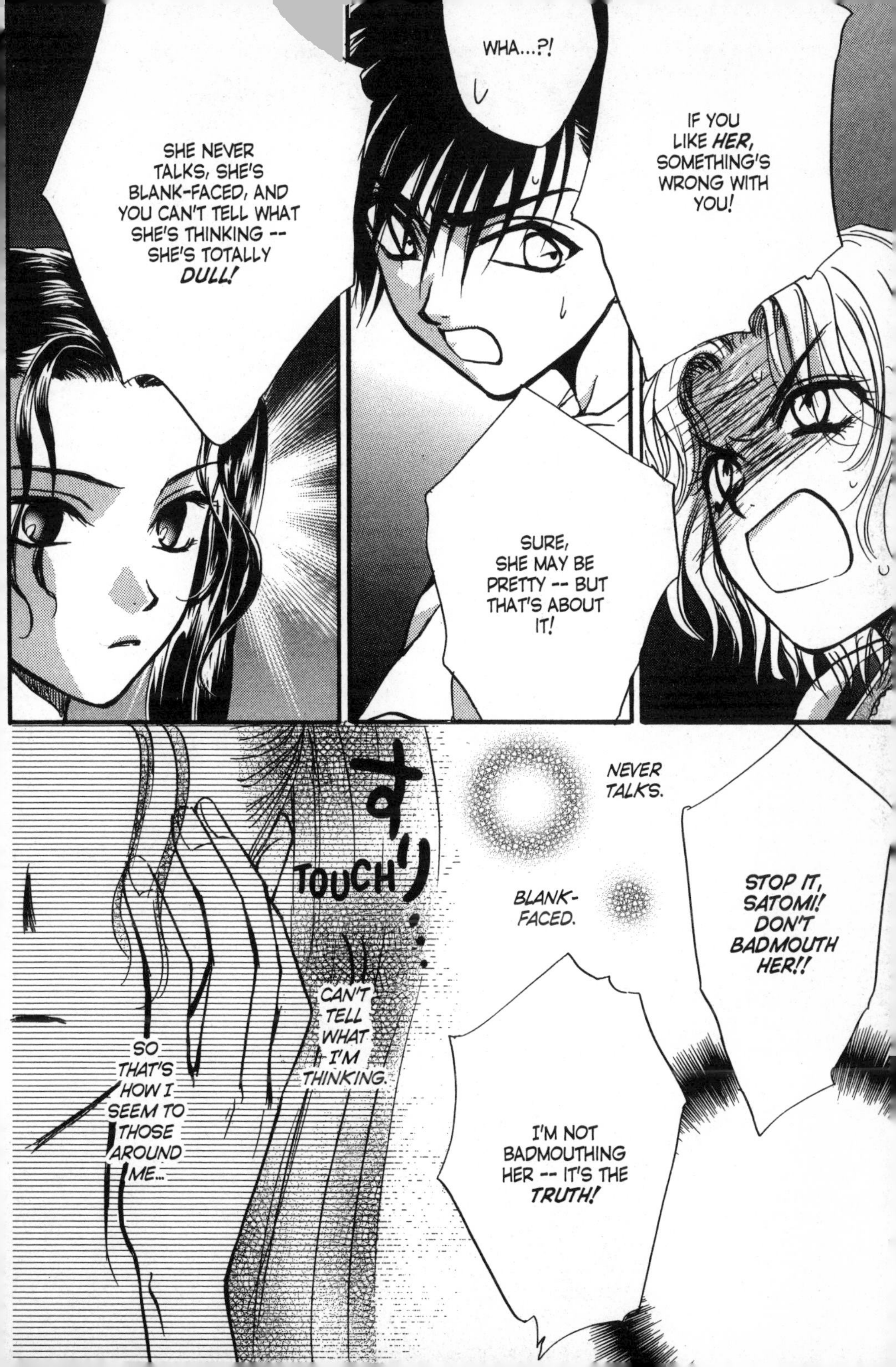
IF YOU LIKE HER, SOMETHING'S WRONG WITH YOU!
SURE, SHE MAY BE PRETTY -- BUT THAT'S ABOUT IT!
WHA...?!
SHE NEVER TALKS, SHE'S BLANK-FACED, AND YOU CAN'T TELL WHAT SHE'S THINKING -- SHE'S TOTALLY DULL!
STOP IT, SATOMI! DON'T BADMOUTH HER!!
I'M NOT BADMOUTHING HER -- IT'S THE TRUTH!
NEVER TALKS.
BLANK-FACED.
すり TOUCH り
CAN'T TELL WHAT I'M THINKING.
SO THAT'S HOW I SEEM TO THOSE AROUND ME...

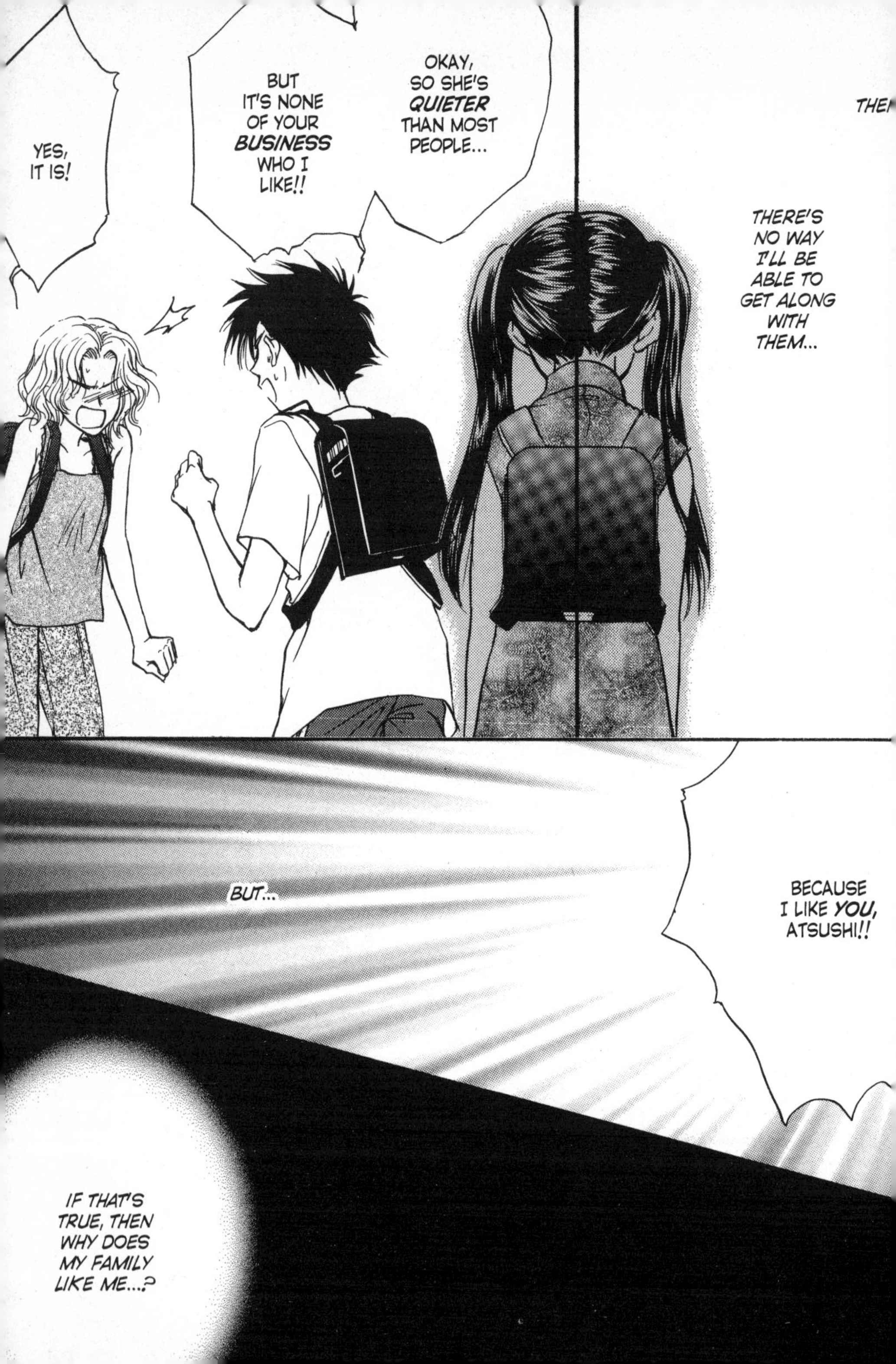
THERE'S NO WAY I'LL BE ABLE TO GET ALONG WITH THEM...
OKAY, SO SHE'S QUIETER THAN MOST PEOPLE...
BUT IT'S NONE OF YOUR BUSINESS WHO I LIKE!!
YES, IT IS!
BECAUSE I LIKE YOU, ATSUSHI!!
BUT...
IF THAT'S TRUE, THEN WHY DOES MY FAMILY LIKE ME...?

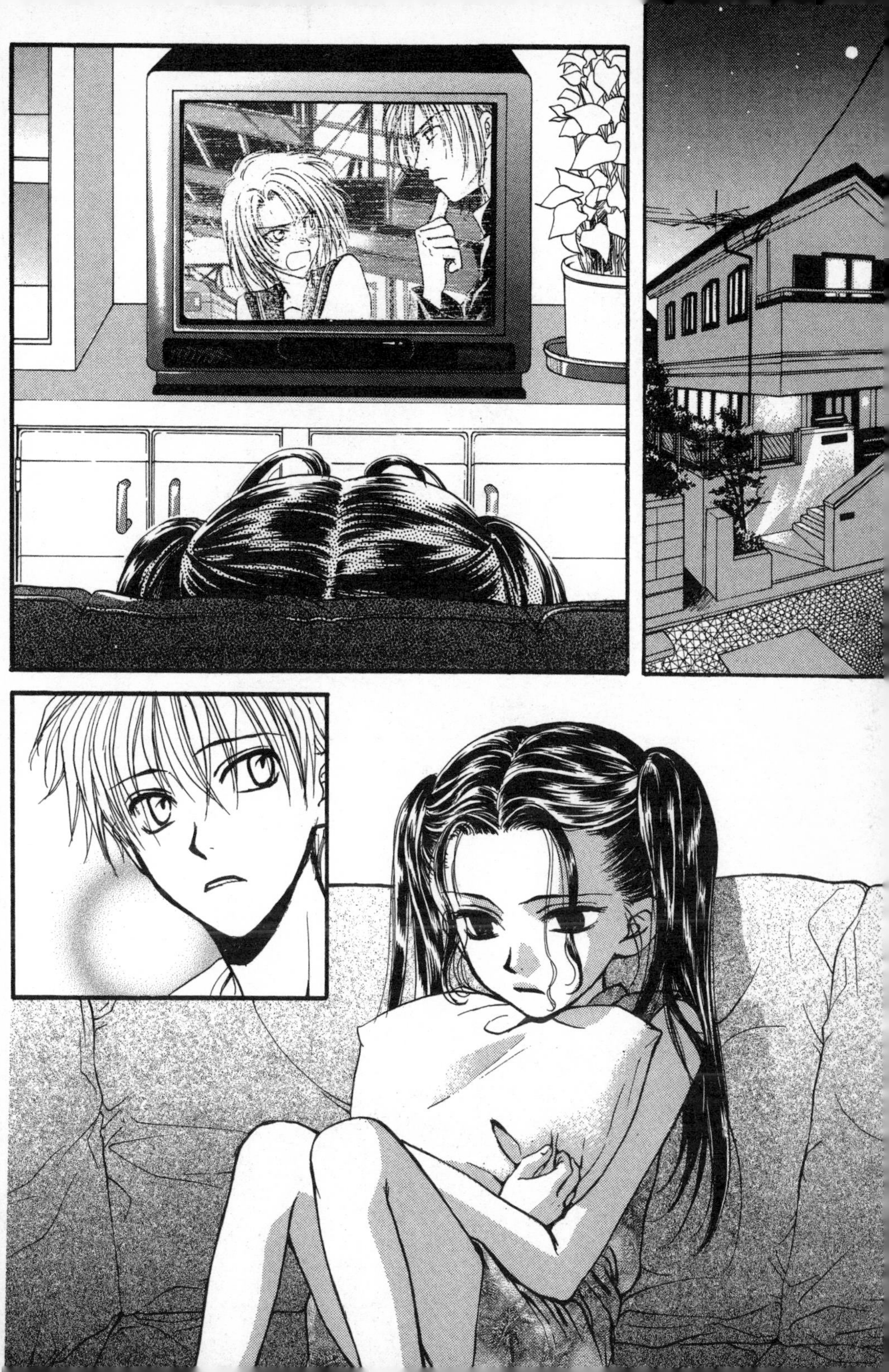

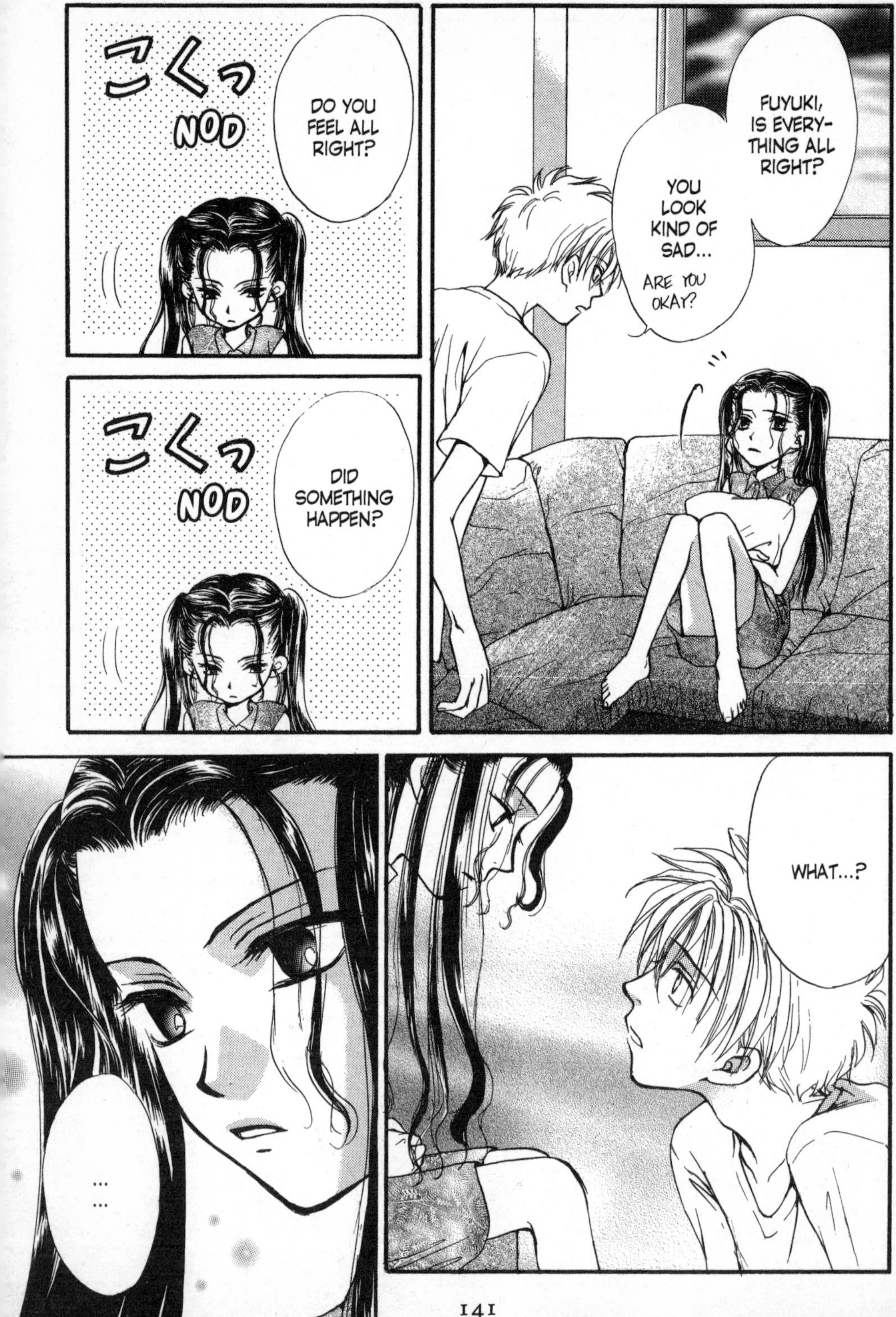
FUYUKI, IS EVERYTHING ALL RIGHT?
YOU LOOK KIND OF SAD...
ARE YOU OKAY?
DO YOU FEEL ALL RIGHT?
こくっ
NOD
DID SOMETHING HAPPEN?
こくっ
NOD
WHAT...?
...
...

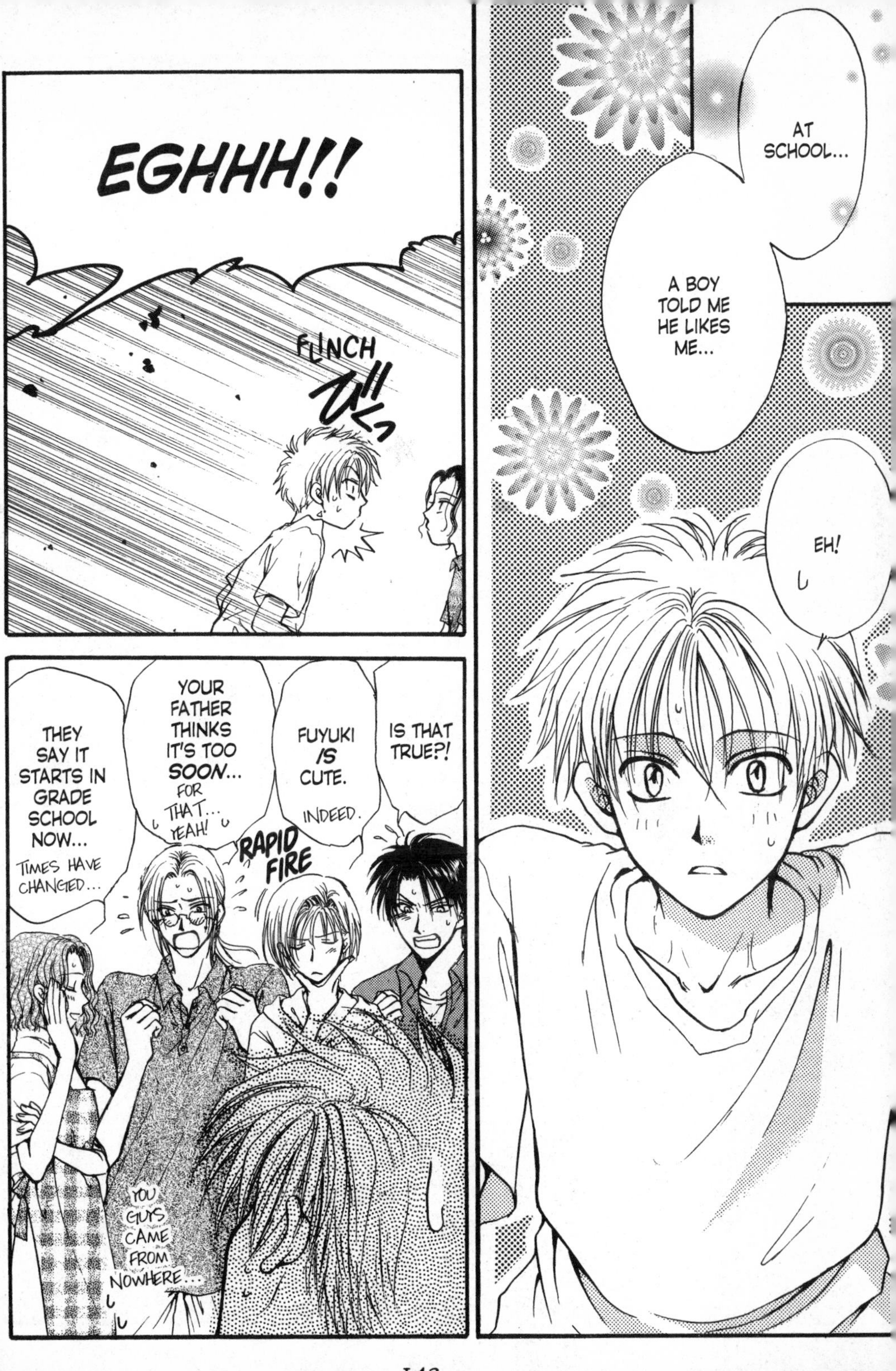
AT SCHOOL...
A BOY TOLD ME HE LIKES ME...
EH!
EGHHH!!
FLINCH
IS THAT TRUE?!
FUYUKI IS CUTE.
INDEED.
RAPID FIRE
YOUR FATHER THINKS IT'S TOO SOON...
FOR THAT... YEAH!
THEY SAY IT STARTS IN GRADE SCHOOL NOW...
TIMES HAVE CHANGED...
YOU GUYS CAME FROM NOWHERE...

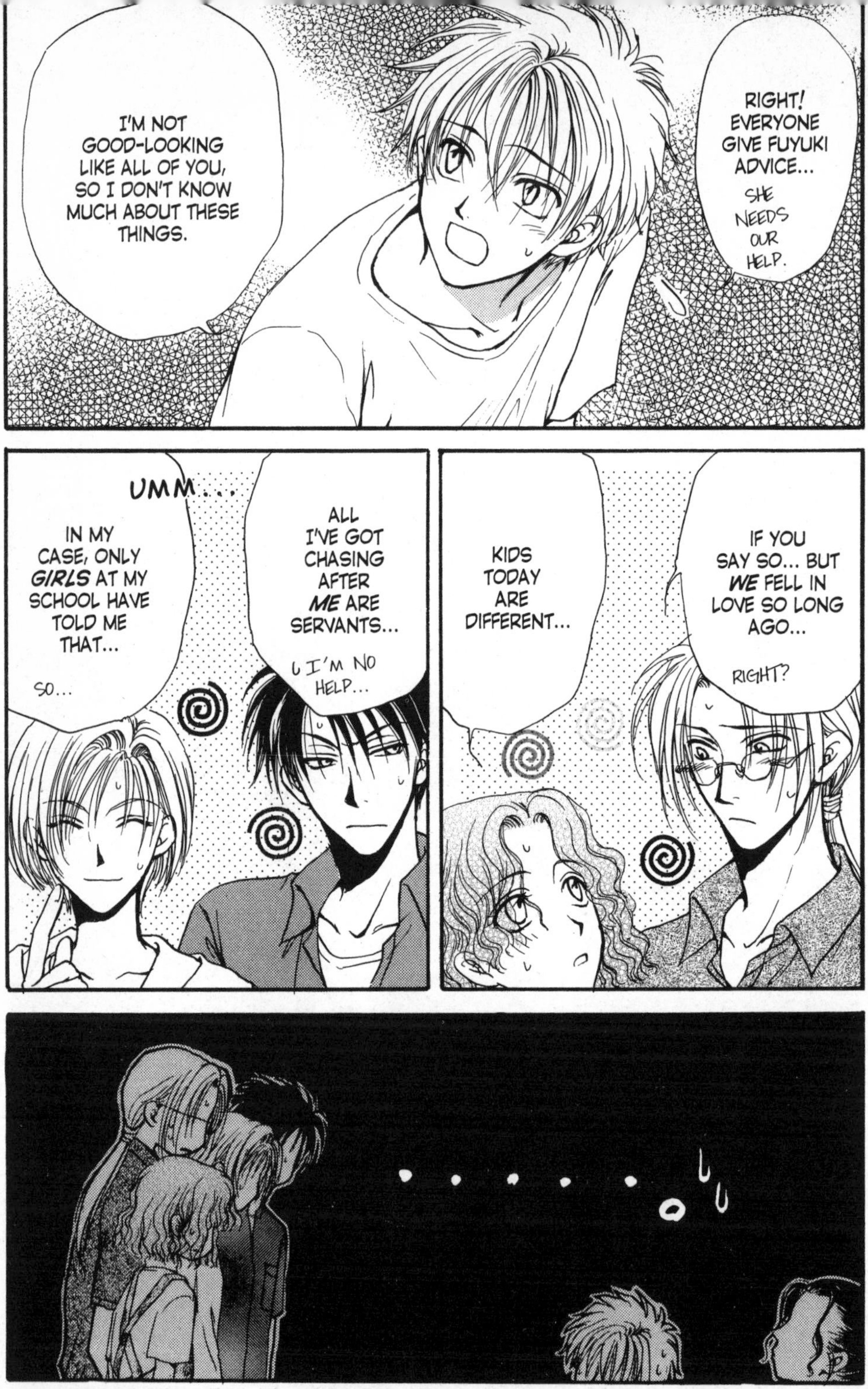
RIGHT! EVERYONE GIVE FUYUKI ADVICE...
SHE NEEDS OUR HELP.
I'M NOT GOOD-LOOKING LIKE ALL OF YOU, SO I DON'T KNOW MUCH ABOUT THESE THINGS.
IF YOU SAY SO... BUT WE FELL IN LOVE SO LONG AGO...
RIGHT?
KIDS TODAY ARE DIFFERENT...
ALL I'VE GOT CHASING AFTER ME ARE SERVANTS...
I'M NO HELP...
UMM...
IN MY CASE, ONLY GIRLS AT MY SCHOOL HAVE TOLD ME THAT...
SO...
......

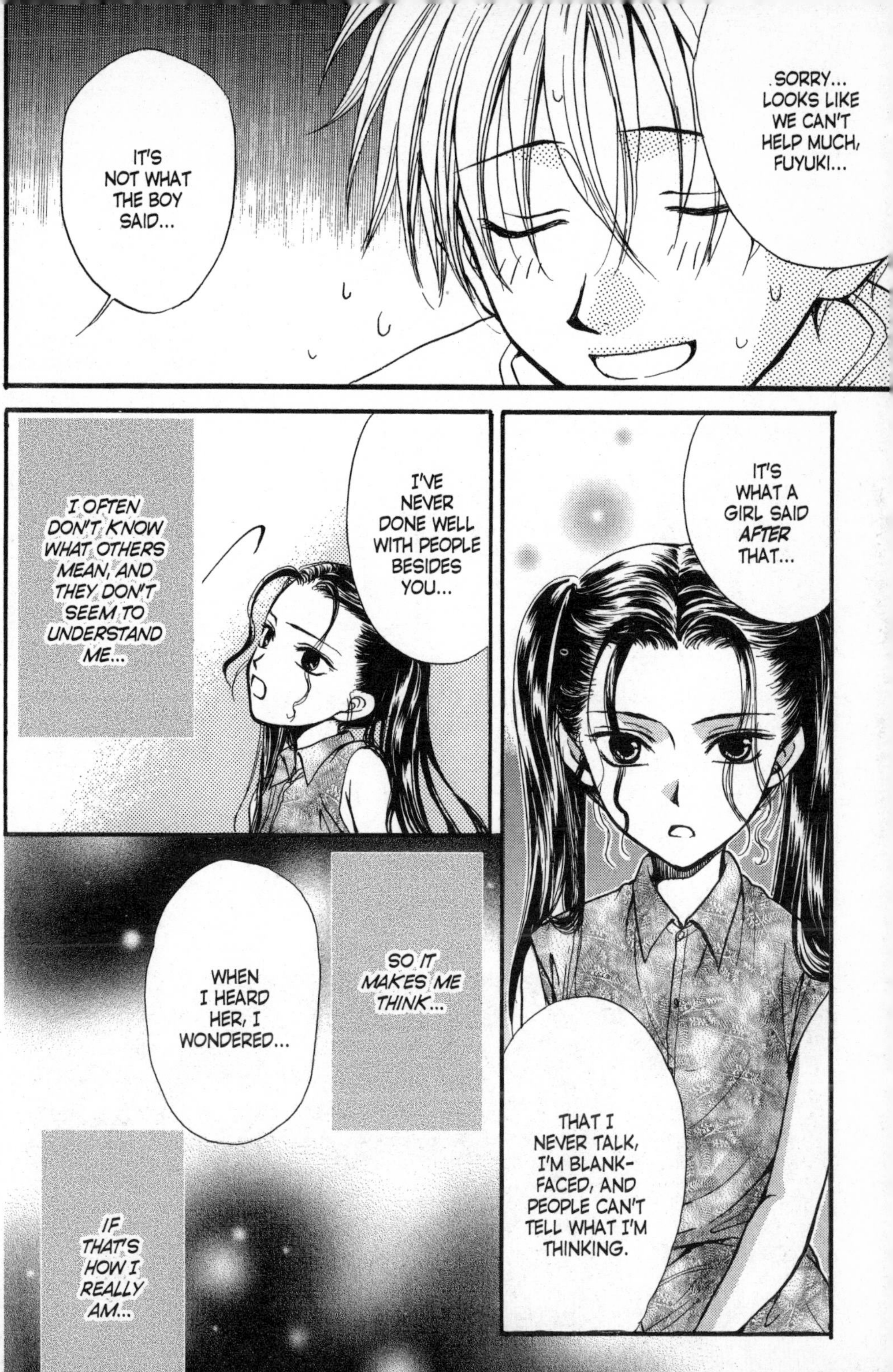
SORRY... LOOKS LIKE WE CAN'T HELP MUCH, FUYUKI...
IT'S NOT WHAT THE BOY SAID...
IT'S WHAT A GIRL SAID *AFTER* THAT...
THAT I NEVER TALK, I'M BLANK-FACED, AND PEOPLE CAN'T TELL WHAT I'M THINKING.
I'VE NEVER DONE WELL WITH PEOPLE BESIDES YOU...
I OFTEN DON'T KNOW WHAT OTHERS MEAN, AND THEY DON'T SEEM TO UNDERSTAND ME...
SO IT MAKES ME THINK...
WHEN I HEARD HER, I WONDERED...
IF THAT'S HOW I REALLY AM...

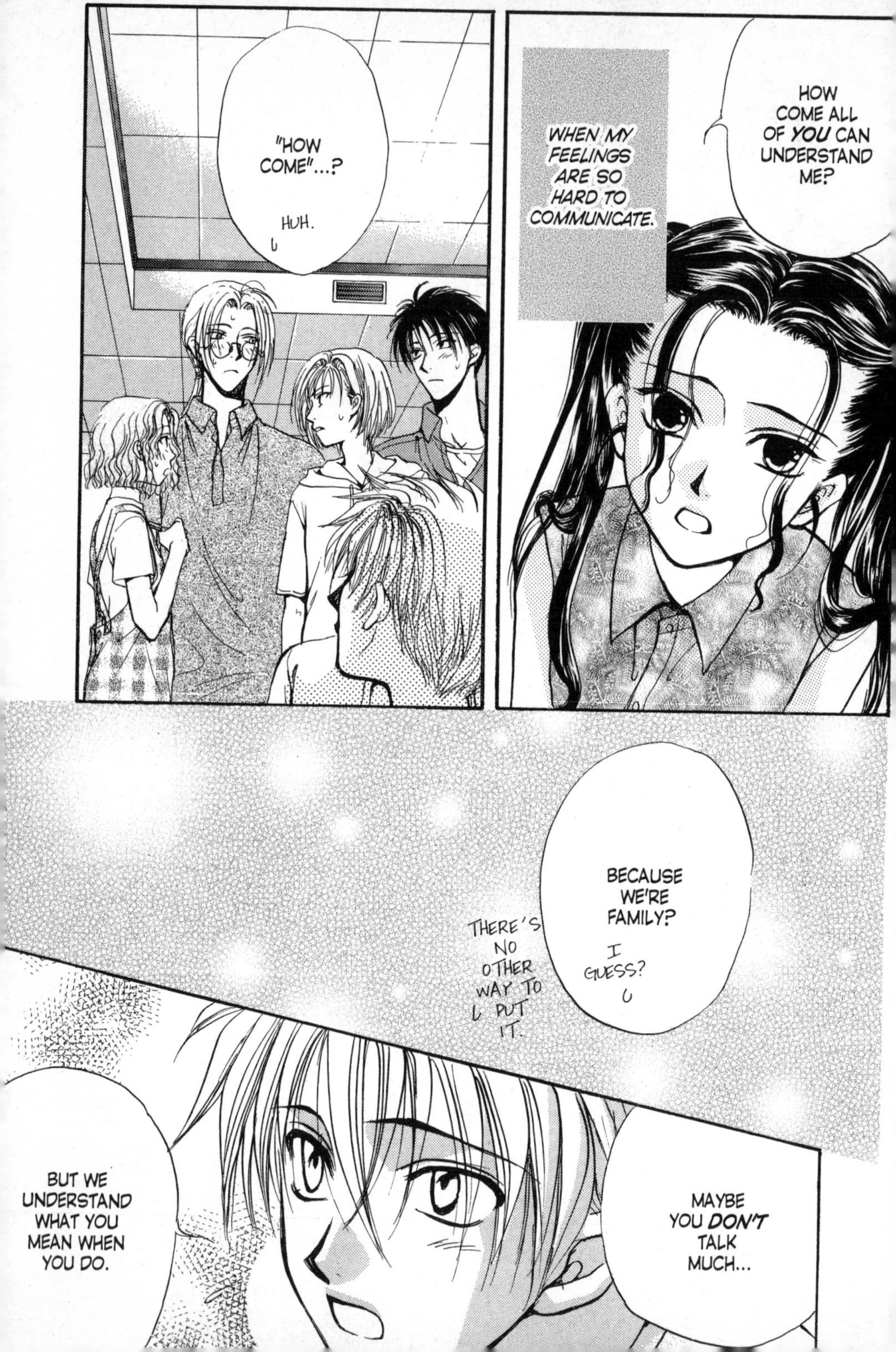
HOW COME ALL OF *YOU* CAN UNDERSTAND ME?
WHEN MY FEELINGS ARE SO HARD TO COMMUNICATE.
"HOW COME"...?
HUH.
BECAUSE WE'RE FAMILY?
I GUESS?
THERE'S NO OTHER WAY TO PUT IT.
MAYBE YOU ***DON'T*** TALK MUCH...
BUT WE UNDERSTAND WHAT YOU MEAN WHEN YOU DO.

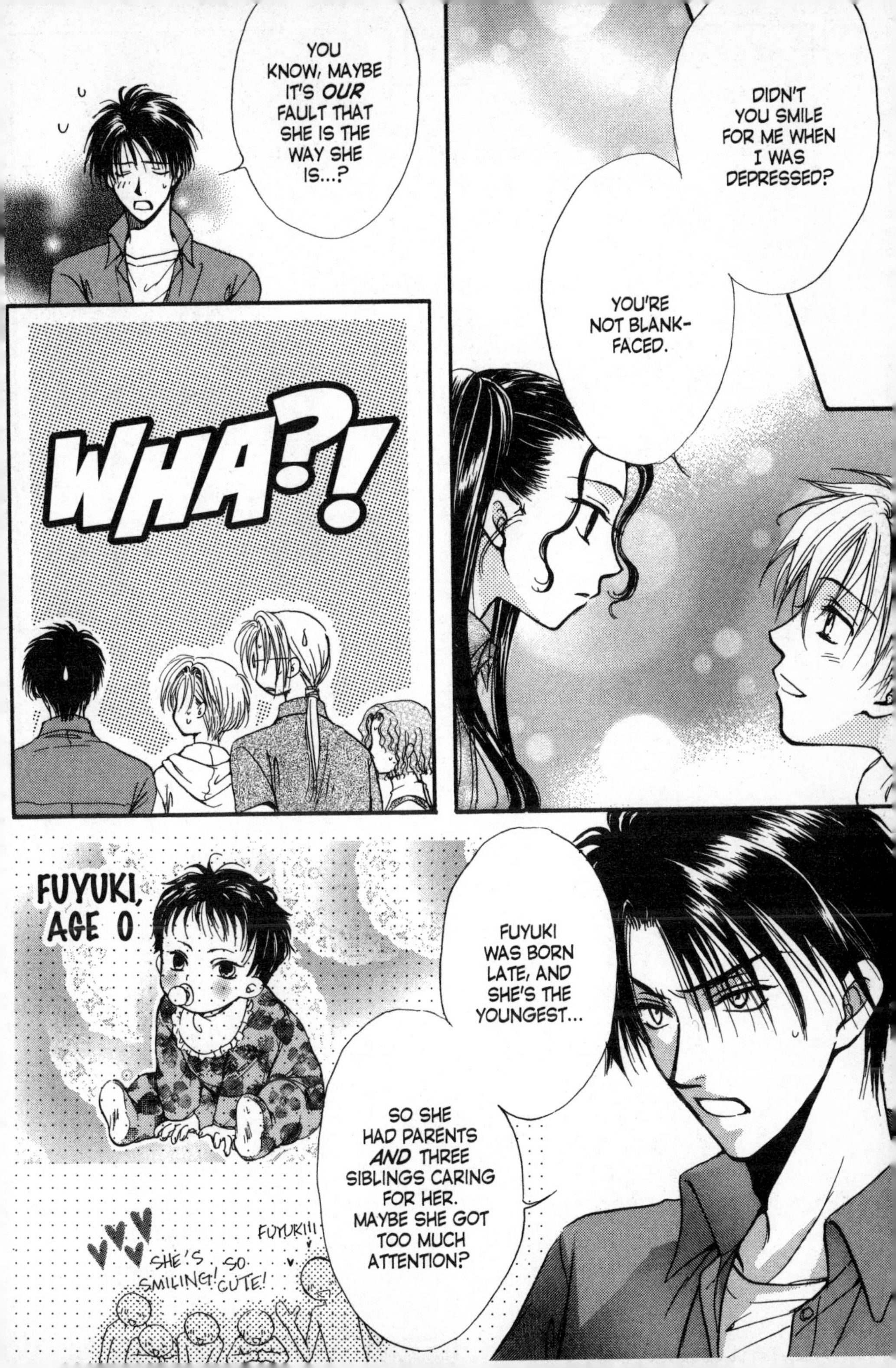
DIDN'T YOU SMILE FOR ME WHEN I WAS DEPRESSED?
YOU'RE NOT BLANK-FACED.
YOU KNOW, MAYBE IT'S *OUR* FAULT THAT SHE IS THE WAY SHE IS...?
WHA?!
FUYUKI WAS BORN LATE, AND SHE'S THE YOUNGEST...
SO SHE HAD PARENTS ***AND*** THREE SIBLINGS CARING FOR HER. MAYBE SHE GOT TOO MUCH ATTENTION?
FUYUKI, AGE 0
FUYUKI!!!
SO CUTE!
SHE'S SMILING!

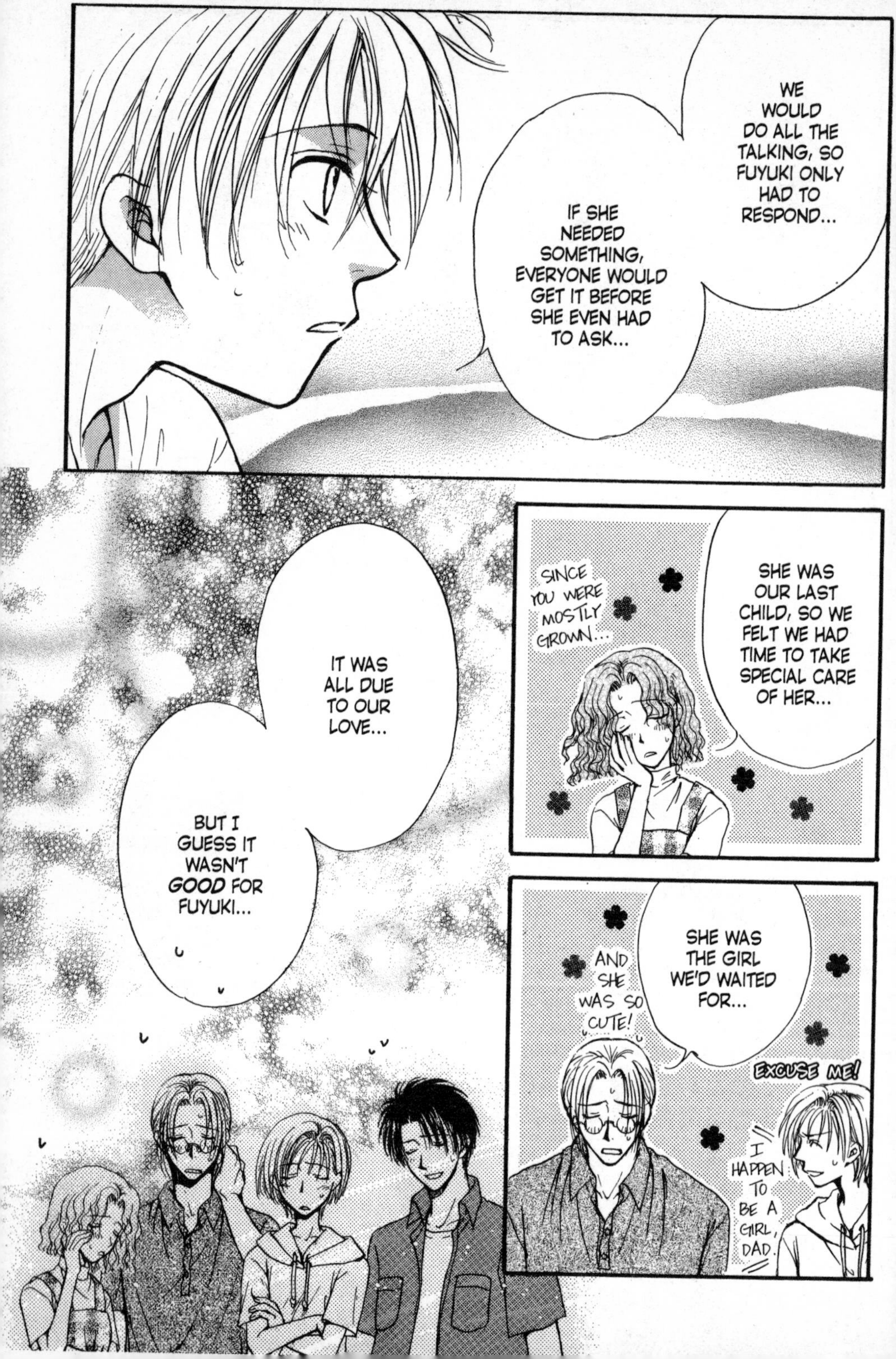
WE WOULD DO ALL THE TALKING, SO FUYUKI ONLY HAD TO RESPOND...
IF SHE NEEDED SOMETHING, EVERYONE WOULD GET IT BEFORE SHE EVEN HAD TO ASK...
SHE WAS OUR LAST CHILD, SO WE FELT WE HAD TIME TO TAKE SPECIAL CARE OF HER...
SINCE YOU WERE MOSTLY GROWN...
SHE WAS THE GIRL WE'D WAITED FOR...
AND SHE WAS SO CUTE!
EXCUSE ME!
I HAPPEN TO BE A GIRL, DAD.
IT WAS ALL DUE TO OUR LOVE...
BUT I GUESS IT WASN'T *GOOD* FOR FUYUKI...

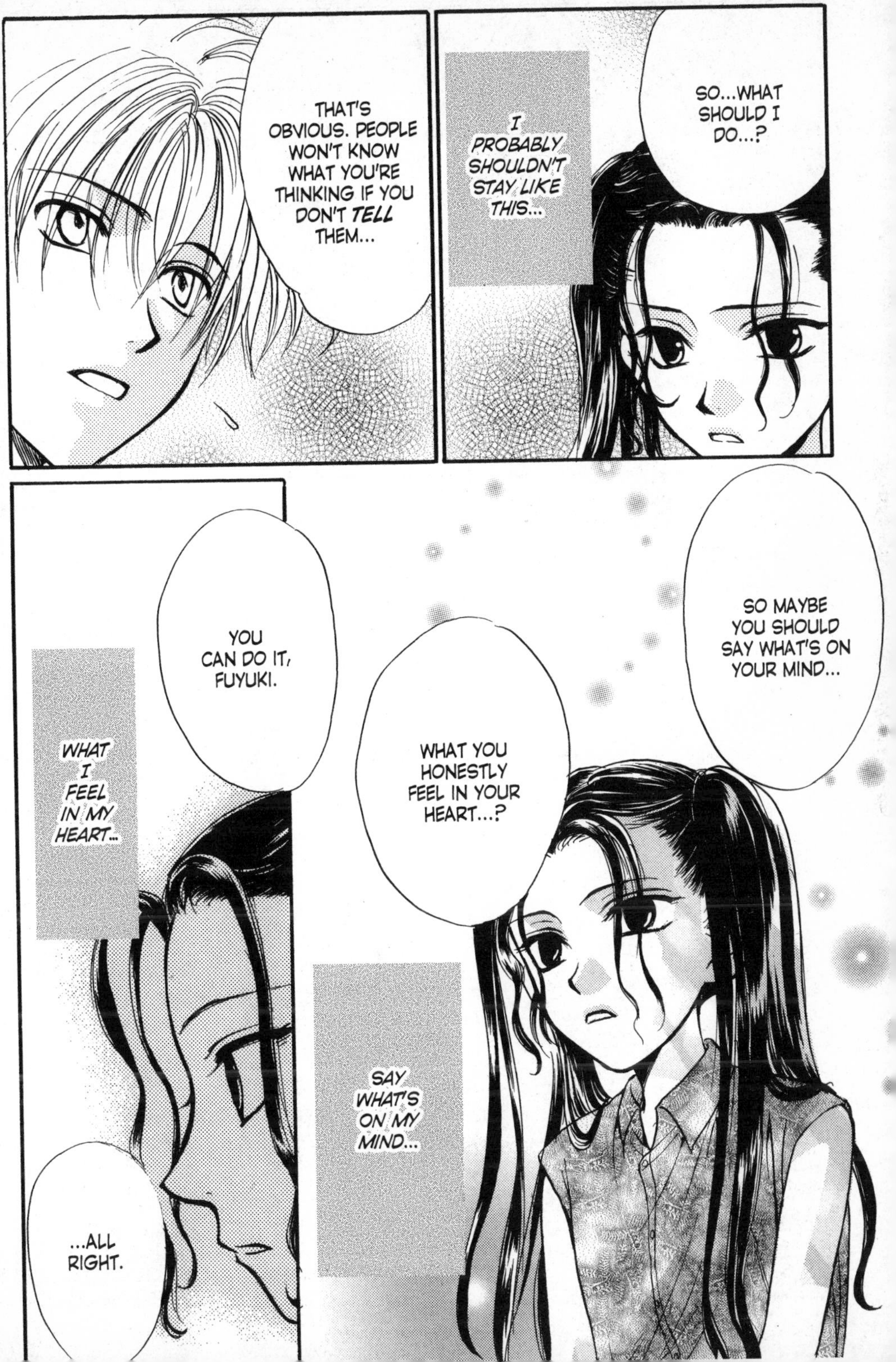
SO...WHAT SHOULD I DO...?
I PROBABLY SHOULDN'T STAY LIKE THIS...
THAT'S OBVIOUS. PEOPLE WON'T KNOW WHAT YOU'RE THINKING IF YOU DON'T *TELL* THEM...
SO MAYBE YOU SHOULD SAY WHAT'S ON YOUR MIND...
WHAT YOU HONESTLY FEEL IN YOUR HEART...?
YOU CAN DO IT, FUYUKI.
WHAT I FEEL IN MY HEART...
SAY WHAT'S ON MY MIND...
...ALL RIGHT.

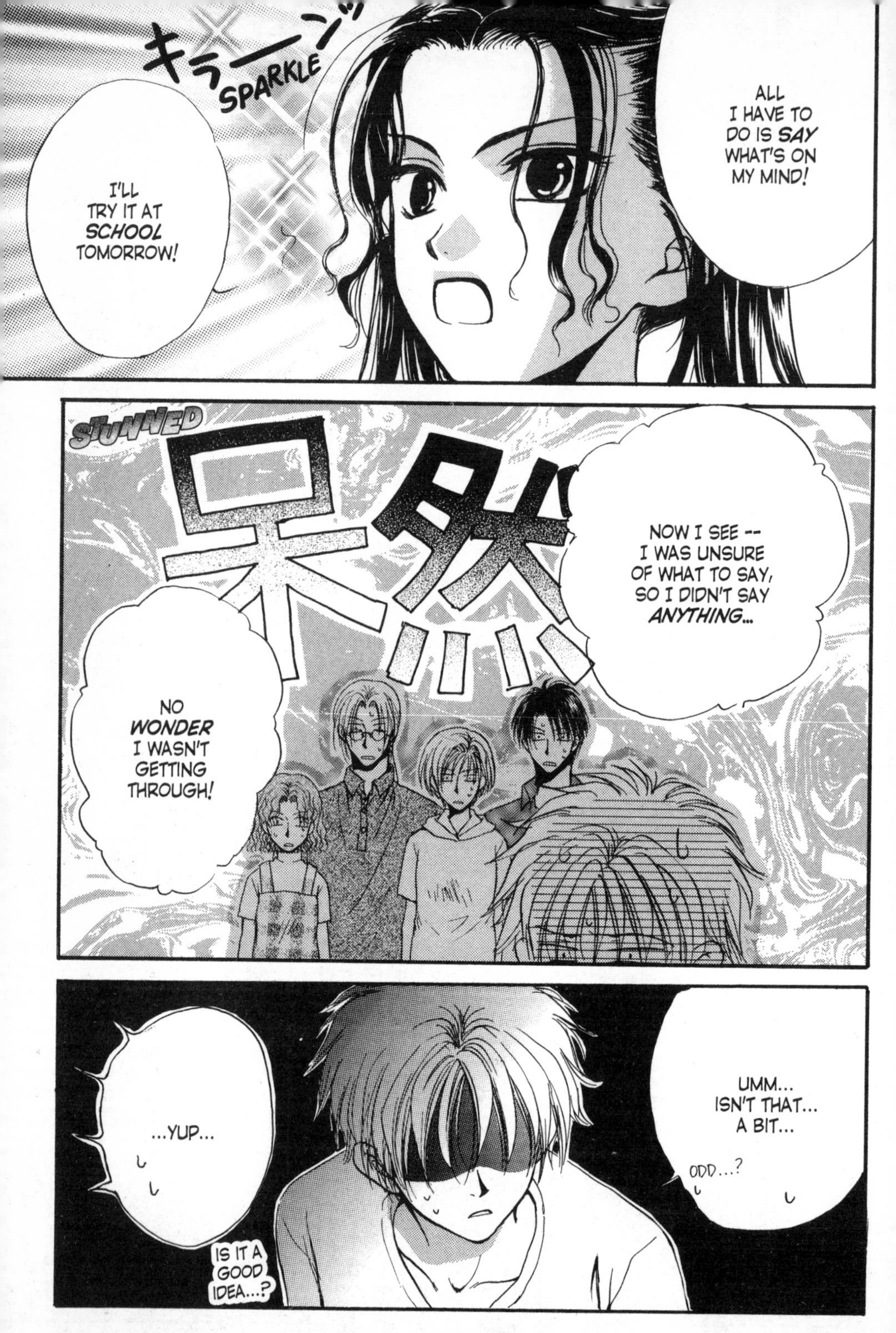
ALL I HAVE TO DO IS SAY WHAT'S ON MY MIND!
キラーン SPARKLE
I'LL TRY IT AT SCHOOL TOMORROW!
NOW I SEE -- I WAS UNSURE OF WHAT TO SAY, SO I DIDN'T SAY ANYTHING...
STUNNED 呆然
NO WONDER I WASN'T GETTING THROUGH!
UMM... ISN'T THAT... A BIT...
ODD...?
...YUP...
IS IT A GOOD IDEA...?

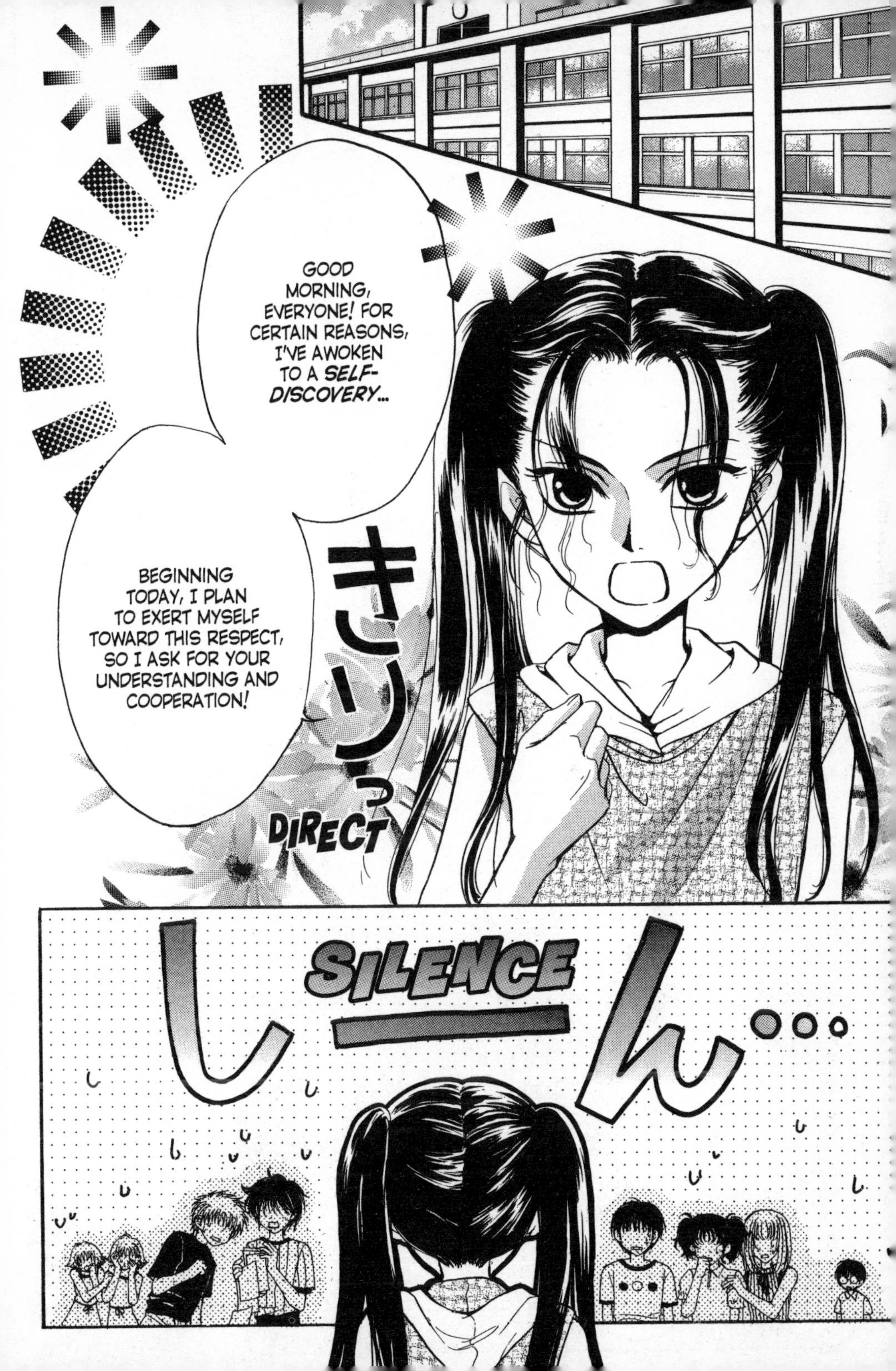
GOOD MORNING, EVERYONE! FOR CERTAIN REASONS, I'VE AWOKEN TO A *SELF-DISCOVERY*...
BEGINNING TODAY, I PLAN TO EXERT MYSELF TOWARD THIS RESPECT, SO I ASK FOR YOUR UNDERSTANDING AND COOPERATION!
きりっ
DIRECT
しーん...
SILENCE

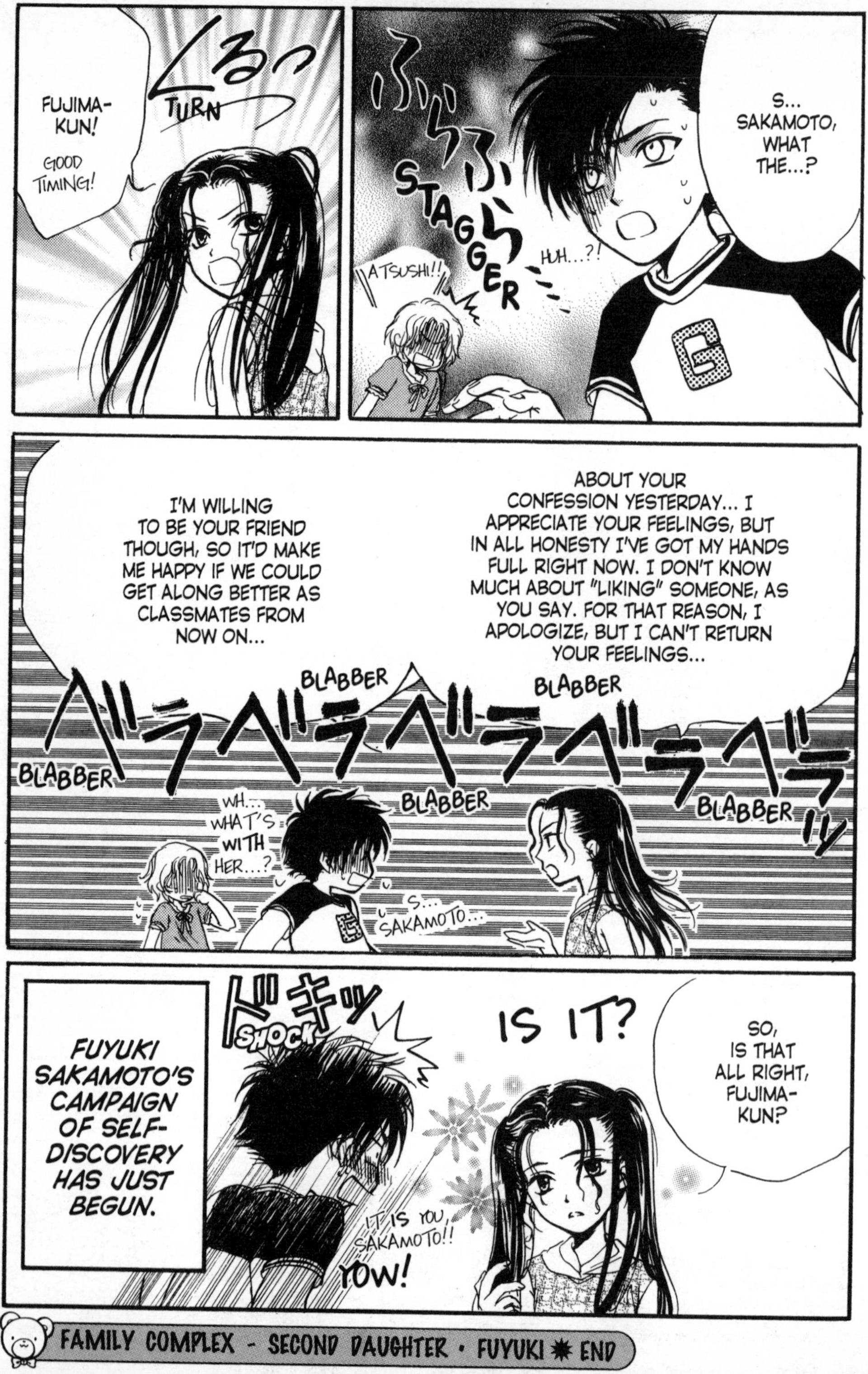
S... SAKAMOTO, WHAT THE...?
HUH...?!
STAGGER
ATSUSHI!!
TURN
FUJIMA-KUN!
GOOD TIMING!
ABOUT YOUR CONFESSION YESTERDAY... I APPRECIATE YOUR FEELINGS, BUT IN ALL HONESTY I'VE GOT MY HANDS FULL RIGHT NOW. I DON'T KNOW MUCH ABOUT "LIKING" SOMEONE, AS YOU SAY. FOR THAT REASON, I APOLOGIZE, BUT I CAN'T RETURN YOUR FEELINGS...
I'M WILLING TO BE YOUR FRIEND THOUGH, SO IT'D MAKE ME HAPPY IF WE COULD GET ALONG BETTER AS CLASSMATES FROM NOW ON...
BLABBER
BLABBER
BLABBER
BLABBER
BLABBER
S... SAKAMOTO...
WH... WHAT'S WITH HER...?
SO, IS THAT ALL RIGHT, FUJIMA-KUN?
IS IT?
SHOCK
IT IS YOU, SAKAMOTO!!
YOW!
FUYUKI SAKAMOTO'S CAMPAIGN OF SELF-DISCOVERY HAS JUST BEGUN.

FAMILY COMPLEX - SECOND DAUGHTER • FUYUKI ✸ END

MIDWORD

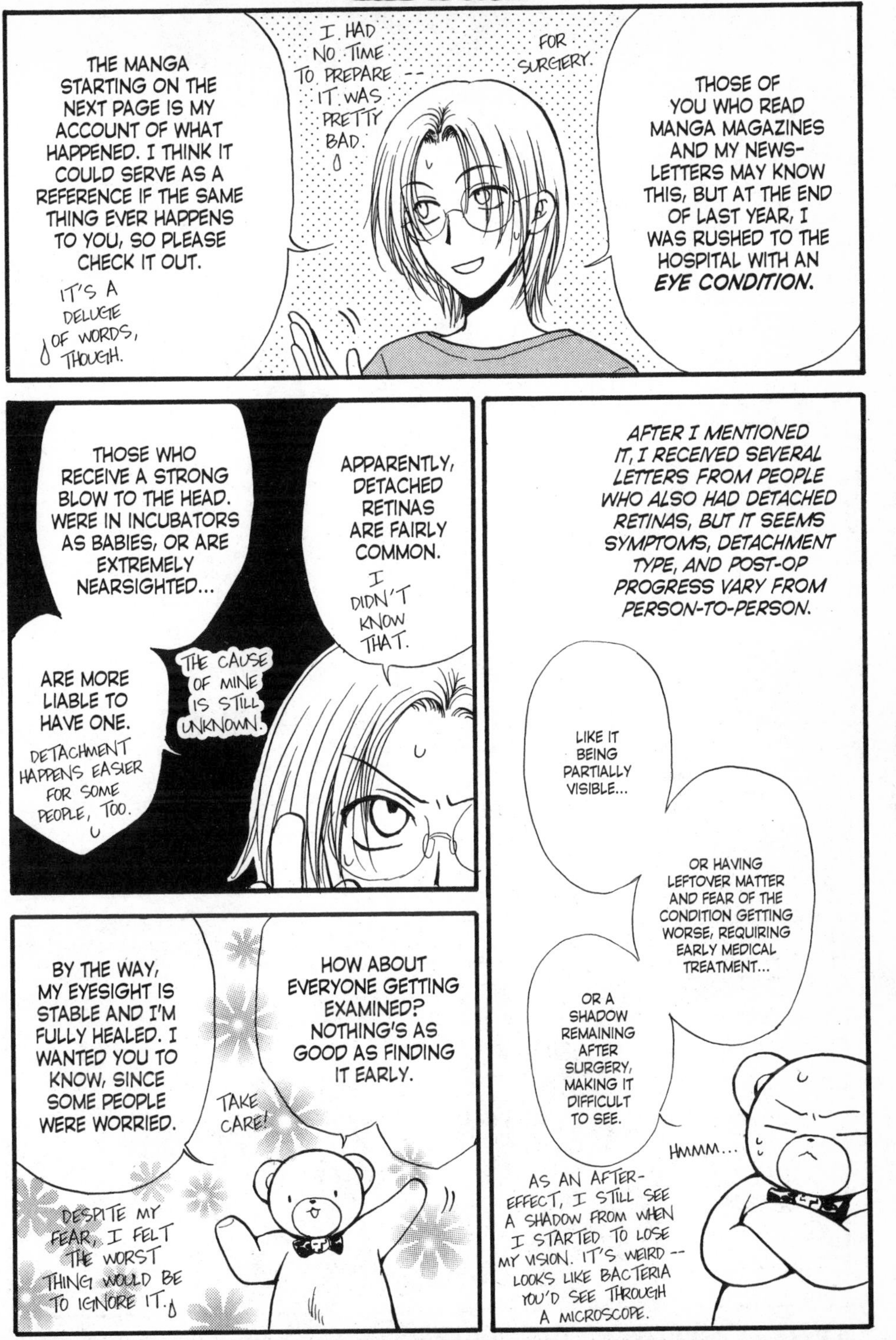
THOSE OF YOU WHO READ MANGA MAGAZINES AND MY NEWS-LETTERS MAY KNOW THIS, BUT AT THE END OF LAST YEAR, I WAS RUSHED TO THE HOSPITAL WITH AN *EYE CONDITION*.
FOR SURGERY.
I HAD NO TIME TO PREPARE -- IT WAS PRETTY BAD.
THE MANGA STARTING ON THE NEXT PAGE IS MY ACCOUNT OF WHAT HAPPENED. I THINK IT COULD SERVE AS A REFERENCE IF THE SAME THING EVER HAPPENS TO YOU, SO PLEASE CHECK IT OUT.
IT'S A DELUGE OF WORDS, THOUGH.
AFTER I MENTIONED IT, I RECEIVED SEVERAL LETTERS FROM PEOPLE WHO ALSO HAD DETACHED RETINAS, BUT IT SEEMS SYMPTOMS, DETACHMENT TYPE, AND POST-OP PROGRESS VARY FROM PERSON-TO-PERSON.
LIKE IT BEING PARTIALLY VISIBLE...
OR HAVING LEFTOVER MATTER AND FEAR OF THE CONDITION GETTING WORSE, REQUIRING EARLY MEDICAL TREATMENT...
OR A SHADOW REMAINING AFTER SURGERY, MAKING IT DIFFICULT TO SEE.
HMMM...
AS AN AFTER-EFFECT, I STILL SEE A SHADOW FROM WHEN I STARTED TO LOSE MY VISION. IT'S WEIRD -- LOOKS LIKE BACTERIA YOU'D SEE THROUGH A MICROSCOPE.
APPARENTLY, DETACHED RETINAS ARE FAIRLY COMMON.
I DIDN'T KNOW THAT.
THOSE WHO RECEIVE A STRONG BLOW TO THE HEAD. WERE IN INCUBATORS AS BABIES, OR ARE EXTREMELY NEARSIGHTED...
THE CAUSE OF MINE IS STILL UNKNOWN.
ARE MORE LIABLE TO HAVE ONE.
DETACHMENT HAPPENS EASIER FOR SOME PEOPLE, TOO.
HOW ABOUT EVERYONE GETTING EXAMINED? NOTHING'S AS GOOD AS FINDING IT EARLY.
TAKE CARE!
BY THE WAY, MY EYESIGHT IS STABLE AND I'M FULLY HEALED. I WANTED YOU TO KNOW, SINCE SOME PEOPLE WERE WORRIED.
DESPITE MY FEAR, I FELT THE WORST THING WOULD BE TO IGNORE IT.

DETACHED RETINA DIARY

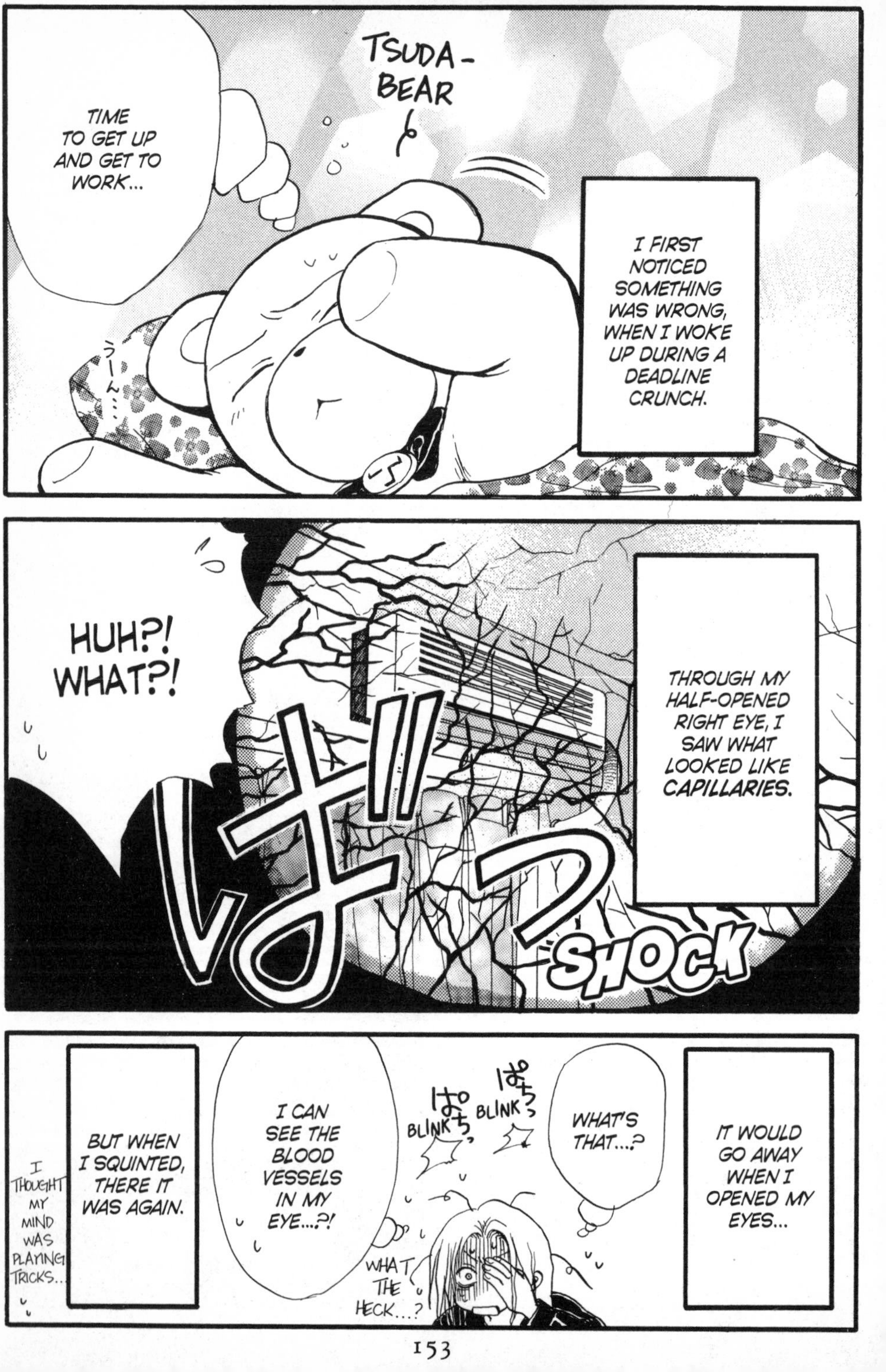

I FIRST NOTICED SOMETHING WAS WRONG, WHEN I WOKE UP DURING A DEADLINE CRUNCH.
TSUDA-BEAR
TIME TO GET UP AND GET TO WORK...
うーん…
THROUGH MY HALF-OPENED RIGHT EYE, I SAW WHAT LOOKED LIKE CAPILLARIES.
SHOCK
ぎっ
HUH?! WHAT?!
IT WOULD GO AWAY WHEN I OPENED MY EYES...
WHAT'S THAT...?
ぱちっ
BLINK
ぱちっ
BLINK
I CAN SEE THE BLOOD VESSELS IN MY EYE...?!
WHAT THE HECK...?
BUT WHEN I SQUINTED, THERE IT WAS AGAIN.
I THOUGHT MY MIND WAS PLAYING TRICKS...

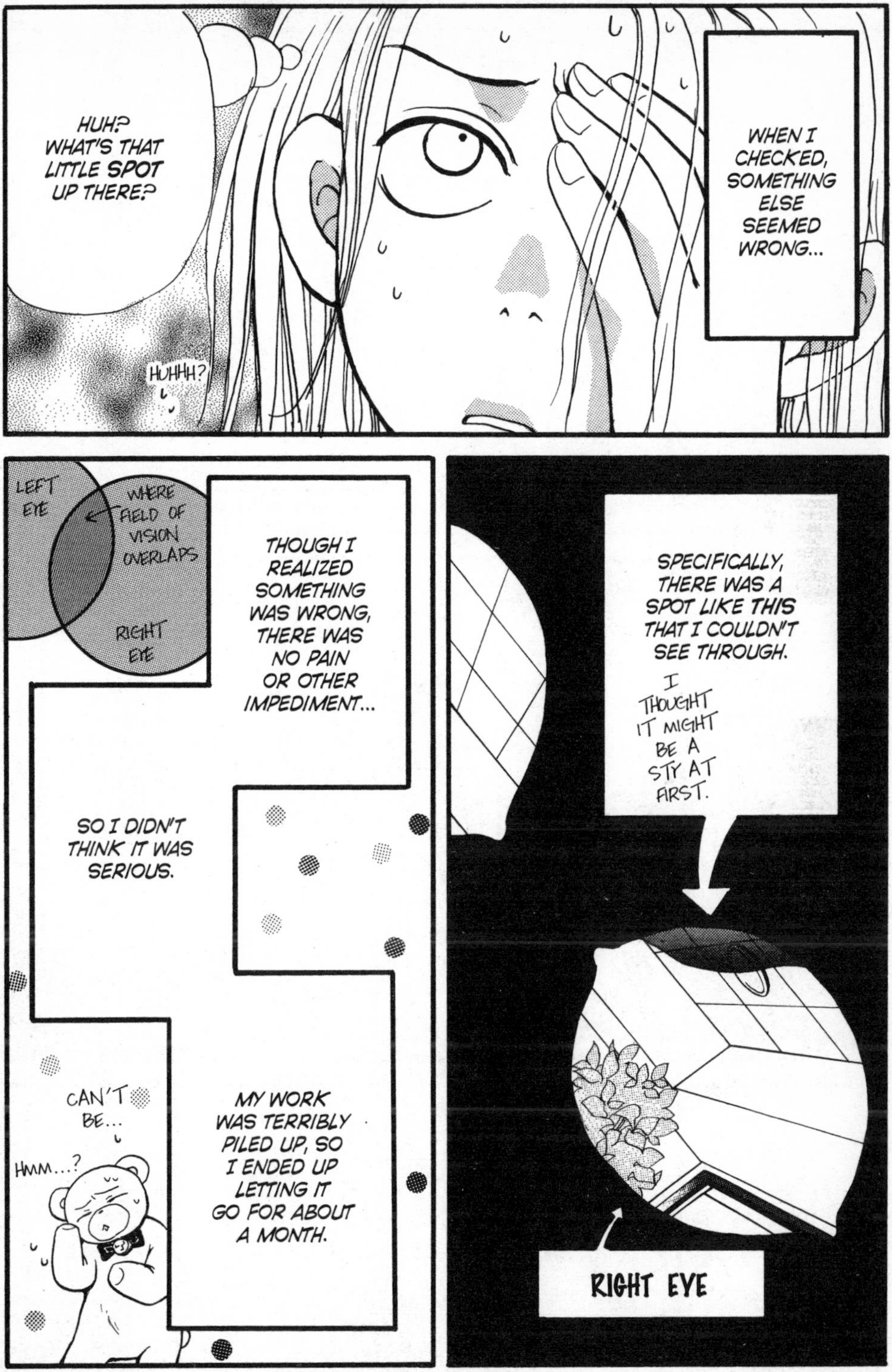
WHEN I CHECKED, SOMETHING ELSE SEEMED WRONG...
HUH? WHAT'S THAT LITTLE SPOT UP THERE?
HUHHH?
SPECIFICALLY, THERE WAS A SPOT LIKE THIS THAT I COULDN'T SEE THROUGH.
I THOUGHT IT MIGHT BE A STY AT FIRST.
RIGHT EYE
THOUGH I REALIZED SOMETHING WAS WRONG, THERE WAS NO PAIN OR OTHER IMPEDIMENT...
LEFT EYE
WHERE FIELD OF VISION OVERLAPS
RIGHT EYE
SO I DIDN'T THINK IT WAS SERIOUS.
MY WORK WAS TERRIBLY PILED UP, SO I ENDED UP LETTING IT GO FOR ABOUT A MONTH.
CAN'T BE...
HMM...?

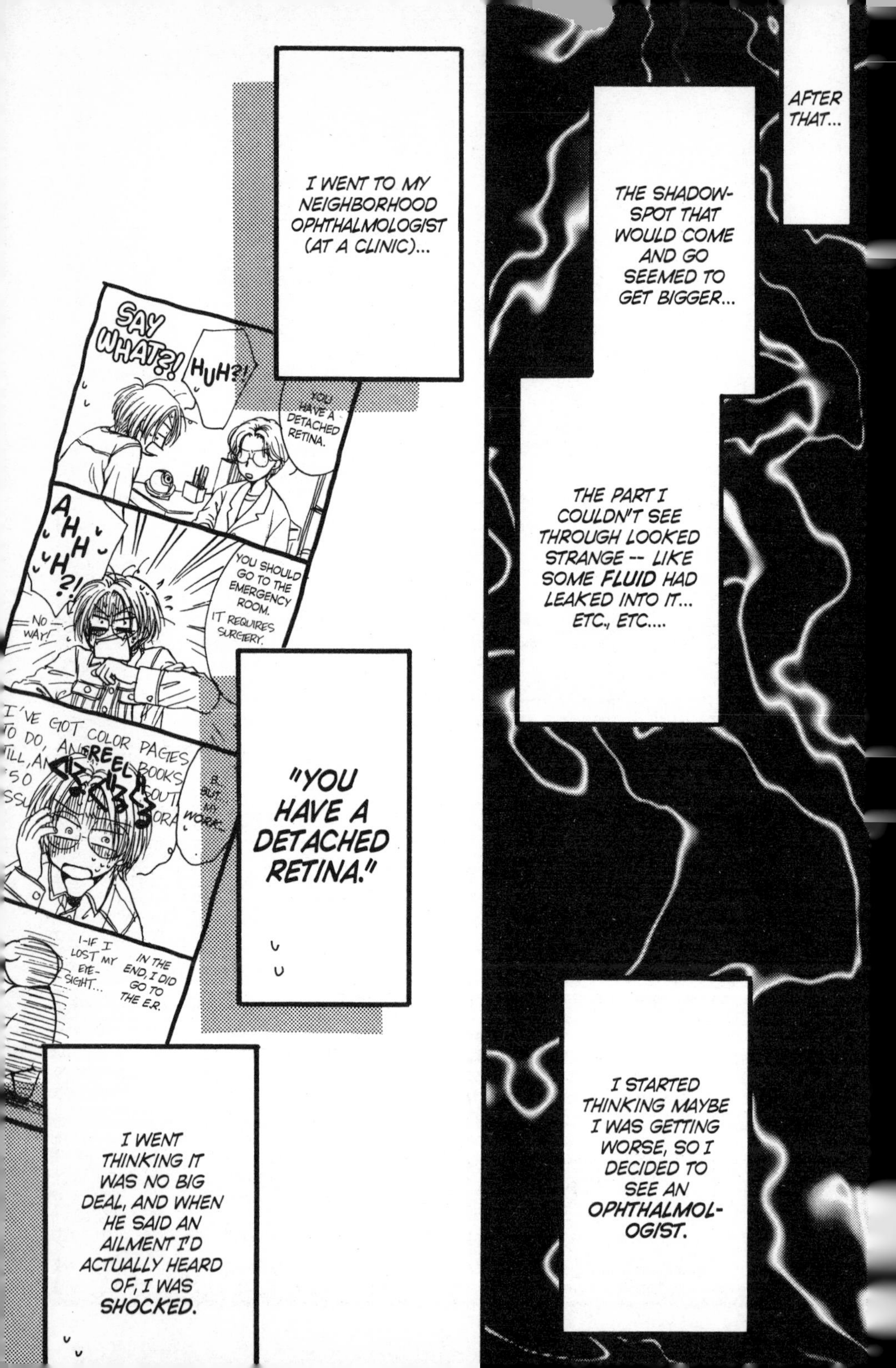
AFTER THAT...
THE SHADOW-SPOT THAT WOULD COME AND GO SEEMED TO GET BIGGER...
THE PART I COULDN'T SEE THROUGH LOOKED STRANGE -- LIKE SOME FLUID HAD LEAKED INTO IT... ETC., ETC....
I STARTED THINKING MAYBE I WAS GETTING WORSE, SO I DECIDED TO SEE AN OPHTHALMOLOGIST.
I WENT TO MY NEIGHBORHOOD OPHTHALMOLOGIST (AT A CLINIC)...
"YOU HAVE A DETACHED RETINA."
I WENT THINKING IT WAS NO BIG DEAL, AND WHEN HE SAID AN AILMENT I'D ACTUALLY HEARD OF, I WAS SHOCKED.
YOU HAVE A DETACHED RETINA.
HUH?!
YOU SHOULD GO TO THE EMERGENCY ROOM. IT REQUIRES SURGERY.
AHHH?!
NO WAY!
B... BUT... MY WORK...
REEL
IN THE END, I DID GO TO THE E.R.
I-IF I LOST MY EYE-SIGHT...

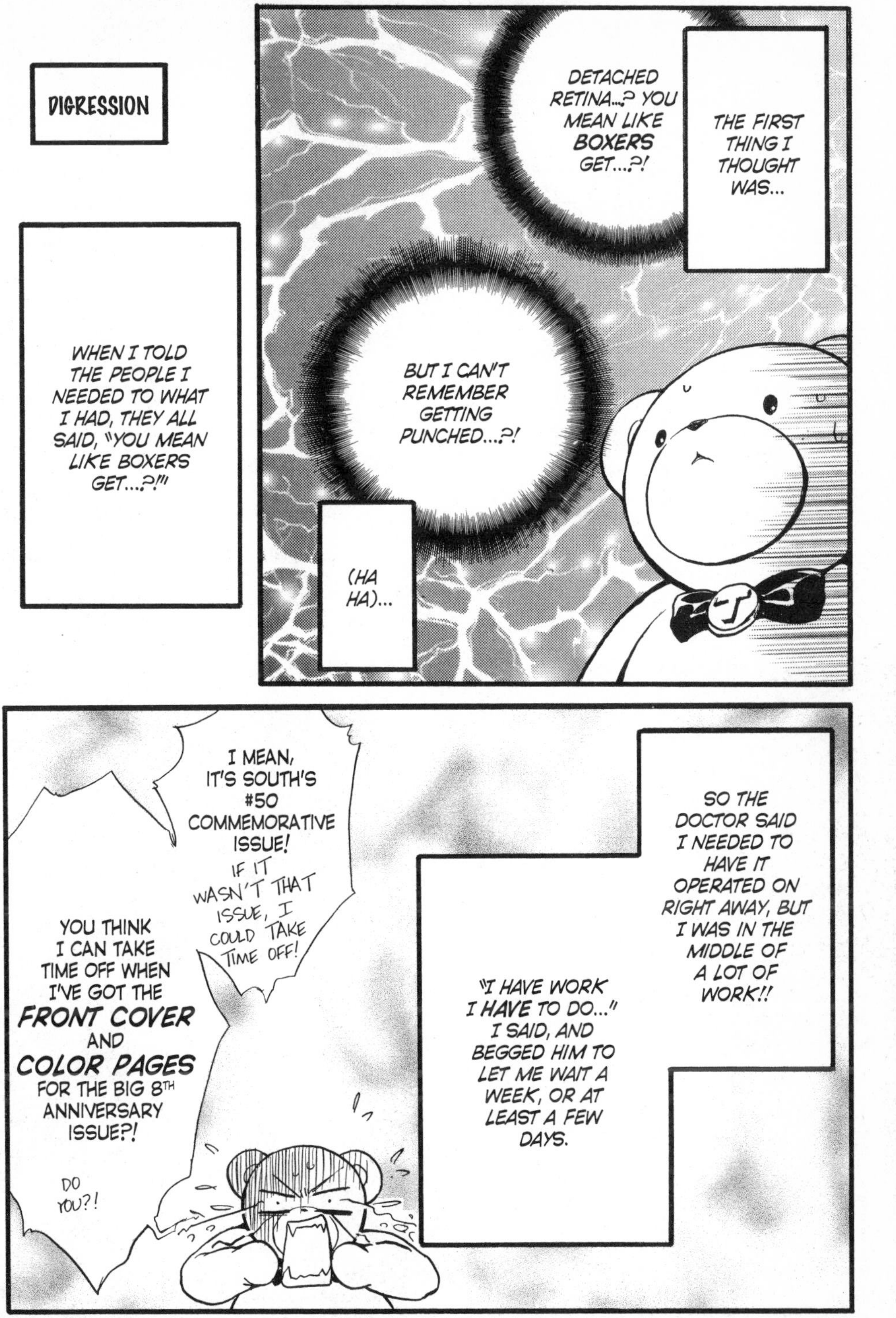
THE FIRST THING I THOUGHT WAS...
DETACHED RETINA...? YOU MEAN LIKE BOXERS GET...?!
BUT I CAN'T REMEMBER GETTING PUNCHED...?!
(HA HA)...
DIGRESSION
WHEN I TOLD THE PEOPLE I NEEDED TO WHAT I HAD, THEY ALL SAID, "YOU MEAN LIKE BOXERS GET...?!"
SO THE DOCTOR SAID I NEEDED TO HAVE IT OPERATED ON RIGHT AWAY, BUT I WAS IN THE MIDDLE OF A LOT OF WORK!!
"I HAVE WORK I HAVE TO DO..." I SAID, AND BEGGED HIM TO LET ME WAIT A WEEK, OR AT LEAST A FEW DAYS.
I MEAN, IT'S SOUTH'S #50 COMMEMORATIVE ISSUE!
IF IT WASN'T THAT ISSUE, I COULD TAKE TIME OFF!
YOU THINK I CAN TAKE TIME OFF WHEN I'VE GOT THE FRONT COVER AND COLOR PAGES FOR THE BIG 8TH ANNIVERSARY ISSUE?!
DO YOU?!

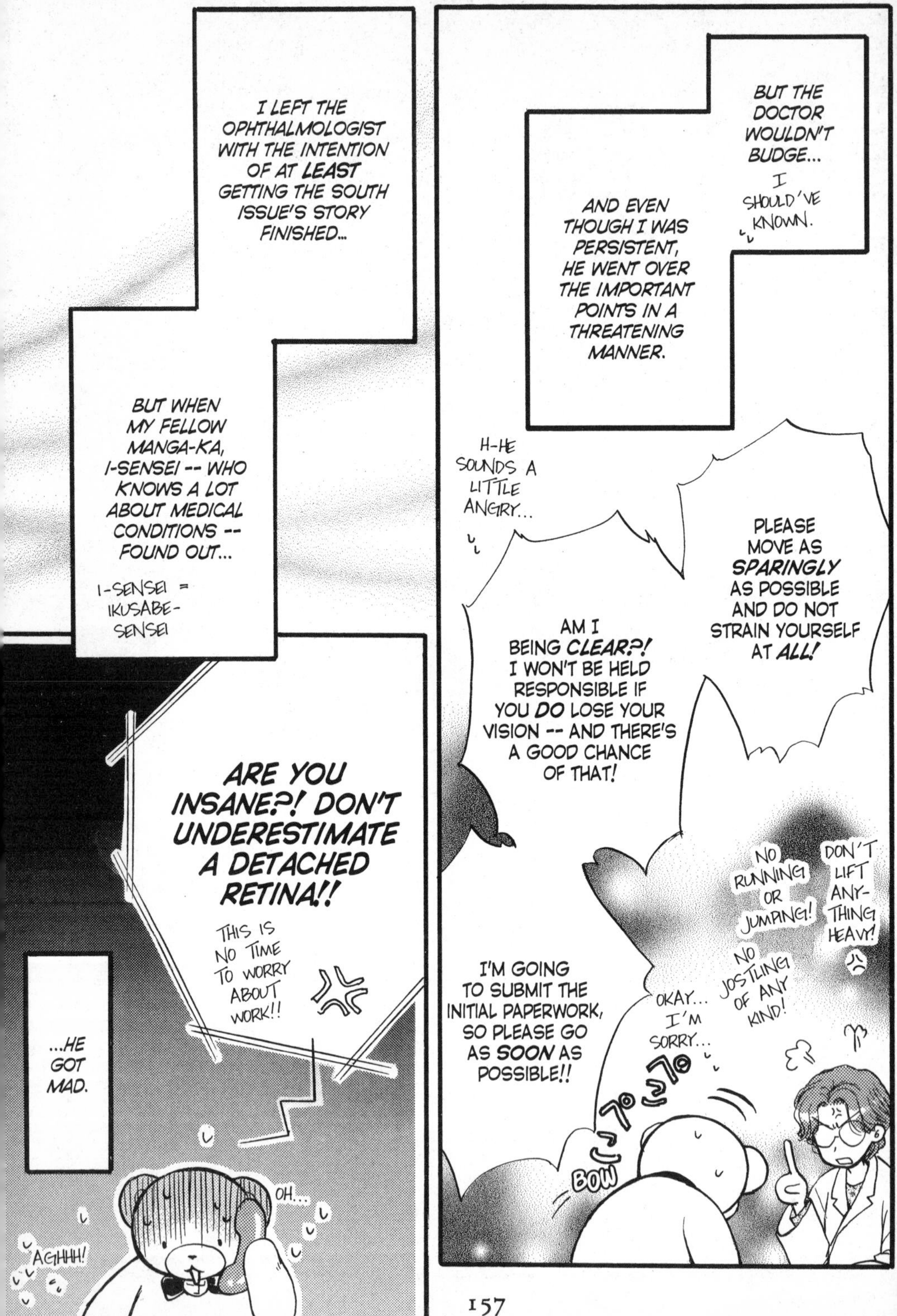
BUT THE DOCTOR WOULDN'T BUDGE...
I SHOULD'VE KNOWN.
AND EVEN THOUGH I WAS PERSISTENT, HE WENT OVER THE IMPORTANT POINTS IN A THREATENING MANNER.
PLEASE MOVE AS SPARINGLY AS POSSIBLE AND DO NOT STRAIN YOURSELF AT ALL!
AM I BEING CLEAR?! I WON'T BE HELD RESPONSIBLE IF YOU DO LOSE YOUR VISION -- AND THERE'S A GOOD CHANCE OF THAT!
H-HE SOUNDS A LITTLE ANGRY...
DON'T LIFT ANYTHING HEAVY!
NO RUNNING OR JUMPING!
NO JOSTLING OF ANY KIND!
I'M GOING TO SUBMIT THE INITIAL PAPERWORK, SO PLEASE GO AS SOON AS POSSIBLE!!
OKAY... I'M SORRY...
BOW
I LEFT THE OPHTHALMOLOGIST WITH THE INTENTION OF AT LEAST GETTING THE SOUTH ISSUE'S STORY FINISHED...
BUT WHEN MY FELLOW MANGA-KA, I-SENSEI -- WHO KNOWS A LOT ABOUT MEDICAL CONDITIONS -- FOUND OUT...
I-SENSEI = IKUSABE-SENSEI
ARE YOU INSANE?! DON'T UNDERESTIMATE A DETACHED RETINA!!
THIS IS NO TIME TO WORRY ABOUT WORK!!
...HE GOT MAD.
OH...
AGHHH!

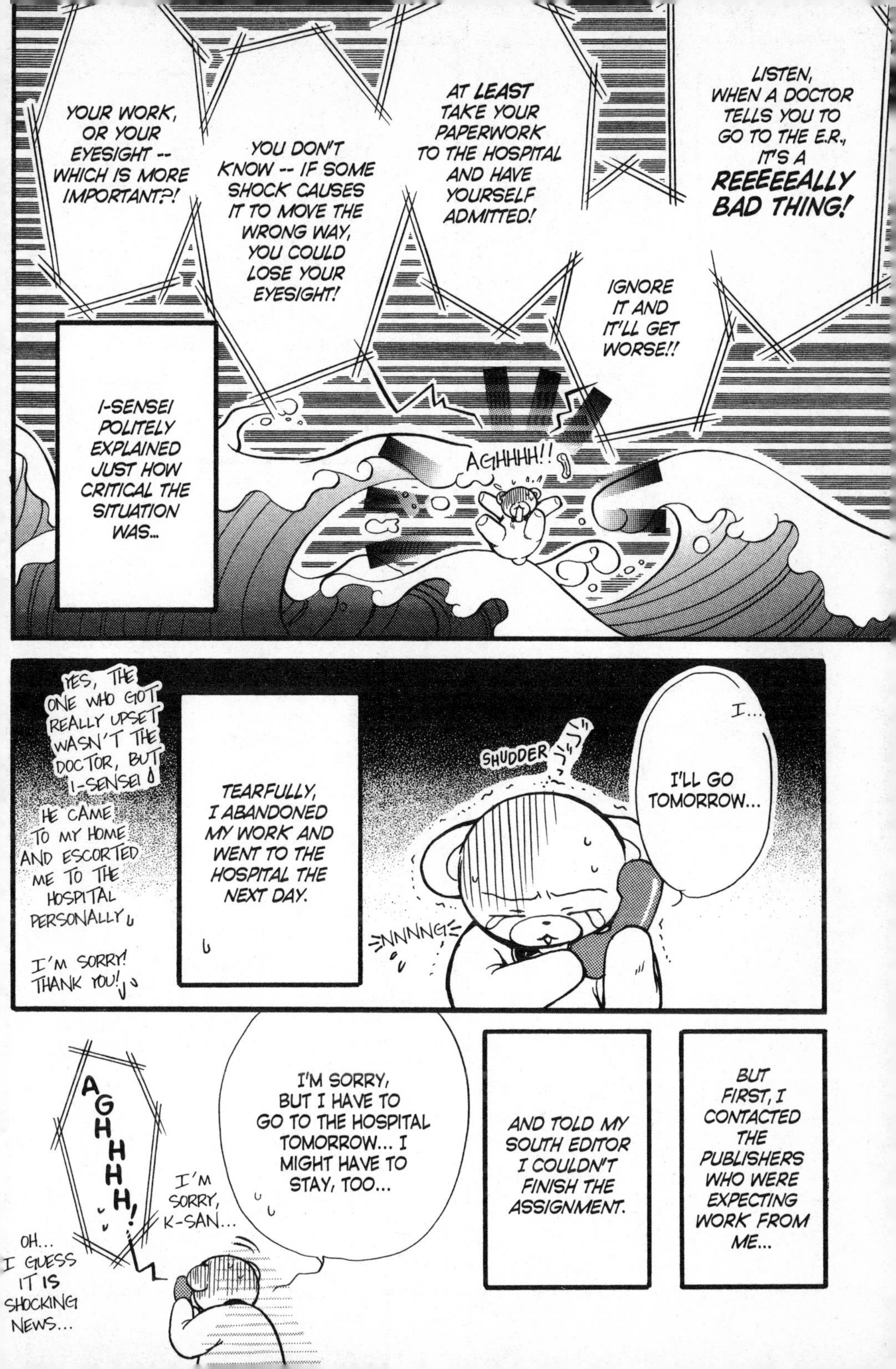
LISTEN, WHEN A DOCTOR TELLS YOU TO GO TO THE E.R., IT'S A REEEEEALLY BAD THING!
AT LEAST TAKE YOUR PAPERWORK TO THE HOSPITAL AND HAVE YOURSELF ADMITTED!
YOU DON'T KNOW -- IF SOME SHOCK CAUSES IT TO MOVE THE WRONG WAY, YOU COULD LOSE YOUR EYESIGHT!
YOUR WORK, OR YOUR EYESIGHT -- WHICH IS MORE IMPORTANT?!
IGNORE IT AND IT'LL GET WORSE!!
AGHHHH!!
I-SENSEI POLITELY EXPLAINED JUST HOW CRITICAL THE SITUATION WAS...
I...
I'LL GO TOMORROW...
SHUDDER
NNNNG
TEARFULLY, I ABANDONED MY WORK AND WENT TO THE HOSPITAL THE NEXT DAY.
YES, THE ONE WHO GOT REALLY UPSET WASN'T THE DOCTOR, BUT I-SENSEI
HE CAME TO MY HOME AND ESCORTED ME TO THE HOSPITAL PERSONALLY
I'M SORRY! THANK YOU!
BUT FIRST, I CONTACTED THE PUBLISHERS WHO WERE EXPECTING WORK FROM ME...
AND TOLD MY SOUTH EDITOR I COULDN'T FINISH THE ASSIGNMENT.
I'M SORRY, BUT I HAVE TO GO TO THE HOSPITAL TOMORROW... I MIGHT HAVE TO STAY, TOO...
I'M SORRY, K-SAN...
AGHHH!
OH... I GUESS IT IS SHOCKING NEWS...

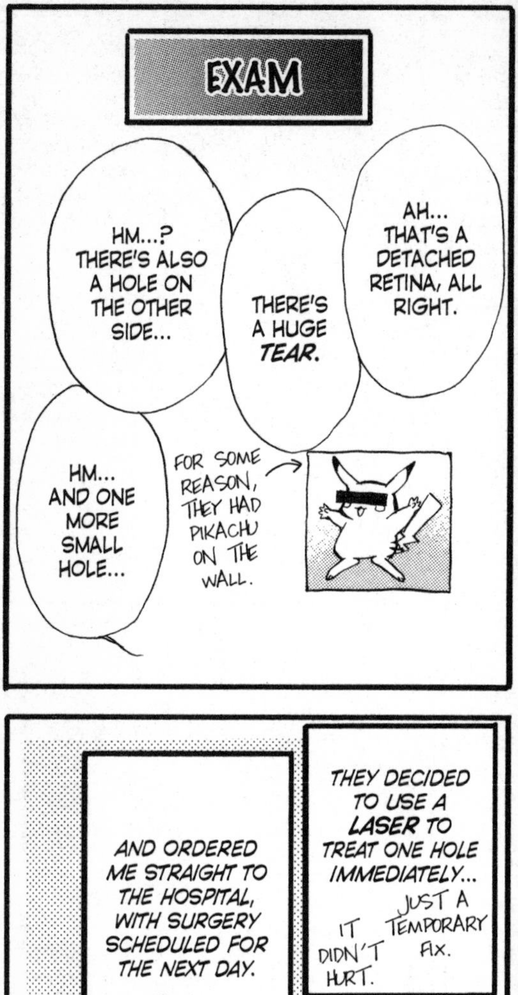
EXAM
AH... THAT'S A DETACHED RETINA, ALL RIGHT.
THERE'S A HUGE TEAR.
HM...? THERE'S ALSO A HOLE ON THE OTHER SIDE...
HM... AND ONE MORE SMALL HOLE...
FOR SOME REASON, THEY HAD PIKACHU ON THE WALL.
THEY DECIDED TO USE A LASER TO TREAT ONE HOLE IMMEDIATELY...
JUST A TEMPORARY FIX.
IT DIDN'T HURT.
AND ORDERED ME STRAIGHT TO THE HOSPITAL, WITH SURGERY SCHEDULED FOR THE NEXT DAY.
TALK ABOUT AN EMERGENCY!
APPARENTLY, I HAD THREE HOLES... NORMALLY THERE'S ONLY ONE...
WHY DOES ABNORMAL STUFF ALWAYS HAPPEN TO ME...?

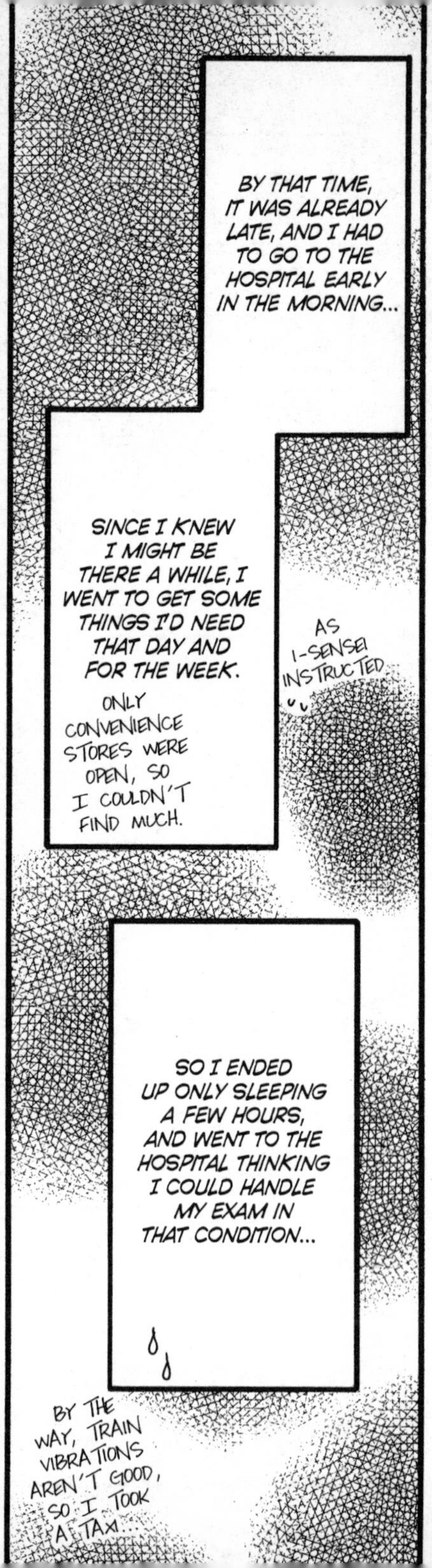
BY THAT TIME, IT WAS ALREADY LATE, AND I HAD TO GO TO THE HOSPITAL EARLY IN THE MORNING...
SINCE I KNEW I MIGHT BE THERE A WHILE, I WENT TO GET SOME THINGS I'D NEED THAT DAY AND FOR THE WEEK.
AS I-SENSEI INSTRUCTED
ONLY CONVENIENCE STORES WERE OPEN, SO I COULDN'T FIND MUCH.
SO I ENDED UP ONLY SLEEPING A FEW HOURS, AND WENT TO THE HOSPITAL THINKING I COULD HANDLE MY EXAM IN THAT CONDITION...
BY THE WAY, TRAIN VIBRATIONS AREN'T GOOD, SO I TOOK A TAXI...

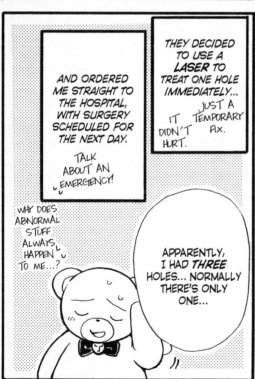

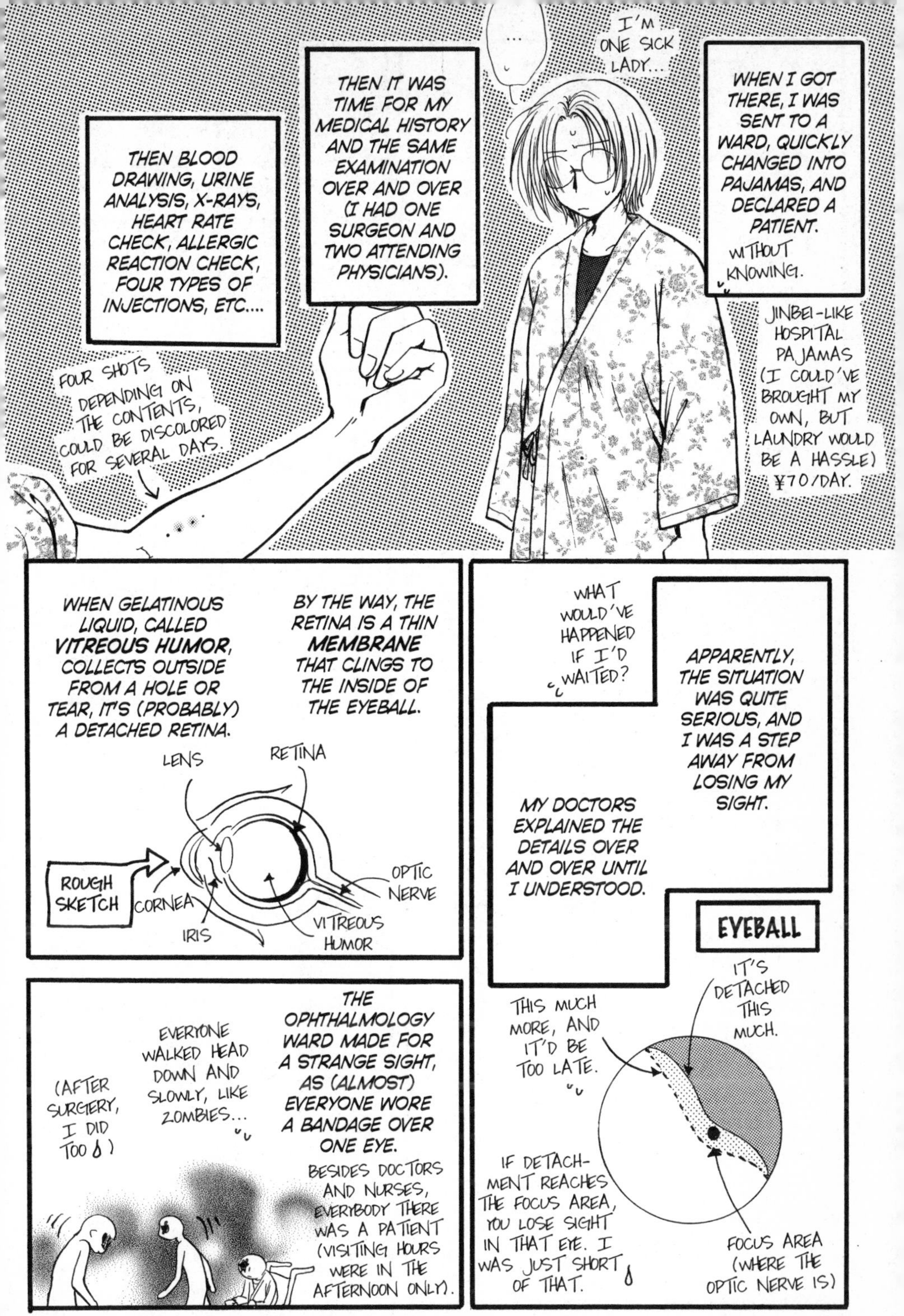

WHEN I GOT THERE, I WAS SENT TO A WARD, QUICKLY CHANGED INTO PAJAMAS, AND DECLARED A PATIENT.
WITHOUT KNOWING.
I'M ONE SICK LADY...
...
JINBEI-LIKE HOSPITAL PAJAMAS (I COULD'VE BROUGHT MY OWN, BUT LAUNDRY WOULD BE A HASSLE) ¥70/DAY.
THEN IT WAS TIME FOR MY MEDICAL HISTORY AND THE SAME EXAMINATION OVER AND OVER (I HAD ONE SURGEON AND TWO ATTENDING PHYSICIANS).
THEN BLOOD DRAWING, URINE ANALYSIS, X-RAYS, HEART RATE CHECK, ALLERGIC REACTION CHECK, FOUR TYPES OF INJECTIONS, ETC....
FOUR SHOTS
DEPENDING ON THE CONTENTS, COULD BE DISCOLORED FOR SEVERAL DAYS.
WHAT WOULD'VE HAPPENED IF I'D WAITED?
APPARENTLY, THE SITUATION WAS QUITE SERIOUS, AND I WAS A STEP AWAY FROM LOSING MY SIGHT.
MY DOCTORS EXPLAINED THE DETAILS OVER AND OVER UNTIL I UNDERSTOOD.
EYEBALL
IT'S DETACHED THIS MUCH.
THIS MUCH MORE, AND IT'D BE TOO LATE.
IF DETACHMENT REACHES THE FOCUS AREA, YOU LOSE SIGHT IN THAT EYE. I WAS JUST SHORT OF THAT.
FOCUS AREA (WHERE THE OPTIC NERVE IS)
BY THE WAY, THE RETINA IS A THIN MEMBRANE THAT CLINGS TO THE INSIDE OF THE EYEBALL.
WHEN GELATINOUS LIQUID, CALLED VITREOUS HUMOR, COLLECTS OUTSIDE FROM A HOLE OR TEAR, IT'S (PROBABLY) A DETACHED RETINA.
LENS
RETINA
ROUGH SKETCH
CORNEA
IRIS
VITREOUS HUMOR
OPTIC NERVE
THE OPHTHALMOLOGY WARD MADE FOR A STRANGE SIGHT, AS (ALMOST) EVERYONE WORE A BANDAGE OVER ONE EYE.
EVERYONE WALKED HEAD DOWN AND SLOWLY, LIKE ZOMBIES...
(AFTER SURGERY, I DID TOO)
BESIDES DOCTORS AND NURSES, EVERYBODY THERE WAS A PATIENT (VISITING HOURS WERE IN THE AFTERNOON ONLY).

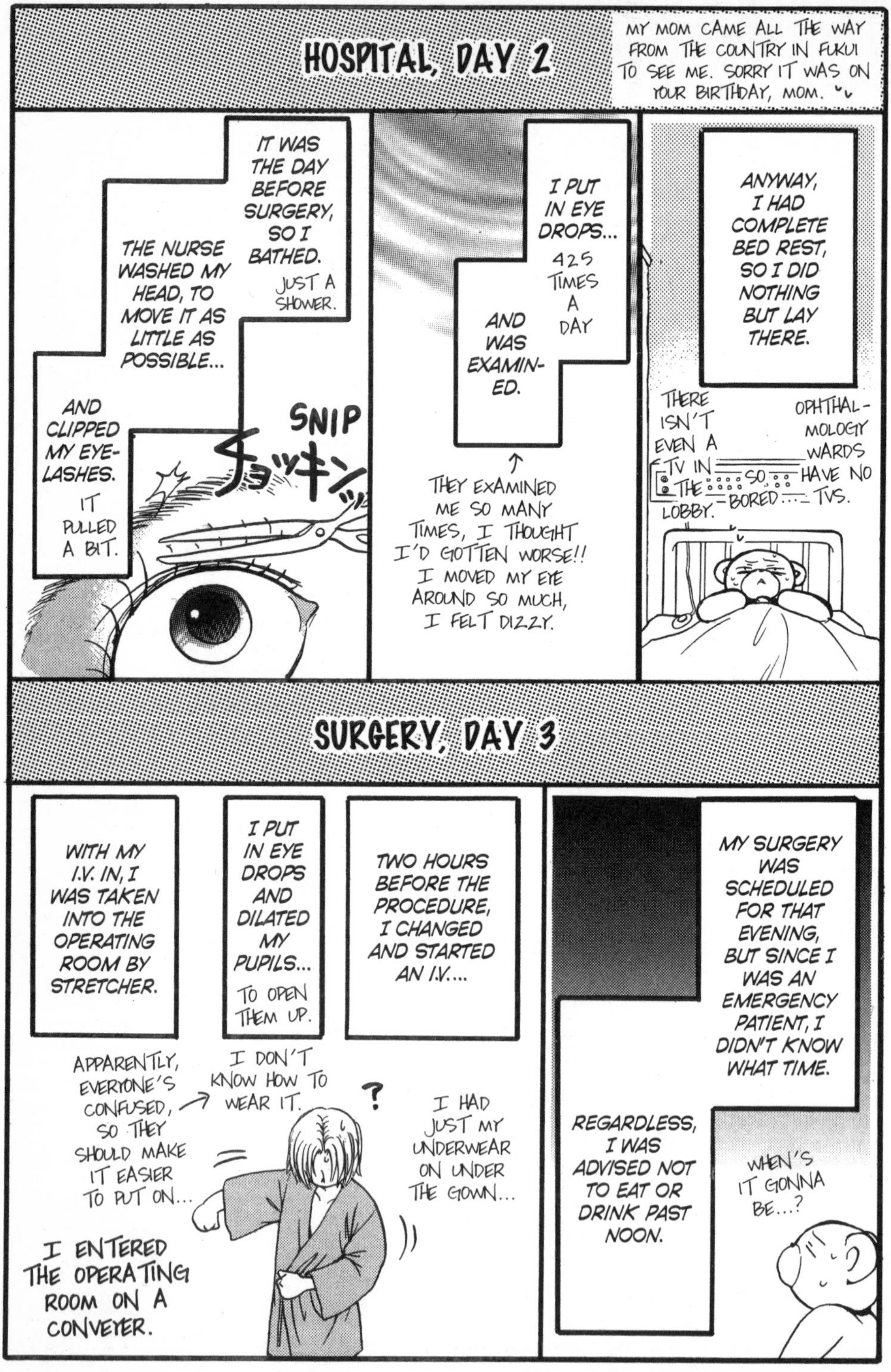
MY MOM CAME ALL THE WAY FROM THE COUNTRY IN FUKUI TO SEE ME. SORRY IT WAS ON YOUR BIRTHDAY, MOM.
HOSPITAL, DAY 2
ANYWAY, I HAD COMPLETE BED REST, SO I DID NOTHING BUT LAY THERE.
OPHTHAL-MOLOGY WARDS HAVE NO TVS.
SO BORED...
THERE ISN'T EVEN A TV IN THE LOBBY.
I PUT IN EYE DROPS...
425 TIMES A DAY
AND WAS EXAMIN-ED.
THEY EXAMINED ME SO MANY TIMES, I THOUGHT I'D GOTTEN WORSE!! I MOVED MY EYE AROUND SO MUCH, I FELT DIZZY.
IT WAS THE DAY BEFORE SURGERY, SO I BATHED.
JUST A SHOWER.
THE NURSE WASHED MY HEAD, TO MOVE IT AS LITTLE AS POSSIBLE...
SNIP
チョッキン
AND CLIPPED MY EYE-LASHES.
IT PULLED A BIT.
SURGERY, DAY 3
MY SURGERY WAS SCHEDULED FOR THAT EVENING, BUT SINCE I WAS AN EMERGENCY PATIENT, I DIDN'T KNOW WHAT TIME.
REGARDLESS, I WAS ADVISED NOT TO EAT OR DRINK PAST NOON.
WHEN'S IT GONNA BE...?
TWO HOURS BEFORE THE PROCEDURE, I CHANGED AND STARTED AN I.V....
I PUT IN EYE DROPS AND DILATED MY PUPILS...
TO OPEN THEM UP.
WITH MY I.V. IN, I WAS TAKEN INTO THE OPERATING ROOM BY STRETCHER.
I HAD JUST MY UNDERWEAR ON UNDER THE GOWN...
?
I DON'T KNOW HOW TO WEAR IT.
APPARENTLY, EVERYONE'S CONFUSED, SO THEY SHOULD MAKE IT EASIER TO PUT ON...
I ENTERED THE OPERATING ROOM ON A CONVEYER.

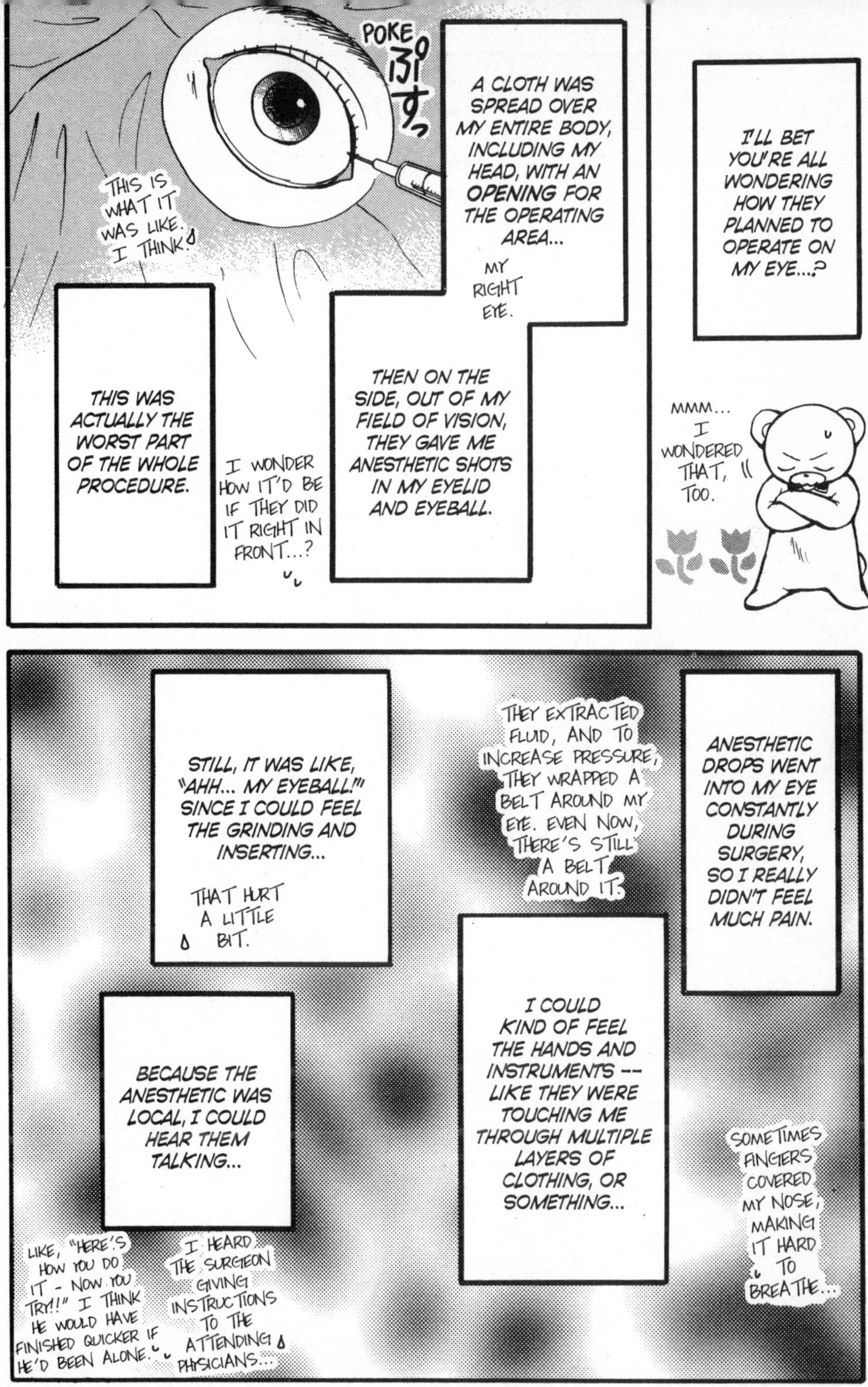

I'LL BET YOU'RE ALL WONDERING HOW THEY PLANNED TO OPERATE ON MY EYE...?
MMM... I WONDERED THAT, TOO.
A CLOTH WAS SPREAD OVER MY ENTIRE BODY, INCLUDING MY HEAD, WITH AN OPENING FOR THE OPERATING AREA...
MY RIGHT EYE.
POKE
THIS IS WHAT IT WAS LIKE. I THINK.
THEN ON THE SIDE, OUT OF MY FIELD OF VISION, THEY GAVE ME ANESTHETIC SHOTS IN MY EYELID AND EYEBALL.
I WONDER HOW IT'D BE IF THEY DID IT RIGHT IN FRONT...?
THIS WAS ACTUALLY THE WORST PART OF THE WHOLE PROCEDURE.
ANESTHETIC DROPS WENT INTO MY EYE CONSTANTLY DURING SURGERY, SO I REALLY DIDN'T FEEL MUCH PAIN.
THEY EXTRACTED FLUID, AND TO INCREASE PRESSURE, THEY WRAPPED A BELT AROUND MY EYE. EVEN NOW, THERE'S STILL A BELT AROUND IT.
STILL, IT WAS LIKE, "AHH... MY EYEBALL!" SINCE I COULD FEEL THE GRINDING AND INSERTING...
THAT HURT A LITTLE BIT.
SOMETIMES FINGERS COVERED MY NOSE, MAKING IT HARD TO BREATHE...
I COULD KIND OF FEEL THE HANDS AND INSTRUMENTS -- LIKE THEY WERE TOUCHING ME THROUGH MULTIPLE LAYERS OF CLOTHING, OR SOMETHING...
BECAUSE THE ANESTHETIC WAS LOCAL, I COULD HEAR THEM TALKING...
I HEARD THE SURGEON GIVING INSTRUCTIONS TO THE ATTENDING PHYSICIANS...
LIKE, "HERE'S HOW YOU DO IT - NOW YOU TRY!!" I THINK HE WOULD HAVE FINISHED QUICKER IF HE'D BEEN ALONE.

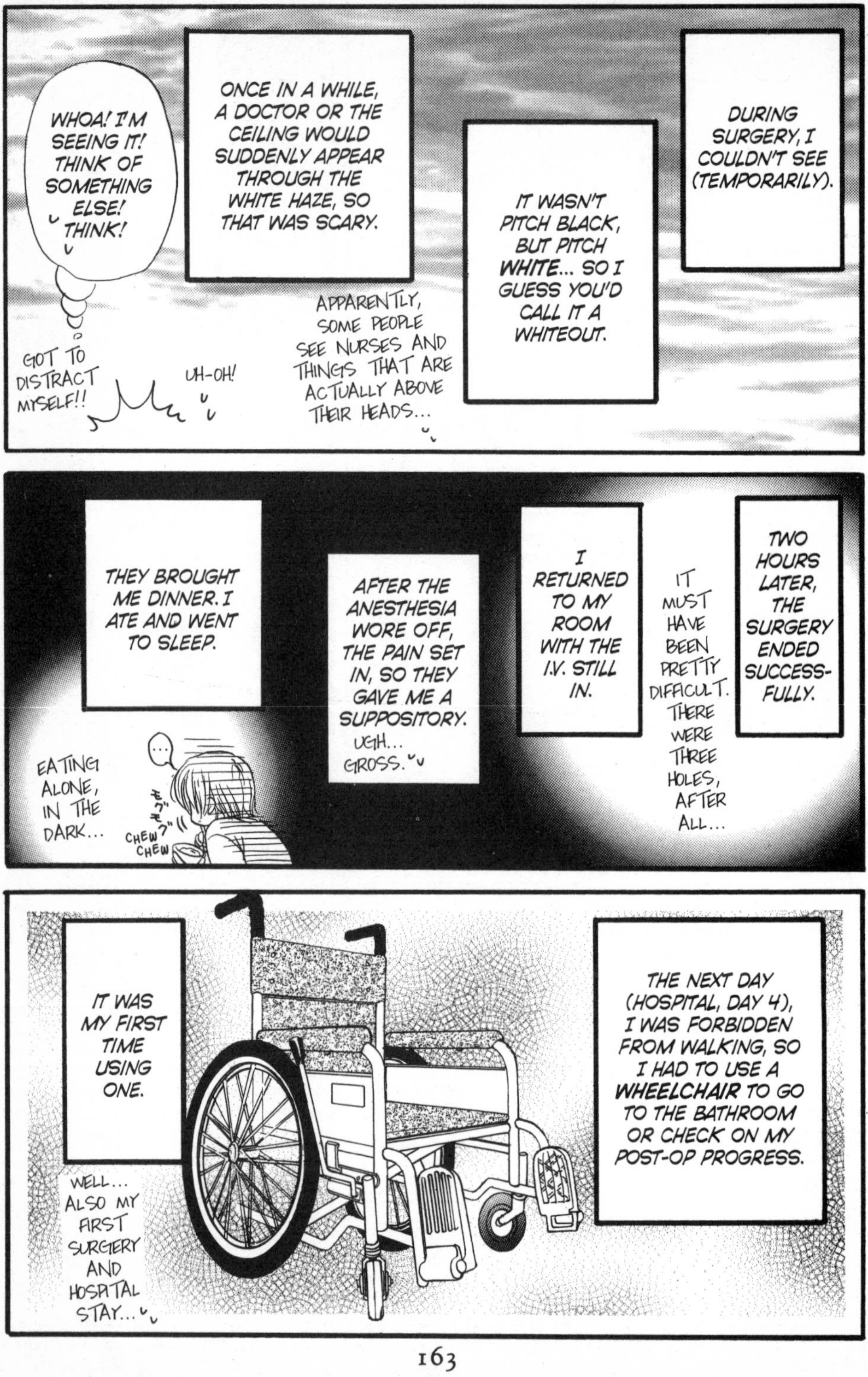
DURING SURGERY, I COULDN'T SEE (TEMPORARILY).
IT WASN'T PITCH BLACK, BUT PITCH WHITE... SO I GUESS YOU'D CALL IT A WHITEOUT.
ONCE IN A WHILE, A DOCTOR OR THE CEILING WOULD SUDDENLY APPEAR THROUGH THE WHITE HAZE, SO THAT WAS SCARY.
APPARENTLY, SOME PEOPLE SEE NURSES AND THINGS THAT ARE ACTUALLY ABOVE THEIR HEADS...
WHOA! I'M SEEING IT! THINK OF SOMETHING ELSE! THINK!
UH-OH!
GOT TO DISTRACT MYSELF!!
TWO HOURS LATER, THE SURGERY ENDED SUCCESS-FULLY.
IT MUST HAVE BEEN PRETTY DIFFICULT. THERE WERE THREE HOLES, AFTER ALL...
I RETURNED TO MY ROOM WITH THE I.V. STILL IN.
AFTER THE ANESTHESIA WORE OFF, THE PAIN SET IN, SO THEY GAVE ME A SUPPOSITORY.
UGH... GROSS.
THEY BROUGHT ME DINNER. I ATE AND WENT TO SLEEP.
...
CHEW CHEW
EATING ALONE, IN THE DARK...
THE NEXT DAY (HOSPITAL, DAY 4), I WAS FORBIDDEN FROM WALKING, SO I HAD TO USE A WHEELCHAIR TO GO TO THE BATHROOM OR CHECK ON MY POST-OP PROGRESS.
IT WAS MY FIRST TIME USING ONE.
WELL... ALSO MY FIRST SURGERY AND HOSPITAL STAY...

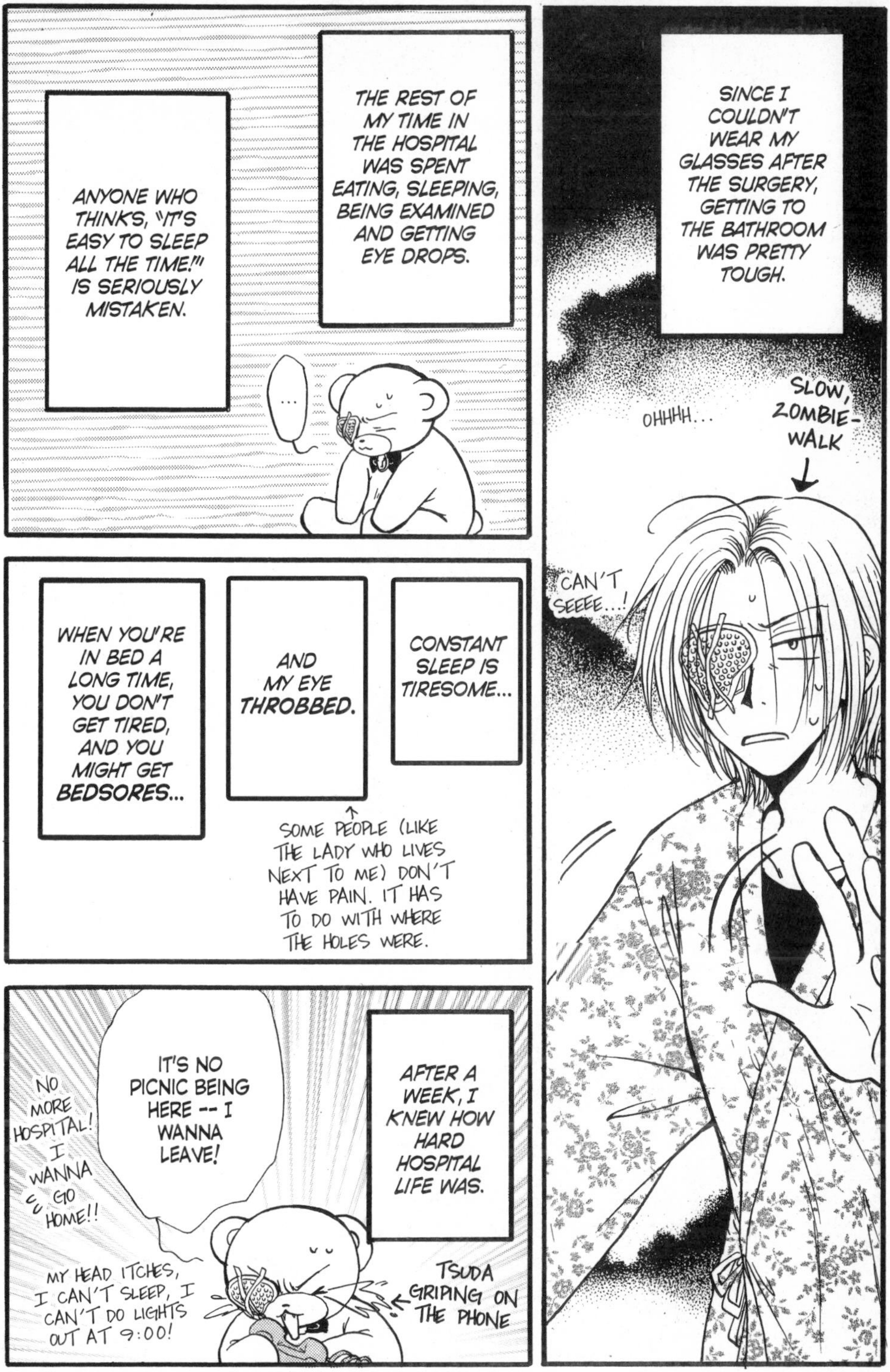
SINCE I COULDN'T WEAR MY GLASSES AFTER THE SURGERY, GETTING TO THE BATHROOM WAS PRETTY TOUGH.
SLOW, ZOMBIE-WALK
OHHHH...
CAN'T SEEEE...!
THE REST OF MY TIME IN THE HOSPITAL WAS SPENT EATING, SLEEPING, BEING EXAMINED AND GETTING EYE DROPS.
ANYONE WHO THINKS, "IT'S EASY TO SLEEP ALL THE TIME!" IS SERIOUSLY MISTAKEN.
...
CONSTANT SLEEP IS TIRESOME...
AND MY EYE THROBBED.
SOME PEOPLE (LIKE THE LADY WHO LIVES NEXT TO ME) DON'T HAVE PAIN. IT HAS TO DO WITH WHERE THE HOLES WERE.
WHEN YOU'RE IN BED A LONG TIME, YOU DON'T GET TIRED, AND YOU MIGHT GET BEDSORES...
AFTER A WEEK, I KNEW HOW HARD HOSPITAL LIFE WAS.
IT'S NO PICNIC BEING HERE -- I WANNA LEAVE!
NO MORE HOSPITAL! I WANNA GO HOME!!
TSUDA GRIPING ON THE PHONE
MY HEAD ITCHES, I CAN'T SLEEP, I CAN'T DO LIGHTS OUT AT 9:00!

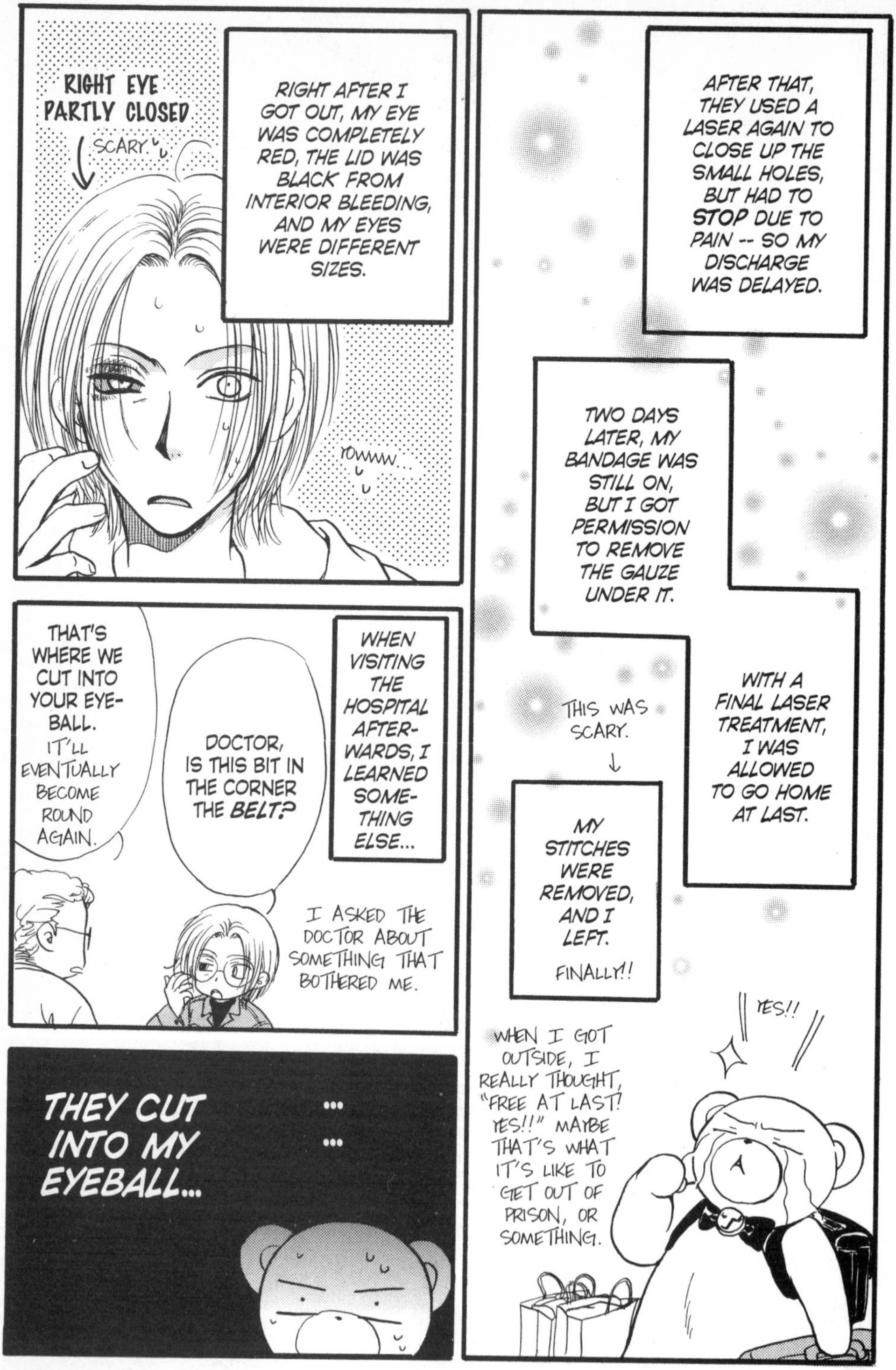

AFTER THAT, THEY USED A LASER AGAIN TO CLOSE UP THE SMALL HOLES, BUT HAD TO STOP DUE TO PAIN -- SO MY DISCHARGE WAS DELAYED.
TWO DAYS LATER, MY BANDAGE WAS STILL ON, BUT I GOT PERMISSION TO REMOVE THE GAUZE UNDER IT.
WITH A FINAL LASER TREATMENT, I WAS ALLOWED TO GO HOME AT LAST.
THIS WAS SCARY.
MY STITCHES WERE REMOVED, AND I LEFT.
FINALLY!!
YES!!
WHEN I GOT OUTSIDE, I REALLY THOUGHT, "FREE AT LAST! YES!!" MAYBE THAT'S WHAT IT'S LIKE TO GET OUT OF PRISON, OR SOMETHING.
RIGHT AFTER I GOT OUT, MY EYE WAS COMPLETELY RED, THE LID WAS BLACK FROM INTERIOR BLEEDING, AND MY EYES WERE DIFFERENT SIZES.
RIGHT EYE PARTLY CLOSED
SCARY.
YOWWW...
WHEN VISITING THE HOSPITAL AFTERWARDS, I LEARNED SOMETHING ELSE...
DOCTOR, IS THIS BIT IN THE CORNER THE BELT?
THAT'S WHERE WE CUT INTO YOUR EYEBALL. IT'LL EVENTUALLY BECOME ROUND AGAIN.
I ASKED THE DOCTOR ABOUT SOMETHING THAT BOTHERED ME.
THEY CUT INTO MY EYEBALL...
...
...

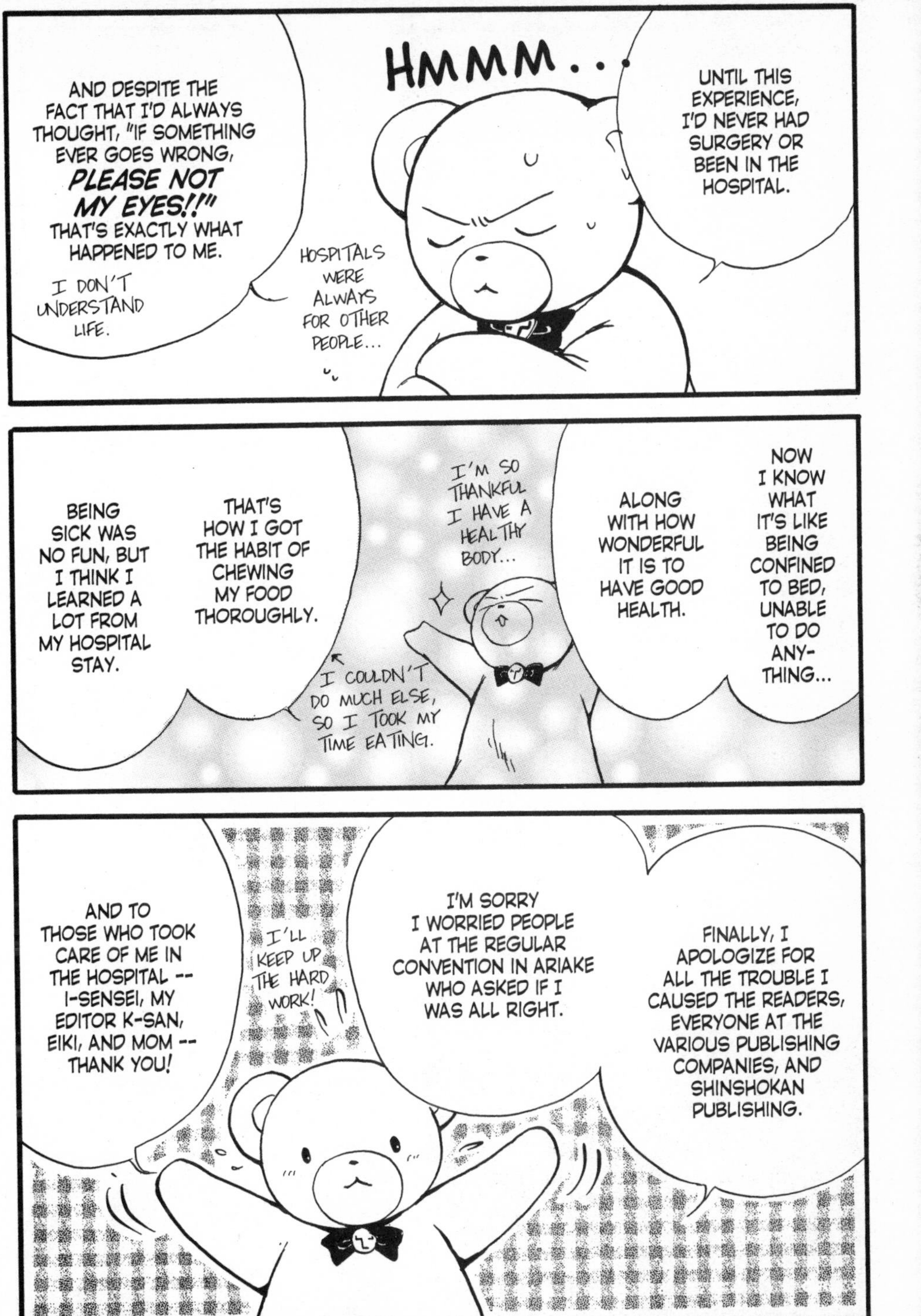
HMMM...
UNTIL THIS EXPERIENCE, I'D NEVER HAD SURGERY OR BEEN IN THE HOSPITAL.
HOSPITALS WERE ALWAYS FOR OTHER PEOPLE...
AND DESPITE THE FACT THAT I'D ALWAYS THOUGHT, "IF SOMETHING EVER GOES WRONG, ***PLEASE NOT MY EYES!!"*** THAT'S EXACTLY WHAT HAPPENED TO ME.
I DON'T UNDERSTAND LIFE.
NOW I KNOW WHAT IT'S LIKE BEING CONFINED TO BED, UNABLE TO DO ANY-THING...
ALONG WITH HOW WONDERFUL IT IS TO HAVE GOOD HEALTH.
I'M SO THANKFUL I HAVE A HEALTHY BODY...
THAT'S HOW I GOT THE HABIT OF CHEWING MY FOOD THOROUGHLY.
I COULDN'T DO MUCH ELSE, SO I TOOK MY TIME EATING.
BEING SICK WAS NO FUN, BUT I THINK I LEARNED A LOT FROM MY HOSPITAL STAY.
FINALLY, I APOLOGIZE FOR ALL THE TROUBLE I CAUSED THE READERS, EVERYONE AT THE VARIOUS PUBLISHING COMPANIES, AND SHINSHOKAN PUBLISHING.
I'M SORRY I WORRIED PEOPLE AT THE REGULAR CONVENTION IN ARIAKE WHO ASKED IF I WAS ALL RIGHT.
I'LL KEEP UP THE HARD WORK!
AND TO THOSE WHO TOOK CARE OF ME IN THE HOSPITAL -- I-SENSEI, MY EDITOR K-SAN, EIKI, AND MOM -- THANK YOU!

DETACHED RETINA DIARY ✸ END

SAKAMOTO FAMILY • MOM & DAD

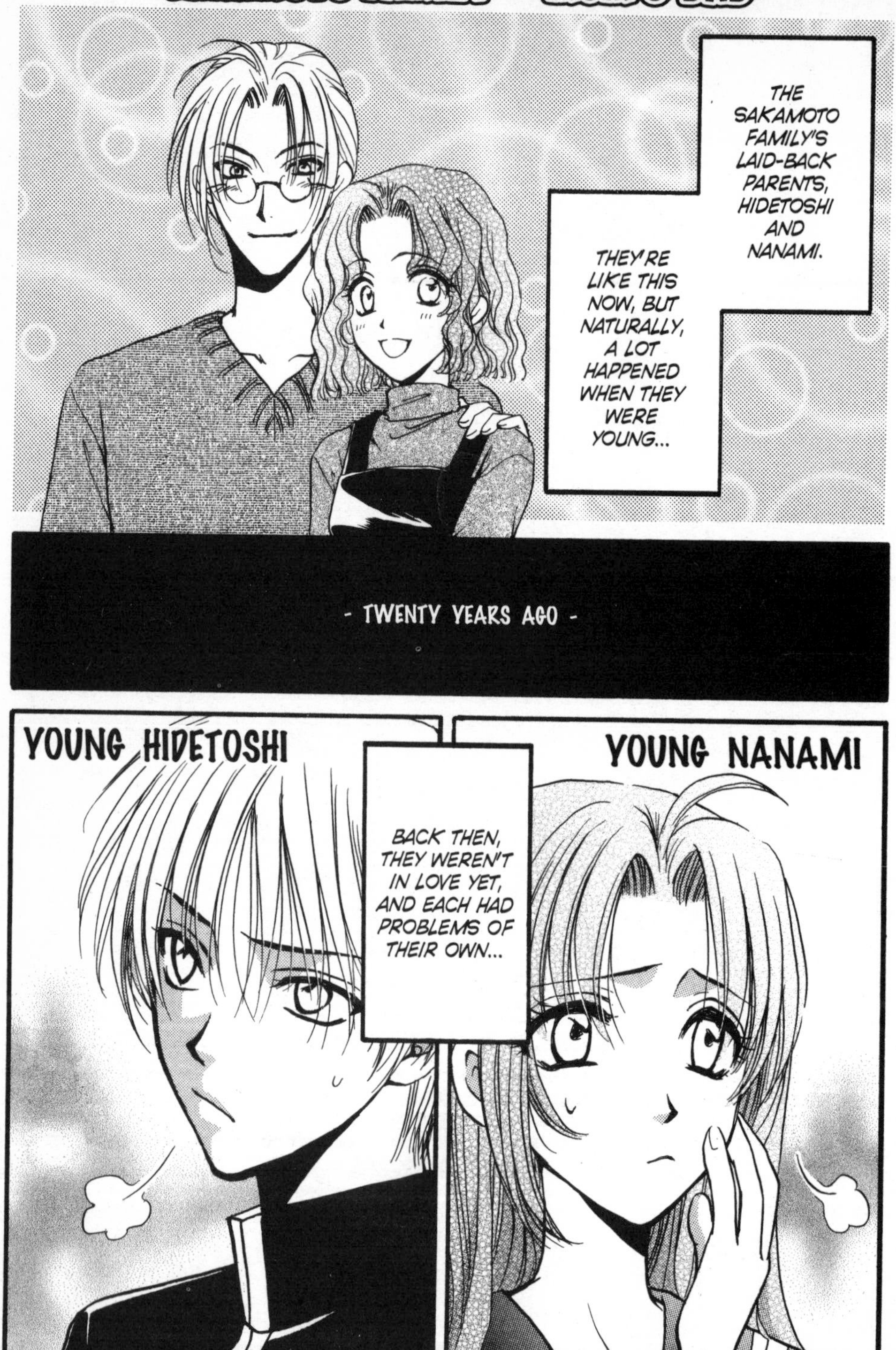
THE SAKAMOTO FAMILY'S LAID-BACK PARENTS, HIDETOSHI AND NANAMI.
THEY'RE LIKE THIS NOW, BUT NATURALLY, A LOT HAPPENED WHEN THEY WERE YOUNG...
- TWENTY YEARS AGO -
YOUNG NANAMI
BACK THEN, THEY WEREN'T IN LOVE YET, AND EACH HAD PROBLEMS OF THEIR OWN...
YOUNG HIDETOSHI

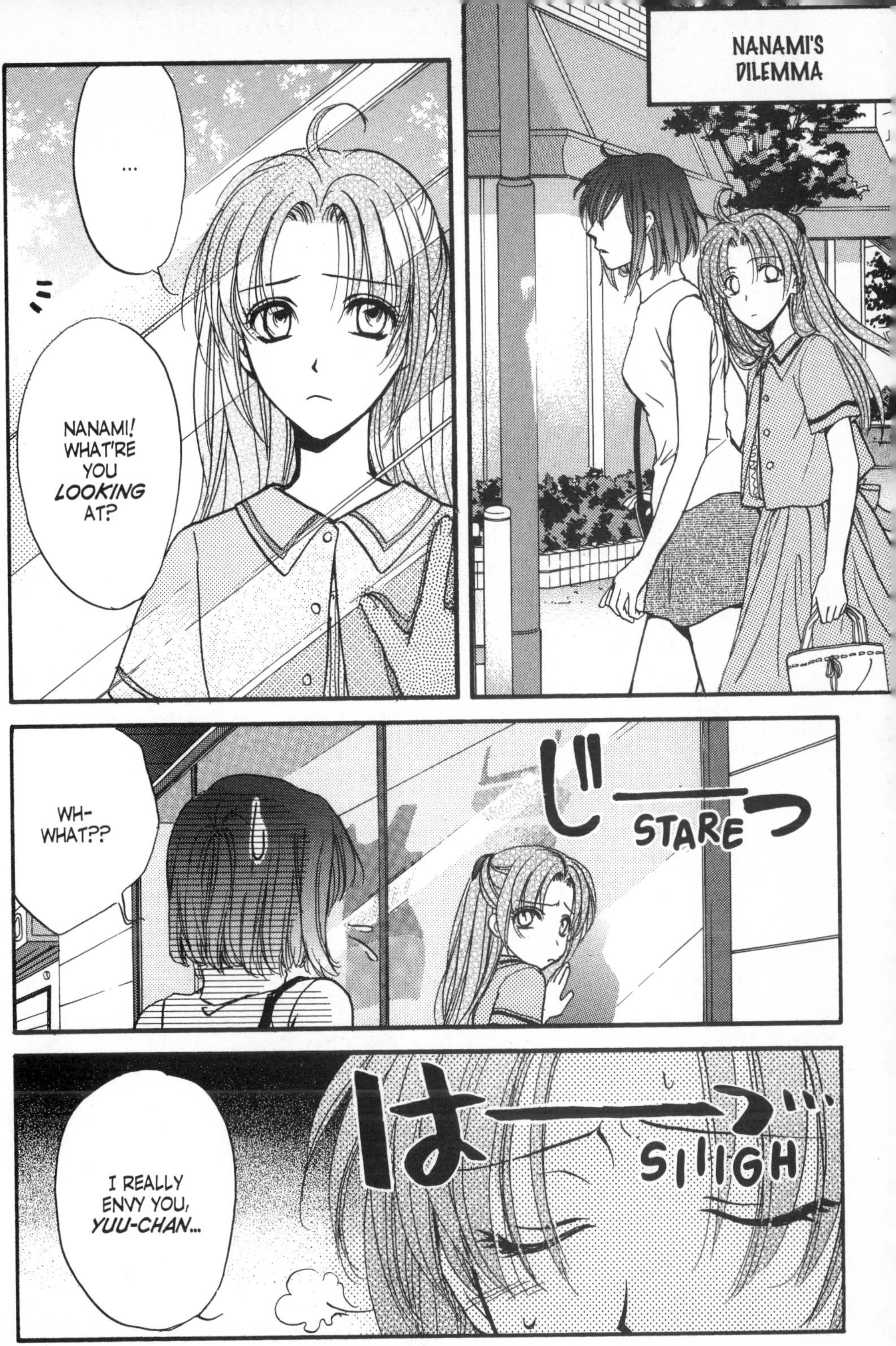
NANAMI'S DILEMMA
...
NANAMI! WHAT'RE YOU *LOOKING* AT?
じーっ
STARE
WH- WHAT??
はーっ
SIIIGH
I REALLY ENVY YOU, *YUU-CHAN*...

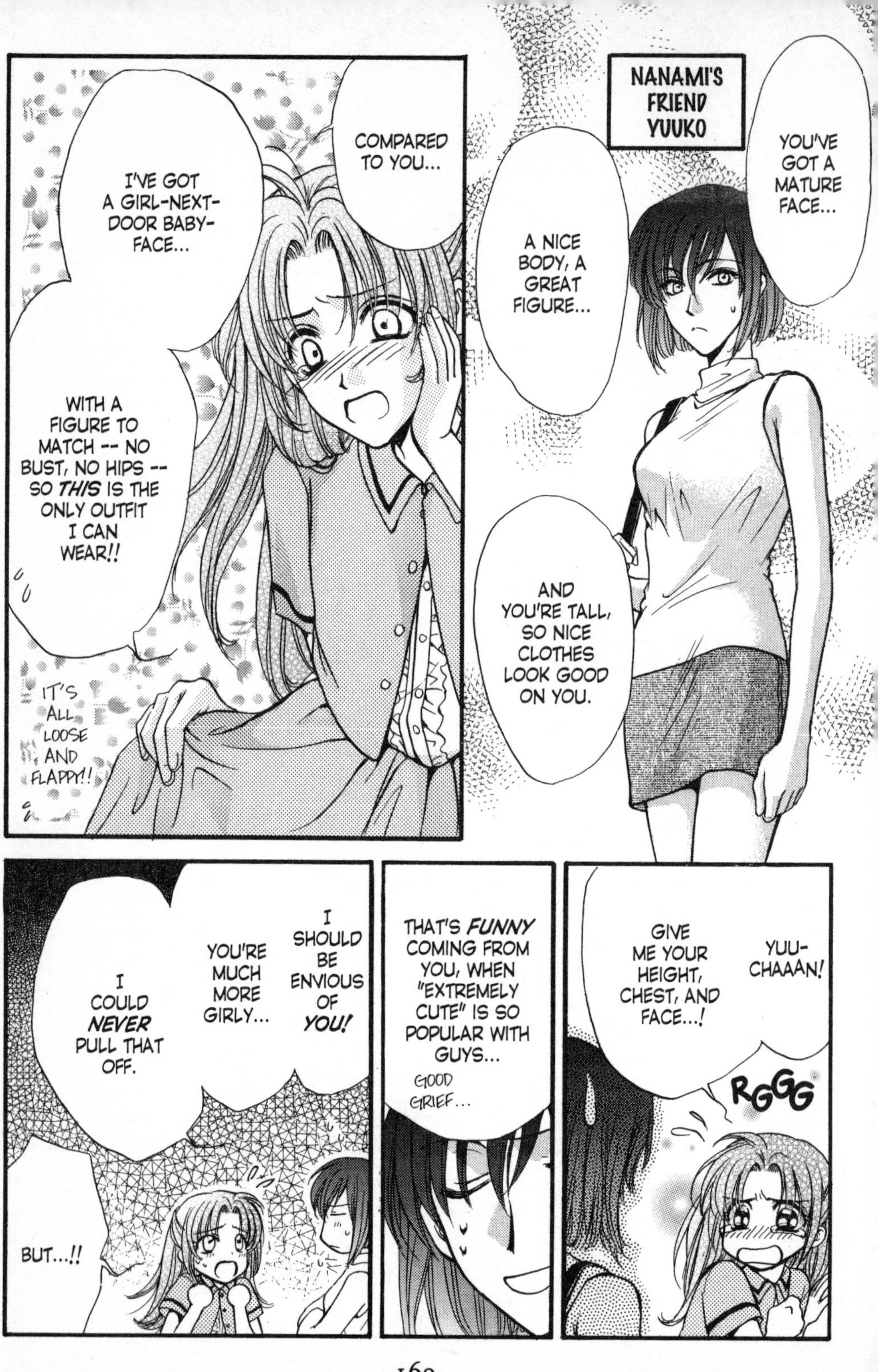
NANAMI'S FRIEND YUUKO
YOU'VE GOT A MATURE FACE...
A NICE BODY, A GREAT FIGURE...
AND YOU'RE TALL, SO NICE CLOTHES LOOK GOOD ON YOU.
COMPARED TO YOU...
I'VE GOT A GIRL-NEXT-DOOR BABY-FACE...
WITH A FIGURE TO MATCH -- NO BUST, NO HIPS -- SO *THIS* IS THE ONLY OUTFIT I CAN WEAR!!
IT'S ALL LOOSE AND FLAPPY!!
YUU-CHAAAN!
GIVE ME YOUR HEIGHT, CHEST, AND FACE...!
RGGG
THAT'S *FUNNY* COMING FROM YOU, WHEN "EXTREMELY CUTE" IS SO POPULAR WITH GUYS...
GOOD GRIEF...
I SHOULD BE ENVIOUS OF ***YOU!***
YOU'RE MUCH MORE GIRLY...
I COULD ***NEVER*** PULL THAT OFF.
BUT...!!

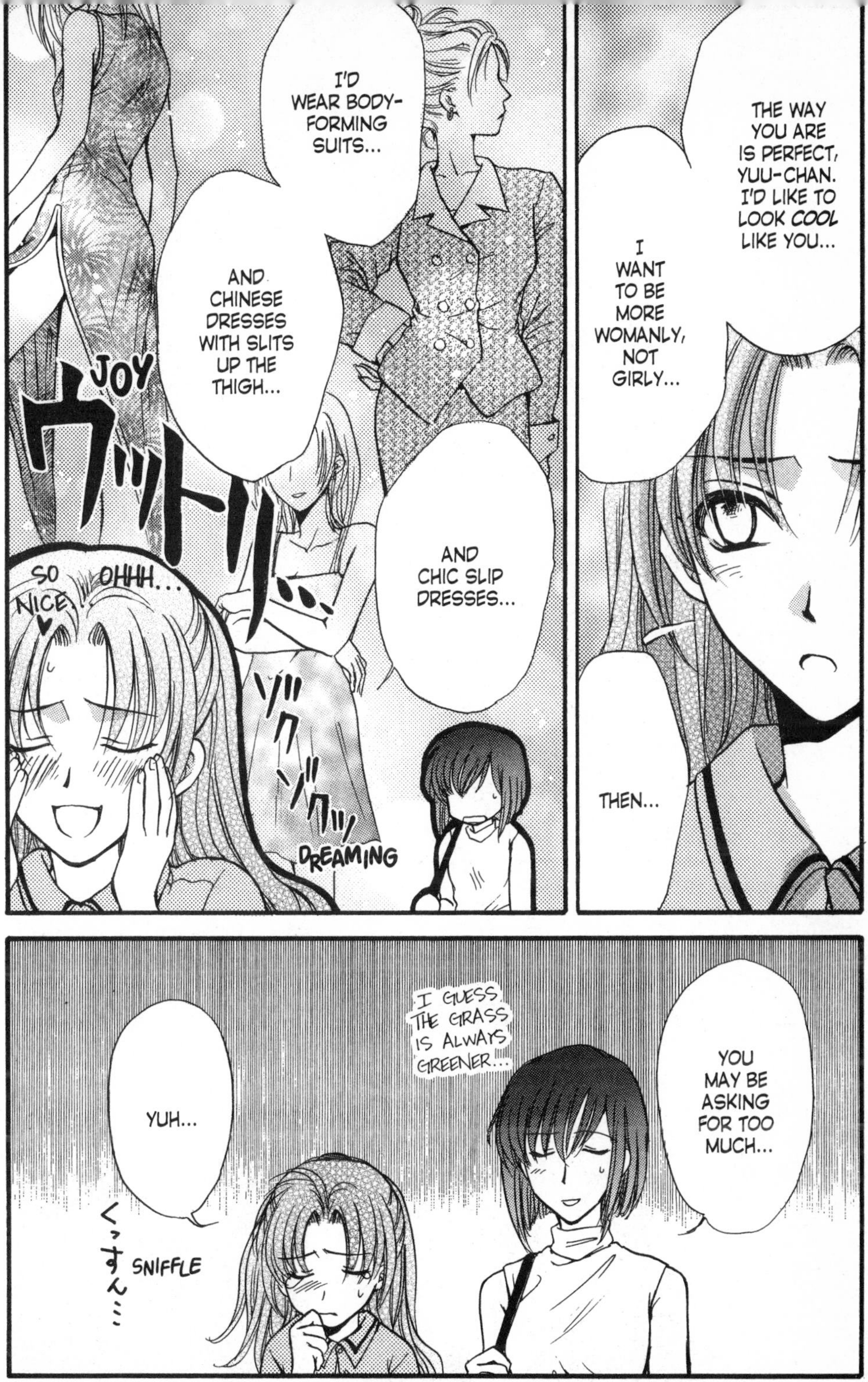
THE WAY YOU ARE IS PERFECT, YUU-CHAN. I'D LIKE TO LOOK *COOL* LIKE YOU...
I WANT TO BE MORE WOMANLY, NOT GIRLY...
THEN...
I'D WEAR BODY-FORMING SUITS...
AND CHINESE DRESSES WITH SLITS UP THE THIGH...
JOY
ウットリ…
SO NICE
OHHH...
AND CHIC SLIP DRESSES...
ゾクゾクッ
DREAMING
YOU MAY BE ASKING FOR TOO MUCH...
I GUESS THE GRASS IS ALWAYS GREENER...
YUH...
くっすん…
SNIFFLE

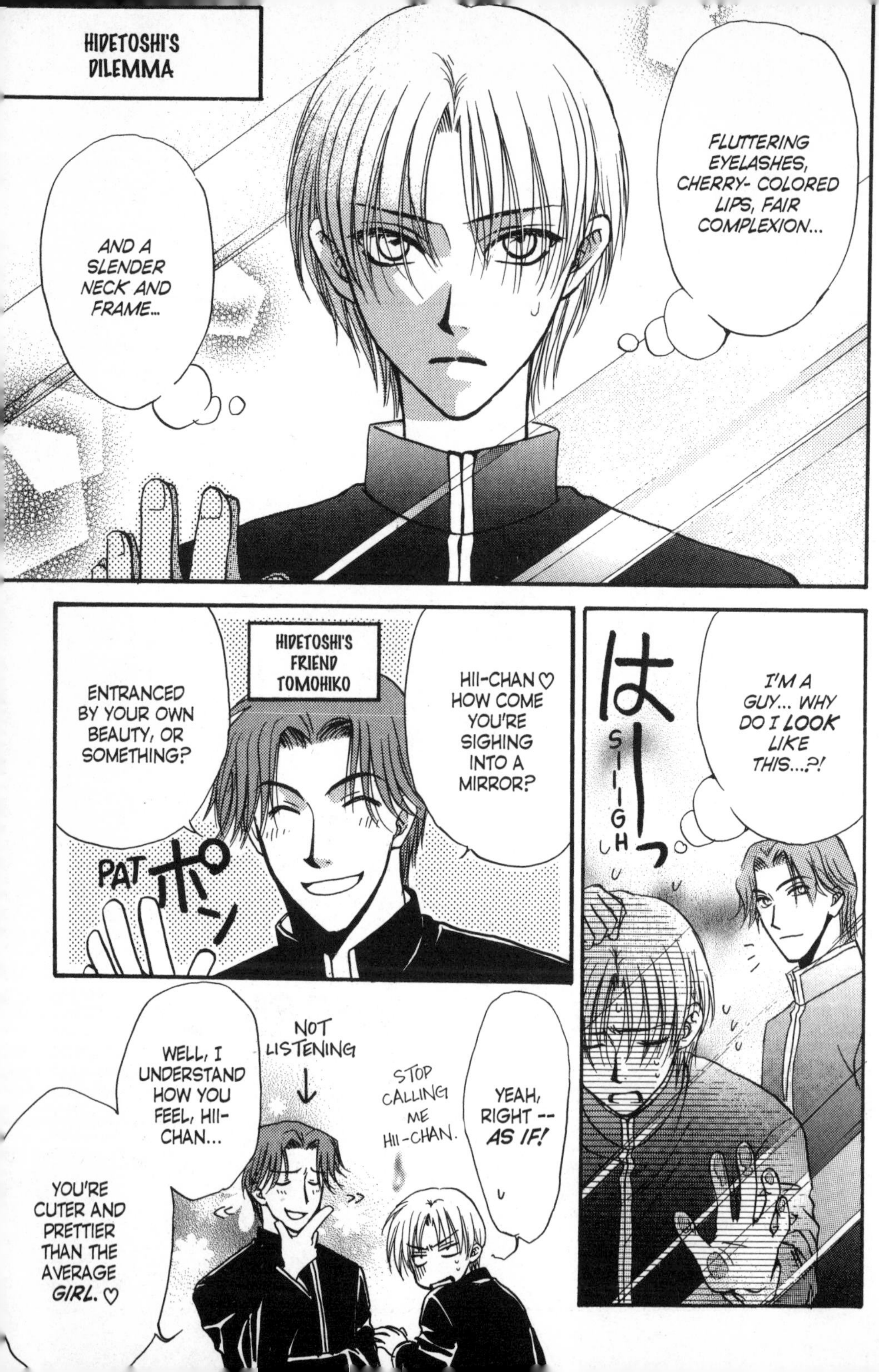
HIDETOSHI'S DILEMMA
FLUTTERING EYELASHES, CHERRY- COLORED LIPS, FAIR COMPLEXION...
AND A SLENDER NECK AND FRAME...
I'M A GUY... WHY DO I *LOOK* LIKE THIS...?!
はーっ
SIIGH
HII-CHAN ♡ HOW COME YOU'RE SIGHING INTO A MIRROR?
HIDETOSHI'S FRIEND TOMOHIKO
ENTRANCED BY YOUR OWN BEAUTY, OR SOMETHING?
ポン
PAT
YEAH, RIGHT -- *AS IF!*
STOP CALLING ME HII-CHAN.
NOT LISTENING
WELL, I UNDERSTAND HOW YOU FEEL, HII-CHAN...
YOU'RE CUTER AND PRETTIER THAN THE AVERAGE **GIRL.** ♡

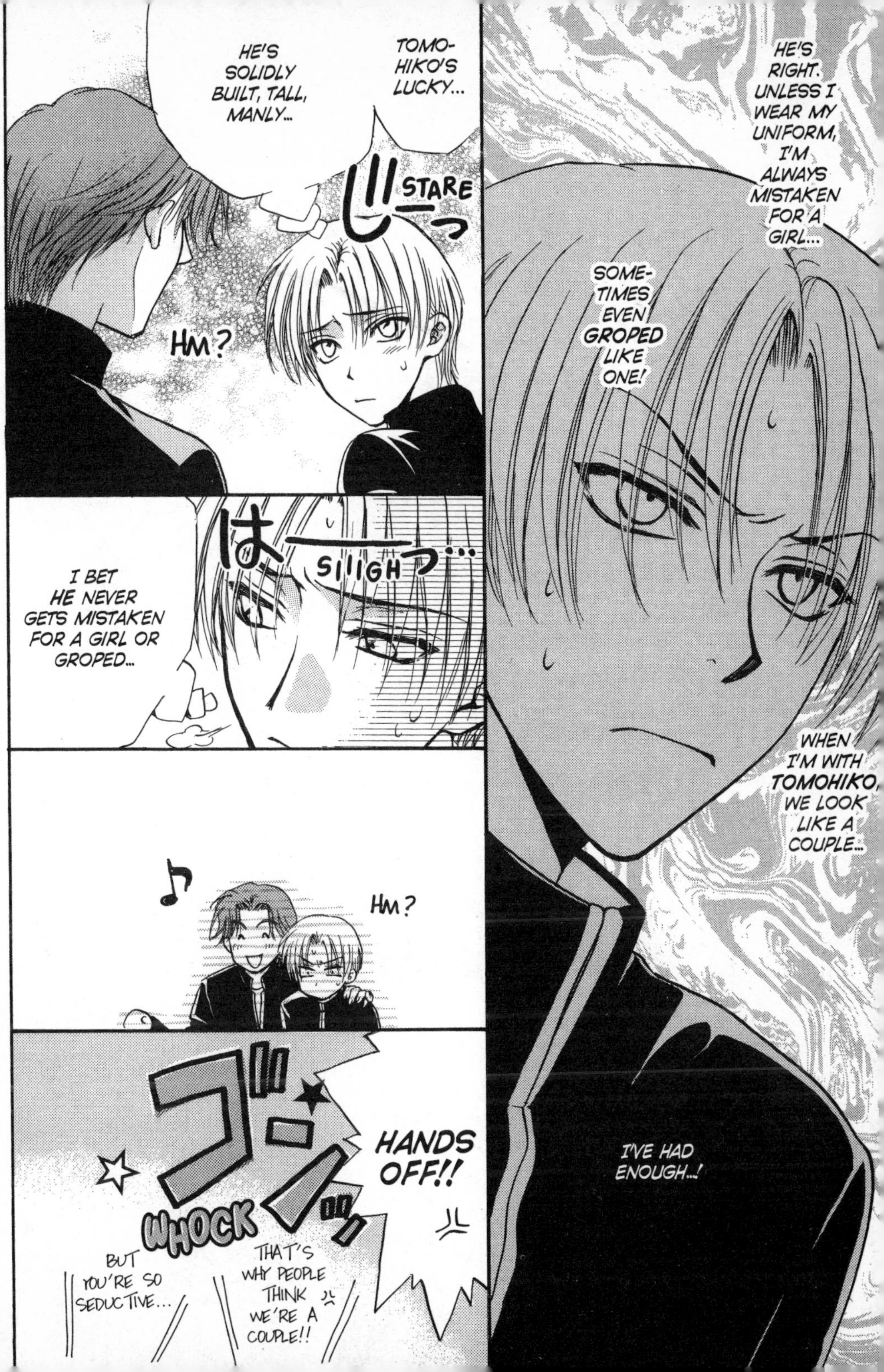
HE'S RIGHT. UNLESS I WEAR MY UNIFORM, I'M ALWAYS MISTAKEN FOR A GIRL...
SOME-TIMES EVEN GROPED LIKE ONE!
WHEN I'M WITH TOMOHIKO, WE LOOK LIKE A COUPLE...
I'VE HAD ENOUGH...!
TOMO-HIKO'S LUCKY...
HE'S SOLIDLY BUILT, TALL, MANLY...
じーっ
STARE
HM?
はーっ…
SIIIGH
I BET HE NEVER GETS MISTAKEN FOR A GIRL OR GROPED...
HM?
ゴッ
WHOCK
HANDS OFF!!
THAT'S WHY PEOPLE THINK WE'RE A COUPLE!!
BUT YOU'RE SO SEDUCTIVE...

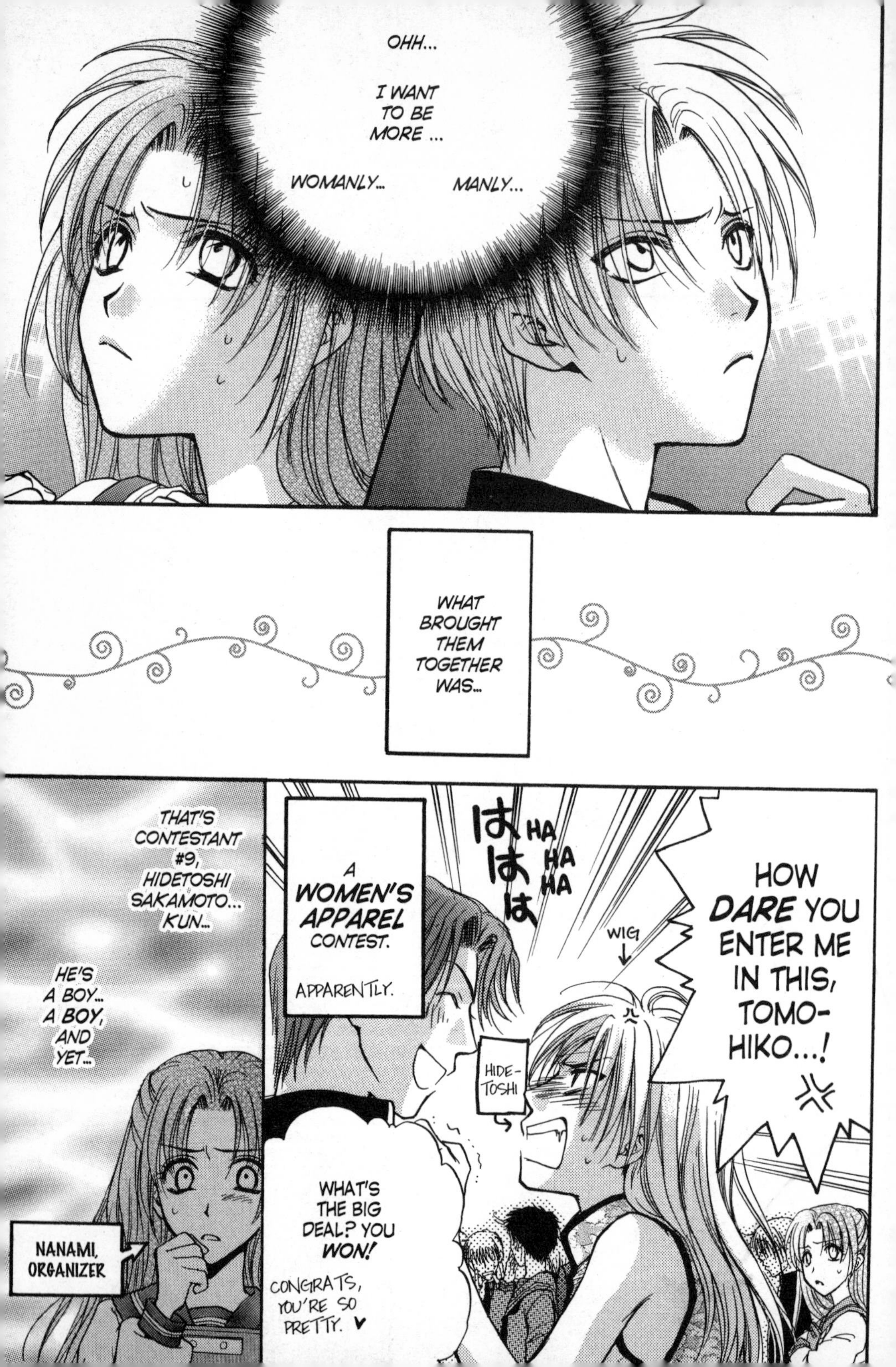
OHH...
I WANT TO BE MORE ...
MANLY...
WOMANLY...
WHAT BROUGHT THEM TOGETHER WAS...
HOW DARE YOU ENTER ME IN THIS, TOMO-HIKO...!
はHA はHA はHA
A WOMEN'S APPAREL CONTEST.
APPARENTLY.
WIG
HIDE-TOSHI
WHAT'S THE BIG DEAL? YOU WON!
CONGRATS, YOU'RE SO PRETTY. ♥
THAT'S CONTESTANT #9, HIDETOSHI SAKAMOTO... KUN...
HE'S A BOY... A BOY, AND YET...
NANAMI, ORGANIZER

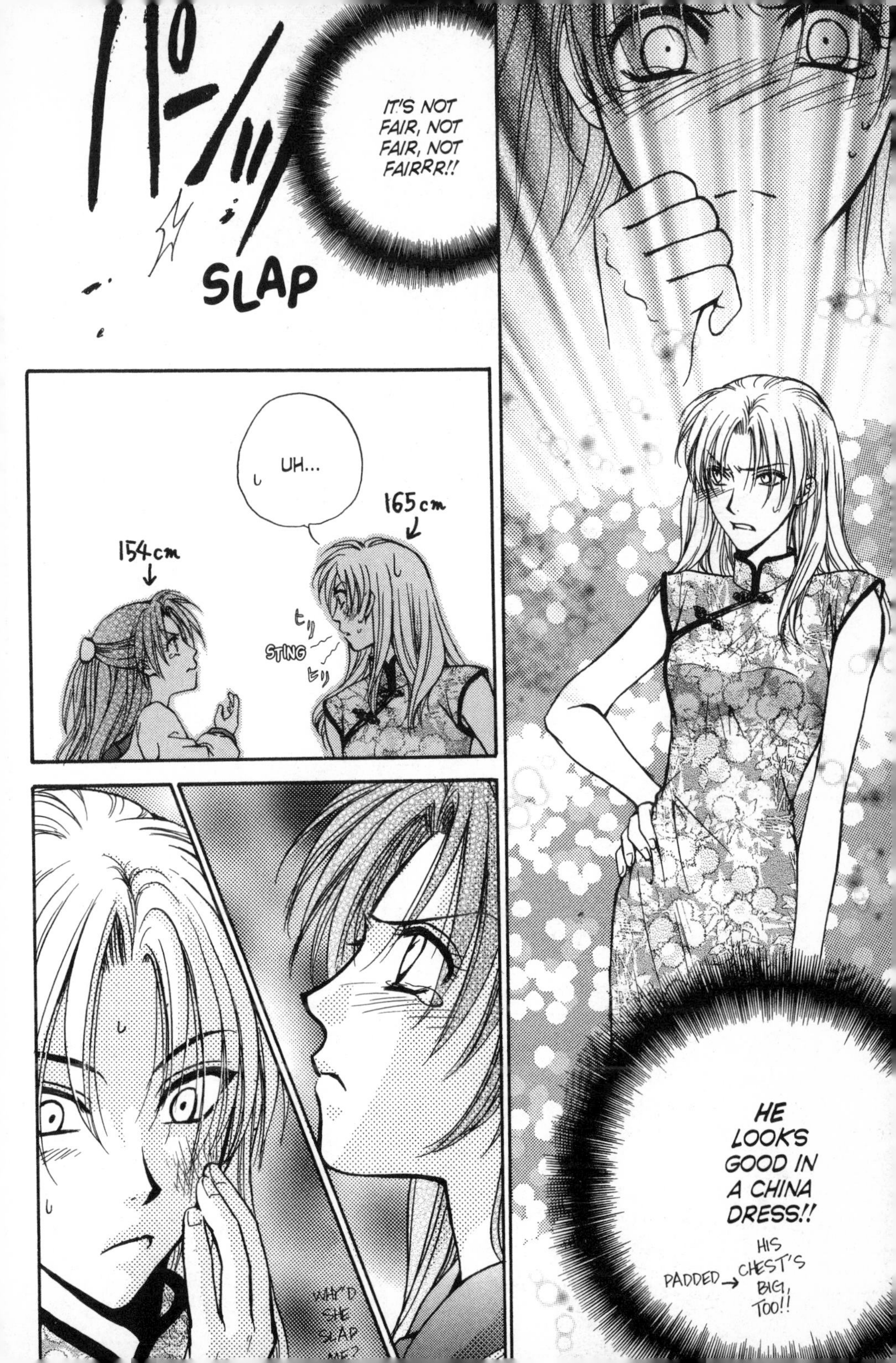
HE LOOKS GOOD IN A CHINA DRESS!!
HIS CHEST'S BIG, TOO!!
PADDED
パーン
SLAP
IT'S NOT FAIR, NOT FAIR, NOT FAIRRR!!
UH...
165cm
154cm
ヒリ
STING
ヒリ
WHY'D SHE SLAP

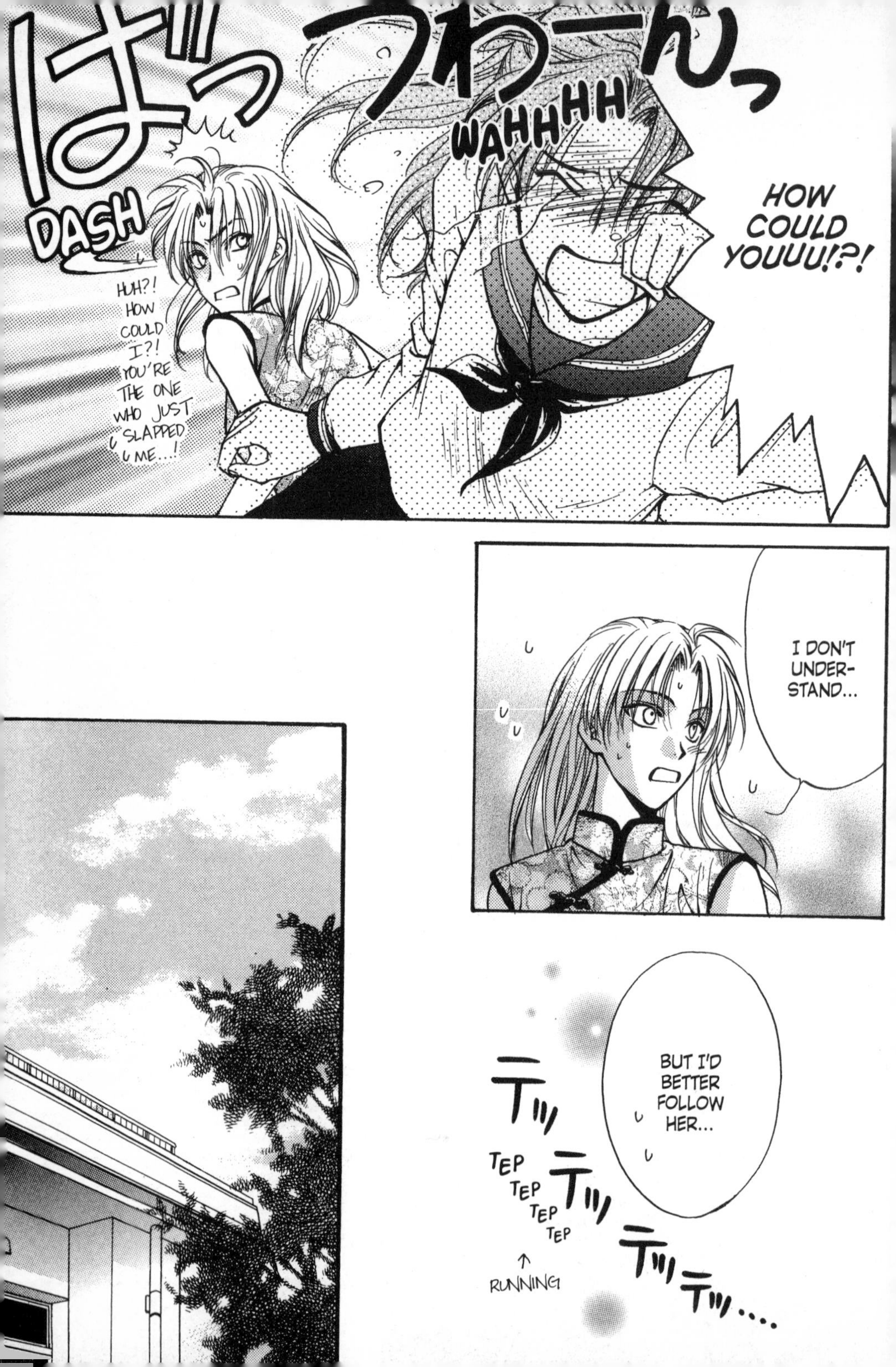
HOW COULD YOUUU!?!
うわーんっ
WAHHHH
ばっ
DASH
HUH?! HOW COULD I?! YOU'RE THE ONE WHO JUST SLAPPED ME...!
I DON'T UNDER-STAND...
BUT I'D BETTER FOLLOW HER...
テッテッテッテッ....
TEP TEP TEP TEP
RUNNING

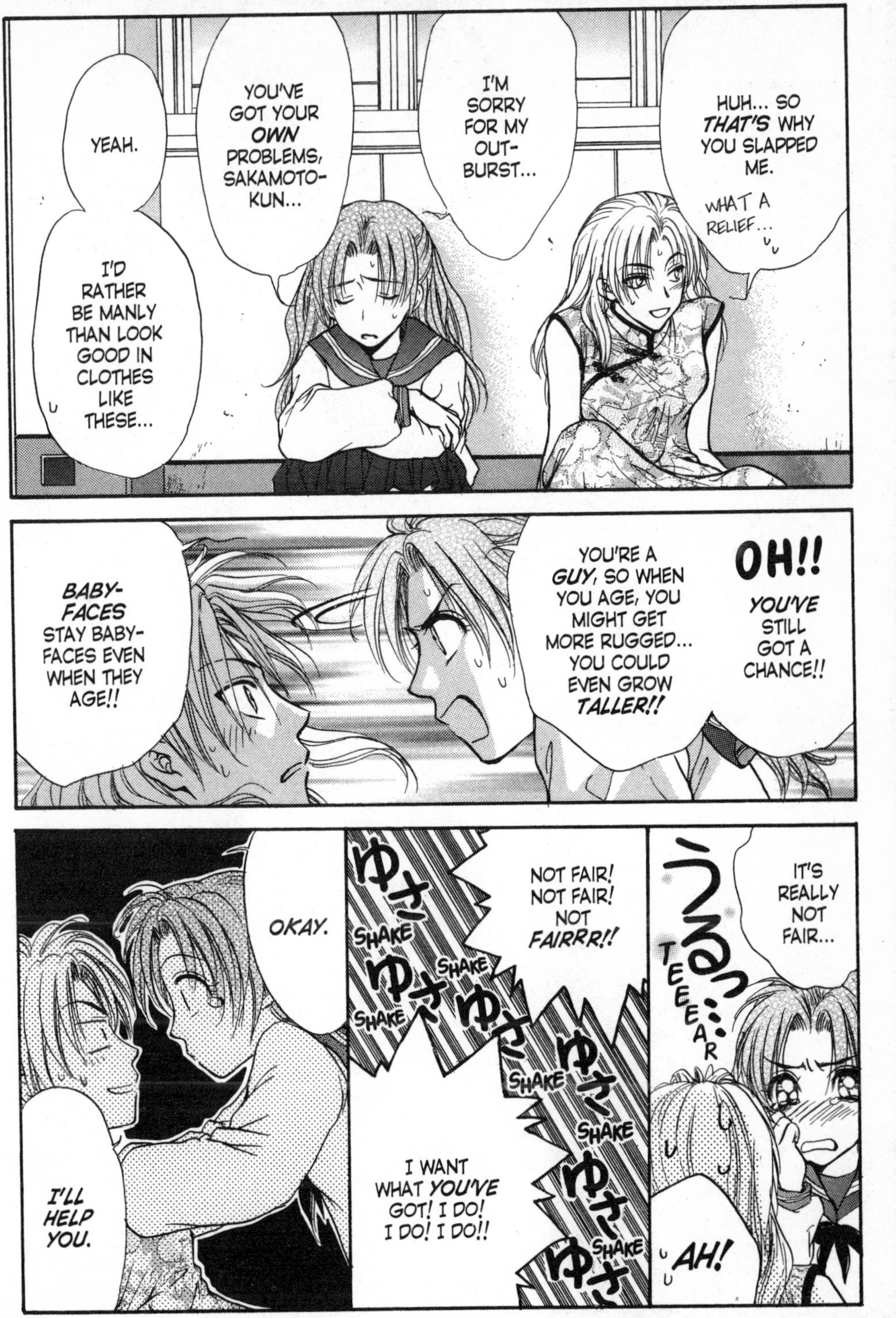
HUH... SO THAT'S WHY YOU SLAPPED ME.
WHAT A RELIEF...
I'M SORRY FOR MY OUT-BURST...
YOU'VE GOT YOUR OWN PROBLEMS, SAKAMOTO-KUN...
YEAH.
I'D RATHER BE MANLY THAN LOOK GOOD IN CLOTHES LIKE THESE...
OH!!
YOU'VE STILL GOT A CHANCE!!
YOU'RE A GUY, SO WHEN YOU AGE, YOU MIGHT GET MORE RUGGED... YOU COULD EVEN GROW TALLER!!
BABY-FACES STAY BABY-FACES EVEN WHEN THEY AGE!!
IT'S REALLY NOT FAIR...
うるっ
TEEEEAR
AH!
NOT FAIR! NOT FAIR! NOT FAIRRR!!
ゆさ SHAKE ゆさ SHAKE ゆさ SHAKE ゆさ SHAKE ゆさ SHAKE ゆさ SHAKE
I WANT WHAT YOU'VE GOT! I DO! I DO! I DO!!
OKAY.
I'LL HELP YOU.

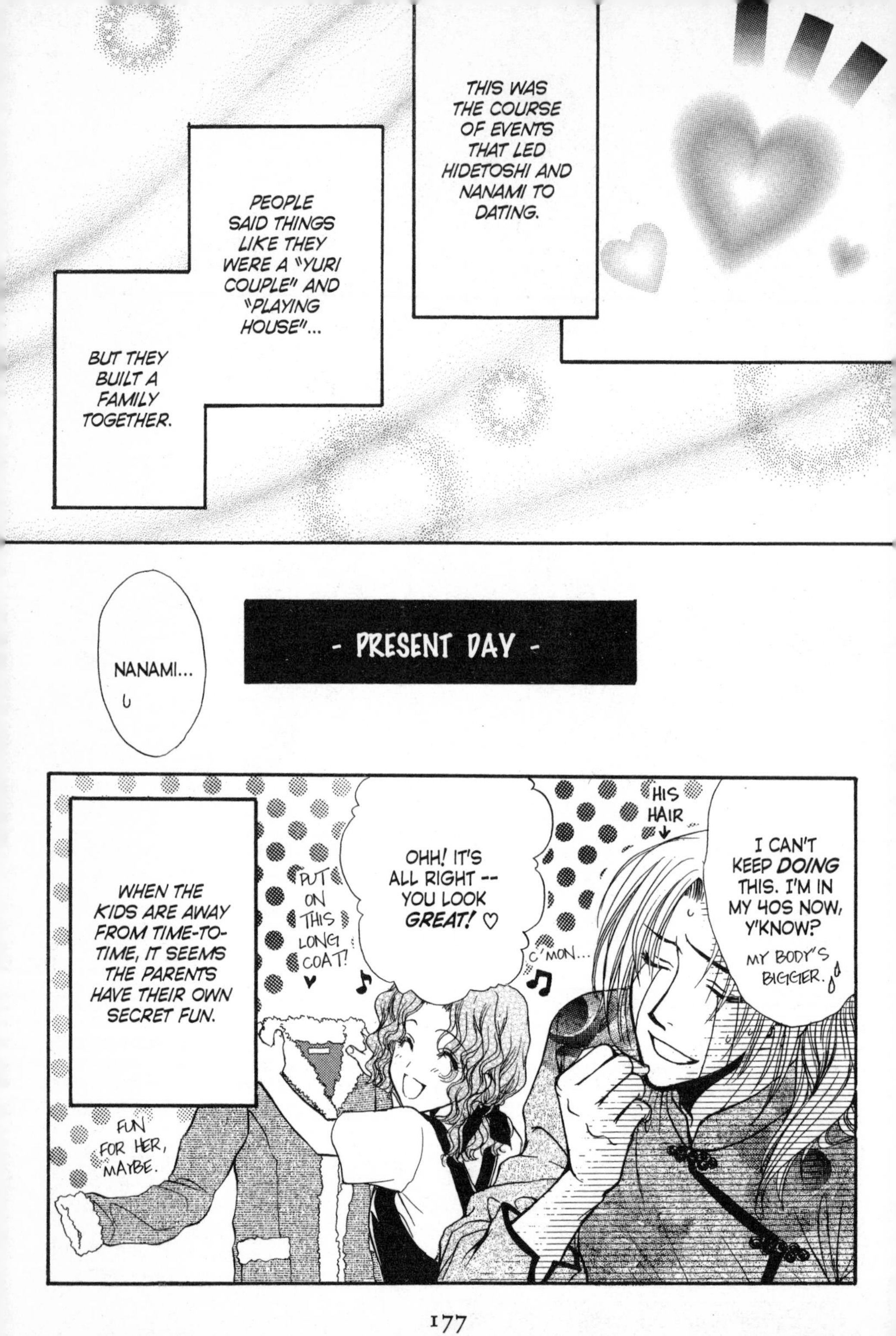
THIS WAS THE COURSE OF EVENTS THAT LED HIDETOSHI AND NANAMI TO DATING.
PEOPLE SAID THINGS LIKE THEY WERE A "YURI COUPLE" AND "PLAYING HOUSE"...
BUT THEY BUILT A FAMILY TOGETHER.
- PRESENT DAY -
NANAMI...
I CAN'T KEEP *DOING* THIS. I'M IN MY 40S NOW, Y'KNOW?
MY BODY'S BIGGER.
HIS HAIR
C'MON...
OHH! IT'S ALL RIGHT -- YOU LOOK *GREAT!* ♡
PUT ON THIS LONG COAT!
WHEN THE KIDS ARE AWAY FROM TIME-TO-TIME, IT SEEMS THE PARENTS HAVE THEIR OWN SECRET FUN.
FUN FOR HER, MAYBE.

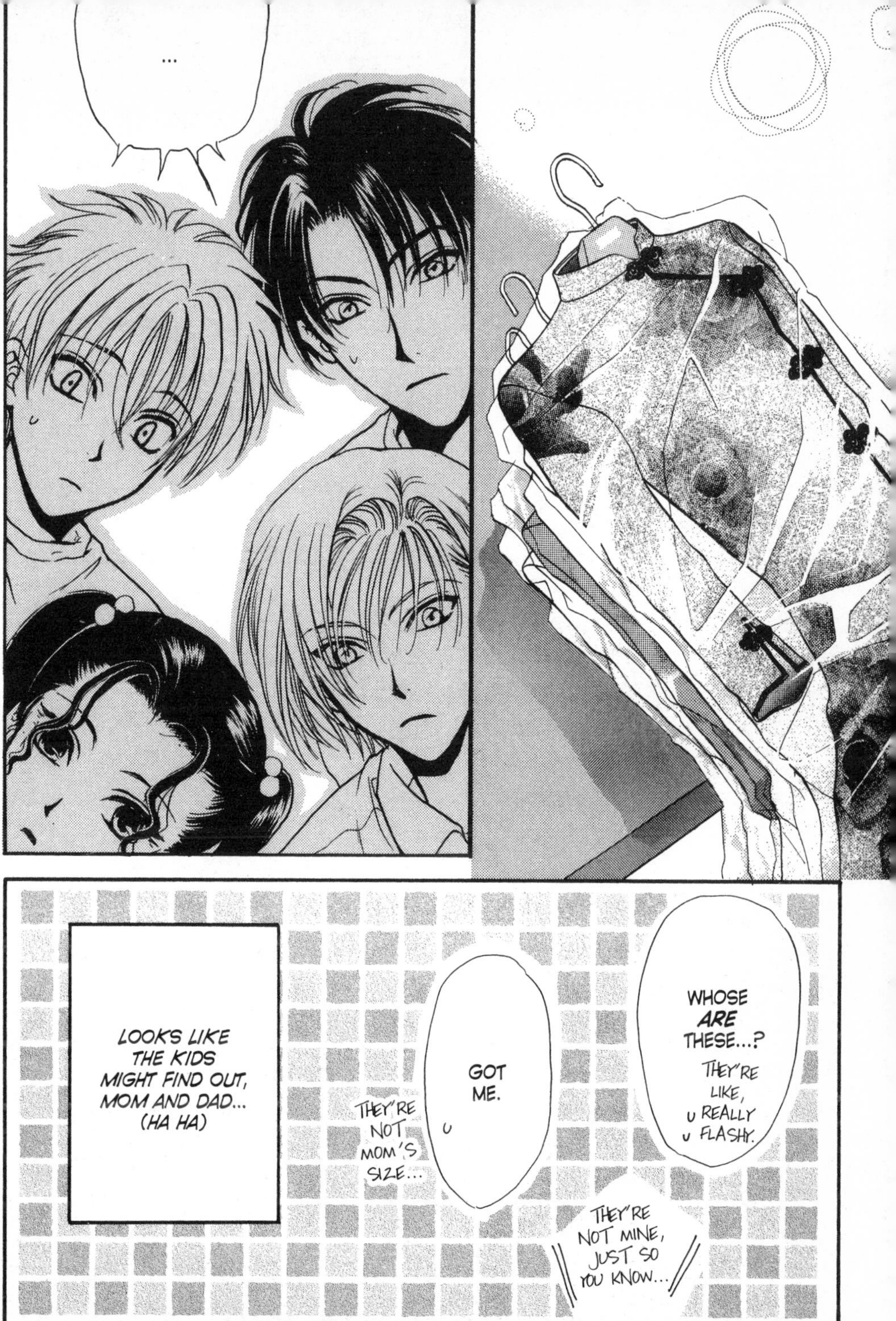
...
WHOSE ARE THESE...?
THEY'RE LIKE, REALLY FLASHY.
GOT ME.
THEY'RE NOT MOM'S SIZE...
THEY'RE NOT MINE, JUST SO YOU KNOW...
LOOKS LIKE THE KIDS MIGHT FIND OUT, MOM AND DAD... (HA HA)

SAKAMOTO FAMILY • MOM & DAD ✸ END

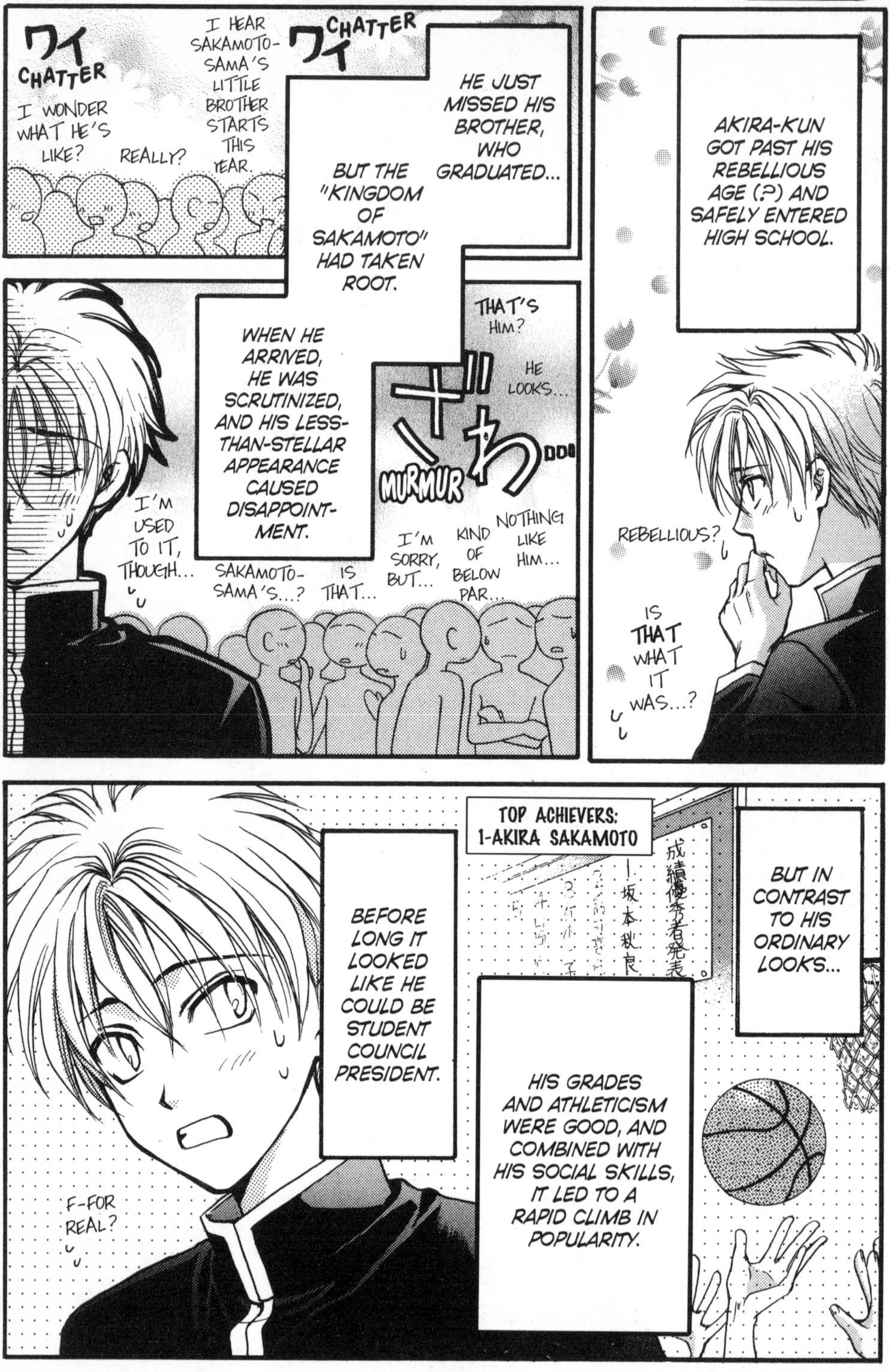
AKIRA-KUN GOT PAST HIS REBELLIOUS AGE (?) AND SAFELY ENTERED HIGH SCHOOL.
REBELLIOUS?
IS THAT WHAT IT WAS...?
HE JUST MISSED HIS BROTHER, WHO GRADUATED...
BUT THE "KINGDOM OF SAKAMOTO" HAD TAKEN ROOT.
ワイ CHATTER
I HEAR SAKAMOTO-SAMA'S LITTLE BROTHER STARTS THIS YEAR.
REALLY?
ワイ CHATTER
I WONDER WHAT HE'S LIKE?
WHEN HE ARRIVED, HE WAS SCRUTINIZED, AND HIS LESS-THAN-STELLAR APPEARANCE CAUSED DISAPPOINTMENT.
THAT'S HIM?
HE LOOKS...
ざわ MURMUR
NOTHING LIKE HIM...
KIND OF BELOW PAR...
I'M SORRY, BUT...
IS THAT...
SAKAMOTO-SAMA'S...?
I'M USED TO IT, THOUGH...
BUT IN CONTRAST TO HIS ORDINARY LOOKS...
TOP ACHIEVERS: 1-AKIRA SAKAMOTO
成績優秀者発表
HIS GRADES AND ATHLETICISM WERE GOOD, AND COMBINED WITH HIS SOCIAL SKILLS, IT LED TO A RAPID CLIMB IN POPULARITY.
BEFORE LONG IT LOOKED LIKE HE COULD BE STUDENT COUNCIL PRESIDENT.
F-FOR REAL?

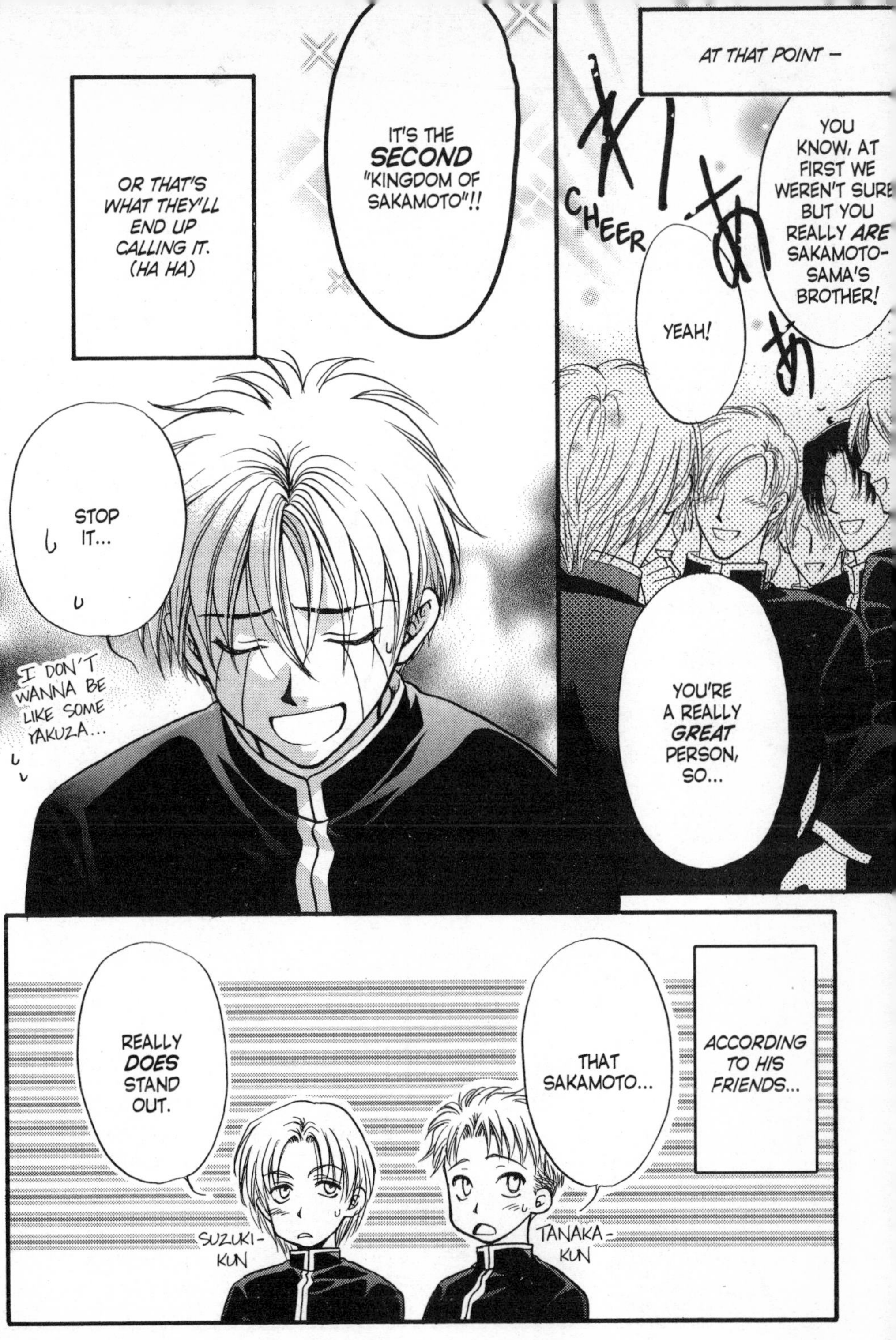
AT THAT POINT –
YOU KNOW, AT FIRST WE WEREN'T SURE BUT YOU REALLY ARE SAKAMOTO-SAMA'S BROTHER!
CHEER
YEAH!
YOU'RE A REALLY GREAT PERSON, SO...
IT'S THE SECOND "KINGDOM OF SAKAMOTO"!!
OR THAT'S WHAT THEY'LL END UP CALLING IT. (HA HA)
STOP IT...
I DON'T WANNA BE LIKE SOME YAKUZA...
ACCORDING TO HIS FRIENDS...
THAT SAKAMOTO...
REALLY DOES STAND OUT.
TANAKA-KUN
SUZUKI-KUN

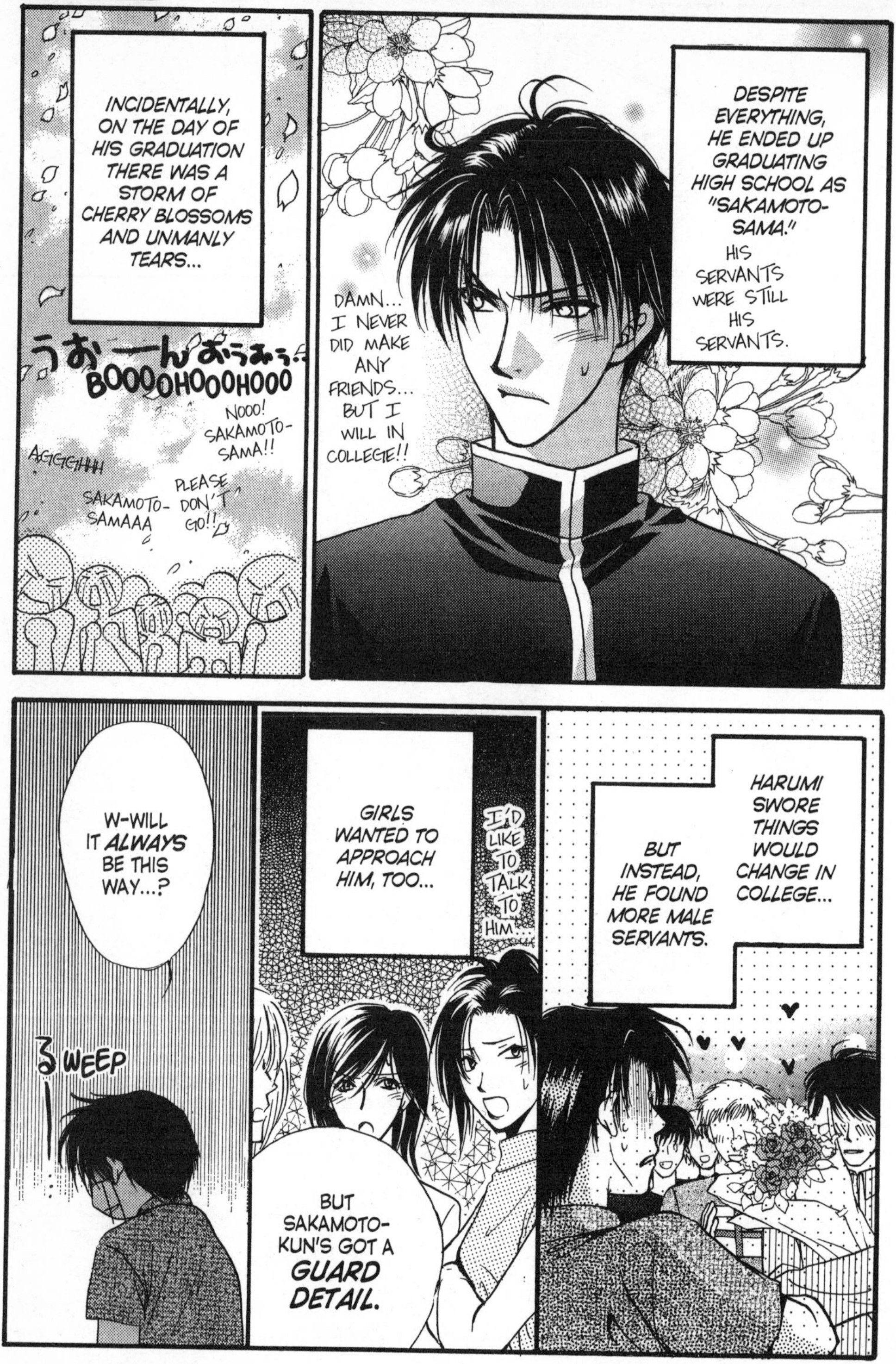
DESPITE EVERYTHING, HE ENDED UP GRADUATING HIGH SCHOOL AS "SAKAMOTO-SAMA."
HIS SERVANTS WERE STILL HIS SERVANTS.
DAMN... I NEVER DID MAKE ANY FRIENDS... BUT I WILL IN COLLEGE!!
INCIDENTALLY, ON THE DAY OF HIS GRADUATION THERE WAS A STORM OF CHERRY BLOSSOMS AND UNMANLY TEARS...
BOOOOHOOOHOOO
NOOO! SAKAMOTO-SAMA!!
AGGGHHH
PLEASE DON'T GO!!
SAKAMOTO-SAMAAA
HARUMI SWORE THINGS WOULD CHANGE IN COLLEGE...
BUT INSTEAD, HE FOUND MORE MALE SERVANTS.
GIRLS WANTED TO APPROACH HIM, TOO...
I'D LIKE TO TALK TO HIM...
BUT SAKAMOTO-KUN'S GOT A GUARD DETAIL.
W-WILL IT ALWAYS BE THIS WAY...?
WEEP

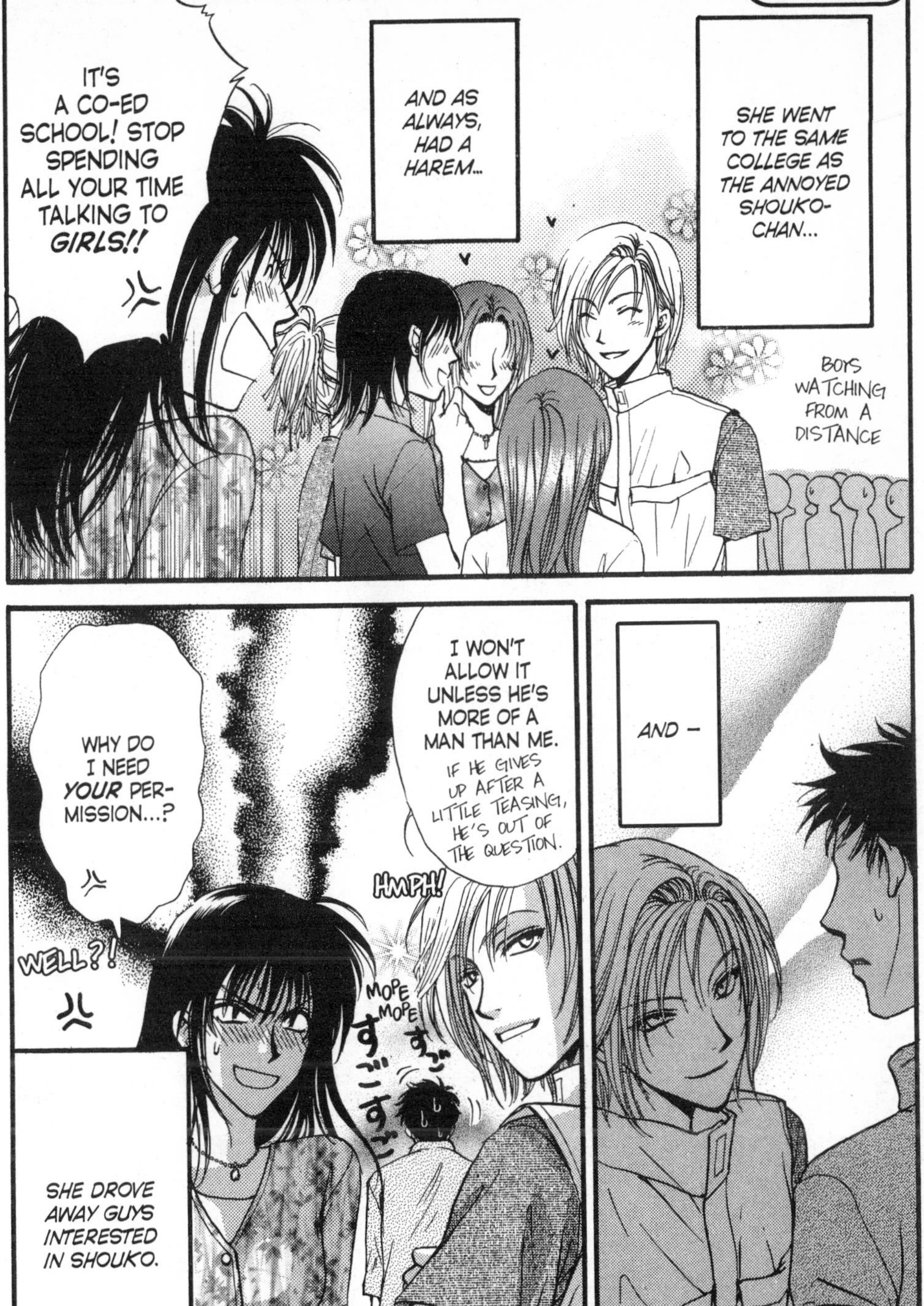
SHE WENT TO THE SAME COLLEGE AS THE ANNOYED SHOUKO-CHAN...
AND AS ALWAYS, HAD A HAREM...
BOYS WATCHING FROM A DISTANCE
IT'S A CO-ED SCHOOL! STOP SPENDING ALL YOUR TIME TALKING TO GIRLS!!
AND –
I WON'T ALLOW IT UNLESS HE'S MORE OF A MAN THAN ME.
IF HE GIVES UP AFTER A LITTLE TEASING, HE'S OUT OF THE QUESTION.
HMPH!
WHY DO I NEED YOUR PERMISSION...?
MOPE MOPE
すごすご すごすご
WELL?!
SHE DROVE AWAY GUYS INTERESTED IN SHOUKO.

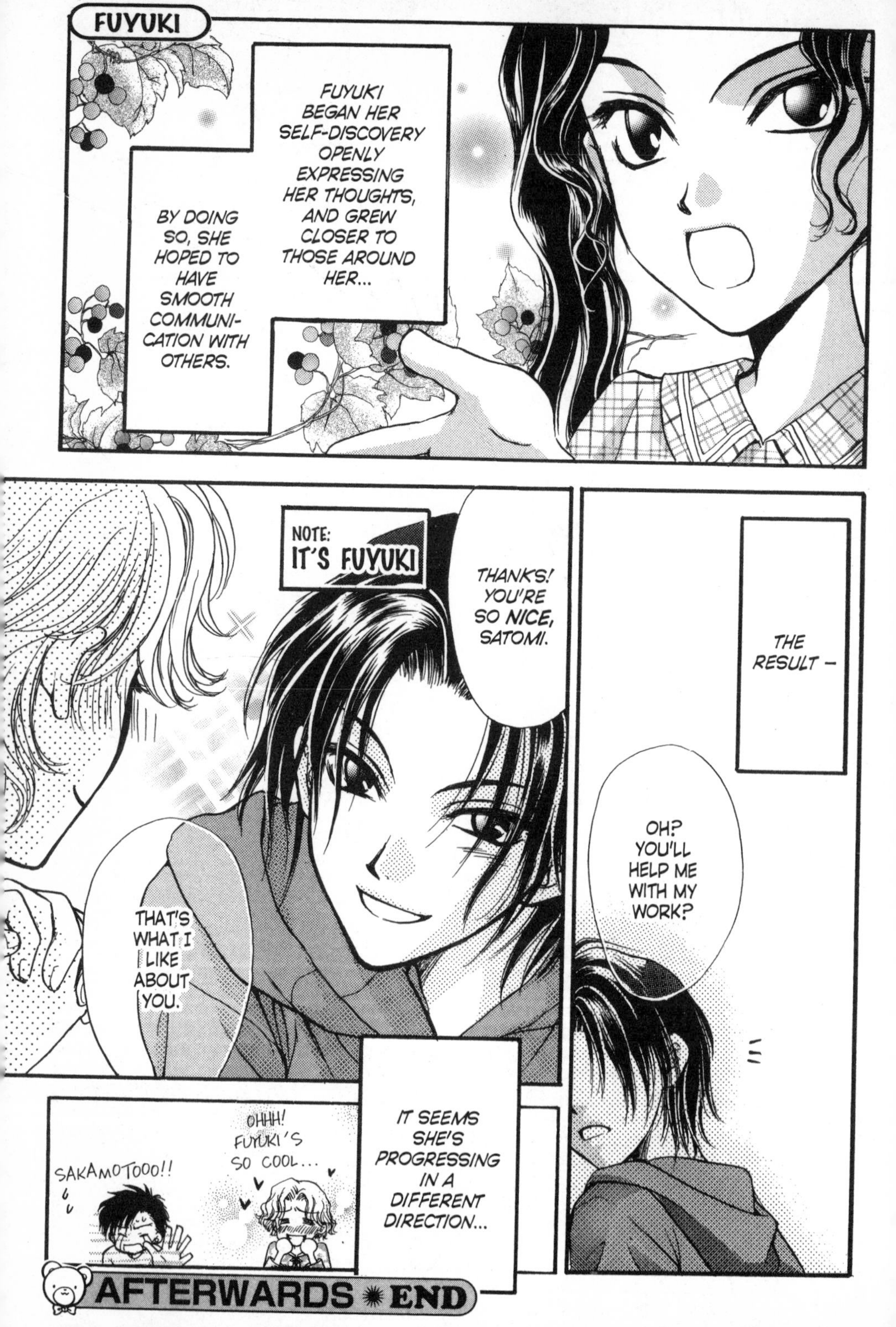
FUYUKI
FUYUKI BEGAN HER SELF-DISCOVERY OPENLY EXPRESSING HER THOUGHTS, AND GREW CLOSER TO THOSE AROUND HER...
BY DOING SO, SHE HOPED TO HAVE SMOOTH COMMUNI-CATION WITH OTHERS.
THE RESULT –
OH? YOU'LL HELP ME WITH MY WORK?
THANKS! YOU'RE SO NICE, SATOMI.
NOTE: IT'S FUYUKI
THAT'S WHAT I LIKE ABOUT YOU.
IT SEEMS SHE'S PROGRESSING IN A DIFFERENT DIRECTION...
OHHH! FUYUKI'S SO COOL...
SAKAMOTOOO!!
AFTERWARDS END

4-PANEL COMIC THEATRE

四コマ劇場

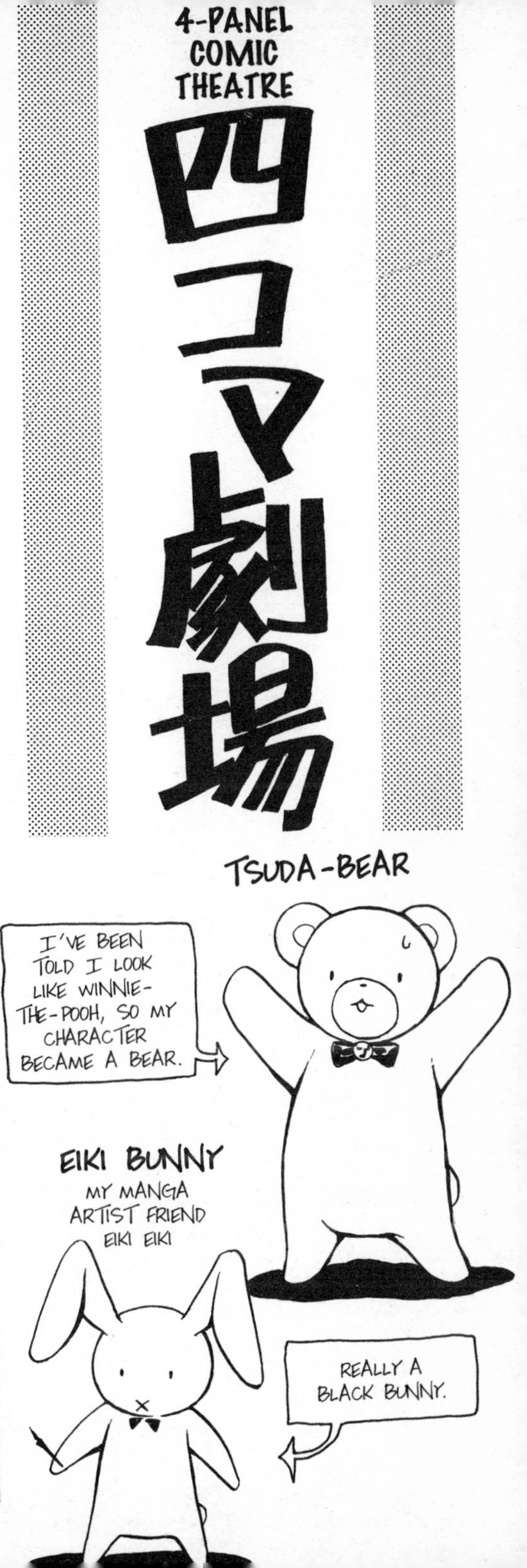
TSUDA-BEAR
I'VE BEEN TOLD I LOOK LIKE WINNIE-THE-POOH, SO MY CHARACTER BECAME A BEAR.
EIKI BUNNY
MY MANGA ARTIST FRIEND EIKI EIKI
REALLY A BLACK BUNNY.

DEADLINE DIARY 1

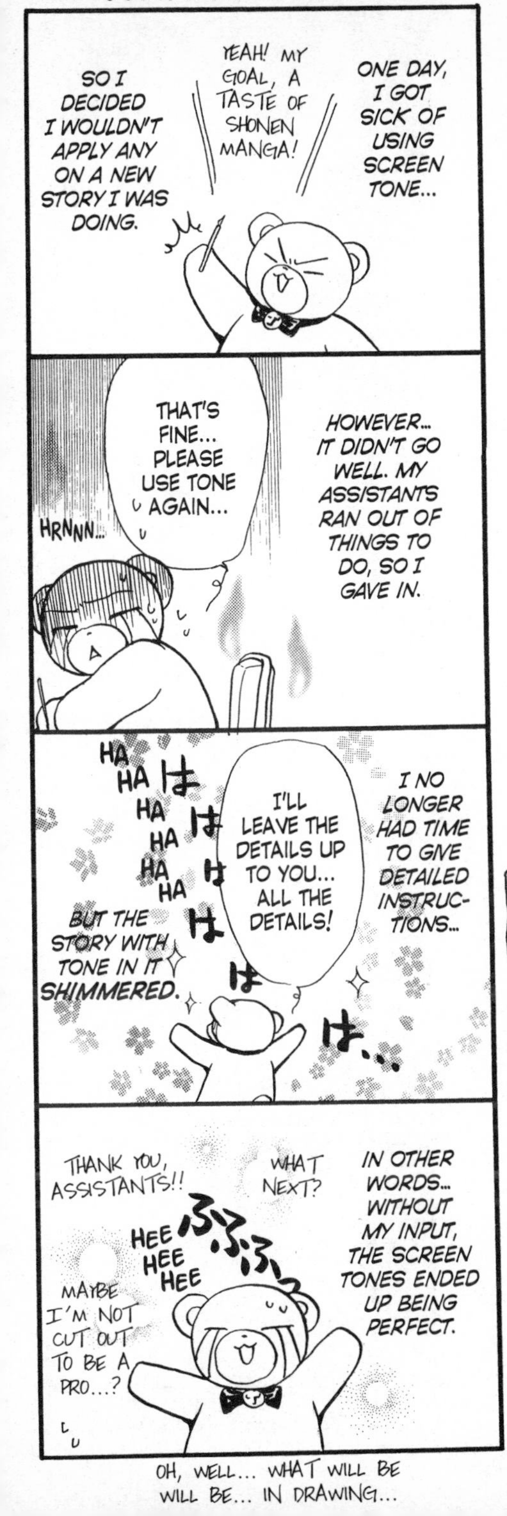
ONE DAY, I GOT SICK OF USING SCREEN TONE...
YEAH! MY GOAL, A TASTE OF SHONEN MANGA!
SO I DECIDED I WOULDN'T APPLY ANY ON A NEW STORY I WAS DOING.
HOWEVER... IT DIDN'T GO WELL. MY ASSISTANTS RAN OUT OF THINGS TO DO, SO I GAVE IN.
THAT'S FINE... PLEASE USE TONE AGAIN...
HRNNN...
I NO LONGER HAD TIME TO GIVE DETAILED INSTRUC-TIONS...
I'LL LEAVE THE DETAILS UP TO YOU... ALL THE DETAILS!
HA HA HA HA HA HA
はははははは...
BUT THE STORY WITH TONE IN IT SHIMMERED.
IN OTHER WORDS... WITHOUT MY INPUT, THE SCREEN TONES ENDED UP BEING PERFECT.
WHAT NEXT?
THANK YOU, ASSISTANTS!!
HEE HEE HEE
ふふふっ
MAYBE I'M NOT CUT OUT TO BE A PRO...?

OH, WELL... WHAT WILL BE WILL BE... IN DRAWING...

FAIRIES?

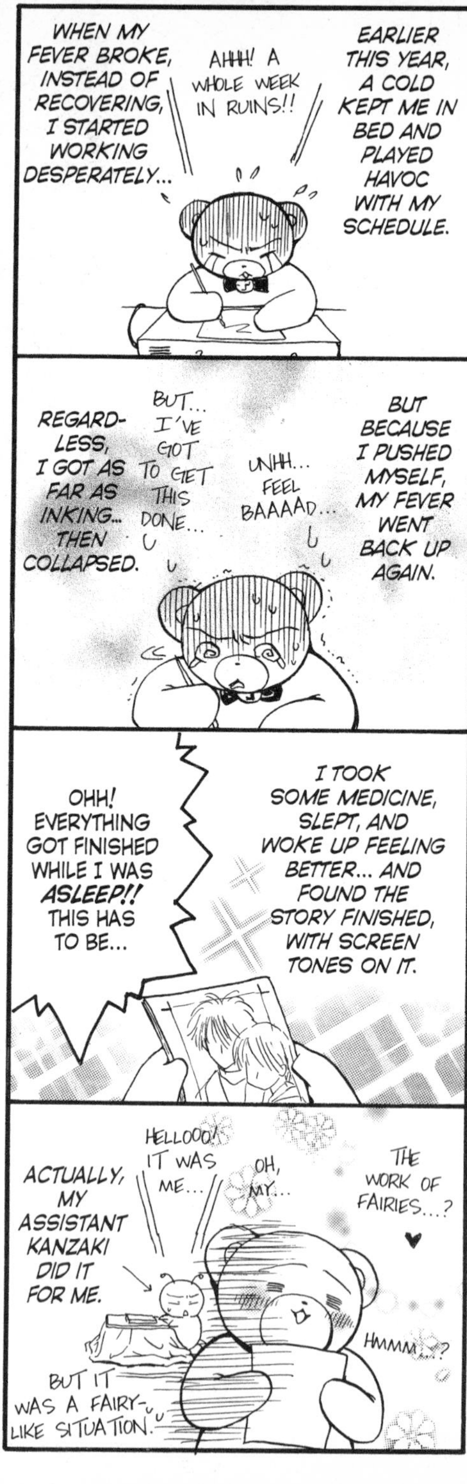
EARLIER THIS YEAR, A COLD KEPT ME IN BED AND PLAYED HAVOC WITH MY SCHEDULE.
AHHH! A WHOLE WEEK IN RUINS!!
WHEN MY FEVER BROKE, INSTEAD OF RECOVERING, I STARTED WORKING DESPERATELY...
BUT BECAUSE I PUSHED MYSELF, MY FEVER WENT BACK UP AGAIN.
UNHH... FEEL BAAAAD...
BUT... I'VE GOT TO GET THIS DONE...
REGARDLESS, I GOT AS FAR AS INKING... THEN COLLAPSED.
I TOOK SOME MEDICINE, SLEPT, AND WOKE UP FEELING BETTER... AND FOUND THE STORY FINISHED, WITH SCREEN TONES ON IT.
OHH! EVERYTHING GOT FINISHED WHILE I WAS *ASLEEP!!* THIS HAS TO BE...
THE WORK OF FAIRIES...?
OH, MY...
HELLOOO! IT WAS ME...
ACTUALLY, MY ASSISTANT KANZAKI DID IT FOR ME.
HMMM...?
BUT IT WAS A FAIRY-LIKE SITUATION.

DEADLINE DIARY 2

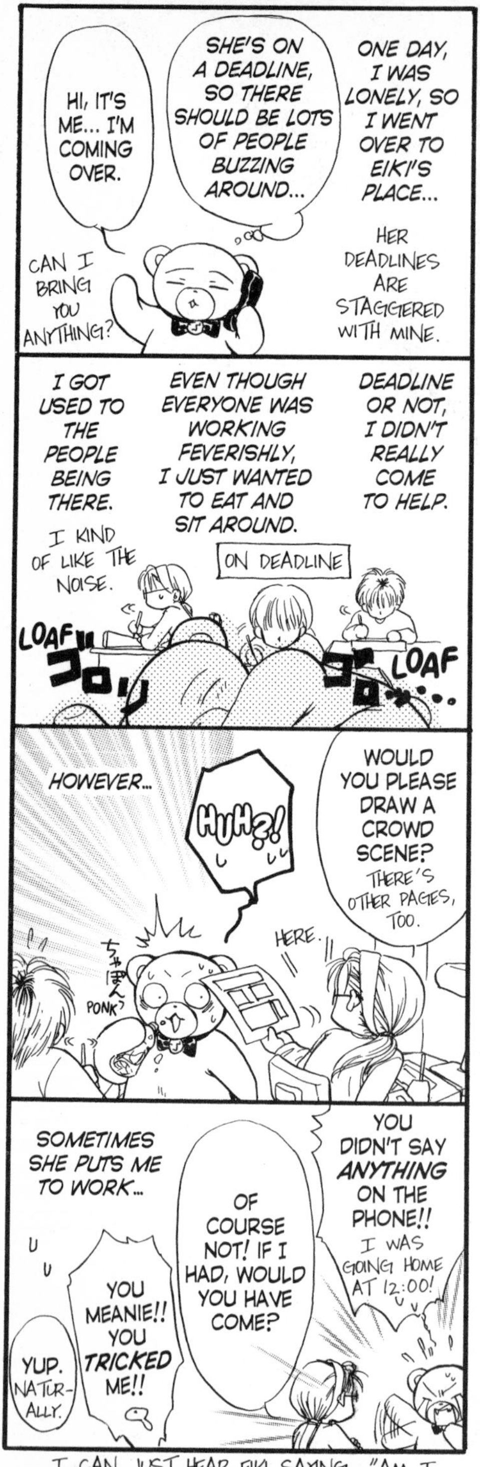
ONE DAY, I WAS LONELY, SO I WENT OVER TO EIKI'S PLACE...
HER DEADLINES ARE STAGGERED WITH MINE.
SHE'S ON A DEADLINE, SO THERE SHOULD BE LOTS OF PEOPLE BUZZING AROUND...
HI, IT'S ME... I'M COMING OVER.
CAN I BRING YOU ANYTHING?
DEADLINE OR NOT, I DIDN'T REALLY COME TO HELP.
EVEN THOUGH EVERYONE WAS WORKING FEVERISHLY, I JUST WANTED TO EAT AND SIT AROUND.
I GOT USED TO THE PEOPLE BEING THERE.
I KIND OF LIKE THE NOISE.
ON DEADLINE
LOAF
LOAF!!
WOULD YOU PLEASE DRAW A CROWD SCENE?
THERE'S OTHER PAGES, TOO.
HERE.
HUH?!
HOWEVER...
PONK
YOU DIDN'T SAY *ANYTHING* ON THE PHONE!!
I WAS GOING HOME AT 12:00!
OF COURSE NOT! IF I HAD, WOULD YOU HAVE COME?
SOMETIMES SHE PUTS ME TO WORK...
YOU MEANIE!! YOU *TRICKED* ME!!
YUP. NATURALLY.

I CAN JUST HEAR EIKI SAYING, "AM I THE BAD GUY AGAIN...?" (HA HA)

IN-SYNC 1

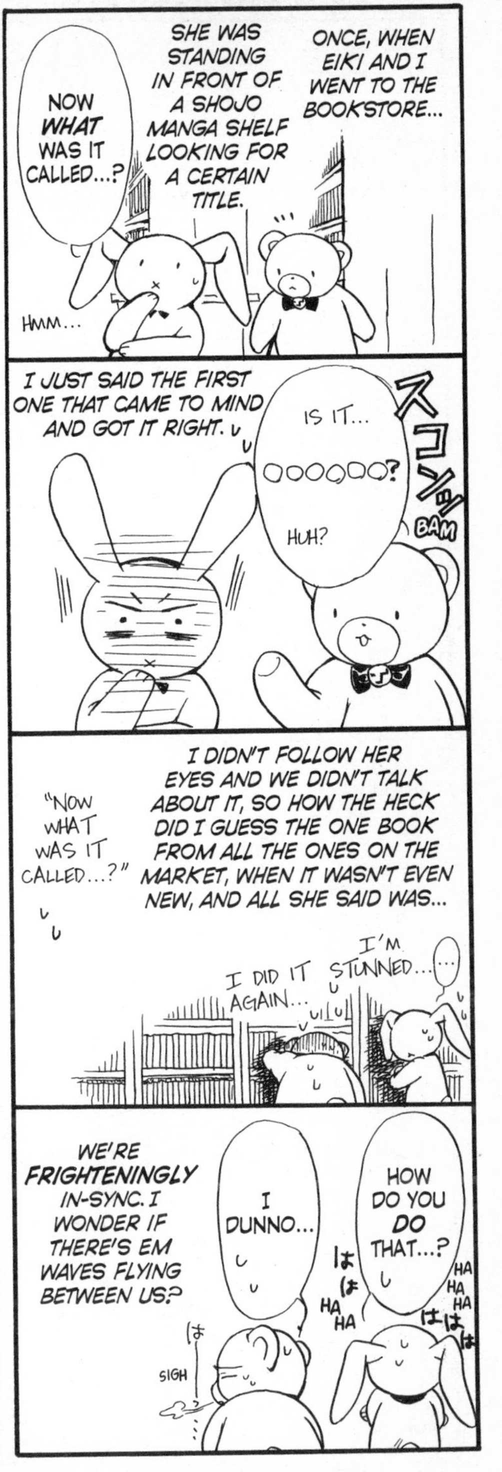
ONCE, WHEN EIKI AND I WENT TO THE BOOKSTORE...
SHE WAS STANDING IN FRONT OF A SHOJO MANGA SHELF LOOKING FOR A CERTAIN TITLE.
NOW WHAT WAS IT CALLED...?
HMM...
スコンッ
BAM
IS IT... ○○○○○○○?
HUH?
I JUST SAID THE FIRST ONE THAT CAME TO MIND AND GOT IT RIGHT.
I DIDN'T FOLLOW HER EYES AND WE DIDN'T TALK ABOUT IT, SO HOW THE HECK DID I GUESS THE ONE BOOK FROM ALL THE ONES ON THE MARKET, WHEN IT WASN'T EVEN NEW, AND ALL SHE SAID WAS...
"NOW WHAT WAS IT CALLED...?"
...
I'M STUNNED...
I DID IT AGAIN...
HOW DO YOU DO THAT...?
HA HA HA
ははは
I DUNNO...
WE'RE FRIGHTENINGLY IN-SYNC. I WONDER IF THERE'S EM WAVES FLYING BETWEEN US?
はは
HA HA
はー
SIGH

IN-SYNC 2

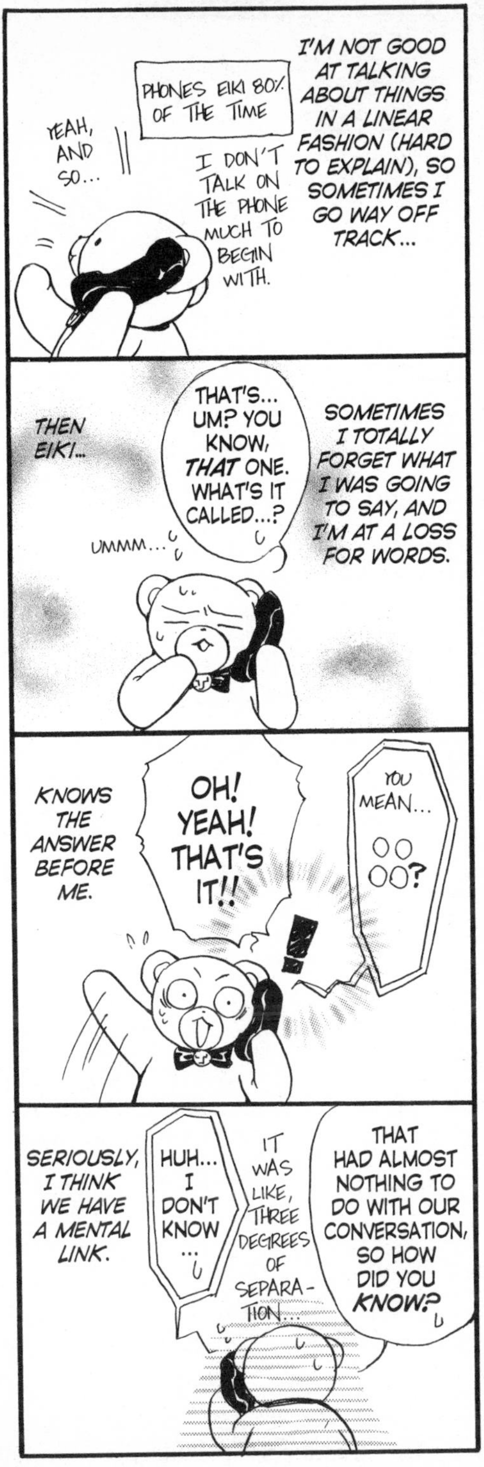
I'M NOT GOOD AT TALKING ABOUT THINGS IN A LINEAR FASHION (HARD TO EXPLAIN), SO SOMETIMES I GO WAY OFF TRACK...
PHONES EIKI 80% OF THE TIME
I DON'T TALK ON THE PHONE MUCH TO BEGIN WITH.
YEAH, AND SO...
SOMETIMES I TOTALLY FORGET WHAT I WAS GOING TO SAY, AND I'M AT A LOSS FOR WORDS.
THAT'S... UM? YOU KNOW, THAT ONE. WHAT'S IT CALLED...?
UMMM...
THEN EIKI...
YOU MEAN... ○○○○?
OH! YEAH! THAT'S IT!!
KNOWS THE ANSWER BEFORE ME.
THAT HAD ALMOST NOTHING TO DO WITH OUR CONVERSATION, SO HOW DID YOU KNOW?
IT WAS LIKE, THREE DEGREES OF SEPARATION...
HUH... I DON'T KNOW...
SERIOUSLY, I THINK WE HAVE A MENTAL LINK.

CHANGE

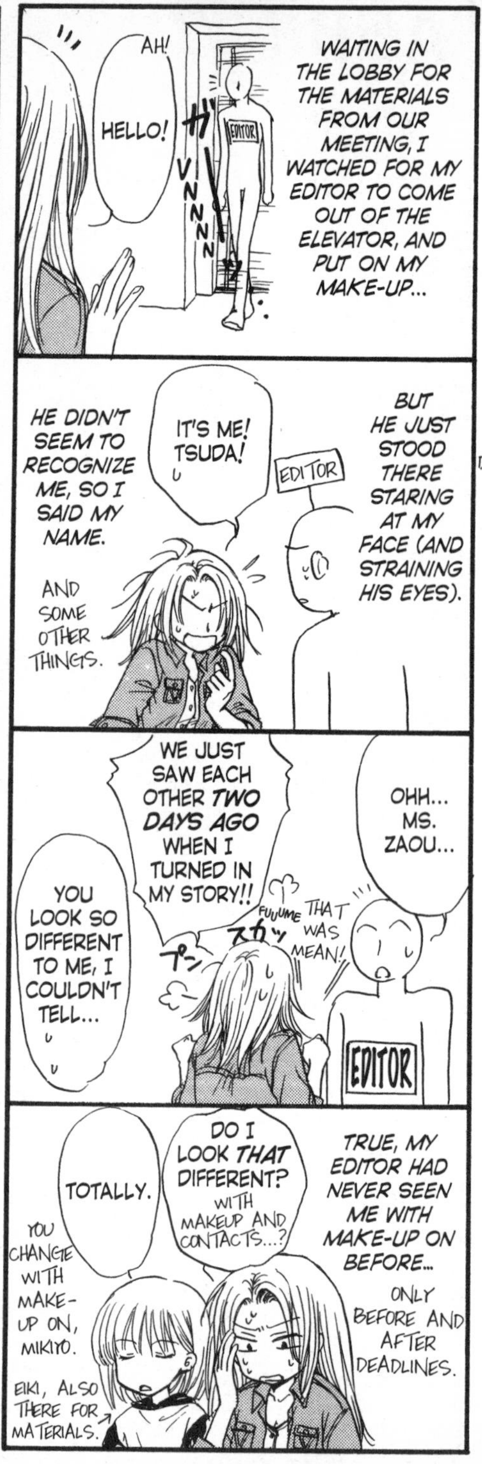
WAITING IN THE LOBBY FOR THE MATERIALS FROM OUR MEETING, I WATCHED FOR MY EDITOR TO COME OUT OF THE ELEVATOR, AND PUT ON MY MAKE-UP...
AH!
HELLO!
ガ
VNNNN
EDITOR
BUT HE JUST STOOD THERE STARING AT MY FACE (AND STRAINING HIS EYES).
EDITOR
IT'S ME! TSUDA!
HE DIDN'T SEEM TO RECOGNIZE ME, SO I SAID MY NAME.
AND SOME OTHER THINGS.
OHH... MS. ZAOU...
THAT WAS MEAN!
FUUUME
スカッ
WE JUST SAW EACH OTHER TWO DAYS AGO WHEN I TURNED IN MY STORY!!
YOU LOOK SO DIFFERENT TO ME, I COULDN'T TELL...
プン
EDITOR
TRUE, MY EDITOR HAD NEVER SEEN ME WITH MAKE-UP ON BEFORE...
ONLY BEFORE AND AFTER DEADLINES.
DO I LOOK THAT DIFFERENT? WITH MAKEUP AND CONTACTS...?
TOTALLY.
YOU CHANGE WITH MAKE-UP ON, MIKIYO.
EIKI, ALSO THERE FOR MATERIALS.

CHANGE (CONTINUED)

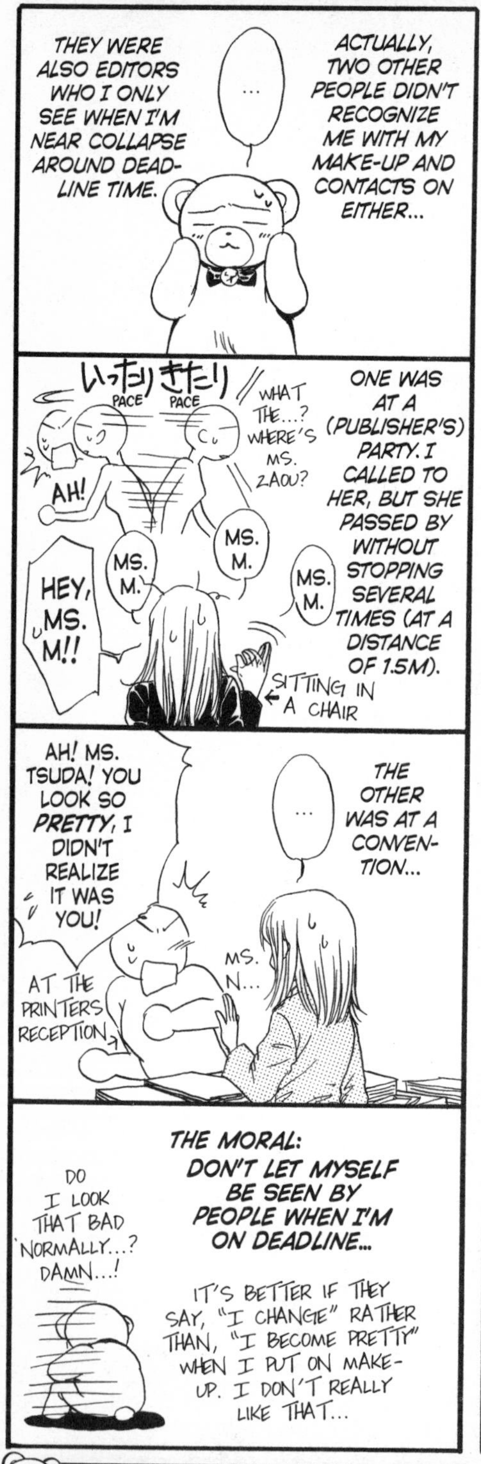
ACTUALLY, TWO OTHER PEOPLE DIDN'T RECOGNIZE ME WITH MY MAKE-UP AND CONTACTS ON EITHER...
...
THEY WERE ALSO EDITORS WHO I ONLY SEE WHEN I'M NEAR COLLAPSE AROUND DEAD-LINE TIME.
ONE WAS AT A (PUBLISHER'S) PARTY. I CALLED TO HER, BUT SHE PASSED BY WITHOUT STOPPING SEVERAL TIMES (AT A DISTANCE OF 1.5M).
WHAT THE...? WHERE'S MS. ZAOU?
いったりきたり
PACE PACE
MS. M.
MS. M.
MS. M.
AH!
HEY, MS. M!!
SITTING IN A CHAIR
THE OTHER WAS AT A CONVEN-TION...
...
AH! MS. TSUDA! YOU LOOK SO PRETTY, I DIDN'T REALIZE IT WAS YOU!
MS. N...
AT THE PRINTERS RECEPTION
THE MORAL: DON'T LET MYSELF BE SEEN BY PEOPLE WHEN I'M ON DEADLINE...
IT'S BETTER IF THEY SAY, "I CHANGE" RATHER THAN, "I BECOME PRETTY" WHEN I PUT ON MAKE-UP. I DON'T REALLY LIKE THAT...
DO I LOOK THAT BAD NORMALLY...? DAMN...!

4-PANEL COMIC THEATRE ✸ END

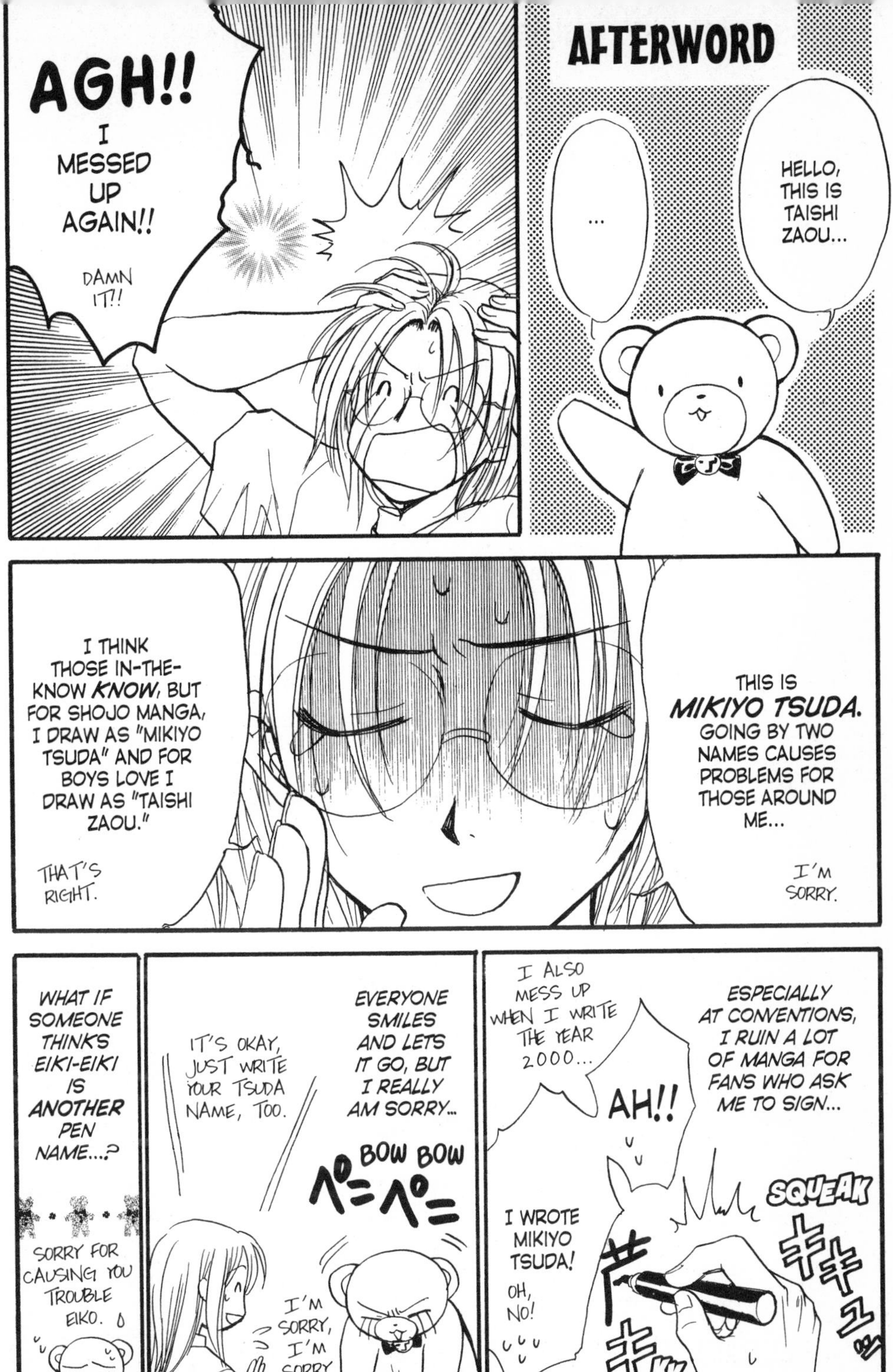
AFTERWORD
HELLO, THIS IS TAISHI ZAOU...
...
AGH!!
I MESSED UP AGAIN!!
DAMN IT!!
THIS IS MIKIYO TSUDA. GOING BY TWO NAMES CAUSES PROBLEMS FOR THOSE AROUND ME...
I'M SORRY.
I THINK THOSE IN-THE-KNOW KNOW, BUT FOR SHOJO MANGA, I DRAW AS "MIKIYO TSUDA" AND FOR BOYS LOVE I DRAW AS "TAISHI ZAOU."
THAT'S RIGHT.
ESPECIALLY AT CONVENTIONS, I RUIN A LOT OF MANGA FOR FANS WHO ASK ME TO SIGN...
I ALSO MESS UP WHEN I WRITE THE YEAR 2000...
AH!!
SQUEAK
I WROTE MIKIYO TSUDA!
OH, NO!
KK
EVERYONE SMILES AND LETS IT GO, BUT I REALLY AM SORRY...
IT'S OKAY, JUST WRITE YOUR TSUDA NAME, TOO.
BOW BOW
I'M SORRY, I'M SORRY.
WHAT IF SOMEONE THINKS EIKI-EIKI IS ANOTHER PEN NAME...?
SORRY FOR CAUSING YOU TROUBLE EIKO.

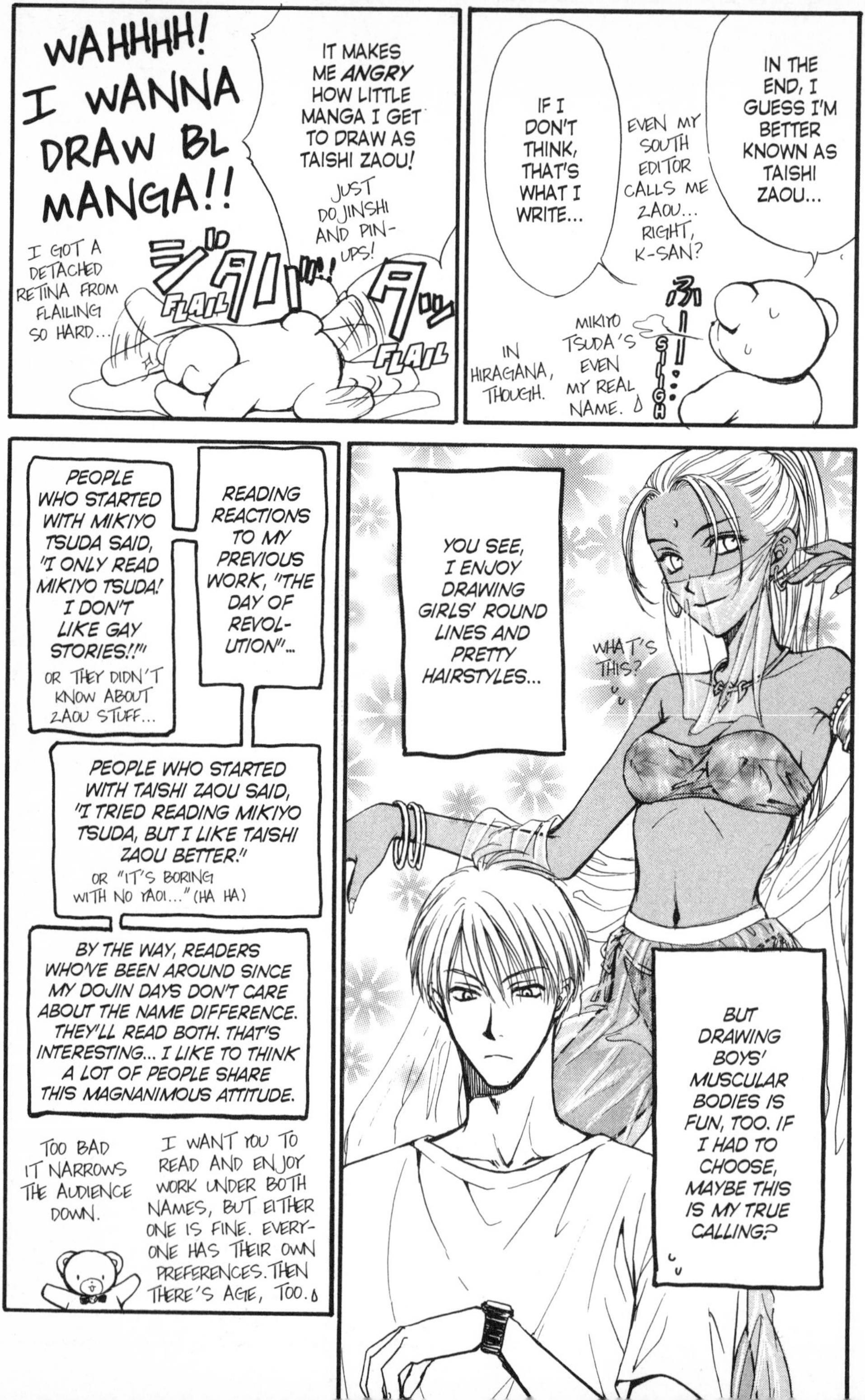

IN THE END, I GUESS I'M BETTER KNOWN AS TAISHI ZAOU...
EVEN MY SOUTH EDITOR CALLS ME ZAOU... RIGHT, K-SAN?
IF I DON'T THINK, THAT'S WHAT I WRITE...
ふー
SIGH
MIKIYO TSUDA'S EVEN MY REAL NAME.
IN HIRAGANA, THOUGH.
IT MAKES ME ANGRY HOW LITTLE MANGA I GET TO DRAW AS TAISHI ZAOU!
JUST DOJINSHI AND PIN-UPS!
WAHHHH! I WANNA DRAW BL MANGA!!
FLAIL
FLAIL
I GOT A DETACHED RETINA FROM FLAILING SO HARD...
YOU SEE, I ENJOY DRAWING GIRLS' ROUND LINES AND PRETTY HAIRSTYLES...
WHAT'S THIS?
BUT DRAWING BOYS' MUSCULAR BODIES IS FUN, TOO. IF I HAD TO CHOOSE, MAYBE THIS IS MY TRUE CALLING?
READING REACTIONS TO MY PREVIOUS WORK, "THE DAY OF REVOLUTION"...
PEOPLE WHO STARTED WITH MIKIYO TSUDA SAID, "I ONLY READ MIKIYO TSUDA! I DON'T LIKE GAY STORIES!!"
OR THEY DIDN'T KNOW ABOUT ZAOU STUFF...
PEOPLE WHO STARTED WITH TAISHI ZAOU SAID, "I TRIED READING MIKIYO TSUDA, BUT I LIKE TAISHI ZAOU BETTER."
OR "IT'S BORING WITH NO YAOI..." (HA HA)
BY THE WAY, READERS WHO'VE BEEN AROUND SINCE MY DOJIN DAYS DON'T CARE ABOUT THE NAME DIFFERENCE. THEY'LL READ BOTH. THAT'S INTERESTING... I LIKE TO THINK A LOT OF PEOPLE SHARE THIS MAGNANIMOUS ATTITUDE.
I WANT YOU TO READ AND ENJOY WORK UNDER BOTH NAMES, BUT EITHER ONE IS FINE. EVERYONE HAS THEIR OWN PREFERENCES. THEN THERE'S AGE, TOO.
TOO BAD IT NARROWS THE AUDIENCE DOWN.

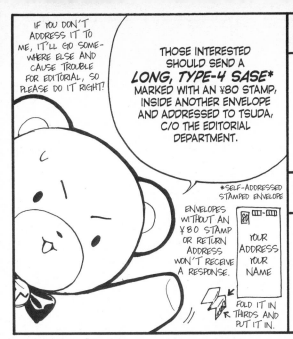

DOJIN INFORMATION

ZAOU GROUP

TAISHI ZAOU'S PERSONAL CIRCLE. MAINLY ANIME PARODY AND SHONEN MANGA-RELATED. I PUBLISH ORIGINAL YAOI IN GENRES I'M INTO AT THE TIME (I ALSO DO LOCAL COMMISSIONS).

KOZOUYA

MY JOINT CIRCLE WITH EIKI-EIKI. WE HAVE SPACE RESERVED FOR ORIGINAL YAOI AT LARGE EVENTS 3-4 TIMES A YEAR (NOTE: WE DON'T MAKE PAPER AT KOZOUYA). BY THE WAY, WE'RE READY TO TAKE A BREAK.

THOSE INTERESTED SHOULD SEND A *LONG, TYPE-4 SASE** MARKED WITH AN ¥80 STAMP, INSIDE ANOTHER ENVELOPE AND ADDRESSED TO TSUDA, C/O THE EDITORIAL DEPARTMENT.
IF YOU DON'T ADDRESS IT TO ME, IT'LL GO SOMEWHERE ELSE AND CAUSE TROUBLE FOR EDITORIAL, SO PLEASE DO IT RIGHT!
*SELF-ADDRESSED STAMPED ENVELOPE
80
YOUR ADDRESS
YOUR NAME
ENVELOPES WITHOUT AN ¥80 STAMP OR RETURN ADDRESS WON'T RECEIVE A RESPONSE.
FOLD IT IN THIRDS AND PUT IT IN.

PEOPLE SEND LETTERS SAYING, "PLEASE BE SURE TO REPLY!!" I'M SORRY... IT'S *IMPOSSIBLE*.
I ASSURE YOU.
I DO READ ALL YOUR LETTERS.
AS YOU CAN SEE, MUCH OF MY TIME IS SPENT WORKING, SO I HAVE VERY LITTLE LEEWAY.
I'M SORRY.

INSTEAD, I PUT OUT AN IRREGULAR NEWSLETTER, SO PLEASE HAVE A LOOK AT IT!
I AIM FOR JAN-MAR-MAY-AUG-NOV.
YOU MIGHT GET THE CREATOR'S INSIDE SCOOP (HA HA).
THOSE WITH INQUIRIES, SEE THE INFO ABOVE. JUST DON'T SEND ONLY A STAMP OR ONLY AN ENVELOPE.
YOU PROBABLY WON'T HEAR BACK!

AFTERWORD ✱ END

WHEN I WENT BACK AND LOOKED OVER THE STORIES FOR THE TANKUBON, THE ART MADE ME WANT TO CRY.
IT'S PARTLY THAT I WASN'T USED TO THE NEW CHARACTERS, AND PROBABLY BECAUSE I WAS PRESSED FOR TIME, BUT STILL!! SO ROUGH!
I GRIPED AND CRINGED AS I FIXED IT. I MEAN, THERE WERE ENTIRE LINES MISSING!
AS FOR THE STORY, I DIDN'T WANT TO DO A LOVE STORY... SO OKAY, I'LL TRY CLINGY FAMILY LOVE. THAT'S WHAT I THOUGHT WHEN I STARTED DRAWING... BUT I'M BAD AT TRYING TO BE SERIOUS. SOMEHOW MY OWN INDULGENCE GETS IN, AND I CAN'T PUSH THE CHARACTERS AWAY. I WANT TO DRAW A MORE PROFOUND STORY... BUT, THAT'S A TASK FOR ANOTHER TIME. DRAWING VARIOUS TYPES OF NEW CHARACTERS WAS A LEARNING EXPERIENCE. I GUESS THE ONES MOST DIFFERENT FROM WHAT I'D DRAWN BEFORE WERE MOM, AKIRA, AND FUYUKI. THEY WERE UNUSUAL TYPES, SO I STRUGGLED... BUT IT WAS FUN. I WANT TO CREATE MORE DISTINCT CHARACTERS NEXT TIME.
I DREW THE MOM AND DAD SEGMENT AS A NEW ADDITION, BECAUSE I GOT BUGGED TO SO MUCH (HA HA). WELL, THE TITLE IS "FAMILY COMPLEX," SO I THOUGHT MAYBE ONLY USING THE KIDS WASN'T GOOD. BUT THANKS TO THAT STORY, I WENT OVER MY REGULATED PAGE COUNT, SO IN ORDER TO MEET THE NEXT TIER, I WOUND UP DRAWING A TOTAL OF 27 MORE PAGES OF THE KIDS, AN AFTERWORD, AND 4-PANEL COMIC THEATER. IT PROBABLY MAKES FANS HAPPY, BUT IT SURE WORE ME OUT. IT WAS FUN, THOUGH! HEE HEE!

ASSISTANTS
KAZUI KANZAKI
SAKI IORI
RINPEI HIRABAYASH

MENTAL ADVISORS (?)
EIKI-EIKI
MY EDITOR, KUMAGAI-SAN
SPECIAL THANKS

FOR THE PROBLEMS I CAUSED DURING FAMILY COMPLEX

NEXT UP WILL PROBABLY BE "THE DAY OF REVOLUTION 2" OR "LOVE IS A STRANGE AND DIFFERENT THING." PLEASE LOOK FOR THEM AND ENJOY!

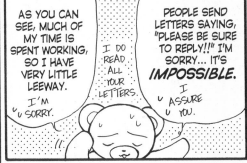

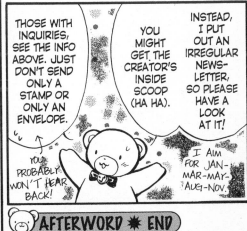

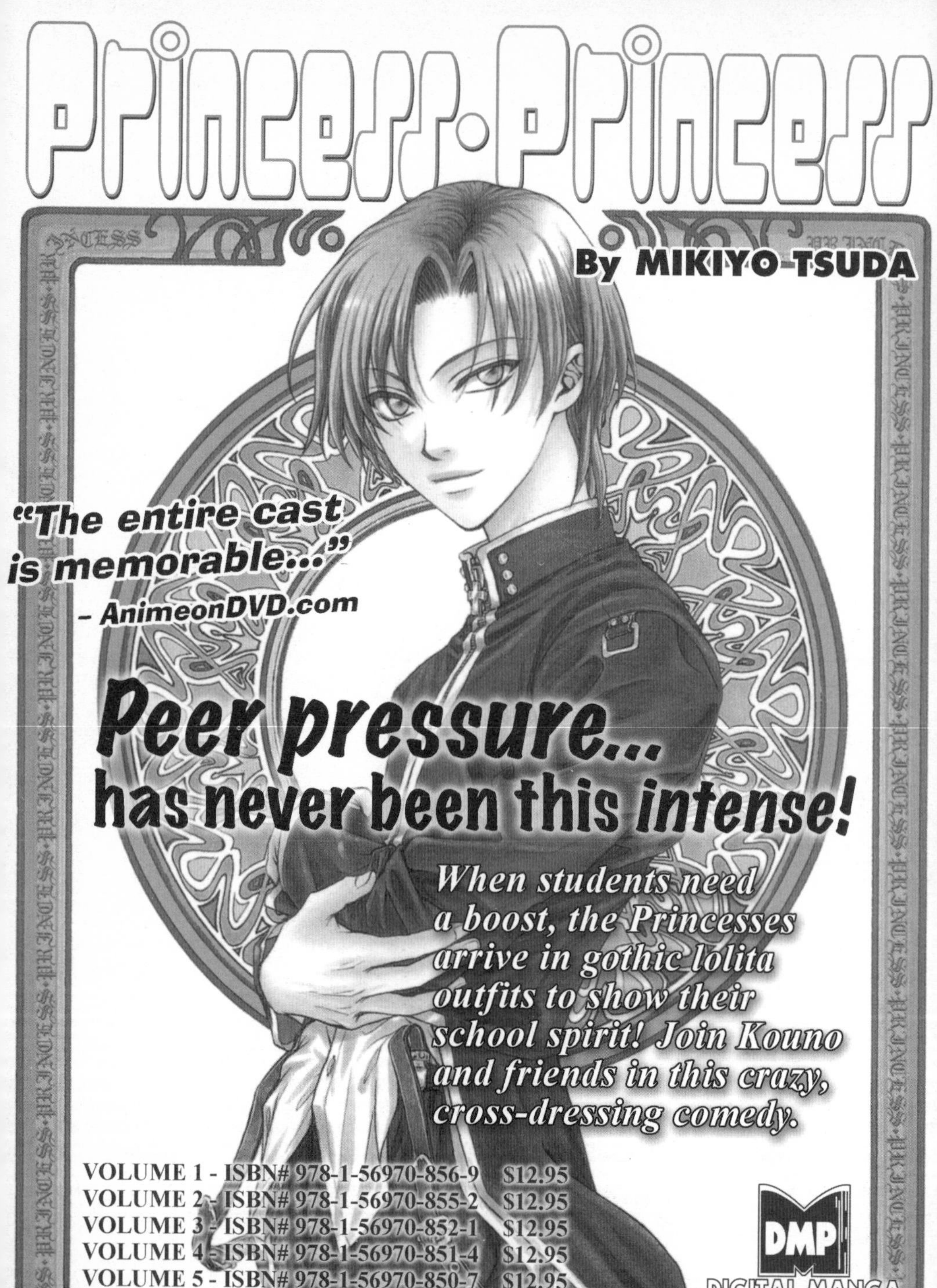
Princess · Princess
By MIKIYO TSUDA
"The entire cast is memorable..."
– AnimeonDVD.com
Peer pressure... has never been this intense!
When students need a boost, the Princesses arrive in gothic lolita outfits to show their school spirit! Join Kouno and friends in this crazy, cross-dressing comedy.
VOLUME 1 - ISBN# 978-1-56970-856-9 $12.95
VOLUME 2 - ISBN# 978-1-56970-855-2 $12.95
VOLUME 3 - ISBN# 978-1-56970-852-1 $12.95
VOLUME 4 - ISBN# 978-1-56970-851-4 $12.95
VOLUME 5 - ISBN# 978-1-56970-850-7 $12.95
DMP
DIGITAL MANGA PUBLISHING
www.dmpbooks.com

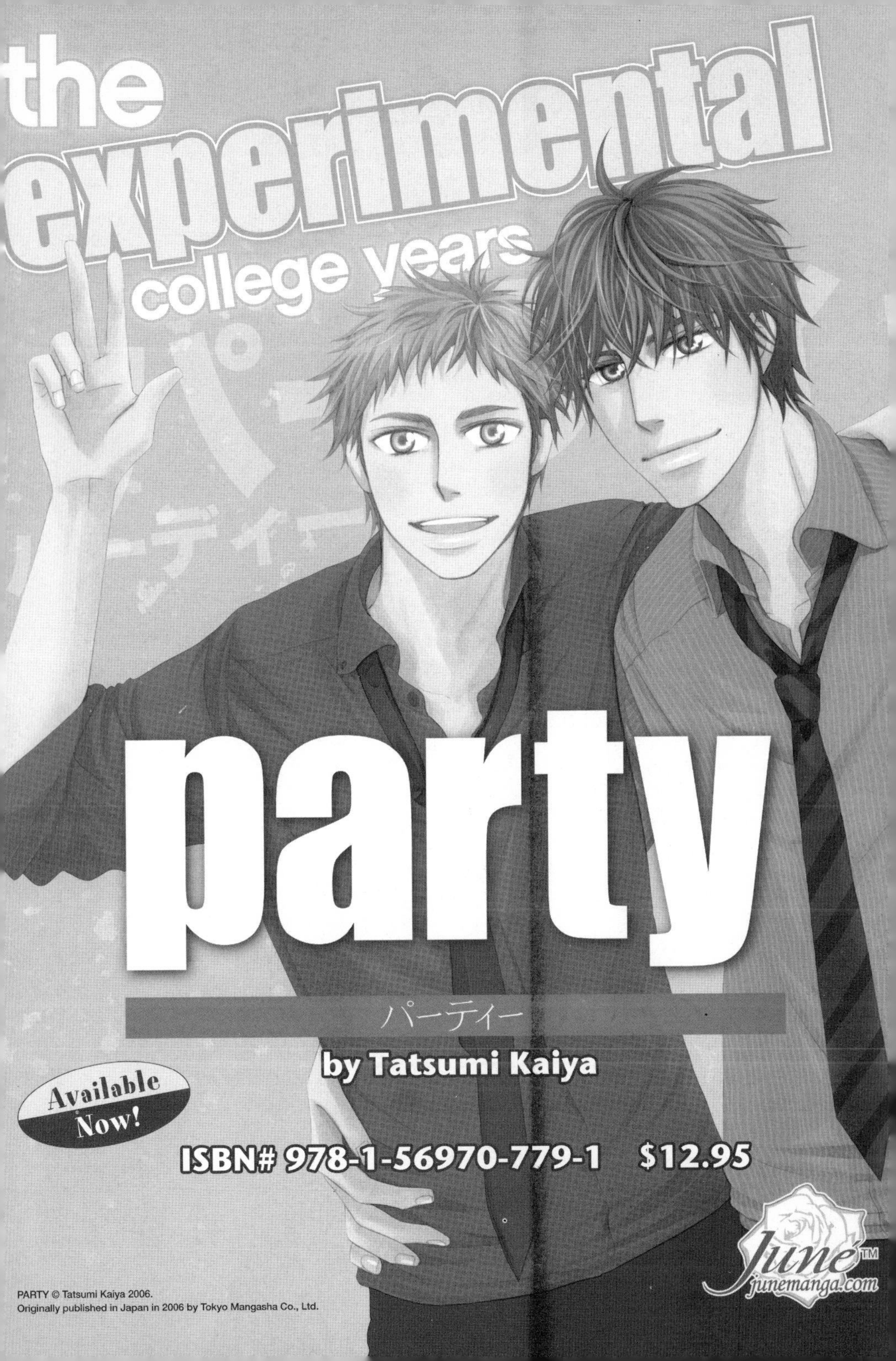

the experimental college years
party
パーティー
by Tatsumi Kaiya
Available Now!
ISBN# 978-1-56970-779-1 $12.95
June™
junemanga.com
PARTY © Tatsumi Kaiya 2006.
Originally published in Japan in 2006 by Tokyo Mangasha Co., Ltd.

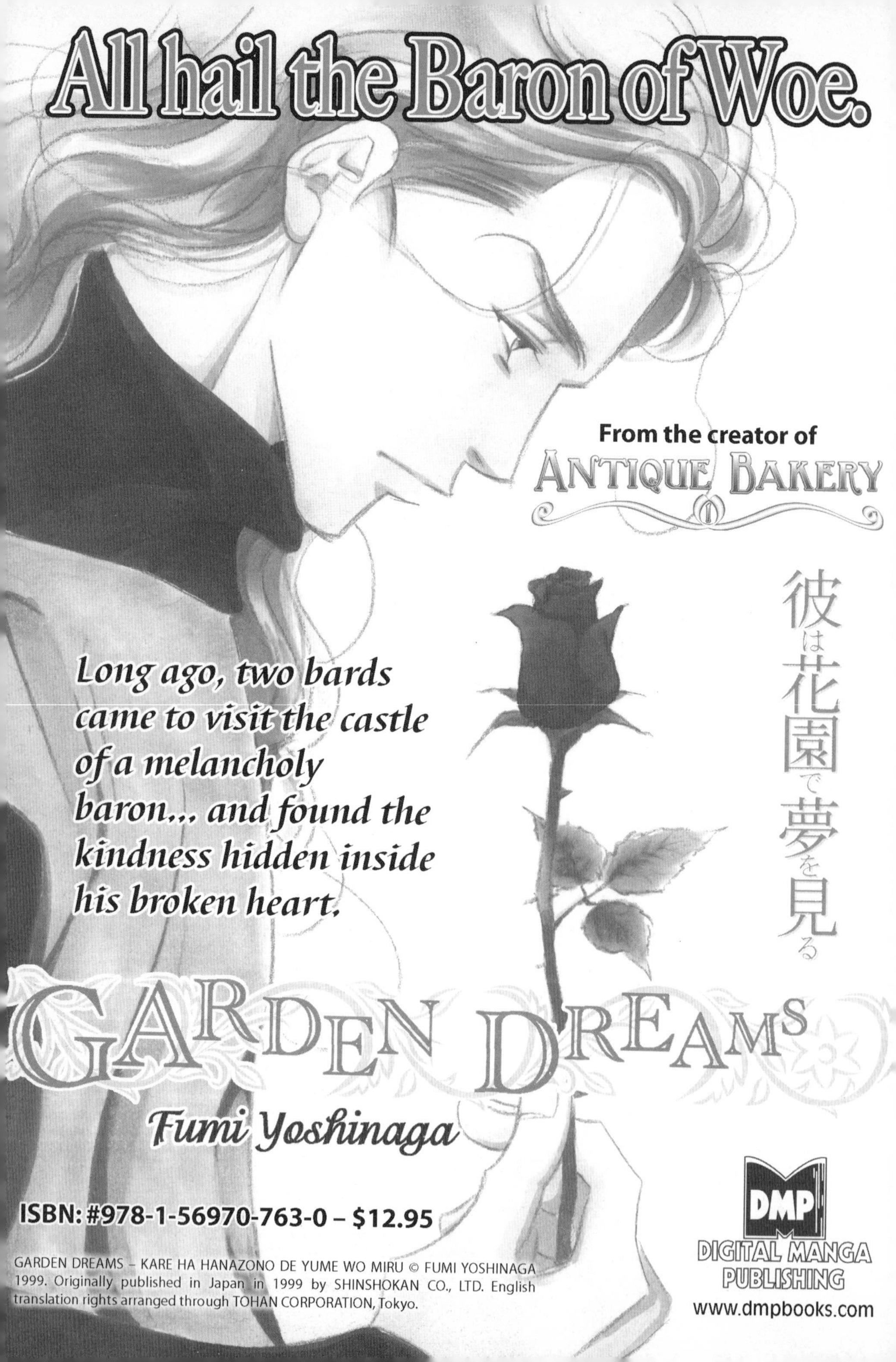
All hail the Baron of Woe.
From the creator of
ANTIQUE BAKERY
彼は花園で夢を見る
Long ago, two bards came to visit the castle of a melancholy baron... and found the kindness hidden inside his broken heart.
GARDEN DREAMS
Fumi Yoshinaga
ISBN: #978-1-56970-763-0 – $12.95
GARDEN DREAMS – KARE HA HANAZONO DE YUME WO MIRU © FUMI YOSHINAGA 1999. Originally published in Japan in 1999 by SHINSHOKAN CO., LTD. English translation rights arranged through TOHAN CORPORATION, Tokyo.
DMP
DIGITAL MANGA PUBLISHING
www.dmpbooks.com

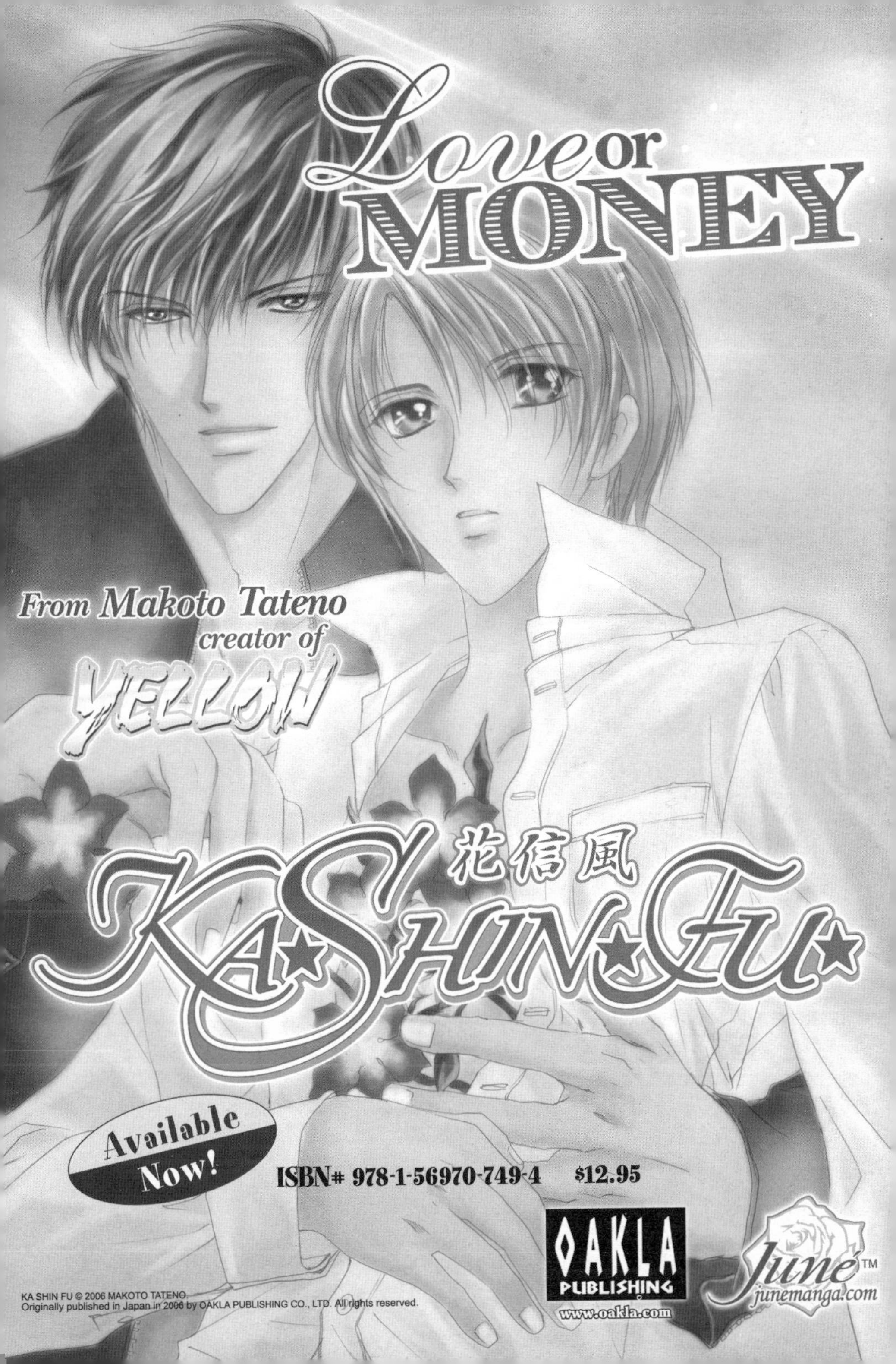
Love or MONEY
From Makoto Tateno
creator of
YELLOW
花信風
KA SHIN FU
Available Now!
ISBN# 978-1-56970-749-4
$12.95
OAKLA PUBLISHING
www.oakla.com
June™
junemanga.com
KA SHIN FU © 2006 MAKOTO TATENO.
Originally published in Japan in 2006 by OAKLA PUBLISHING CO., LTD. All rights reserved.

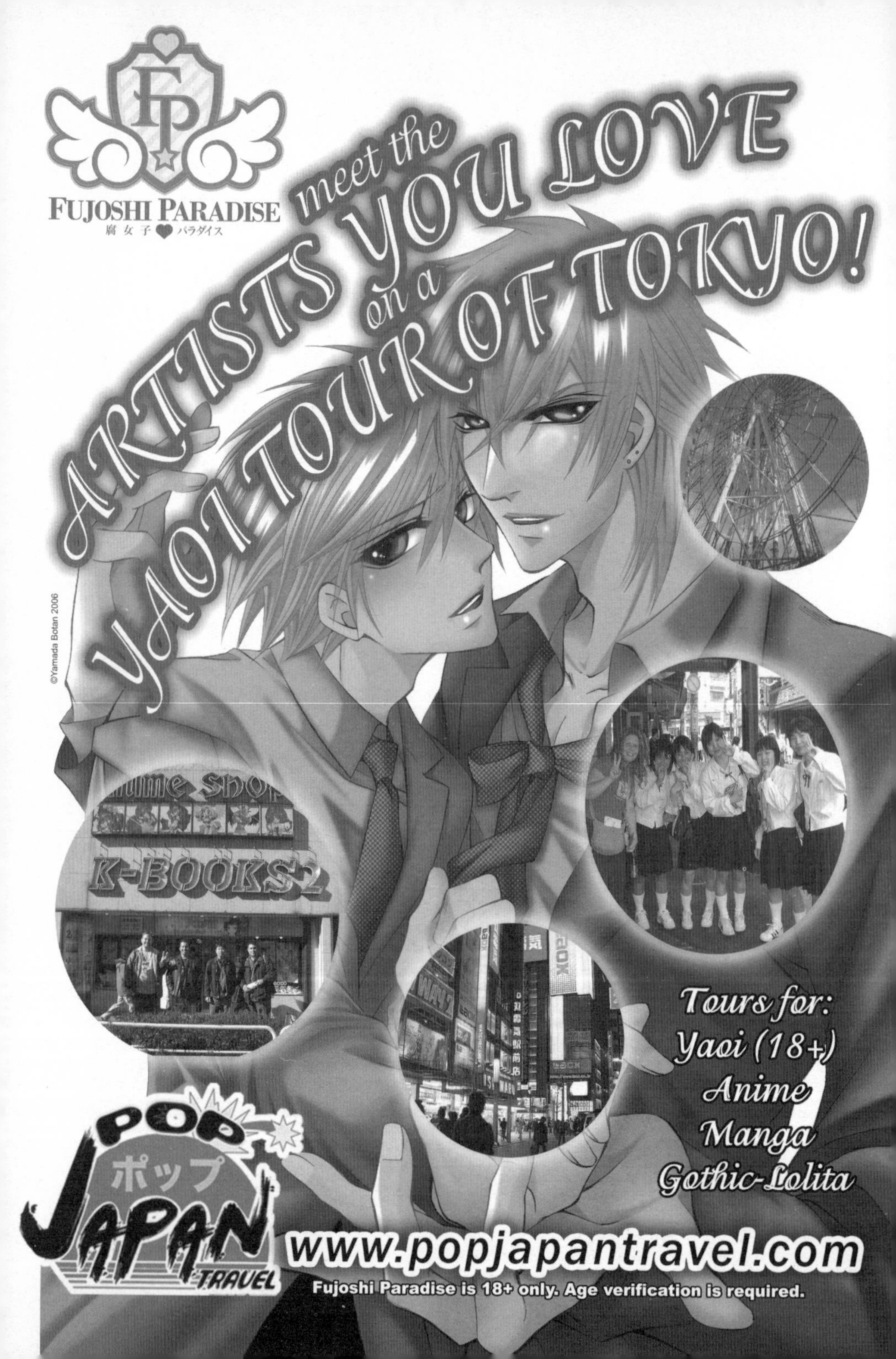

FUJOSHI PARADISE
腐女子❤パラダイス
meet the
ARTISTS YOU LOVE
on a
YAOI TOUR OF TOKYO!
©Yamada Botan 2006
K-BOOKS 2
Tours for:
Yaoi (18+)
Anime
Manga
Gothic-Lolita
POP ポップ JAPAN TRAVEL
www.popjapantravel.com
Fujoshi Paradise is 18+ only. Age verification is required.

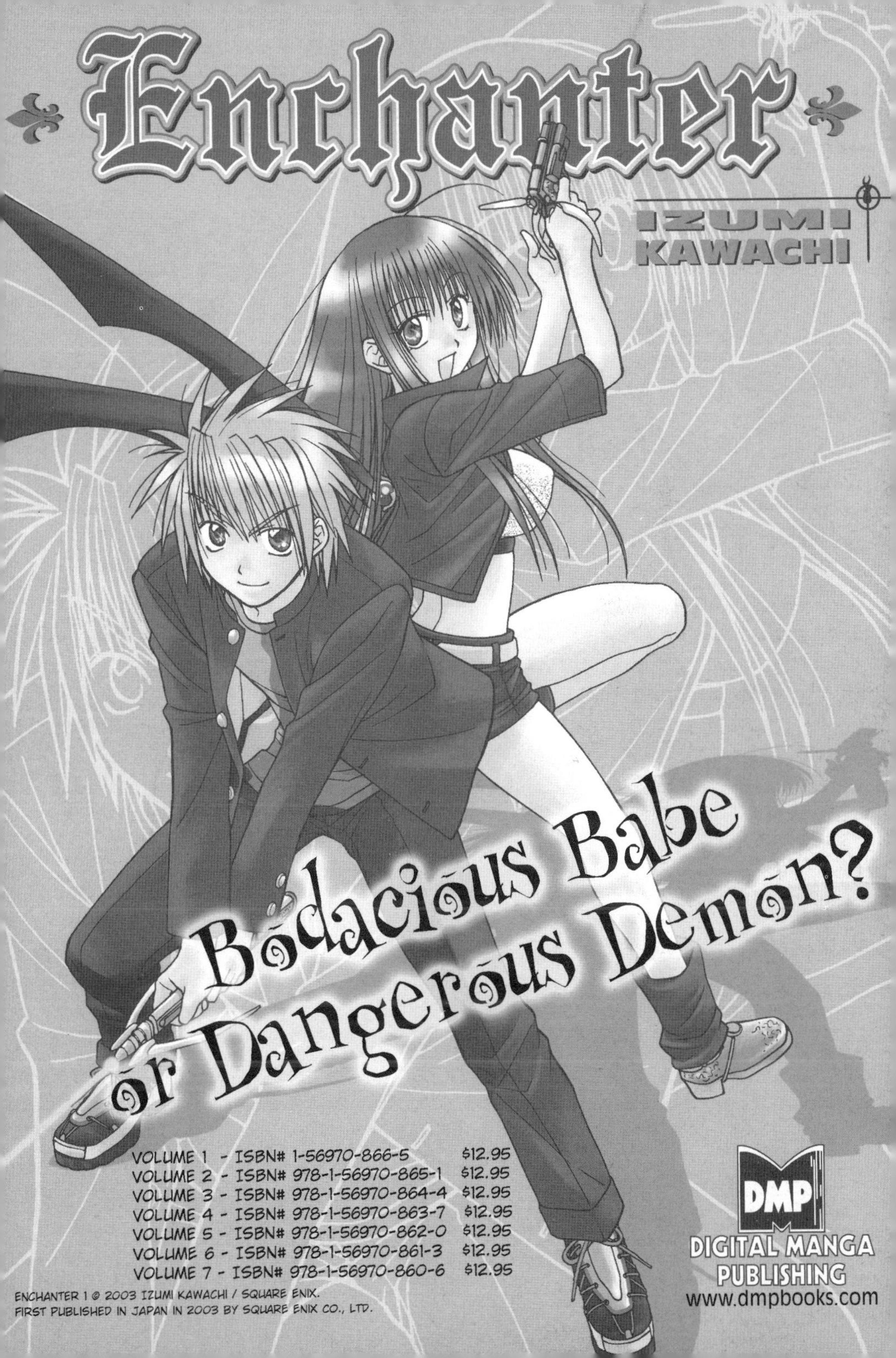
Enchanter
IZUMI KAWACHI
Bodacious Babe or Dangerous Demon?
VOLUME 1 - ISBN# 1-56970-866-5 $12.95
VOLUME 2 - ISBN# 978-1-56970-865-1 $12.95
VOLUME 3 - ISBN# 978-1-56970-864-4 $12.95
VOLUME 4 - ISBN# 978-1-56970-863-7 $12.95
VOLUME 5 - ISBN# 978-1-56970-862-0 $12.95
VOLUME 6 - ISBN# 978-1-56970-861-3 $12.95
VOLUME 7 - ISBN# 978-1-56970-860-6 $12.95
ENCHANTER 1 © 2003 IZUMI KAWACHI / SQUARE ENIX.
FIRST PUBLISHED IN JAPAN IN 2003 BY SQUARE ENIX CO., LTD.
DMP
DIGITAL MANGA PUBLISHING
www.dmpbooks.com

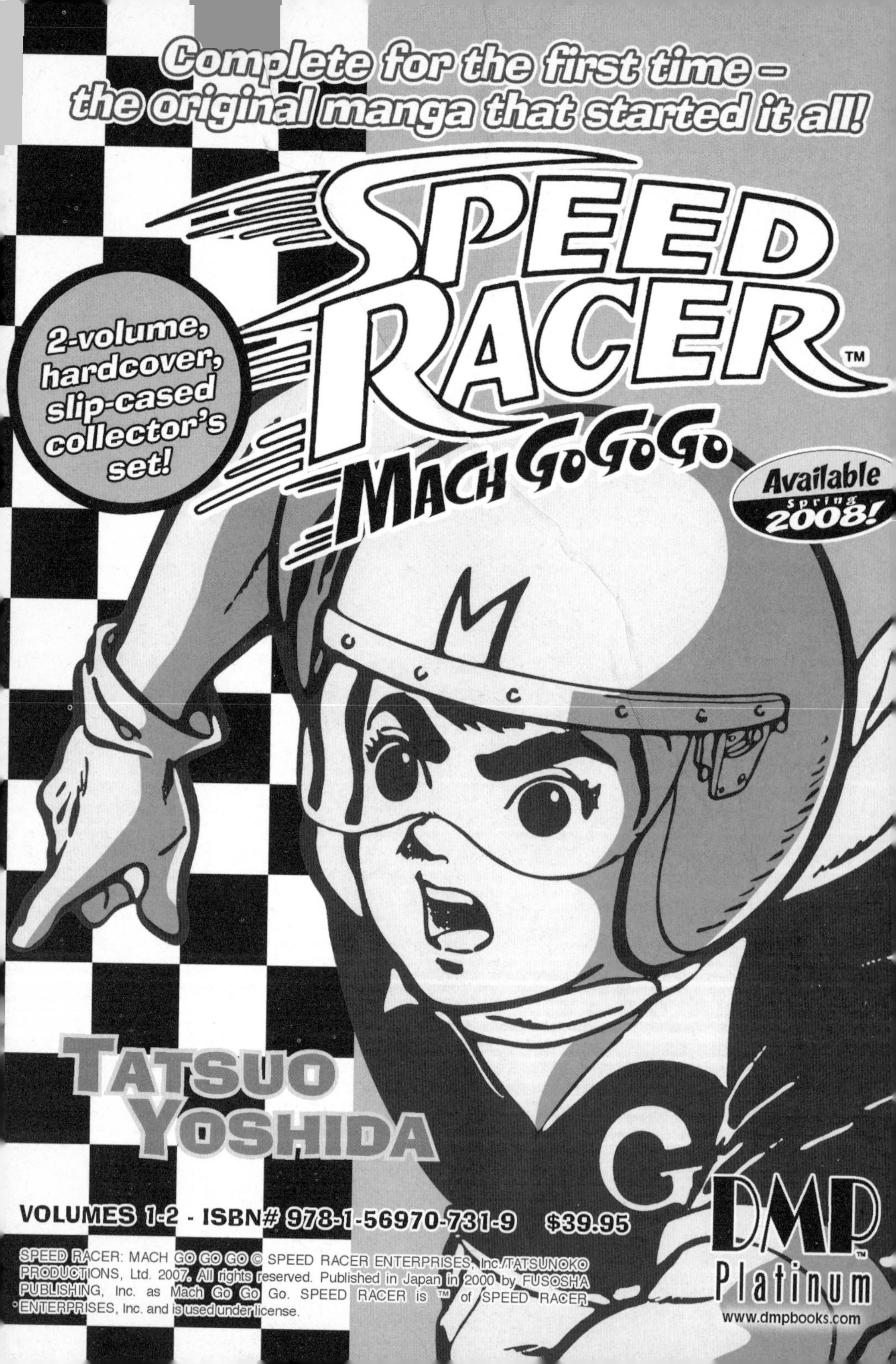

Complete for the first time – the original manga that started it all!
SPEED RACER™
MACH GOGOGO
2-volume, hardcover, slip-cased collector's set!
Available Spring 2008!
TATSUO YOSHIDA
VOLUMES 1-2 - ISBN# 978-1-56970-731-9 $39.95
SPEED RACER: MACH GO GO GO © SPEED RACER ENTERPRISES, Inc./TATSUNOKO PRODUCTIONS, Ltd. 2007. All rights reserved. Published in Japan in 2000 by FUSOSHA PUBLISHING, Inc. as Mach Go Go Go. SPEED RACER is ™ of SPEED RACER ENTERPRISES, Inc. and is used under license.
DMP™ Platinum
www.dmpbooks.com

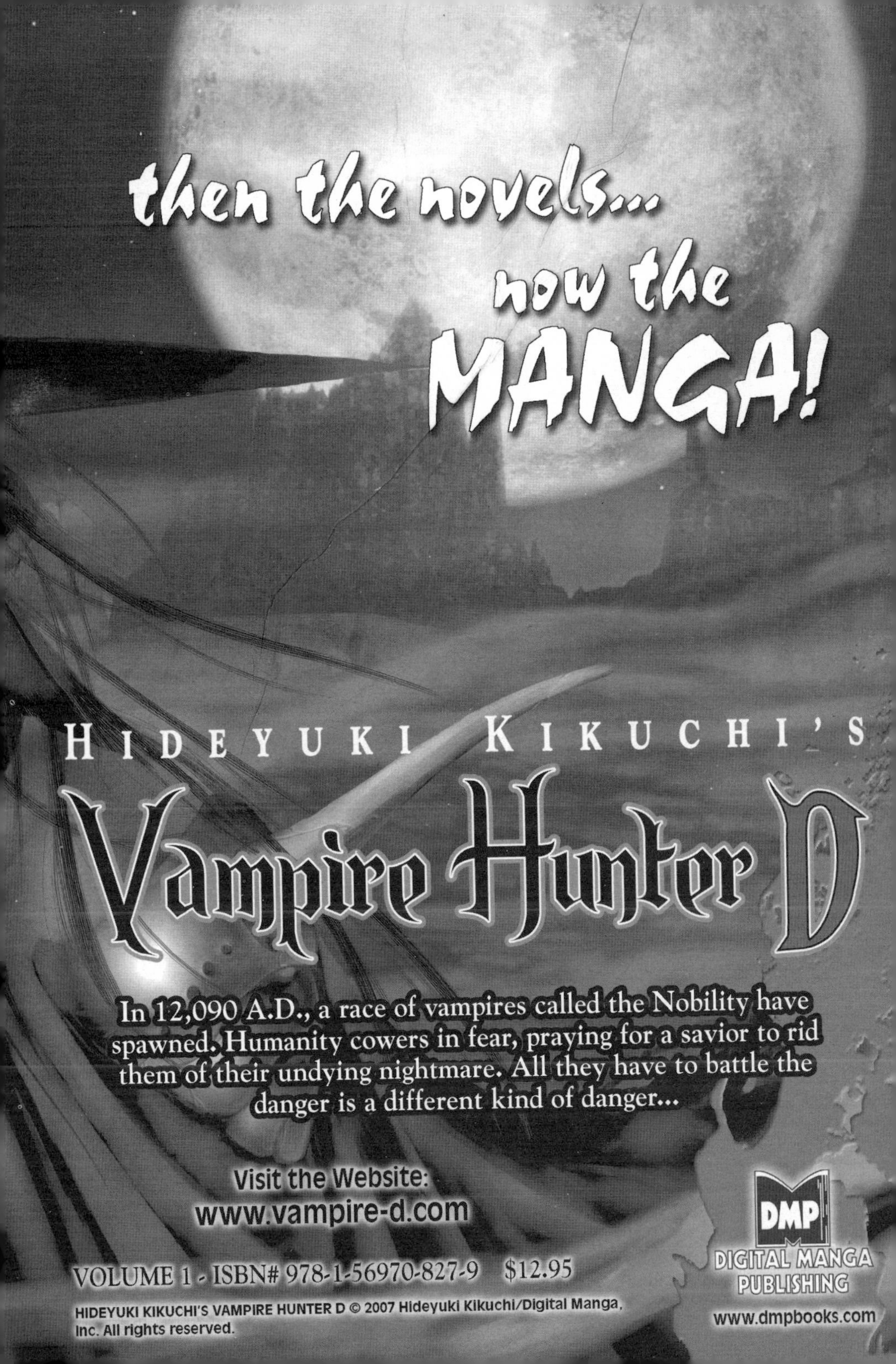
then the novels...
now the
MANGA!
HIDEYUKI KIKUCHI'S
Vampire Hunter D
In 12,090 A.D., a race of vampires called the Nobility have spawned. Humanity cowers in fear, praying for a savior to rid them of their undying nightmare. All they have to battle the danger is a different kind of danger...
Visit the Website:
www.vampire-d.com
VOLUME 1 - ISBN# 978-1-56970-827-9 $12.95
HIDEYUKI KIKUCHI'S VAMPIRE HUNTER D © 2007 Hideyuki Kikuchi/Digital Manga, Inc. All rights reserved.
DMP
DIGITAL MANGA PUBLISHING
www.dmpbooks.com

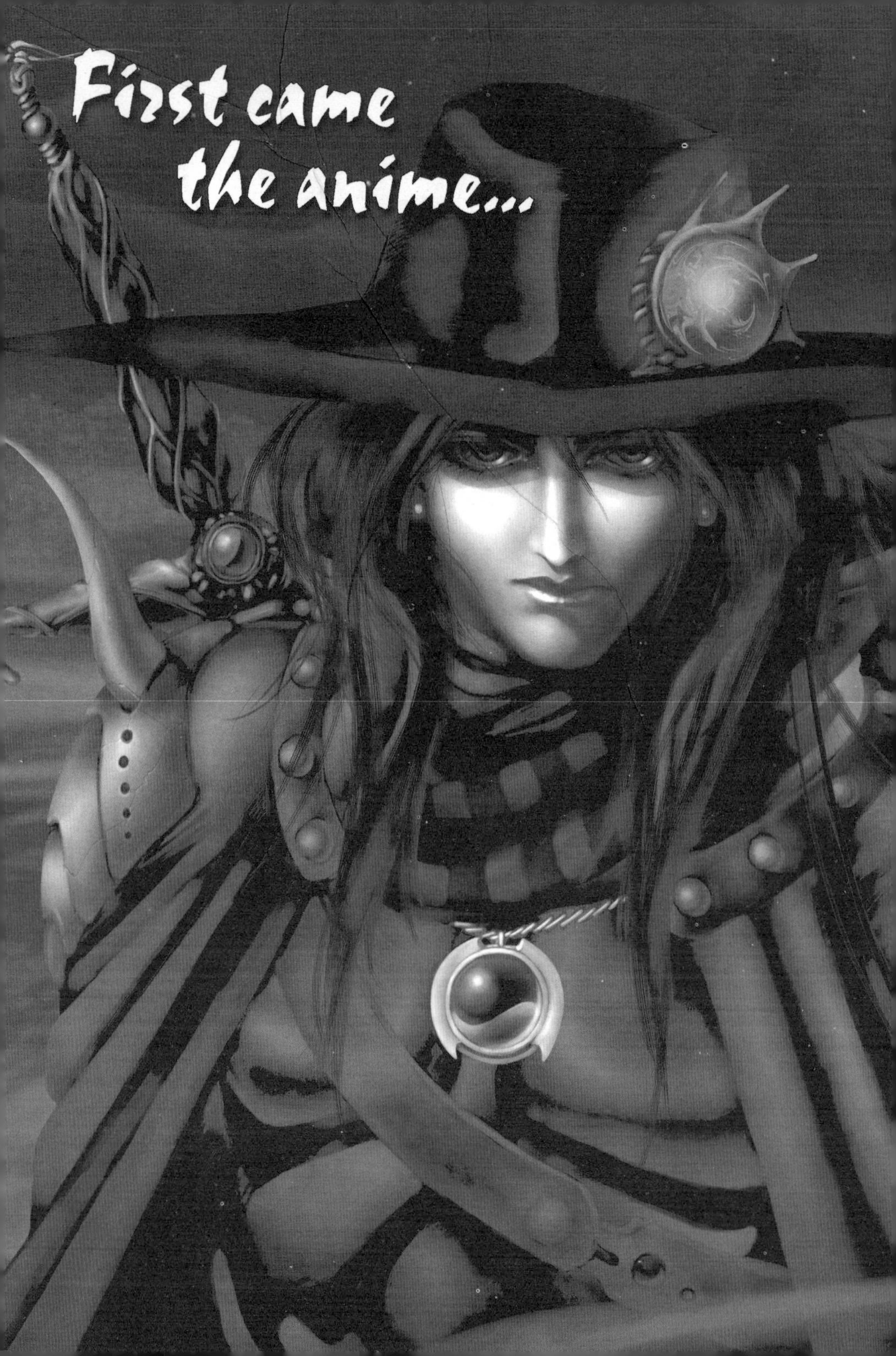
First came
the anime...

STOP

This is the ba[ck] [of the b]ook!
Start from th[e oth]er side.

NATIVE MANGA
readers read manga
from *right to left*.

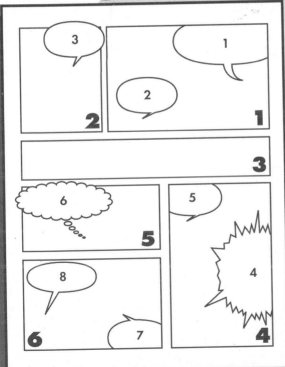

If you run into our *Native Manga* logo on any of our books... you'll know that this manga is published in it's true original native Japanese right to left reading format, as it was intended. Turn to the other side of the book and start reading from right to left, top to bottom.

Follow the diagram to see how its done. **Surf's Up!**

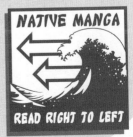

NATIVE MANGA

READ RIGHT TO LEFT